S0-AXT-299

81
277

The Caribbean
After
Grenada

ROBERT MANNING
STROZIER LIBRARY

JUL 17 1989

Tallahassee, Florida

The Caribbean
After
Grenada

REVOLUTION,
CONFLICT,
AND
DEMOCRACY

Edited by
Scott B. MacDonald,
Harald M. Sandstrom,
and
Paul B. Goodwin, Jr.

PRAEGER

New York
Westport, Connecticut
London

ROBERT MANNING
STROZIER LIBRARY

2183

JUL 17 1989 C35

1988

Tallahassee, Florida

Library of Congress Cataloging-in-Publication Data

The Caribbean after Grenada : revolution, conflict, and democracy /
Scott B. MacDonald, Harald M. Sandstrom, and Paul B. Goodwin, Jr.,
editors.
    p. cm.
  Includes bibliographical references and index.
  ISBN 0-275-92722-9 (alk. paper)
  1. Caribbean Area—Politics and government—1945–   2. Grenada—
Politics and government—1974–   3. Grenada—History—American
invasion, 1983—Influence. 4. Caribbean Area—Foreign
relations—1945–   I. MacDonald, Scott B. II. Sandstrom, Harald M.
III. Goodwin, Paul B., 1942–
F2183.C35 1988
972.9′052—dc 19   88–11986

Copyright © 1988 by Scott B. MacDonald, Harald M. Sandstrom, and Paul B. Goodwin,
Jr.

All rights reserved. No portion of this book may
be reproduced, by any process or technique, without
the express written consent of the publisher.

Library of Congress Catalog Card Number: 88-11986
ISBN: 0-275-92722-9

First published in 1988

Praeger Publishers, One Madison Avenue, New York, NY 10010
A division of Greenwood Press, Inc.

Printed in the United States of America

The paper used in this book complies with the
Permanent Paper Standard issued by the National
Information Standards Organization (Z39.48-1984).

10 9 8 7 6 5 4 3 2 1

Contents

Preface

This book seeks to contribute to a balanced and informed dialogue about "the lessons of Grenada" and the problems of revolution, conflict and democracy faced by contemporary Caribbean societies. By consciously seeking contributions from a range of ideological viewpoints, we have striven to avoid the one-sidedness that often characterizes treatises on controversial topics. The authors and editors hail from a variety of disciplines, including history, political science, sociology, and economics. While most are academics, junior and senior, two have served in the U.S. government: Sally Shelton-Colby as Ambassador to the Eastern Caribbean States, and Robert Pastor as the Director of Latin American and Caribbean Affairs on the National Security Council, both during the Carter years. We have included all geographic regions from the islands farthest out in the Atlantic to the Central American republics, all major regime types, and all cultural/linguistic areas. We hope the result will be useful to our colleagues as a text or supplement in courses on comparative politics, the Caribbean, the Third World, development and underdevelopment, political economy, and political sociology, as well as to the inquiring general reader.

On April 14, 1984, the Center for Latin American and Caribbean Studies at the University of Connecticut sponsored a one-day symposium entitled "Grenada—A Post-Mortem." This book dates from that day of reflection on the dramatic events of October 1983. Part I is a re-presentation of some of the papers delivered in 1984, fleshed out and updated to reflect current Caribbean realities, with the addition of Sally Shelton-Colby's introductory chapter and Robert Pastor's conclusion. In this section we tackle the self-destruction of the New Jewel Movement's revolution (1979–1983), the ensuing invasion/intervention/rescue mission, and the impact of Grenada in and beyond the Caribbean, both before and after the October 1983 cataclysm.

In Parts II and III we have drawn on further original contributions to go beyond the focus of the conference. Part II deals with the attempts of the societies closest to Grenada to contend with challenges of revolution, conflict, and democracy. Part III goes farther afield to examine Caribbean societies most distant from Grenada and the Caribbean policies of the European Community, The Soviet Union/Cuba, and the United States.

We wish to express our gratitude to several individuals and institutions. Insightful comments at the original symposium by Gordon K. Lewis, John Plank, and Fransisco Scarano steered us away from a number of pitfalls. Wendell Bell of Yale University has been a constant source of inspiration. Nancy Lilliquist typed the entire manuscript efficiently and cheerfully. Special thanks by Scott MacDonald for the support given him by Connecticut National Bank and American Security Bank, and for the time and insights shared by Lionel Hurst, the Trade Consul for Antigua and Barbuda in Miami, Ambassadors to the United States and the Organization of American States James O'Neill Lewis from Trinidad and Tobago and Joseph Edmunds from St. Lucia, and Prime Minister Dr. Kennedy Simmonds of St. Kitts–Nevis; by Harald Sandstrom to his Grenada class which worked through an earlier version of the manuscript, to the University of Hartford for the Vincent B. Coffin grant that enabled him to do research in Grenada, and to Jan Carew for his nuggets of wisdom and kind encouragement; and by Paul Goodwin to the Center for Latin American and Caribbean Studies at the University of Connecticut. Most importantly, of course, we wish to thank the authors for their signal contributions to Caribbean studies and our families for their forbearance.

Introduction
Scott B. MacDonald, Harald M. Sandstrom, and Paul B. Goodwin, Jr.

I.

The purpose of this book is to examine the major political and economic developments in the Caribbean since the events of October 1983 in Grenada. That "tempest in a teacup" generated a host of instant analyses, most of which necessarily lacked depth and perspective.

This book differs from these predecessors in at least three ways. Most importantly, it broadens the perspective from concentration exclusively on Grenada. The microcosm of Grenada is important, but its importance is seen more clearly when placed in a larger context. We have sought to analyze the impact of Grenada's tragedy in concentric circles of increasing scope, starting with its neighbors and progressing to the more distant shores of the Caribbean Sea and to East-West relations with the Caribbean—the "ripple effects," to borrow Robert Pastor's phrase, of a very small pebble in a very large pond.

The second difference is that the passage of time afforded us the advantage of writing informed current history rather than instant analysis. Beyond the benefit of perspective and the ability to study *effects* and *reactions* over a few years, even this brief hiatus allows us to see a bit more clearly now that the dust has had time to settle. Furthermore, data not previously available are now in the public domain, such as the Grenada papers. Events such as Bouterse's ouster of the Cubans from Suriname can be seen against the backdrop of the Cuban role in Grenada. Time can warp, allowing special pleaders a chance to sow confusion about what really transpired. However, it also allows the analyst a chance to sort the wheat from the chaff.

The third difference from many previous studies where Grenada was the centerpiece is that in this book there is no pervasive ideological mode governing the editors' selections or the authors' perceptions. This does not constitute a vain attempt to be all things to all people. Nor does it mean that the editors or authors are without bias. Writing history (current or otherwise) and social analysis, despite claims to the contrary, is a subjective exercise, rarely presented without ideological or personal coloration. Thus leftists or progressives tend to portray the invasion of Grenada as a deliberate imperialist attempt to crush a small Caribbean nation which was seeking to create an egalitarian society after centuries of external exploitation—a contemporary Goliath smiting little David. To right-wingers, Grenada was no David but a Trojan horse waiting to spring its trap. The Eastern bloc presence in this view indicated that Grenada had joined Moscow's "camp," and the airport was obviously to be a staging area for Cuban adventurism and export of revolution to Latin America and Africa. Intervention was therefore justified, especially as it preempted an "Iran-like" hostage taking of American medical students. Who can prove that either of these perspectives is wrong? Not everybody laughed at Garry Trudeau's characterization (in the "Doonesbury" comic strip) of the Grenada invasion as "sort of a special olympics for the military."

II.

The origins of the New Jewel Movement (NJM) and its ultimate self-destruction together with an aggressive U.S. role in the region that culminated in invasion/intervention reflect both historical continuities and discontinuities.

U.S., Jamaican, and Eastern Caribbean forces have departed from Grenada, and an elected government has again assumed power in the island-state. But questions as to the continued viability of Westminster-style democracy continue, and revolutionary challenges to establish power remain a distinct possibility. The words of Régis Debray capture the complexity of the historical processes at work in the Caribbean in the aftermath of Grenada.

We are never completely contemporaneous with our present. History advances in disguises; it appears on stage wearing the mask of the preceding scene, and we tend to lose the meaning of the play. Each time the curtain rises, continuity has to be re-established.[1]

In a sense, in the aftermath of October 1983, the curtain was raised again and in the post-Grenada act, continuity has been re-established as many of the problems and questions of the past have resurfaced—or in some cases never went away.

III.

Allow us a moment to develop a worst-case scenario which might prove to be frighteningly accurate in the near future.

A continuing and deepening crisis in the Caribbean has discredited democratic, pro–U.S. governments. Island economies are largely non-viable, and restrictive immigration policies in mainland states have led to severe population pressure on resources. Unemployment and underemployment are at all-time highs.

The picture is not much better on the larger islands of Hispaniola or Jamaica. U.S. Marines patrol the streets of Port-au-Prince. In the poverty-stricken Haitian countryside a leftist insurgency has emerged and ties with Cuba are rumored. Instability in Haiti deepened after the fall of the Duvaliers as successor governments failed to develop responsible social or economic policies. In the neighboring Dominican Republic a deepening economic crisis, food shortages, high consumer prices, an onerous foreign debt burden, and severe austerity have brought the government to the brink of collapse. Anti–United States demonstrations have become an almost daily occurence in the streets of Santo Domingo. In Jamaica, a recently elected People's National Party government has renewed diplomatic relations with Cuba and increased trade with the Soviet Union.

In the Eastern Caribbean, with the exception of Barbados, Westminster-style leaders have fallen one by one in elections which brought to power populist politicians beholden to Cuba and Nicaragua for revolutionary guidance. Failed promises have brought the New Jewel Movement back into existence in Grenada. The energy-exporting economies of Trinidad and Tobago and the Netherlands Antilles have gradually deteriorated. Drug trafficking has continued to spread throughout the region. Honduras and Nicaragua prepare for war. Mexico reels under the impact of the continued corrupt practices of the ruling Institutionalized Revolutionary Party (PRI). Libyan involvement has increased in Suriname and the Eastern Caribbean. The prestige of the United States is at an all-time low. A great malaise has settled over the region. Conditions encourage intervention and revolution.

All of the above is informed fiction. However, the scenario is not as outrageous and frivolous as it may appear at first glance. What could bring the Caribbean and surrounding regions to this stage in the near future?

Certainly many of the region's problems are internally generated. But the United States must bear a portion of the blame. Ill-considered and poorly conceived politics in the mid–1980s may produce unexpected and unpleasant results. Episodic interest in the Caribbean, as symbolized by both the invasion of Grenada and the Caribbean Basin Initiative, masked an essential lack of concern for the region and its people. Neglect, self-serving protectionism, problems of debt, and the inability of the United States to perceive problems in other than an East-West context will demand their price. Destabilization, both political and economic, as well as the social problems engendered in poverty, lack of opportunity, declining health and educational standards will encourage penetration by groups and powers unfriendly to the United States. The high expectations generated in the aftermath of Grenada have failed to come true.

The October 1983 U.S.–led invasion of Grenada deposed a regime that had deteriorated to a Marxist–Leninist military dictatorship, reaffirmed Washington's long-standing claim to hegemony in the Caribbean, and sent the message that "America is back" as a power to contend with in international affairs. The projection of U.S. military power was echoed both by rhetoric and by the development of economic policies such as the Caribbean Basin Initiative (CBI), which promised to help the region's states advance on a capitalist/democratic path.

Initially the rhetoric was backed by action. The Reagan administration played a positive role in Haiti by applying pressure on President-for-Life Jean-Claude Duvalier to depart peacefully—though it was unable or unwilling to stem the violence and corruption of the Duvalieristas in first the aborted election and then the fundamentally flawed election of early 1988. Democratic elections in 1986 in the Dominican Republic were warmly supported by the United States. Under the auspices of the CBI, there was an easing of some restrictions on entry of Caribbean-produced textiles into the U.S. market.

Unfortunately, countercurrents in U.S. policy have outweighed these positive initiatives. If unchecked, they have the potential to destabilize the Caribbean. The Grenada invasion created expectations in the region that the United States was going to bring about sweeping changes. The inability or unwillingness to remain constant in translating rhetoric into reality, however, created both skepticism and tension. Protectionist lobbies in the United States gutted many of the positive programs originally envisioned in the CBI. Both the Bahamas and the Netherland's Antilles lost their offshore financial advantages and were barred from U.S. petroleum markets. The Dominican Republic, Guyana, Belize, Trinidad, Jamaica, St. Christopher (St. Kitts)–Nevis, and all the Central American Republics and Panama—all dependent to varying degrees on the U.S. sugar market—were jarred by congressional legislation that sharply reduced their quotas. The negative impact of U.S. sugar policy was immediately evident in closed plants, layoffs, unemployment, and reduced government revenues. Most of the region's governments realize the need to diversify their economies. They have made significant strides in textiles, apparel, and footwear. However, strong lobbies have also attempted to close these doors. Additionally, the U.S. trade embargo on Nicaragua has hurt U.S. allies, such as Dominica, St. Vincent, and St. Lucia. They now have to compete with a surplus of Nicaraguan bananas in their traditional European markets. Furthermore, several U.S. corporations have retreated from the region: Gulf and Western from the Dominican Republic, Lago Oil from Aruba, Esso from Curaçao, and Intel from Barbados.

U.S. Caribbean policy in the aftermath of Grenada has not been without its successes, however. Some nations have benefited from new employment opportunities and have managed economic growth. Antigua and Barbuda, and St. Lucia are notable. Nor should the United States be held solely responsible for the Caribbean's problems. Local leadership elites have also made their own share of economic miscalculations and other mistakes. Other problems are simply a matter of climate, geography, and size.

The brief period of Pax Americana imposed on the region in 1983 began to wear thin by 1988. Problems swept aside and not seriously addressed began to reemerge. The Caribbean, briefly an area of focused U.S. attention, is again back page news. Only with a new round of political and economic crises, with possible East-West overtones, will the United States be shaken from its lethargy.

IV.

Caribbean reality continues to be formed by its history. Yet the events of 1983 also mark a watershed. The changes wrought by Grenada are examined in the remainder of this volume. Sally Shelton-Colby offers insights into the Eastern Caribbean setting of the NJM revolution, Harald Sandstrom analyzes the movement's ideology, and David Lewis its foreign policy. Wendell Bell's focus is on U.S.–Grenadian relations and the character of the decision to intervene. The final chapter in Part I, by Robert Pastor, discusses the impact on the Caribbean of the revolution's demise and the intervention.

Part II, "Revolution, Conflict, and Democracy in the Caribbean," provides country studies of the Caribbean region since 1983. Georges Fauriol covers Jamaica; Edward Dew examines Suriname; Aaron Segal explores events in Haiti; G. Pope Atkins analyzes the Dominican Republic; and Scott MacDonald, Erik Kopp, and Victor J. Bonilla cover the Caribbean's eastern tier.

"Issues on the Periphery" comprise Part III. In this section the scope is widened to include U.S. foreign policy in the Caribbean, the question of whether or not the Grenada debacle was a defeat for Soviet-Cuban foreign policy, and the role of the European Economic Community in the Caribbean basin. Jonathan Lemco's observations on the Contadora process in Central America raise pertinent issues such as democracy, development, and self-determination of small-state actors in the international arena. Eva Loser's chapter on Panama is equally relevant. That nation's strategic location and control of the Canal are of utmost concern to the United States and the Caribbean states, regardless of who Panama's leader is at a particular time.

Seweryn Bialer wrote: "The teaching of history, or, for that matter, political science and sociology, is almost without exception the distillation of the past." He also noted that the application of the lessons of the past to the present and future was highly important.[2] Bialer was writing about the Soviet Union. Yet his words have merit for the Caribbean since Grenada. There is a continuity with the past, which has been reestablished, especially with a renewal of the debate over what the future may bring: revolution, conflict, and/or democracy. This volume seeks to be part of that debate.

V.

We would be derelict if we were to leave it at that. Readers new to Caribbean studies may be forgiven some confusion as they strive to grapple with an extremely diverse and complex region. While Sally Shelton-Colby's chapter does an admirable job of introducing the Eastern Caribbean, some more general background is called for before we wade into particulars.

What are the most important facts a beginning student of the Caribbean needs in his/her "toolkit?" We feel they should include a geographic sense of what constitutes "the Caribbean," a basic grasp of British/French/Spanish/U.S. differences in colonial pattern, and an appreciation of the immense impact of colonial rule on the indigenous societies in terms of culture (especially language and religion), political forms, and socioeconomic patterns.

What is "The Caribbean?" We define it as the islands (the Greater and Lesser Antilles—i.e., the vast arc from the tip of Florida to the northern rim of South America) plus, strangely, the Guianas on the northeastern rimland of South America (Guyana—formerly British Guiana, French Guiana, and Suriname—formerly Dutch Guiana) and Belize, "the odd man out" in Central America due to its British colonial heritage. The reason for their inclusion is that they do not fit the Hispanic mold of the rest of that continent in terms of cultural, historical, and commercial links. Recently the Reagan administration has sought to popularize the term *Caribbean basin* for essentially the same geographic expanse. We prefer the simpler *Caribbean.*

Central America is generally considered a distinct region. We include it in our definition of the Caribbean and in our coverage as part of the periphery, viewed from Grenada. Our rationale is the mutual relevance of events in these two areas, exemplified by the widespread interpretation of the U.S.–led invasion of Grenada as prelude to armed intervention in Nicaragua.

It may be helpful to name the islands referred to above. The greater Antilles consist of Cuba, Hispaniola (Haiti and the Dominican Republic), Jamaica, the Cayman Islands, Puerto Rico, and the Virgin Islands. The lesser Antilles are comprised of Anguilla, Antigua and Barbuda, Dominica, Montserrat, St. Lucia, St. Vincent and the Grenadines, Grenada, St. Kitts–Nevis (St. Christopher), plus various French departments and Dutch territories. The final group consists of the islands on the South American continental shelf: Trinidad and Tobago; Barbados; and the Dutch islands Aruba, Curaçao, and Bonaire. We hasten to add a caveat: We have been unable, within these covers, to include attention to all societies that fit our definition. Specifically, the following, with regret, are not covered: The Bahamas, Bermuda, Belize, the British and U.S. Virgin Islands, the Cayman Islands, the Turks and Caicos Islands (these are often overlooked in comprehensive studies of "the Caribbean"), and Puerto Rico.

Differences in Cultural, Social, Economic, and Political Patterns

Each colonial master brought a different language and cultural heritage: British, French, Spanish, and Dutch. Beyond these differences of kind, there is also a rich variety of mixtures within each island and territory, as Creoles (Europeans born in the Caribbean) blended the mother tongues from Europe with those of African slaves and indigenous Caribs. Many citizens of the region still identify themselves as English or French, for instance, and shaking the idea that "British (or European) is best" remains a fundamental problem of collective identity and self-esteem.

Social stratification owes much to slave days, when interaction between plantation owners and slaves produced a mixed-race group called, in the Anglophone regions, Coloureds, and "lighter is better" became the criterion of social status. The French Caribbean led the way in seeking more positive identification with the African heritage, and black power movements in the Anglo areas followed suit. However, economic achievement and social stratification are still determined significantly by the hue of one's skin—and the fact that most states are still heavily reliant on

export of agricultural goods and minerals means that the range of vocational choice and social mobility remains quite limited. Further complications arose when the slaves were freed, and indentured servants
were imported from India. Guyana and Trinidad and Tobago are well-
known for their large Indian populations and communal politics (supporting candidates by racial identity—what is called "apanjaht" in Suriname; see Edward Dew's Chapter 7).

Political forms are as varied as the cultural and linguistic norms. For
example, Cuba and Nicaragua (also Grenada between 1979 and 1983)
practice full-fledged Marxist-Leninist vanguard party rule; a number of
states are trying democratic capitalism (e.g., Jamaica, Grenada, Belize,
the Bahamas), using British-style Westminster parliamentary structure;
Suriname and Guyana have exhibited versions of praetorianism—that
is, societies so unable to agree on who has the legitimate right to rule
that they are prone to military rule; and Haiti is struggling to find
channels of participation after years of total domination by Papa Doc
and Baby Doc Duvalier—a halfway house, an unresolved dialectic, only
a few years behind the Dominican Republic on the other half of the
island, where the Trujillo legacy is still not buried. So variety indeed
makes for very spicy alternatives among the Caribbean nations.

As we now narrow our focus, in the next chapter, to the Eastern
Caribbean, and then proceed to study the area "from Grenada out," we
hope this brief survey of the region's salient characteristics will enable
the reader to navigate the Caribbean Sea with a reasonably reliable com-
pass.

NOTES

1. Régis Debray, *Revolution in the Revolution?: Armed Struggle and Political Struggle in Latin America* (New York: Grove Press, 1967), p. 19.

2. Seweryn Bailer, *The Soviet Paradox: External Expansion Internal Decline* (New
York: Alfred A. Knopf, 1986), p. 375.

PART I
THE IMPLICATIONS OF GRENADA:
REVOLUTION AND INVASION

1
An Introduction to the Eastern Caribbean
Sally Shelton-Colby

INTRODUCTION

The Eastern Caribbean, despite its miniscule size and lack of economic resources, has become an important item on the foreign policy agendas of several Western Hemisphere powers, including the United States, Canada, Venezuela, and Cuba. The withdrawal of the United Kingdom from the Eastern Caribbean; the attainment of independence by most of the very small English-speaking states; the 1979 revolution in Grenada, the growth of Cuban influence there, and the subsequent "rescue mission"; three coup attempts and mass civic protest that resulted in the fall of a government in Dominica; and political turmoil in St. Lucia—coupled with fragile economic systems and widespread poverty—have underlined the region's potential for political turmoil and instability.

This introductory chapter will set the stage for the following chapters on specific Eastern Caribbean island nations: Grenada, St. Lucia, St. Vincent and the Grenadines, Dominica, Antigua-Barbuda, St. Kitts–Nevis, Anguilla, and Montserrat. Collectively known as the Windwards and the Leewards, these islands' historical experience and shared political and economic characteristics provide a useful framework for evaluating the ability of very small nations to manage political and economic stresses as well as threats to their national security. All have populations, gross national products, and per capita income levels that, though varied, are more closely related to each other than to the rest of the Caribbean. The Windwards and Leewards, at times politically united, at times separate, have a shared colonial history which conditioned contemporary political and economic realities.[1] Both island groups are similar socially and economically. Their history is only tangentially linked to the larger Caribbean islands and almost not at all to the smaller islands, such as the Turks and Caicos or the British Virgin Islands. Geographically, they cover a 500-mile-long swath in the easternmost part of the Caribbean archipelago. Their populations range from 12,000 (Montserrat) to 123,000 (St. Lucia); their gross national products from $526 million to 1.25 billion; and land surface from 102 to 600 square kilometers. To put these figures into perspective, the total population of the islands is less than that of South Dakota: the population of St. Vincent is roughly equivalent to that of Hialeah, Florida; that of Dominica to Charlestown, South Carolina; that of St. Lucia to Macon, Georgia; and even that of far larger Barbados to Jersey City, New Jersey.

THE COLONIAL BACKGROUND

The Leewards, historically, experienced almost continuous British rule except for a brief interregnum when St. Kitts (St. Christopher) was occupied by the British and the French simultaneously. This contrasts sharply with the Windwards which experienced both British and French colonial rule. The Leewards were also probably settled before the Windwards and experimented with federation earlier than other parts of the Caribbean.

There have been two Leeward Island federations. The first was established in the seventeenth century and the second in the late nineteenth century, lasting until 1956.[2] The Leewards are typically smaller than the Windwards, are closer together (from one Leeward Island others can be observed), and seem to have a greater degree of inter-island contact than the Windwards. Although climatically they are drier and tend to experience severe water shortages, the foundation of the economy has traditionally been plantation agriculture.[3] This is still the case in St. Kitts where sugar is the largest earner of foreign exchange in contrast to Antigua where sugar production has almost disappeared and the sugar estates are now in the possession of the government. Antigua-Barbuda and Montserrat have had some modest success at attracting foreign investment and tourism though all the islands' highly dependent, undiversified economies have traditionally relied on externally sourced balance of payments support for financial survival.

Two of the Leewards face ongoing secessionist tendencies: Nevis has traditionally insisted on either independence from St. Kitts (which has already lost Anguilla) or self-rule while Barbuda strenuously sought separation from Antigua prior to independence. The Grenadines have at times tried to distance themselves from St. Vincent as has Cariacou from Grenada. The smaller islands feel they lack the proper representation in the national legislatures due to the difference in population sizes, and that their share of the national budget is usually smaller than it should be.[4] Insular rivalry is likely to continue as a source of tension for the foreseeable future, though further fragmentation of country units is remote.

The Windwards have not enjoyed the same experience with federation nor have they experienced the virtually uninterrupted colonial rule of the Leewards (though the Windwards were under a common British governor for a time).[5] The Windwards, lusher and larger than the Leewards in terms of both geography and population and at a greater distance from each other, have a less homogeneous pattern of colonialism, as the islands seesawed between the British and the French. Dominica changed hands four times, St. Lucia nine, St. Vincent and the Grenadines four and Grenada five. As a result they are more culturally heterogeneous than the Leewards and a French-based patois is spoken by preference in many of the rural areas.[6] Moreover, certain linkages to the French metropole remain, as reflected by the attendance of St. Lucia's prime minister, John Compton, at the Francophone summit held in Paris on February 18, 1986.[7] In addition to the language difference, the Windwards have closer relations with nations outside the Windwards and Leewards system. St. Vincent, for example, has especially close ties with Barbados, and Grenada with Trinidad and Tobago.

THE ECONOMIC SCENE

For most of the islands in the Eastern Caribbean political independence has obviously not brought economic independence. A significant improvement in economic performance has occurred thanks to the plunge in the price of oil and improved tourism revenues. Nevertheless, island economies remain highly fragile and dependent on external sources of concessional aid. There has been only limited success at economic diversification and economies remain overwhelmingly dependent on tourism, sugar, or banana production. Consumption absorbs almost all gross domestic product while investment and much of recurrent expenditures are financed largely from external resources in the form of grants or concessional development assistance.

Examining the reasons for this continuing—and perhaps growing— dependence on external financial flows, one finds a daunting series of factors that cumulatively pose major obstacles to achieving satisfactory levels of economic growth and development. These include severely limited economies of scale deriving from internal and regional markets too small for import-substitution or export-oriented industrial production; an extremely limited range of raw materials; inefficient use of existing resources; declining agricultural productivity in some of the islands (though improved in others); and limited technical capabilities both in the public and private sectors. Moreover, the islands suffer diseconomies of scale leading to high per capita cost of public administration and social infrastructure; low levels of national savings; a limited range of economic activities and a virtually total lack of intersectoral linkages (i.e., limited structural transformation); and a high percentage of exports and imports relative to GDP. Frequent natural disasters devastate or seriously damage local economies. While some islands have developed a significant tourism industry, others have only limited capacity for tourism development. None has been successful at attracting the needed levels of foreign capital and technology for the development of the productive sector. Revenue continues to be exceeded by expenditure and all the islands face serious budgetary deficits. In sum, the economies of the Eastern Caribbean nations, in spite of some improvements, remain fragile and susceptible to changes in the international economic environment. Expected cuts in U.S. development assistance levels as a result of budgetary pressures in the United States could take a serious toll on the island economies.

Agriculture, the mainstay of the Eastern Caribbean, has declined on some islands (though it improved in others).[8] The decline in acreage under cultivation (and, in some areas, productivity) is linked to the lack of an adequate agricultural policy on the part of some island governments to help ease the transition from estate economies to smaller landowner production. Agricultural extension services are weak to nonexistent in almost all the islands and the requisite technical inputs into modern farming are not available. In addition, most agricultural holdings may be too small to be economically efficient. In many cases there is no clear land tenure policy or system with the result that a majority of small farmers have neither clear title to the land nor guaranteed long-term lease arrangements, thus making it difficult to obtain credit for modernization of farming methods. The incentive to invest and increase production is also reduced. The World Bank estimated that it is possible to triple food crop production in some islands and to increase it significantly in others. Another part of the explanation, therefore, is related to a particular cultural problem: many West Indians associate agricultural work with slavery, a crippling legacy of the colonial experience. No Caribbean government has as yet succeeded in devising an effective strategy for coping with this aspect of the problem.

Another major impediment in the development process is the generally sluggish private sector. In fact, manufacturing tends to employ a very small percentage of the total work force. Private sectors play a limited role in the productive capacity of island governments due to the small size of the economies, the lack of raw materials, shortages of managerial and technical skills, and virtually nonexistent capital markets. To the extent that any of the islands have been able to develop a manufacturing sector, it has generally been of the "enclave" type, that is, a production structure based on imports of raw materials which are then assembled by low wage local labor and reexported. Such enclave industries provide important employment opportunities but also cause some revenue loss to governments; governments tend to compete with each other to provide tax and other incentives to foreign corporations, the most common being 10–15 year, full or partial, tax holidays and low cost factory shells. Moreover, in spite of several years of effort to draw new investments into the manufacturing sector of the islands, results have been poor, even under the U.S. government's Caribbean Basin Initiative. The distance of the Eastern Caribbean from mainland U.S. markets, noncompetitive wage rates and inadequate economic infrastructure are major disincentives to prospective investors. In addition, a disintegrating Caribbean Common Market (CARICOM) and growing intra-Caribbean protectionism deny regional market opportunities to island manufacturers.

Severely limited technical capabilities in both the public and private sectors are also a very significant obstacle in the development process. Although out-migration has been an important safety valve in countries where birth rates are high (Dominica and Grenada, for example) migration also has its negative aspects since those who migrate tend to be those with the skills so desperately needed at home. The lack of skills in the public sector has been one of the main reasons for the heretofore severe shortage of planning capacity. Caribbean planners have stressed the absence of technical resources to accumulate basic data on social and economic conditions in their countries and the lack of any significant planning capability as serious problems for development strategists. They attribute the lack of adequate planning not only to the migration of technicians but also to an absence of a consistent political commitment to planning, inferring that politics often takes precedence over the technical merits of development plans.[9] Although planning units now exist in most of the Eastern Caribbean, they are a new phenomenon; in several countries they have existed for some time on paper but are only just beginning to be staffed. The question remains as to whether they will be utilized effectively.

The shortage of technical expertise is also felt by multilateral donor institutions and donor countries whose aid dispersal rates are often unduly slow because of inadequate technical resources in the recipient governments for project identification and development. Some Eastern Caribbean economic development ministries have until recently had no trained economists and many civil servants have only a high school degree.

The high per capita cost of public administration is a financial burden the island-states of the Eastern Caribbean could do without. This situation derives fom the historical practice of each territory being governed from London as one entity in a confederation. Many have argued that a gigantic historical error was made when the British Caribbean attained independence piecemeal and not as a single unit.[10] Government in most of the Eastern Caribbean tends to be the most important employer. Roughly 75 percent of government spending goes to financing administrative and social services. The percentage is high because of separate governments on each island, each with its associated bureaucracy.

Tourism also plays an important role in the regional economy. It is a major source of foreign exchange earnings for some island economies. However, not all islands have the white sand beaches that seem to be required by tourists. Tourism therefore remains underdeveloped, with few exceptions. The obvious risk in developing tourism as the main pillar of the economy is the susceptibility to international economic recession. The 1981–1982 recession, for example, took a serious toll on tourism earnings in all the Caribbean as tourist arrivals plunged well below normal levels.

A review of the relationships among the three main pillars of the Eastern Caribbean economies—agriculture, industry, and tourism—points to a severe lack of intersectional linkages.[11] For example, 90 percent of the food consumed in the Eastern Caribbean's tourist industry is believed to be imported rather than produced locally. Handicraft also tends to be imported from Asia or Latin America. The lack of intersectoral linkages derives from the islands' close dependence on the colonial power, the United Kingdom, to which they have been tied vertically, rather than to horizontal links with each other.

A low level of national savings and a high ratio of consumption to GDP are also serious economic handicaps. The main sources of financing have been foreign governments and investors, and remittances from nationals living abroad.[12] Although reliable data on remittances are scarce, it appears that approximately 15–20 percent of household income in one Eastern Caribbean nation, for example, comes from remittances and about 40 percent of the finances of low income, women-run households in another derives from the same sources. The share may be even larger than these figures indicate. It appears that nationals are scarcely contributing to the financing of their own development. It may be one of the ironies of the increased donor attention to the Eastern Caribbean that enlarged aid flows may reduce the incentive to save, thereby tending to perpetuate dependency.

With public sector spending focused on infrastructure and basic human needs programs, there has been insufficient funding for revenue-earning production to help sustain high levels of government spending. Many islands have had to resort to substantial short-term external borrowing. In the past, island governments tended to have relatively low external debt levels, living as they did off British budgetary support, but even under colonial rule there were deficits. Increasingly, they have resorted to deficit financing to maintain public expenditures. The Eastern Caribbean islands have a history of recurrent budgetary problems. The impact of natural disasters and international economic stresses has further aggravated those problems. The most dramatic case is that of Dominica, where the average annual deficit has been about EC $3 million but reached EC $20 million in 1979 as a result of devastation by hurricanes. Per capita income figures, while relatively high by Third World standards, distort the actual standard of living and level of economic development. The fundamental problem confrontng the area is an inappropriate, antiquated economic structure which can neither meet the basic needs of the people nor demonstrate sufficient resilience in the face of external economic decline.

THE POLITICS OF CHANGE

Self-government is a recent political phenomenon in the Windwards and Leewards dating from the 1960s. London maintained control over defense and external affairs until formal independence. With most of the islands now independent, the legal responsibilities of the United Kingdom for defense of existing democratic systems has vanished. In its wake questions are being raised about the strength and appropriateness to small island nations of that inherited system and of its ability to deal with challenges to its survival. A review of the political processes and social systems in the islands reveals both strengths and weaknesses that will help determine the political evolution of the Eastern Caribbean.

There is widespread debate among Caribbean scholars as to how deeply rooted democratic values and systems are among West Indians and what the prospects are for those systems to survive.[13] Analysts who take an optimistic view emphasize the survival generally of democratic systems in the face of severe economic decline and political turmoil. They point to the vehement rejection of groups advocating radical political and economic change by West Indian electorates in a dozen elections since the Grenadian Revolution of 1979. They stress the embrace by West Indians of democratic values and institutions that reinforce democratic systems.

Those who take a pessimistic view point to continuing high unemployment (in most islands), drug abuse, and other indices of economic and social decline; institutional corruption in parts of the Eastern Caribbean and a willingness by some political leaders to bend the law to their own ends; the high percentage of youth who have not known the colonial experience, who may have a more clearly defined sense of Caribbean identity than their elders and who may be desirous of experimentation with "indigenous" political and economic models; the growing drug trafficking through the area; new evidence of organized crime money being filtered through offshore banking operations; and finally the limited technical capabilities of local governments to handle an armed rebellion like that on Union Island in 1979 or to cope with the newer challenges of drug trafficking and organized crime activities.

There is only limited empirical evidence available to support either hypothesis. Nevertheless, certain tentative conclusions can be drawn, based on a weighing of the forces of tradition versus the forces of change. Even many rabid anticolonialists argue that West Indians are a conservative people, embracing traditional models and alliances and reluctant to experiment with alternative structures and systems. In many respects, what occurred in Grenada with the New Jewel Movement was an aberration from the regional norm which was characterized by an acceptance of the Westminster parliamentary system. Anthony Maingot has used the apt term "modern conservative societies" to describe the islands' people.[14] One should not discount the influence of the relatively benign British colonial experience in terms of shaping the views of West Indian elites. Oriented towards the United Kingdom through education, training, and family ties as well as commercial links and aid flows, West Indians are just beginning to turn toward the United States, a move hastened by the United Kingdom's unwillingness to participate in the 1983 Grenada invasion.

Moreover, the Westminster parliamentary system has served the area well by providing a relatively high level of social services and by generally responding to and respecting the will of the people through regular elections required under local constitutions. As Scott MacDonald has noted, "Outside of the Caribbean, there are few areas in the Third World that may be regarded as having a preponderance of open political systems where electoral competition is strong, a loyal opposition exists, and change of government is peaceful and regular, while at the same time, governments seek to improve the standard of living for their citizens."[15] The most celebrated instance of flagrant abuse of this system (Grenada under Eric Gairy) is probably a *sui generis* case and the exception to a pattern of political order reflecting a significant degree of stability within a democratic context—one that is virtually without precedent in the Third World.

This pattern is reinforced by the existence of strong trade union movements, shaped and encouraged by their British and North American counterparts. These movements have not only formed the main base of support for democratic political parties throughout Eastern Caribbean states, but also, given the absence of well developed grass roots parties in most countries, may be the prime institution within which political and social attitudes are molded. Furthermore, a relatively high degree of literacy and level of social services, though not always adequate, have resulted in declining infant mortality and greater life expectancy than in many parts of the Caribbean and Central America. This tends to reinforce existing social patterns, and the primarily religious role of the churches contrasts starkly with that of the reformist, politicized Catholic Church in Central America. The Eastern Caribbean is also characterized by a significant degree of racial homogeneity. Racial consciousness can be noted, but the racial tensions and antagonisms of Guyana, Suriname, and Trinidad and Tobago are not present.

Other factors, however, raise questions about the viability of the West-minster tradition and the ability of democratic governments to manage conflict and to survive as democracies. The potential for conflict in the West Indies derives from various sources, and capabilities to deal with conflict are limited. The Eastern Caribbean's experience with problem solving and crisis management has not been extensive because of its relatively recent emergence from colonial status. The road to self-government in the Windwards and Leewards has been slow. From the mid-Victorian period (1870s), the Windwards and Leewards were administered from London as a Crown Colony. As Gordon Lewis noted, in terms of the West Indian island-states' political and nationalistic development, they lagged twenty years behind the larger countries of the Caribbean. In fact, universal adult suffrage was not granted until as late as 1951. After World War II, U.S. pressure, the influence of educated and politically aware West Indian expatriates, and the rise of militant trade unions produced a change in the political climate, and power passed from the brown middle class to the black working class in most instances. Self-government came only in the late 1960s with the development of the concept of the "associated state." London maintained responsibility for security and external affairs, two important attributes of sovereignty. Dominica became fully independent only in 1978, St. Lucia and St. Vincent in 1979, Antigua in 1981 and St. Kitts–Nevis in 1983. Independence is recent and experience with full self-government, especially in the area of security, is limited.

The style of government in the islands is both stabilizing and destabilizing. Politics is highly personalistic, nonideological, and centralized. True cabinet government is rare; the general pattern in the Eastern Caribbean is one of strong (some would say authoritarian) prime ministerial government. This contrasts with larger, more modern societies where politics tends to be the result of interaction among groups. It is at the cabinet level, moreover, where most decisions, no matter how trivial, are made. For example, cabinets normally decide whether civil servants traveling abroad will fly first-class or coach! Furthermore, in view of the minute size of island nation governments and societies and the dominant role of the government in shaping the economy (absent any significant private sector role), the government, that is, the prime minister, is a powerful force with broad influence over all aspects of the society and body politic. Decisions will often be made on the basis of politics rather than merit, on the grounds of what is good for the party in power rather than what is good for the country and frequently on the prime minister's personal likes and dislikes rather than on the basis of informed orderly procedure. Even the politically neutral civil service is not immune from political wrath; the term "victimization" is a West Indian invention which describes revenge politicians take on civil servants suspected of harboring sympathies for the opposition party.

As long as the political leadership enjoys the confidence of the people, that is, as long as it enjoys legitimacy not only through the electoral process but also through a thoughtful and fair decision-making process and implementation procedure, personalized politics can be a stabilizing force. However, there may be a tendency in some islands toward institutional corruption. If a government is believed to be guilty of administrative corruption and that corruption is sufficiently blatant and egregious, then a breakdown in the political order will tend to occur. One obvious example is Grenada during the 1960s and 1970s.

Gordon Lewis quite correctly points to Eric Gairy and his performance as head of government as proof of the fragility of new constitutional systems.[16] A 1962 U.K. inquiry into political unrest in Grenada (the United Kingdom suspended the constitution) provides evidence of Gairy's illegal use of government monies, victimization of the civil service, and systematic flaunting of certain government regulations and other violations of public trust.

Another example is Dominica in 1979, when Prime Minister Patrick John attempted to force Parliament to accept new laws which would have served both to expand John's authority and to have severely restricted certain civil rights guaranteed under the Dominican constitution. The result was mass popular protest that resulted in violence and death for several civilians at the hands of the Dominican Defense Force. This was followed by an extralegal change of government and a period of prolonged turmoil unprecedented in Dominica's—or the Eastern Caribbean's—modern history up to that point.

Personal political ambitions have potential for weakening processes and institutions of government. St. Lucia experienced three years of turmoil and a virtual breakdown in administration due to serious factionalism within the government beginning in 1979. An attempt by the St. Vincent government to pass legislation muzzling the press and unions produced a broad popular reaction which could have produced a period of serious instability had the government not been forced to withdraw the legislation. Faith in democracy then may ultimately relate to the commitment of political leadership to respect legal procedure both in the letter and the spirit of the law.

Another source of potential conflict could arise out of what appears to be a growth in drug trafficking through the area and some increase in local production and consumption.[17] Local growers have challenged the security forces in Dominica, and drug traffickers are believed to have been behind one of the coup attempts against that island's government.

Other threats come from corporate charlatans and organized crime elements who attempt to reap economic benefits from exploitation of poor island-states desperate for foreign investment but lacking the capability of evaluating the bona fides of the potential investor. It is Dominica again that has had unhappy experiences with these elements, some of whom had connections to the Ku Klux Klan, others with possible contacts to organized crime. Foreign criminal elements appear to have been interested in "investments" in some of the other islands as well.

It is economic decline, however, which has elicited the most attention as a potential source of conflict in the Eastern Caribbean. Scholars, analysts and politicians have long debated whether it is economic decline, economic growth or some combination thereof which generates or contributes to tension, conflict, and crisis. A review of recent conflict in the Caribbean would seem to indicate that where revolutionary change has occurred (Grenada and Suriname), economic issues have not been the immediate or most obvious cause. Furthermore, in a dozen recent national elections, which coincided with serious economic decline or stagnation, radical leftist parties were strongly rejected and traditional parties were overwhelmingly elected or reelected. Nevertheless, a survey of Eastern Caribbean opinion shapers almost unanimously reflects a clear belief that economic deterioration, if not checked, over the long term will lead to a breakdown in political order and the rise of alternative, radical economic and political models. Some believe that, if present governments are not able to bring about a material improvement in present economic and social conditions, the same West Indian electorate will endorse left-leaning parties promising reform. Others predict more Grenada-style coups: A small armed group easily overpowers a relatively weak local police force, suspends the existing political system and begins to implement reforms, basing its action on an appeal for national unity, social justice, political reform, economic progress—and probably a rejection of the traditional means of achieving those objectives.

There is one interesting historical precedent for establishing a linkage between economic decline and political instability in the Eastern Caribbean. During the second half of the 1930s, widespread violence and riots in the region were attributed by many historians to worsening economic conditions, which parallel in some respects the current world

economic situation. The late thirties were marked by dramatically increased unemployment resulting largely from a fall in world prices
for West Indian exports; a sharp increase in the rate of population
growth due to declining infant mortality; a marked increase in urbanization; and forced repatriation of West Indians from the United
States and Latin America in the face of the Great Depression. The
spread of education and the beginnings of mass media (radio) produced hopes and ambitions that could not be met. Apathy turned
into violence when existing governments proved to be unresponsive
to the polity's demands.

One striking difference between then and now of course is the absence
of the British colonial administration to maintain order. The capability
of present island governments to maintain order in the face of conflict,
be it purely internally or externally supported, has been extremely limited. Until recently not even a coast guard capacity for marine rescue
or coastal patrol purposes has existed. Although each government possessed one or two police patrol craft, they have traditionally been small,
slow, and often as not dry-docked for need of repairs. U.S. and U.K.
efforts to support the development of an Eastern Caribbean Regional
Security System augur well for improved cooperation on security threats
in the future. This endeavor has been given impetus by events in Grenada which underlined the inability of the Eastern Caribbean to provide
for its own security.

EXPLORING THE OPTIONS

Contributing to concern about sources of conflict which the islands
face are high birthrates, growing urbanization, reduced migration outlets
as a result of U.S. legislation, and a demographic bulge in the younger
segment of the population (about 60 percent of the population is under
the age of fifteen years) where unemployment may be twice as high as
the national average. (One prime minister believes it to be as high as 90
percent.) Although migration has traditionally reduced the rate of population growth to a reasonably manageable level of 2 percent annually,
this disguises the probability that the urban population may be growing
at 4 to 5 percent annually. This is reflected as well in the anticipated
higher rate of growth in the labor force in the 1980s than in the 1960s
and 1970s. U.S. and U.K. moves to restrict migration are closing (at least
to some degree) the traditional safety valve with a resultant increase in
pressures on the Eastern Caribbean governments to provide employment as well as improved social services.

Another source of potential conflict in the Eastern Caribbean is Cuba,
if it were to shift its current policy away from one dealing with established
governments to one actively supporting revolution in the region. Cuba's

influence at present cuts both ways. There is admiration, partic-ularly among the young, for Cuba's achievements in the fields of education, health and housing. But there is also awareness of and concern among many West Indians over Cuba's close alignment with the USSR and the lack of civil liberties under its restricted political system. Although some Eastern Caribbean leaders fear Cuba's support for radical leftist groups at home, all acknowledge that Cuba's influence is generally weak. They point to the fact that in every island election since 1979 voters have rejected Cuba-oriented, leftist parties. In some cases candidates did not receive enough votes even to recoup their electoral deposits.

Whether or not the Eastern Caribbean of the 1980s and 1990s ex-periences either a repeat of the political turmoil of the 1930s or another Grenada will depend in part on the responsiveness and commitment of their governments to economic growth and development and adherence to constitutional procedures. But it will also depend in a large degree on the responsiveness of external actors, principally in the United States, to the economic and security needs of the region. To deal with the array of potential and actual sources of conflict confronting them, island gov-ernments must move promptly toward a broad range of political, eco-nomic and social reforms in order to maintain the legitimacy and strengthen the effectiveness of existing systems.

On the economic side, the most urgent need is for a broad restruc-turing and diversification of the economy. To achieve this, the islands of the Eastern Caribbean must shift from their present intense concen-tration on consumption to a priority on productive investment. The share of public sector spending on productive investment should in-crease. Agricultural revitalization may be the most important way to start the drastic economic overhaul the island-states need. Land tenure policy should be rationalized and claraified so that access to credit is assured and incentive provided for farmers to increase production. Adequate credit should be made available through revamped government pro-grams. Agricultural extension services should be enhanced and enabled to provide technical assistance and inputs. Agricultural diversification should be encouraged, where possible, away from traditional mono-crop patterns. Where land is held by the Crown, it should be distributed in economically sized units rather than being allowed to lie fallow. Mar-keting facilities urgently need to be developed in order to facilitate the sale of both export and local produce. Fisheries development is another area deserving priority attention. Appropriate social policies should be shaped to provide much needed education, health and other social pro-grams, at present seriously inadequate in rural areas.

Governments must become more aggressive in their efforts to stim-ulate local and attract foreign investment by creating the political and economic climate conducive to investment. Establishing and financing national development corporations with aggressive "selling" operations in overseas countries is an important place to start. Governments should also provide appropriate fiscal incentives, coordinated with other Eastern Caribbean nations to avoid competitiveness leading to excessive revenue loss. Island governments should establish well-staffed planning units in order to gather necessary social and economic data, formulate national development goals, outline public sector investment programs and undertake project identification and development to take advantage of external sources of development assistance. This should also include a priority to develop an appropriate national energy policy to include measures aimed at conservation, pricing, and the creation of alternative indigenous energy sources.

Governments must also upgrade the capabilities of civil servants and of the private sector work force. A good start would be to move toward revamping the antiquated secondary school curriculum in order to emphasize the teaching of vocational skills. A conscious effort should be made to improve the training of civil servants, a need which a number of donor governments and institutions recognize and for which they are developing training programs. A similar kind of thrust should be made vis-à-vis training private sector managers in entrepreneurial skills, perhaps via a technical college in the area.

A more rational, planned policy of generating local revenue must be developed to deal with the alarming increase in budgetary deficits. Existing taxes could be more progressively assessed and efficiently collected and new taxes could be levied. For example, the income tax should be reimposed in those countries where is has, for political reasons, been eliminated. It will then be incumbent on governments to ensure that additional revenue collected will be used for productive investment and not only to meet recurrent budgetary expenditures.

Finally there is urgent need for governments to expend regional economic, political, and coast guard cooperation, as envisioned in the new Organization of Eastern Caribbean States Treaty, as well as in the CARICOM Treaty. Given the paucity of trained human resources in the Eastern Caribbean, development of pools of experts in various areas is particularly important. All island governments have endorsed the concept as have many donor governments and leading institutions, but progress in implementation has been painfully slow. Regional pools of experts would bring needed technical resources to the area and would reduce the cost per government. In addition, regional cooperation would expand market size and exports, thereby increasing the prospects of achieving economies of scale. It should also ultimately reduce the level of competitiveness relative to incentives to attract foreign investment.

The regional Coast Guard should be strengthened for coastal patrol, marine rescue, fisheries enforcement, and narcotics interdiction functions. Such a regional entity should also include joint training and intelligence sharing in order to enhance capabilities and minimize costs. Priority should also be placed on maximum standarization of equipment to achieve interchangeability of spare parts and repair services. Added to all this, the capabilities of the police forces in the region should be upgraded, particularly in new criminal areas such as hostage-taking, drug interdiction and terrorism.

CONCLUSION

Eastern Caribbean governments should be sensitive to the potential for loss of legitimacy from measures and practices which will result in an erosion of democratic values and popular support for democratic political systems. Respect for free trade union movements, an independent press, opposition political party activity, a politically neutral civil service not subject to victimization, and avoidance of the misuse of the police and manipulation of constitutional procedures would help to strengthen extant democratic value systems and institutions in the Eastern Caribbean. Moreover, it would be desirable for political parties to develop stronger grass roots party organizations in order to encourage voter participation and to avoid the development of mass-based radical movements deriving strength from public disenchantment with traditional parties that have become isolated, ossified, and elitist.

Lastly, the United States, with significant political and strategic interests in the Eastern Caribbean, must reinforce its commitment to the strengthening of democratic institutions and the economic development process. It should encourage a greater involvement by the National Endowment for Democracy to work with democratic political parties, trade unions, and other groups. It must commit the economic resources necessary to achieve the requisite level of economic growth through an appropriate mix of regional and bilateral aid, of project and budgetary assistance, of support for the public sector and for the private sector. As the region's largest donor, it should join the Caribbean Development Bank and play a more active role in helping to strengthen it and other regional institutions. It should use its considerable influence in the area to make a maximum push for revitalization of CARICOM and more serious efforts at political cooperation, if not unification. It should take the basic concept of the CBI and expand its coverage to make it much more meaningful than it currently is. And it should link the economic benefits the Caribbean is eligible to receive under the CBI to the Caribbean's taking meaningful steps toward greater political and economic cooperation. The U.S. should continue its efforts to build up the regional Coast Guard and should expand its cooperation with the United Kingdom in providing police training. Its commitment to the area will strengthen not only the tiny microstates of the Eastern Caribbean but also the United States' own ability to protect its interests there.

NOTES

1. See A.J. Payne, *The Politics of the Caribbean Community 1961–1979: Regional Integration Among New States* (New York: St. Martin's Press, 1980), pp. 1–25.

2. Payne, *The Politics of the Caribbean Community.*

3. For a more in-depth study of the Caribbean's food situation, see W. Andrew Axline, *Agricultural Policy and Collective Self-Reliance in the Caribbean* (Boulder, Colorado: Westview Press, 1986).

4. Payne, *The Politics of the Caribbean Community*, pp. 1–25.

5. Payne, *The Politics of the Caribbean Community*, pp. 1–25.

6. David Loventhal, *West Indian Societies* (New York: Oxford University Press, 1972), pp. 77–79.

7. David Housego, "French Seek to Set Up a Commonwealth," *Financial Times*, February 18, 1986, p. 3.

8. Frank Long, "The Food Crisis in the Caribbean," *Third World Quarterly* (October 1982), Vol. 4, no. 4, p. 758. Also see Report by a Group of Caribbean Experts, *The Caribbean Community in the 1980s* (Georgetown: Caribbean Community Secretariat, 1981).

9. This problem is not indigenous to the Eastern Caribbean, but is observable in other parts of the developing world as well. For Central America, see Gairy Wynia, *Politics and Planners: Economic Development Policy in Central America* (Madison: University of Wisconsin Press, 1972).

10. Sir Kenneth Blackburne, "Changing Patterns of Caribbean International Relations: Britain and the 'British' Caribbean" in Richard Millett and W. Marvin Will, *The Restless Caribbean: Changing Patterns of International Relations* (New York: Praeger, 1979), p. 204.

11. See William Demas, *The Economics of Development in Small Countries* (Montreal: McGill University Press, 1965).

12. See country chapters in *Latin and Caribbean 1984* (Saffron Walden, Essex (U.K.): World of Information, 1984).

13. See Paget Henry and Carl Stone, eds., *The Newer Caribbean: Decolonization, Democracy and Development* (Philadelphia: Institute for the Study of Human Issues, 1983); and Anthony Payne and Paul Sutton, eds., *Dependency Under Challenge: The Political Economy of the Commonwealth Caribbean* (Manchester: Manchester University Press, 1984).

14. Personal communication with Anthony Maingot.

15. Scott B. MacDonald, *Trinidad and Tobago: Democracy and Development in the Caribbean* (New York: Praeger, 1986), p. 1.

16. Gordon K. Lewis, *The Growth of the Modern West Indies* (New York: Monthly Review Press, 1965), p. 160.

17. Joseph B. Treaster, "Jamaica, Close Ally, Does Little to Halt Drugs," New York *Times*, September 10, 1984, pp. 1 and 12.

2
The Ideology of Grenada's Revolution: Dead End or Model?
Harald M. Sandstrom

INTRODUCTION

A Prefatory Note

- March 13, 1979: Maurice Bishop and a group of left-wing radical intellectuals took over the government of tiny Grenada.
- October 19, 1983: Prime Minister Maurice Bishop was killed by a firing squad of fellow revolutionaries.
- Late October, 1983: U.S. armed forces, joined by soldiers and police from the Eastern Caribbean islands plus Jamaica, administered the coup de grace to the revolution.

It was a shortlived revolution. It was unique in the annals of revolutionary history. In its four and a half years, it raised questions about Caribbean societies' proneness to left-wing radical solutions, the tolerance of the United States and regional status quo forces to such experimentation, and the lessons to be drawn from this brief episode for the Caribbean and beyond.

These questions are reminiscent of those that arose after Chilean Marxist President Salvador Allende was killed in a 1973 military coup enjoying U.S. advice and consent. Allende, contrary to Bishop and associates, had won power through a national election, thus providing important evidence for Marxists promoting "the parliamentary road to socialism," a debate going back to Lenin's revolutionary Bolshevik's confrontation with the more gradualist Mensheviks. When Allende was slain and brutal right-wing repression arose under General Augusto Pinochet (who became president), Leninist revolutionaries were able, in effect, to say, "I told you so."

After the Grenadian revolution took and subsequently lost power by force, did the gradualist "parliamentary road" argument gain new impetus? Logic would lead us to expect a yes answer. However, (a) logic has not been known to govern men's action in international affairs or revolution, and (b) the answer to such questions clearly depends on our understanding of what happened in Grenada.

In this chapter I examine the ideology of Grenada's revolution with a view to estimating the consequences of the revolution's rise and fall for Caribbean and other Third World societies. My hypothesis is that elitist leadership assumptions in Marxism-Leninism clash with the egalitarian thrust of popular decision making in populism, the leading ideology in the Third World, and that the Grenadian revolution's demise can be traced to this clash. I predict that Marxist-Leninist revolutions in other Third World societies will meet a similar fate.

I do not believe these are ideological statements, though they will obviously be interpreted as such by Marxist-Leninists. I do not deny that I disagree with Marxist-Leninists, though I share much of their egalitarian intent, admire the sincere dedication many revolutionaries bring to their cause, and in particular acknowledge the achievements—especially in employment, education, and health—of the Grenadian revolution. Despite these disagreements, I have tried my best to approach, understand, and set forth the complex and intensely controversial tenets of the Grenadian revolutionaries with an open mind and without any wish to distort the record or stack the cards. The subject is much too important to play such games. I therefore ask the reader to approach the sometimes difficult task of reading through this chapter with as open a mind as possible. No generalizations based on one case can be valid. Yet I believe important lessons can be learned from this case.

The Importance of Grenada's Revolution and Its Ideology

Beyond what was said above, we may judge the significance of this Lilliputian revolution and the "Guns of October" invasion that ended it under three headings: space, time, and theory.

Space. The regional/hemispheric implications of events in Grenada clearly seem to have been judged significant by the leaders of the United States and its Caribbean allies. Why else was such a ferocious attack launched against the island? Was not the operation's code name, "Urgent Fury," an accurate reflection

• of anger over a mouse that roared, a tiny Melos taunting mighty Athens? (For a most enlightening dialogue about the Melos-Athens confrontation, drawing out the lesson of what happens when the weak challenge the strong, as in Thucydides' *History of the Peloponnesian War,* see *PS: Political Science & Politics* 17, 1 [1984]: 10–17; and ibid., 3 [1984]: 586–96.) Maurice Bishop frequently exclaimed to approving crowds "We're not in anybody's backyard!", and indicated his awareness that Grenada's "independent and nonaligned path" was anathema, particularly to "this present administration of President Ronald Reagan" which saw Grenada's foreign policy "as a moral insult."[1]

- of anxiety over "socialism with a human face" spreading from its base in the first socialist revolution in the English-speaking black Caribbean to other black majority, English-speaking, problem plagued societies in the area—perhaps even blacks and other minorities in North America? Bishop pointed with pride to "imperialism" being "doubly worried" because they feared Grenada "may prove to be an example to the rest of the region," and because Grenada's largely black population, unlike the people in Nicaragua and Cuba, was able to speak English "directly to...the people of the USA overall,...to the exploited majority," and especially to the "twenty-seven million black people who are a part of the most rejected and oppressed section of the American Population." For that, he said, "U.S. imperialism has a particular dread...."[2] His saying it does not make it so. However, with a few changes to account for ideological differences, it is not unlikely that these sentiments were expressed in U.S. foreign policy circles.

- of the consequent need to insure that the Grenadian revolution's ideology be seen as a dead end rather than a model?

Clearly, the U.S. and Caribbean governments chose to attack because they deemed it to be in their national interest to eradicate this irritant before it became a more serious threat. Presumably, the status quo powers meant also to send a meaningful signal to left-wing governments in Guyana and Suriname, to Nicaragua at the opposite end of the Caribbean Sea, and perhaps to Cuba. It is therefore no exaggeration to say that the Grenadian revolution and its aftermath sent waves through the Caribbean and beyond vastly disproportionate to the pebble size of the island. This was no forgettable aberration. It was a watershed act of U.S. foreign policy the implications of which will be felt and studied for years to come.

Time. Since the invasion/intervention/peace mission/rescue mission (One's label betrays one's disposition. Most Grenadians protested my use of the word "invasion."), an enormous amount of printed material has become available for the would-be anlyst of the revolution. U.S. forces removed tons of documents from the inner sanctums of the New Jewel Movement (NJM) and the People's Revolutionary Government (PRG), for the first time giving us a front seat to observe the development of a Marxist-Leninist revolution. These documents are now available in the U.S. National Archives, and we are far enough removed from the events that some perspective is possible.

On the other hand, we are still in the midst of aftershocks. At this writing, fourteen revolutionaries are languishing on death row for allegedly having ordered or carried out Prime Minister Bishop's assassination. Working with such recent data about such intensely controversial matters places a scholar in a dilemma. Lives and futures of real people may be affected by his analysis. Does prudence dictate delay? On the other hand, if any of his findings might help shed some light on contemporary controversies, would not delay be an irresponsible evasion? I decided it would be. I was privileged to get feedback from some of the accused on my interpretation of their ideology. Combining their views with the enormously rich and only partially tapped archival material allows me to present an analysis benefiting from resources previously unavailable to scholars dealing with this or any other revolution. The time is right to present this material.

Theory. Revolutionary ideology should not be studied in isolation. Meaning is provided by context, comparison, and contrast. Context includes socioeconomic conditions and history as well as questions concerning the nature of revolution. These questions, in turn, include the controversy over the importance of such a seemingly esoteric and intangible phenomenon as ideology vis-à-vis "more real" factors. There is endless debate among scholars about whether ideology really matters as action orientation, or whether it is primarily used as post-hoc rationalization for action taken in pursuit of realpolitik or personal self-seeking. For instance, there are those who contend that what happened in Grenada in the fall of 1983 was due almost exclusively to Bernard and Phyllis Coard's thirst for power. By focusing on ideology, I do not mean to deny the role of self-serving power motivation.

Given the French Revolution's precedent of "devouring its children," we may wonder if we did not witness a modern day parallel to Robespierre guillotining fellow revolutionary Danton, the orator of the Parisian populace. If Bernard Coard and Maurice Bishop (the orator of the Grenadian populace) had agreed on ideology, would both Bishop and the revolution have survived? The words of Danton haunt us: "All will go well as long as men say 'Robespierre and Danton'; but woe to me if ever they should say 'Danton and Robespierre'."[3]

Furthermore, ideology may serve several purposes. For instance, public statements fall into the agitprop category of accommodating revolutionary ideology to the public's perception, with all the qualifications necessitated by the prevailing political culture, level of education, and so on.

The documents brought back by the invading forces show individuals and groups engaged in a macabre dialogue that seemingly inexorably leads to violent confrontation and death. With "Forward Ever! Backward Never!" emblazoned all over Grenada, its revolution took the final step backward, into death and oblivion. Or did the Grenadian revolution really die? Are embers still smoldering under the ashes, capable of being fanned into flames even after a considerable hiatus? If Grenada's revolution "died" with its maximum leader, Prime Minister Maurice Bishop, what was the role of ideology?

THE RISE AND FALL OF THE NEW JEWEL REVOLUTION

The Status Quo Ante

Maurice Bishop and his colleagues would be the first to insist that no ideology can be understood apart from the material reality that gave it birth. As this chapter focuses on ideology, and as the previous chapter has set forth the material base in some detail, we shall survey only some of the more prominent factors in the prerevolutionary situation: the socioeconomic conditions, especially factors of race and class; the Gairy heritage; and the Black Power origin of the New Jewel Movement.

Socioeconomic Conditions. Grenada's economy, like colonial economies elsewhere, was structured for delivery of cash crops to the world market. Regardless of the ideological color of its government, its core has been primary products (nutmeg, cocoa beans) and tourism. Both of these sources of national income are inherently unstable. When world market prices for commodities drop, Grenada suffers; when political instability sets in, the tourists flee, and Grenada suffers. Foreign aid has matched the miniscule size of the island. Like so many other unviable minieconomies, Grenada has survived on a benevolent climate, lots of fruit, hard work, resourcefulness, and good luck.

The historical evolution of Grenada's lopsided economic structure yielded an equally skewed social structure. Like most of the Anglophone Caribbean, Grenada features a mass-to-elite stratification pattern with such a high correlation between racial pigmentation and class/status that it is almost invariably safe to assume dark means poor.[4]

Gordon Lewis described Grenada's social atmosphere not so much as a class conflict between worker and capitalist as one of "seigneurial paternalism and political clientelism...the 'little man' against the 'big boys.' " The basic human resource of the economy was "semi-subsistence small proprietors and land workers, who were neither pure peasantry nor pure proletariat but a crude mixture of both." On this broad base, a social pyramid was built from a small industrial working class; a lower middle class of mostly badly paid and ill-trained civil servants, teachers, police, and public service workers; a small group of foreign-educated university people; a small shopkeeper class; and on top, a *"comprador* bourgeois group of estate owners and merchant import-export capitalists imbued with the invoice mentality, hardly a sophisticated national bourgeoisie."[5]

In terms of political structure, Grenadians inherited centralization of power from the colonial period. The Crown Colony system (1877–1951) was based on the extensive power of the British-appointed governor who answered only to his government, as did his legislative and executive councils. Gradually (1925) some elected members were included in the legislative council, the number being increased in 1936, but without any change in the allocation of power. Voting, based on high income and property, remained the privilege of the light elite. Distinctions based on race and class remained virtually coincidental.[6] Received wisdom has it that the stronger and more mutually reinforcing such divisions are, the greater is the likelihood of political intolerance.[7]

The Gairy Heritage. Sir Eric Mathew Gairy left a deep footprint on Grenada, largely because he stamped very hard. Prior to Gairy, politics had been an elite, primarily urban occupation. The most prominent political figure, Theophilus Albert Marryshow, for all his remarkable achievements, was essentially ignorant of Grenada outside its capital, St. Georges, and spent 33 years (1925–1958) as a "symbol of the 'sophisticated urban gentlemen,' holding the gates against the 'unlettered country-booky.' " Then, in 1951, Gairy burst on the scene. He pushed the gates wide open through championship of mass revolt and universal enfranchisement, thereby rendering irrelevant pre–1951 politicians of Marryshow's class, values, and style.[8]

Gairy channeled the anger of the black agroproletariat, first into acts of anti-elite violence and a general strike, then into a trade union whose leverage he used to exact a series of economic and political concessions.[9] He was one of the "folk," in Smith's distinction, snubbed by the elite for his black skin, speech, and "weird" beliefs as well as for his obvious hostility to their economic domination.[10] Yet he prevailed over the elite, and Grenada was forever changed.

Surveying the record (wreckage?), it is easy to emerge with an armful of negatives. Some of them are comic. West Indian intellectuals—the new elite—like to ridicule Grenada's first prime minister as a farcial entertainer, an "airhead" who filled the space between his ears with "cult of personality" delusions of grandeur, UFOs, and alcohol-induced flights of fancy. Some are tragic. Gairy had undeniable charisma. His following was personalist and strong. However, rather than remaining the champion of the underclass, he used his popularity to create a "hero and crowd" dictatorship,[11] "exploiting and destroying the very people for whom he fought in 1951,"[12]

New Jewel Movement sympathizers are particularly explicit in describing how horrible the conditions were under Gairy's tutelage.

Massive unemployment (49% of the workforce, 70% unemployment among women) decreasing educational opportunities, sexual exploitation of women, secret police brutality, murders and disappearances, profiteering by monopolists and widespread corruption made life intolerable for the masses of people.... [13]

Obviously, Gairy was not responsible for *all* of this, but much of it must be laid at his doorstep since the consensus is that he had the power to make a difference, and chose not to. There is no denying the quaintness and cockeyed priority of his extraterrestrial concerns, the cruelty and terror of his repression, and the self-seeking and demagoguery of his rule.

However, the New Jewel Movement was successful in gaining power in 1979 not only because it opposed the venal and cruel rule by a dictator who seemed mentally unbalanced. A more balanced and historically accurate account must include Gairy's significant earlier achievements of trade union organizing and political institution building. The socioeconomic and political circumstances in Grenada seemed, in retrospect, to call out for someone capable of mobilizing the population for change. That the change was not entirely wholesome is not as important for the purposes of our analysis as the fact that large segments of the population were, indeed, mobilized.[14] Without Gairy and the institutions he created, there would have been no Bishop and NJM. In this sense we may speak of "the necessity of Gairy."

The Black Power Origin of the New Jewel Movement. "Black Power," to many North American and British observers, is a dated concept that summons up Stokely Carmichael and the U.S. civil rights confrontations of the 1960s. That version of Black Power emphasized a fair share for blacks and the black community—purely domestic concerns.[15]

The Commonwealth Caribbean version is quite different, most obviously due to different historical experience. Blacks in the West Indies are the majority, while in the United States they constitute a minority. Perhaps more importantly, the Commonwealth Caribbean societies only recently emerged from colonialism while the United States, once a colony, is now widely viewed as an imperial power. Moreover, Caribbean societies are characterized by heavy economic dependency on the First World. Added together, these are ingredients for an explosive mixture based on the perception that real independence was not achieved when the Union Jack was hauled down in the early 1960s and the national flags of the Commonwealth Caribbean were unfurled. There is nothing dated about this perception.

Caribbean Black Power, then, focuses its anger on what it is seen as exploitation by white foreign capitalists and their local handmaidens, the "houseslave" black governments and the national bourgeoisie from which their members come and in whose behalf they rule. These local "agents of imperialism" are said to facilitate foreign economic domination in return for economic gain and political/military protection. In the process, they exploit and oppress the lower classes. The ideology of Caribbean Black Power, accordingly, stresses revolutionary antiimperialism and anticapitalism (class struggle), superimposed on antiracism.[16]

Many Caribbean Black Power activists were drawn from the ranks of intellectuals, recently returned from pursuing advanced degrees abroad. A number of them, spread over the four campuses of the University of the West Indies, formed the New World Group as a framework for relatively moderate scholarly criticism of West Indian subservience to metropolitan powers.[17]

In Grenada, similarly, the early currents that flowed together to form the New Jewel Movement were generated by intellectual idealists, convinced that social change and betterment for the Grenadian people had to come through the development of grassroots democracy combined with active opposition to imperialism. Anthony Maingot called Bishop and his early NJM colleagues "utopians," bent on clearing up the Gairy mess: "They were educated and traveled, they had intellectualized ideas and development plans as varied as classical Marxism-Leninism, Tanzanian Christian Socialism, West Indian "New World" grassroots developmentalism and American Black Power formulations."[18]

The Radicalization of the Jewel. The intellectuals returning home from abroad in the late 1960s and early 1970s found a society suffering from 55 percent unemployment and serious alienation, focused on Gairy. The response was an inchoate process of group formation in search of meaningful change and safe allies, given the danger of arousing a backlash from Gairy. By twists and turns, or by successive shakes of the kaleidoscope, the New Jewel Movement took form. A brief survey of the process will give us some insight into the values and objectives that kindled the revolutionary takeover in 1979.

A May 1970 demonstration of solidarity with the potent Black Power uprising in neighboring Trinidad jolted Gairy into seeking emergency powers legislation. He also doubled the police force and announced the existence of a paramilitary squad of the "roughest and toughest roughnecks," the Mongoose Gang, created in 1967 but kept out of public view until 1970. Whether it was audacity or ignorance that caused him to declare in 1970 that he had won Black Power for Grenada in 1951, this demonstration and Gairy's reaction to it may be seen as a turning point. Gairy was for the first time challenged on his own turf, the demonstrators bidding for the support of Gairy's rank and file among the peasantry and workers.[19]

An outgrowth of the solidarity movement responsible for the Black

Power demonstration, the Grenada Forum was formed in June 1970 in the hope of using a newspaper as a foundation for building a new political movement. Bishop was a participant. Though the Forum lasted only half a year, it was seen as part of "a general trend towards radicalization of the young petty bourgeois intellectual elements within the region...." The nurses' demonstration of December 1970, around the time of the Forum's demise, was another direct spinoff from the Black Power demonstration in May of that year. Maurice Bishop and Unison Whiteman (cofounders of the NJM) demonstrated with the nurses and were arrested, as were a number of nurses. Bishop defended the nurses and won aquittals for all. The Forum was succeeded by the Movement for the Advancement of Community Effort (MACE) in early 1972. This group saw a two-stage process of change which focused first on socioeconomic research and then on application through political education of the masses. The young professionals and intelligentsia were becoming more committed to mass-based organization.[20]

In March 1972, yet another group emerged: the Joint Effort for Welfare, Education, and Liberation (JEWEL), whose most prominent leader in terms of his later role was economist Unison Whiteman. JEWEL was rural-based and drew most of its support from Whiteman's own parish.[21] It sought to provide an alternative to Gairy's patronage by mobilizing the peasantry and agro-proletariat in cooperatives.

In October 1972, Maurice Bishop and his law partner Kenrick Radix, both members of MACE, led its metamorphosis into the Movement for the Assembly of Peoples (MAP). This, for the first time, was an openly political group seeking state power and transformation of the Westminster system (an imitation of the British parliamentary democracy) "into one based on more popular control through assemblies of the people." Jacobs and Jacobs saw this as showing a "definite socialist drift."[22]

The reformist and progressive outlooks of MAP and JEWEL were sufficiently similar to make a coalition natural despite the fact that they had barely come into existence, and still had somewhat imprecise political programs. Moreover, Unison Whiteman, as a member of both organizations, provided a link that facilitated the merger. Accordingly, on March 11, 1973 they blended into the New Jewel Movement (NJM). The new party's Manifesto called for (1) radical redistribution of land into cooperative farms to grow food and limit expensive food imports; (2) nationalization of banks and insurance; (3) trade with countries offering the cheapest prices—a device "for challenging imperialist domination of Grenada"; and (4) "condemnation of imperialist activities the world over and concrete proposals to build a State system immune to such domination and based on popular control." Such popular control would come through abolition of party politics and the creation of People's Assemblies, ensuring permanent involvement of the people in democratic decision making.[23]

This Manifesto may have been anticapitalist, but "whatever else it was, this was not a Marxist-Leninist blueprint: There was no role for a 'vanguard' party, and it did not project ongoing class conflict and the eventual dictatorship of the proletariat."[24]

The Seizure of Power

As Grenada moved toward independence with Eric Gairy's political opposition mobilizing and growing stronger, repression by his hooligan Mongoose Gang grew commensurately. An NJM mass meeting entitled People's Congress was held on November 4, 1973. It was attended by some 8000 Grenadians in spite of strenuous efforts by Gairy's forces to scare people into staying away. A "People's Indictment" of 27 charges was read, calling on Gairy to resign by November eighteenth or face a general strike. Indictment #27 was particularly eloquent: "The Gairy Government was BORN IN BLOOD, BAPTIZED IN FIRE, CHRISTENED WITH BULLETS, IS MARRIED TO FOREIGNERS AND IS RESULTING IN DEATH TO THE PEOPLE."[25]

On "Bloody Sunday," November 18, 1973, the day the general strike was to go into effect, six NJM leaders seeking to coordinate the strike with business leaders were attacked, beaten, thrown in jail bleeding and semiconscious, denied both bail and medical services, and had their heads shaved with broken glass. This reign of terror was Gairy's political suicide. It created living martyrs, and virtually ensured that the general strike called for would take place and be successful. Moreover, political opposition was galvanized. In revulsion over the government's brutality, a broad coalition formed, including the Chamber of Commerce, the Civil Service Organization, and anti-Gairy unions. Calling itself the Committee of 22, this "established bourgeoisie" launched demands for reform, within the system.[26]

In the midst of another strike, this time for three months, Maurice Bishop's father, Rupert Bishop, was murdered on "Bloody Monday," January 21, 1974. The strike paralyzed the nation and almost succeeded in toppling Gairy. The achievement of independence on February 7, 1974, did not alter the situation. Gairy was able to shore up his regime through alliances with the repressive governments of Chile and South Korea. The NJM and its allies, having come so close, had to settle back and build support.[27]

The period between 1974 and 1979 saw greater polarization, with Gairy violence continuing unabated and NJM members organizing assiduously. The NJM's grassroots mobilization was concentrated primarily in urban areas, where the party's radical intellectuals succeeded in organizing workers in anti–Gairy unions. It failed to make any significant inroads among the peasantry and agroproletariat, controlled by former Prime Minister Gairy and his Grenada United Labour Party (GULP). It did, however, draw large crowds at public meetings; it developed a widely read newsletter; it established organizations for women and youth; and it had support groups in most villages and towns.[28]

According to some of the nineteen NJM leaders and army officers charged with murdering Maurice Bishop, the NJM was able to bring thirty thousand people into the streets in anti-Gairy demonstrations after the brutal beatings of six NJM leaders. In 1976, despite massive electoral fraud, the NJM–led alliance captured six parliamentary seats to Gairy's nine (the NJM victors were Maurice Bishop, Bernard Coard, and Unison Whiteman), making Bishop opposition leader. The March 13, 1979 seizure of power was led by 46 NJM members assaulting the Army barracks while three thousand almost entirely unarmed workers, unemployed youth, and farmers seized the police stations and the secret police in response to the NJM's call over the radio. To the nineteen, this was clear evidence of a strong popular base.[29]

For all Gairy's bravado and repression, the end came not with a bang, but with a whimper. While this handful of armed people, led by Hudson Austin (a road engineer who became Commander of the People's Revolutionary Army), were engaged in a virtually bloodless coup, Gairy was absent. He had traveled to the United Nations to express his concern over UFOs.

Whither the New Jewel Revolution? Early Directions

There is a consensus among revolution scholars that an ideological blueprint for a new society and significant social change in this new direction are defining characteristics of a revolution.[30] The early public face of the revolution was radical, but certainly not hardcore Marxist-Leninist the way the documents seized from party headquarters show it to be in its later stages. As we explore the first period of NJM rule, there are several things to keep in mind. (1) Revolutionaries do not think alike. They come from different backgrounds and join in a coalition held together by an overarching ideology and the common desire to overcome the "establishment." (2) Revolutionaries and revolutions do not spring ready-made out of even fertile soil. They mature and radicalize over time, at uneven rates and at different levels of intensity. Among people who have been prepared to lay down their lives for a cause, the difficulties of implementing lofty goals in a recalcitrant mini-island society located in a turbulent sea south of a giant, intrusive neighbor were sure to engender tensions. This is the human side of the Grenada revolution, easily forgotten amidst labels of "Leninist," "Stalinist," "one-manism," and "elitism." In the end, only four years after seizing power, the tensions manifested themselves in a seemingly arid debate over divining "the correct Marxist-Leninist path." After a drawn-out squabble, there was mayhem and murder. It did not start that way.

There were some early hints of issues that emerged as central later on. In 1979 Selwyn Strachan, Grenada's minister of mobilization, told an interviewer from the U.S. Socialist Workers Party *Intercontinental Press* that the goal was transition to socialism, but the path led through "the democratic phase of the struggle, preparing the masses for the transition...."

In other words, we see us moving toward socialism, using the mixed-economy approach, the noncapitalist path at this stage. And that, of course, will help us increase the strength of the working class in our country, prepare us for the advancement to socialism, where we can eventually have the dictatorship of the proletariat.[31]

The agenda was thus clear: advance to a full-fledged Marxist-Leninist system. What did not seem clear, given the record of the next four years, was the rate of that advance—that is, how long the more moderate stage would last with its mixed economy (socialist-capitalist compromise) and bourgeois allies.

According to Jacobs and Jacobs, "the principal socialist characteristic of the NJM was its stated commitment to, and practice of, democratic centralism." They cite the close personal and political relationships among the leaders, their need for collaboration and coordination leading to mutual confidence, the danger they all shared, and their awareness of need for support, understanding, and active involvement of the masses as conducive to practicing democratic centralism as a "guiding principle rather than a dogma." In particular, they emphasize the input from the broad masses of the party membership, based on tiered organization reaching into all villages and towns through cells, assuring a "strong degree of 'people control' over the NJM." They celebrate this "impressive democratic orientated edifice," and bemoan Grenada's sad experience with elitism which makes it "perfectly understandable why there is great vigilance within the NJM to ensure that it does not emerge to subvert the NJM objectives."[32]

This early, sympathetic analysis did not spot the problems that arose later in the areas of democratic centralism and elite (vanguard)-mass relations. It is arguable that it was precisely elitist leadership that killed the revolution. It is also worth pointing out that according to the canons of democratic centralism, *party members* constitute the "people control," not the undifferentiated masses.

In view of the crucial importance of the leadership issue in bringing

NJM rule to a bitter end, our analysis of the NJM Central Committee (CC) struggle will focus on that issue. Leadership, however, is not an isolated phenomenon. It implies followers, in this case both in the NJM party and among the masses. The relationship between leader and follower, desired and actual, is essential to grasp to understand the nature of leadership and the problems encountered. Accordingly, we must first tackle the theory of vanguard leadership in a Marxist-Leninist organization and its corollary, the theory of democratic centralism, and then explore the relationship between these and popular democracy. The struggle over joint leadership will then be considered. Throughout this discussion, I shall present general principles as I understand them, the NJM leaders' version of these, and contradictions and problems between and among these versions.

Intellectual Elitism, the Vanguard Theory, and Democratic Centralism

The members of the party referred to each other as Comrade, presumably to stress the equality of all "revo" participants. This is of course common practice in all Marxist-Leninist groups. The irony is that the "revo" leaders who used this epithet were more equal than others, to use George Orwell's justly famous *Animal Farm* expression. They were mostly brown middle-class people who were products (with notable exceptions) of a British educational system often criticized for being designed to create an intellectual elite with ready transition available to elite status in socioeconomic and political realms, if such status was not possessed before entering the educational process.

Our point here is to draw attention to the seductive linkage between British-style intellectual elitism and the Marxist-Leninist vanguard theory of democracy. It is seductive because a theoretical justification was provided by Lenin which coincided with dispositions inculcated through higher education. The following imaginary "address to the people" spells out the rationale of the vanguard theory. "Trust me. Through no fault of your own, you cannot handle the larger questions of public policy. The material conditions of scarcity ensure that you are exploited, work strenuously for survival, and are therefore rendered incapable of understanding the dialectical contradictions of society, much less being able to prescribe corrective social action. We, the vanguard of the proletariat, will lead you to the promised land." What a comfortable rationale Lenin provided for elitist egalitarians to lead the masses without having to ask their consent. They need to be told, not asked.

Democratic centralism is the necessary corollary to the vanguard idea. If only the vanguards are capable of understanding the dialectic forces of history and the material conditions of society which these forces are shaping, they need to present a united front to the masses in order to retain their legitimacy. The vanguard claim requires unanimity to sustain itself. Hence the need for a party decision-making system of democratic centralism that provides for open discussion by party members prior to a decision, and no questioning of the consensus once a decision has been made.

The Grenadian revolutionary leaders themselves defined democratic centralism (DC) as follows:*

It is the basic, fundamental organisational principle of a Marxist Leninist Party that combines in an indissoluble unity unner party democracy (elections, reports, broad free frank discussion, initiative, active participation in party life and work) with centralised leadership, strict single discipline (one programme, one set of rules for all, subordination of minority to majority, higher bodies decisions binding on lower bodies, the line of march, one single leading body, unity of views, aims and action).

At the end of these notes is an abbreviated section entitled *"What is D.C.,"* concluding with *"Why."* The response, apparently by someone named Justin or Austin (Hudson?), reads:

1. combines inner p. dem with str. [strength?]
2. allows for expression of the whole party and ensure monolithic unity & inner p. dem.[33]

Monolithic unity and inner party democracy. How tragic to read these words in the aftermath of the disunity and inner party conflict of 1982–1983, leading to the revolution's demise.

Let us now put some bits and pieces together by way of commentary on the Grenadian application of these principles of vanguard rule and democratic centralism. First, a post hoc commentary from the Cuban

---

*From a handwritten set of notes under the heading STUDY ON DEMOCRATIC CEN-TRALISM, appearing opposite a page of notes outlining an agenda of monthly and bimonthly study groups. Hence it appears authoritative—probably by a senior member of the CC (B. or P. Coard?).

This is an appropriate time to introduce a disclaimer about fidelity to the sources vs. correct English usage. This document is the first of many to be presented from microfiche copies of Grenadian originals in the U.S. National Archives. Many documents are hand-written, and many of those especially are very hard to read, due both to illegible writing and poor copy quality. Since much of this material was written in haste (minutes, etc.) without benefit of revision, and certainly with no expectation of uninvited readers scru-tinizing it, it seems inappropriate and unnecessary to clutter it up with scholarly *sics* every time a spelling or grammatical error occurs. The reader should be aware, therefore, that all quotations from the Grenada documents are rendered "in the raw." Whenever a word or passage is difficult to decipher, a question mark will be entered in brackets.

Communist Party through its embassy in Grenada: "In our view, it was actually a matter of conflicting personalities and conceptions of leadership methods—not exempt from other subjective factors—rather than substantial conflicts." Why a conflict over leadership methods cannot be substantial is not explained. The Cuban CP also said Bishop reported to the Cuban embassy in Grenada that he had never imagined the seriousness of the differences with his party colleagues as they developed during his trip abroad. It went on to say, "No doctrine, principle or position proclaimed as revolutionary, nor any internal division can justify such brutal procedures as the physical elimination of Maurice Bishop and of the outstanding group of honest and worthy leaders who died yesterday."[34] The anger and grief seem genuine. The initial statement concerning personalities and leadership methods appears to contradict the later focus on "doctrine, principle, or position"—that is, ideology. However, ideology also addresses leadership methods in the Marxist-Leninist vanguard theory.

What did the Grenadian revolutionaries say about vanguard leadership? The top-down pattern of rule was emphasized in "Guidelines for Strengthening and Building the Party and Putting It on a Lenin Marxism-Leninist Rooting." It contains the following injunction: "The Central Committee should ensure that decisions taken reach to lower bodies and Party comrades and that ideas, suggestions, and criticisms should be sent through (a) Study Groups, (b) Work Committees, (c) Parish GM, (d) Party GM, and (e) the secretariat."[35]

The minutes of the Political/Economic Bureau for August 3, 1983 addressed the need for worker education, with comrade James complaining that only 50 percent of the people in the public sector were attending classes. A crash course in ideology was also discussed. The "Guidelines for Broadening the Scope and Deepening the Context of the Involvement of the People in the Revolutionary Process," signed by E. J. Layne, discussed "the mass organisations that different sectors of the people are to be mobilised in, including mass activities such as rallies, and revolutionary education for the people."[36]

The tone is definitely manipulative. Maurice Bishop's "Line of March" speech, for example, listed as its first task "sinking the ideas of Marxism-Leninism among the working class and the working people." The main vehicle would be socialism classes. He cited as one of the reasons for Nasser's revolution being rolled back that "the party was not in fact built along Leninist vanguard lines."[37]

There is no denying that the NJM, in 1982–1983, was assiduously engaged in cultivating a mass base through the Young Pioneer Program and the national Youth Organization. "Higher levels of Worker Democracy" trumpeted the NJM paper, through production, emulation committees and general meetings.[38]

The big question, however, is the disposition toward the masses. Tell or listen? Though much sincere listening surely went on in the cells and mass meetings, it is the ideas of vanguard leadership and democratic centralism that come through loudly and clearly in the tone of the party documents. The leadership of the People's Revolutionary Army (PRA) went as far as to say the decisions of the Central Committee have the force of law. Why, then, debate the point further? Because the nineteen NJM leaders took strenuous exception to my interpretation of these ideas. Here, therefore, are their rejoinders.[39]

Our party, they said, sees absolutely no contradiction between the vanguard party concept and the concept of popular democracy. The vanguard party is not an elitist concept, separating party from people. It is an organized force for dialectically interacting with the people, for promoting constant two-way dialogue between leadership and people. We never can be a truly popular revolution without such dialogue, they said.

I did not have time at our hurried encounters to debate the point. But is not the dialectic a concept of contradiction? Dialectical interaction with the people, then, does not seem a positive phenomenon.

Next: There is absolutely no contradiction in the view of our party between democratic centralism and popular democracy. Of course, logical consistency demands that. The only justification the nineteen advanced for this point was that there was election of higher groups (Central Committee, Political Bureau) by the membership, which must approve all important decisions at general meetings, and majority rule always applies.

The question was never addressed, nor was it in the documents or in other Marxist-Leninist literature I have consulted over the years, of how large and how representative was the party? Inner party democracy is well and good. If there is no institutionalized way to hold the party accountable to the people at the initiative of the people, but instead only rallies, mass meetings, and forums organized by the party, what is the meaning of popular democracy? Obviously there is a chasm of interpretation between confirmed Marxist-Leninists and mere human beings, but surely we are talking about a rather fundamental difference between top-down and bottom-up. How can a top-down system not be elitist, and how can it be a popular democracy?

The nineteen continued: Contrary to popular propaganda, there were absolutely no ideological conflicts within the NJM leadership. Not a hard-line/moderate, not a populist vs. democratic centralist, not a dependency vs. orthodox Marxist type. Maurice Bishop never at any time questioned the correctness of the vanguard party concept, nor did he or anyone else see it as conflicting with popular democracy. Coard never pressed the party about leadership by a small elite, and Bishop had no "romantic tendency" to rely on the masses. Those distinctions never existed.

As we enter the esoteric world of populist theory later in this chapter, let us remember Bishop's activity in the Movement for the Assembly of Peoples (MAP) and shortly thereafter in the early New Jewel Movement. If his concern with decision making by village and urban councils or People's Assemblies as substitutes for a national government was genuine, did he ever really lose that "romantic" idealism? Such grass roots power is clearly at odds with the elitism of vanguard party rule, whose correctness allegedly was never questioned by Bishop. The possibility of Bishop hiding his true color from the Grenadian people until after the successful overthrow of Gairy is a realistic alternative. This is the argument of a recent history of the West Indies.[40]

Furthermore, Bishop certainly favored contact with the masses. Perhaps he was only doing it because he was so awfully good in front of a crowd? That raises the question of charisma, or "gift of grace" in the original Greek—a highly elitist concept. Bishop's strength in this category was freely acknowledged by the nineteen. They argued the party needed Maurice especially for his platform skills, while Coard would contribute his organizational ability to the proposed joint leadership. Michael Massing, a free-lance writer who observed Bishop and the revolution prior to the cataclysmic end, concluded that Bishop was immensely popular; the revolution was not.[41]

Joint Leadership: Prelude to Finale

Whether the Grenadian revolution serves as a model or represents only a dead end has much to do with our assessment of how it ceased to be. That its demise had much to do with a struggle for leadership can hardly be denied. It is therefore crucial to understand the nature of this struggle and the New Jewel Movement's attempts to resolve it. Here is where the captured Central Committee minutes are indispensable. Regrettably, they make rather tedious reading.

As early as the April 22, 1982, meeting of the CC, there is evidence of problems surfacing that were to take on increasing importance through the next year and a half. Comrade Ewart "Headache" Layne proposed that the state of the party be placed on the agenda. This appears to be the opening shot of a sustained campaign to reform the party and its leadership. Layne took the lead. He cited poor quality and quantity of work, poor planning and organization, arrogance (especially in the Youth Committee), and lack of study. Several comrades agreed, including Fitzroy Bain, Tan Bartholomew, and "Bogo" Cornwall. Phyllis Coard extended the criticism further to include "the petty bourgeois attitude still existing

in a number of comrades, including the leadership," "last minute organisation," and "our attitude toward self-criticism." Bernard Coard followed his wife, agreed with and praised Layne, and stressed that the main
problem was "we are trying to do too much." Interestingly, and importantly for what followed, Maurice Bishop agreed.[42]

Open discussion of schisms in the party and its potential break-up
took place at meetings in July and August, 1983. The Party was said to
have "demonstrated many weaknesses—ideologically, politically and or-
ganizationally. At the same time, the emergence of deep petty bourgeois
manifestations . . . in the Party had led to two ideological trends." These
trends are not identified in the document, but in the U.S. government
published version, the information was supplied: one Marxist-Leninist
and the other not. The nineteen took strong exception to that. This,
they said, was a reference to petit bourgeois behavior of some members,
not leaders. By September it was realized that this was largely a manifestation of overwork and exhaustion among members. The comment
at the August twenty-sixth meeting by Lt. Col. Liam James, deputy secretary of Defense and Interior, that "we are *seeing the beginning of the
disintegration of the party*" was not linked to that two-trend comment at
an earlier meeting. Indeed, James was immediately followed by Selwyn
Strachan, who said "sections of the party have begun to rebel against
the higher organs of the party," and "this silent rebellion will grow into
open rebellion and if we do not address it now it will be resolved in a
petty bourgeois way."[43]

At this meeting of the Central Committee, August 26, 1983, questions
were raised about why comrade Bernard Coard had resigned from the
CC and Political Bureau (PB). He responded that he felt he was planning
and running everything. He chastised "the slack and weak functioning
of CC and MB [Maurice Bishop]," members coming to meetings "hands
and minds swinging." While burdened by taking initiatives and making
decisions, he was also the "axe-man" in disciplinary matters, for which
he received criticism. All this was contrary to a M-L party. Yet the more
he struggled against this vacillation and failure to implement even agreed
decisions such as engaging in regular disciplined ideological study, the
more some PB comrades "interpreted this as his fighting for leadership."

The meeting further considered the "main problem": Bishop's leadership. His "tremendous strengths" were lauded, such as his ability to
inspire and unite the masses and to represent the revolution regionally
and internationally. With growing complexities, these strengths were not
adequate. In effect, it was said, the party had had joint leadership for
four and a half years, Coard being given credit for forming the first M-
L study group in 1974 [OREL], with providing the ideological guidance
for the party manifesto, and for struggling for the formation of the
Organization Committee (O.C.) in 1978, lifting the party's level of or-

ganization, a key factor of winning power. Accordingly, the joint leadership model was just a formalization of existing reality.[44]

At the crucial CC meeting of September 14–17, 1983, which passed the Joint Leadership resolution, Layne expressed concern about building a Marxist-Leninist vanguard vs. petit bourgeois elements in the country. He also said the CC was on the path of right opportunism. Liam James identified the main problem as Maurice Bishop's leadership. He lacked "(1) Leninist level of organisation and discipline, (2) great depth of ideological clarity, and (3) brilliance in strategy and tactics." Major Cornwall added that he lacked the ability to supervise and "stay up" on his workload. He also criticized the comrades for their timidity in criticizing Bishop because he did not take criticism well. Phyllis Coard added that idealism was the problem. She read off a litany of complaints about the weaknesses of the revolution's programs and organizations, concluding with a direct attack on Bishop for not having "taken responsibility, not given the necessary guidance, ... is disorganized very often, avoids responsibilities for critical areas of work ... " such as teaching study discussion.

Unison Whiteman, one of Bishop's staunchest allies, agreed with the criticisms, but expressed opposition, suggesting the CC should not be left without blame. Maurice Bishop agreed, and said he needed time to reflect on the joint leadership proposal. George Louison was the only member to argue and vote against the proposal. Fitzroy Bain was unsure how it would work. Layne insisted that if the CC did not act on his proposal, it would be guilty of right opportunism. Louison took exception, and used "vulgar" language to express his anger.[45] It should be noted that Bernard Coard was not present at this meeting.

According to the nineteen, a full meeting of the party on September 25, 1983, which lasted for fifteen hours, overwhelmingly endorsed a joint leadership proposal (Bishop and Whiteman voting in favor), and was followed by partying and merriment at Bishop's home. The following day candidate members unanimously approved. The reason, said the nineteen, why the party so overwhelmingly approved the joint leadership proposal was the failure of the leadership to control the rapid expansion of the work. Acute overwork led to mental and physical exhaustion, party resignations and, in Bishop, to a tendency to refuse to make decisions, which created an atmosphere of crisis.

Then Bishop, Whiteman, and Louison, among others, left for a long-scheduled trip to Hungary to seek aid. Upon their return Bishop reneged on the joint leadership agreement, catapulting the CC and party into a maelstrom of vituperation and confrontation. *The Side You Haven't Heard: Maurice Bishop Murder Trial* contains much potent information indicating a pattern of lying by George Louison, who was the only CC member to vote against joint leadership.[46] Bishop was accused of starting a rumor about the Coards being out to assassinate him. One of his body guards, Errol George, signed a sworn statement to that effect.[47] The result was that the CC voted to place Bishop under house arrest while they tried to come up with a way to handle this extremely volatile situation. Unison Whiteman mobilized a crowd, freed Bishop, who led the crowd to capture the Army headquarters at Fort Rupert without a shot being fired. Two armored troop carriers recaptured the fort, and Bishop and NJM leaders loyal to him were lined up and shot. Fourteen of the nineteen accused of this murder have been condemned to death.

Was This a Coup? It is worth noting that many of Bishop's key critics were prominent members of the People's Revolutionary Army (PRA). Ewart Layne was a lieutenant colonel and the NJM's Political Bureau (PB) person in the PRA. Lt. Col. Liam James was a CC member and boss of the interior department (police and intelligence). Other PRA CC members included the commander of the PRA, General Hudson Austin, and Major David "Tan" Bartholomew. Major Leon "Bogo" Cornwall, slated to become chief political education officer of the PRA, returned from his post as ambassador to Cuba just as the crisis discussions peaked.

This is not to hint that a coup had been planned, but to indicate that the armed forces leadership was very well represented at the top of the party, appeared to be quite cohesive, and thus was poised to move decisively when things fell apart. It should be especially noted that a delegation from the Central Committee that visited Maurice Bishop the evening of October eighteenth (the night before he was killed) to discuss a compromise solution to the crisis was composed entirely of PRA officers: Layne, Austin, James, and Bartholomew.

Layne appears to have been most prominent throughout the process of party housecleaning. He initiated the agonizing self-analysis of the CC, and was, along with Liam James, called "the real power" in the CC and PRA by George Louison, one of the few former NJM leaders who is both alive and free to conduct interviews.[48] General Austin had in effect not been in charge of the Armed Forces for more than a year. At the September twenty-fifth meeting of the full NJM party, he complained that he had concentrated on being minister of construction, giving little time to the armed forces, and he was "very concerned about this." He cited the lesson of Poland when its revolution was in danger [the armed forces stepped in], and urged strengthening of the armed forces.[49]

Layne's own words, in a sworn statement, lend some credence to the claim that he was in fact the strongman, not Austin, as U.S. media repeatedly stated. According to this statement, during the October 19, 1983, crisis General Austin, "fearing firm measures... allowed me to have my way, recognising the tremendous respect I have amongst the men.... It was from there on I could say that I took over the situation completely." Layne then (still according to the sworn statement) ordered three armored cars to retake the fort, to "battle it out" if there was resistance, and to liquidate the leaders of the uprising. Later he reported success to Austin, and recommended that the army "take power for a brief period in order to control the situation."[50]

As in other cases, we have a credibility problem here. Layne has offered two disclaimers, one to the court, August 29–September 10, 1986, and one in a letter to the governor general, Sir Paul Scoon, dated November 17, 1983. In both he claims to have been tortured by policemen from Barbados, and to have signed his sworn statement under duress. In his court statement he said the Bajans wanted him to sign a statement that his soldiers went to Fort Rupert with blood in their eyes. He further claimed to have reacted with shock to the news that Bishop and seven others were dead. His statement to the court confirmed that he was, in fact, "in day to day charge of the Army," and that he ordered the recapture of Fort Rupert. His letter to Scoon was sent the morning after Layne claimed to have endured thirteen hours of rough interrogation, which included beatings and threats of electric shock. He said he was periodically told what they wanted: "a statement implicating the whole leadership of the party in murder of Maurice Bishop, telling me it was me who gave orders to assasinate Maurice Bishop and that these orders came from Bernard Coard and Hudson Austin.... I finally agreed to writing it implicating myself only because I could not bere the horror or writing lies about others." Layne also said the policemen boasted about the beatings they had already administered to three of his soldiers, and about what they were going to do to Bernard Coard and Hudson Austin.[51] Corroboration came from Bernard Coard's unsworn statement from the dock, which insisted that when the medical records became available, it will become evident that there was "physical damage done to people in this dock at the time of taking the so-called voluntary statements from them, statements which the court accepted as given voluntarily and is part of the evidence against us in this trial."[52]

The postmortem commentaries tend, understandably, to be a bit shrill. A handwritten layout "For Political Work in PRAF," possibly by Ewart Layne who was the chief political officer, said "Maurice Bishop, Unison Whiteman, and other opportunists and bourgeois elements planned to use the masses who were confused as a mob to massacre the Central Committee, the party and Armed Forces. If they had succeeded this would have meant the definite turn back of the revolution and bourgeois role of the country as well as further exploitation of the working people." It discussed the link-up of bourgeois, opportunist, and counter revolutionary elements with imperialism, and offered comparisons with the French Revolution, where the masses stormed the fort but the bourgeoisie took power, and more recent events in Hungary, Czechoslovakia, and Poland.[53]

In response to Bishop's reversal on the joint leadership decision, some of the strongest support for the CC and party membership reaction came from the armed forces. One statement in particular deserves to be quoted almost in full. A "Resolution of the People's Revolutionary Armed Forces Branch of the New Jewel Movement," passed October twelfth (a week before the assassination), declared unswerving support for the September 14–16 CC decision, and noted:

> We recognise and uphold that based on the fundamental Leninist principle of democratic centralism that decision of our Party's Central Committee have the force of law and form the basis of the activity and conduct of all party bodies and of every single party member, candidate member and applicant regardless of their services and posts.... Never would we allow cultism, egoism, the unreasonable and unprincipled desires of one man or a minority to be imposed on our Party thus stiffling inner party democracy and endangering the party and revolution and holding our country to ransom....
>
> The People's Revolutionary Armed Forces Branch of NJM awaits the decision and orders of the Central Committee![54]

When the political leadership of the armed forces spoke that forcefully, trouble was clearly on the way. Here, presumably, were Layne, James, Austin, Cornwall, and Bartholomew, plus lesser ranks, the men with the guns, the same men who formed the delegation to negotiate with Bishop on October eighteenth in behalf of the CC. It is probably not unfair to extrapolate from this extremely strong statement of support for CC "hardball" to the executions on October nineteenth. If the PRA branch of the NJM "awaits the decision and orders of the Central Committee" on this matter, is it reasonable to presume the PRA members acted independently in lining Bishop and entourage up against the wall?

We should also note Ewart Layne's rejoinder to charges that this was a coup. In coups, he said, the armed forces are on the attack. We, Layne argued, were trying to defend ourselves, to recapture PRA headquarters. Soldiers who could have stayed inside the armored personnel carriers sat on top of them and waved to the people—and some got shot. They did not go to Fort Rupert to conduct a massacre.[55]

Perhaps the most reasonable conclusion to draw from all this is that the pressure on the Central Committee from a united and vindictive leadership of the armed forces helped to remove the restraints on decision makers and implementors alike, leading to brutal bloodshed. There is no way we can exit from this ambiguity short of definitive evidence emerging from the appeal of the death sentences—and the probability of that is rather slim.

Lessons from the Struggle over Joint Leadership? It is hard to know how to interpret such an internal struggle, especially since we now have reason to wonder whom to believe. Was it primarily a personal power struggle couched in ideological mumbo-jumbo? That was the contention of Lyden Ramdhanny, one of the two businessmen (described in the "Line of March" speech as a "big capitalist") included in the cabinet by Maurice Bishop in order to look good to the outside.[56] "There was no question of ideology," Ramdhanny said. "It was simply a grab for power."[57] What weight should we give to this opinion? There is no evidence Ramdhanny was sufficiently schooled in ideology to recognize a vanguard if he saw one. Moreover, he served in the People's Revolutionary Government (PRG) Cabinet (Minister of Tourism), not in the party Central Committee or Political Bureau, the nerve centers where crucial dialogue and decision making took place. Scholars and journalists have therefore given his statement too much weight.

However, Ramdhanny's claim was supported by one of Bishop's closest followers, George Louison, minister of agriculture in the PRG. It was not a question of right against left, he said; the Coard group "wanted to seize power for themselves, to use the revolution for their own purposes. . . ." According to Louison, while Coard's rhetoric was "ultraleft," he would have acted very much like Bishop if he had gained power.[58] To keep things in balance, it should be noted that George Louison was vilified by the other survivors in the NJM leadership for allegedly having been the chief culprit in persuading Bishop to reverse himself on joint leadership, precipitating the crisis. He has been able to speak freely since the invasion, while his detractors have been held incommunicado in jail. He was removed from the NJM Central Committee October 12, 1987, for lying about CC members in the process of trying to persuade Bishop.[59] So far we have not found a credible witness.

There was further corroboration from Maurice Bishop's press secretary, Don Rojas: "There were differences in the approaches to implementing certain policies, differences in method and style," he said. "Maurice Bishop was more flexible, more understanding of the need to make tactical moves. Bernard Coard saw things in more clear-cut terms. On fundamental ideological issues, there were no major differences."[60]

At the risk of becoming too predictable, again we have a credibility problem. Rojas was able to get away to Czechoslovakia, and has been accused of CIA connections and of complicity in the violence that precipitated, or at least was used as justification for, the U.S. invasion. He is alleged to have been "sticking up workers at the telephone company with a gun" at the very moment the crown was taking Maurice Bishop from his home, and in his hand was a statement saying the people took Bro. Bishop from his home and up to Fort Rupert—*before* they went to Fort Rupert. The allegation concludes: "So this shows that the storming of Fort Rupert was planned in advance by other elements outside, and that this same man was working as part of that [?] same group whose purpose was to cause bloodshed that day."[61] I have seen no independent corroboration for any of these charges. They are cited only to indicate it is genuinely hard to know whom to believe.

Massing, the free-lance writer who interviewed all three of these sources concluded that "both, then, were committed Marxists, but the traditions from which they came—Bishop's nationalistic populism and Coard's ideological dogmatism—proved irreconcilable."[62] Massing may have been right for the wrong reasons.

PLACING THE REVOLUTION IN THEORETICAL CONTEXT: POPULISM

The key to understanding Grenada's development from the Gairy years to the death of Bishop and the NJM revolution is populism. It is a very slippery concept. It means so many things. Among those who have been referred to as populist are such diverse characters as Eric Gairy, Maurice Bishop, Michael Manley, Alexander Bustamante, Juan Peron, George Wallace, and Jimmy Carter.

The standard work on populism is by Ionescu and Gellner. Their dramatic and definitely inspired opening sentence, "A spectre is haunting the world—populism," introduces their assertion that populism is the leading ideology of the new states. Their introduction confirms my contention that practically anything could be called populism without being wrong. Yet there is a wealth of instructive and applicable ideas in this corpus. Ionescu and Gellner organize their analysis around six principal questions or points:

1. Was/is populism primarily an ideology or a movement, or is it both?
2. Was/is populism a recurring mentality emerging in societies in which the middle social factors were either missing or too weak?
3. In terms of political psychology, there is an element of political persecution mania—a feeling that identifiable or unidentifiable conspiracies are at work, deliberately and tenaciously, against the people. The basic attitude is one of apprehension toward unknown outside forces.
4. There is in populism a strong element of negativism: it is anticapitalist, antiurban, xenophobic, and anti-Semitic. [Clearly, not all populists or populist movements fit all of these traits.]
5. Populism worships the people. The objects of worship: the meek and the miserable—because they are miserable and persecuted by the conspirators. The more miserable, the more worshipped.
6. "Finally, until now this recurring mentality usually disappeared in history by absorption into stronger ideologies or movements." The disappearance was in three directions: socialism, nationalism, and peasantism.[63]

Other populism scholars have echoed, expanded upon, and added to these points. Edward Shils emphasized the supremacy of the will of the people "over every other standard, over the standards of traditional institutions and over the will of other strata. Populism identifies the will of the people with justice and morality." He also emphasized the desirability of a "direct" relationship between people and leadership, unmediated by institutions.[64] Peter Worsley qualified Shils by suggesting the inclusion of "pseudo-participation" (demagogy, "government by television," etc.). This is strongly reminiscent of the leader-follower relationship between Eric Gairy and his supporters, so vividly painted by Singham in his *Hero and the Crowd*. Popular *participation* is the key, says Worsley, "not only 'direct' relationships between people and leadership (which must, inevitably, in any complex, large-scale society be predominantly sheer mystification or symbolism)...."[65]

Several authors have plugged a gap in Ionescu and Gellner by emphasizing the egalitarian and redistributive thrust of populism. Gavin Kitching, having dug for populist roots deep in the rural soil of Russia, has argued that modern neopopulism, owing its stimulus to development concerns of Third World leaders since the late 1960s, shows "a far greater concern than ever before ... [for] the incapacity of large-scale, capital-intensive industrialization to provide sufficient or sufficiently remunerative employment." Kitching's key point:

[B]oth populism and neo-populism share an over-riding concern with problems of inequality in distribution, and a desire for a future in which the eradication of poverty is combined with forms of social and economic organization able to guarantee a considerable equality of income and wealth in a world of small-scale property.[66]

Carl Stone framed his analysis of democracy and socialism in Jamaica in the relationship among populism, liberalism, and authoritarianism— the basic elements to which all major tendencies since the nineteenth century can be reduced. Political change is a dialectical process where "contending social interests seek to alter the balance and mix among these basic elements. Political stability is attained when a political system is able to achieve a synthesis of these antagonistic elements after cycles of conflicts and contradictions." Populism, according to Stone,

is a political tendency which seeks to elevate ... the status, power, and interests of those social groups that are located at the bottom end of a social hierarchy and to assault and attack interests and groups that are highly placed at the upper end of the social hierarchy.... Populist tendencies can be articulated by revolutionary movements and ideologies such as Marxism, by reformist movements such as Social Democratic political parties, or by cultural, racial, or religious movements that assume a political character.

As for authoritarian tendencies, they can be found in *all* political systems in varying degrees. Authoritarianism or elitism is the antithesis of populism.[67]

Finally, Hilbourne Watson has cautioned that while populism in the sense of redistributive economic justice has been a facilitating mechanism for use in the dialogue of class struggle, it never produces changes in the relations of production. It may even push in the direction of the right: witness Guyana, where populism, in Watson's view, has alienated the workers, the capitalists, the imperialists—indeed, only the state class is *not* alienated. Watson views populism as a halfway house, an in between ideology: anticapitalist but not socialist, and therefore useful to those who would be critical of capitalism but who do not have the strength of conviction or following to seek fundamental alteration of the economic structure of the society.[68]

Most of these points, except possibly for Watson's, almost seem designed to fit Grenada. The middle social factors are indeed weak in Grenada; there was, under the revolutionary regime, a strong sense of conspiracy by outside forces—quite correct, as it turned out; Maurice Bishop may be said to have "worshiped" the people; and his populism was indeed absorbed into the Marxist-Leninist paradigm, whose proponents commanded more power (especially military) than Bishop's faction. Note, especially, how the Bishop-Coard tug-of-war appears to fit Stone's model of struggle between populism and authoritarianism, or elitism. This is the time to remember Maurice Bishop's and Unison Whiteman's earlier track record (in MAP and JEWEL) of relying on the masses for input and Bernard Coard's stress, as the ideology teacher he was for the rest of the party, on a correct Leninist vanguard/democratic centralist approach of leadership. A definite fit with Stone's model. It deserves to be noted, however, that the smallness of the intellectual/professional elite in a society of peasants probably contributed to steering the New Jewel Movement in the direction of Leninist elitism (vanguardism).

We return to Kitching for a summary of populism's universal appeal:

The ideas recur so frequently simply because a similarity of problem and context gives rise to a similarity of intellectual response. For leaders and policymakers with the need or desire to change societies made up overwhelmingly of peasants and other small-scale producers, there will always be a certain attraction in a tradition of thought which suggests both that change and development is possible and that all that is conceived as best in existing institutions and practices may be maintained, and that this double objective can be fulfilled without creating massive extremes of wealth and poverty."[69]

On the assumption that the case has been made for populism having been a major feature of the NJM's ideology, the implications of Kitching's words for the replicability of the Grenada revolution are too obvious to need emphasis.

CONCLUSIONS: WAS THE GRENADIAN
REVOLUTION'S IDEOLOGY A DEAD END OR MODEL?

Let me first draw attention to a telling point made by West Indian scholars Paget Henry and Carl Stone. They bemoan their colleagues' inability to achieve any consensus on reworking Latin American dependency theory and Marxist political economy paradigms "to capture and reflect accurately the specifics of the Caribbean situation." In the absence of such consensus, they say, widely varying policy recommendations are presented, leading to constant debate.[70] This was written just before the Grenadian revolution came apart, almost as if that event were an echo or a fulfillment of the theorists' lament. Whether matters would have taken a different turn if such a theoretical-ideological consensus had preexisted the NJM seizure of power in 1979 is as impossible and futile to answer as are all "what if" questions of history. Besides, the complaint of Henry and Stone is as valid in the late eighties as it was when it was written. The only difference the Grenada debacle may have made is to lend greater urgency to the search for consensus.

When you deal with such esoteric phenomena as ideology, it is difficult to know what constitutes conclusive proof of anything. There is no way this kind of study can be structured using the *ceteris paribus* (all other things being equal) pattern, or holding other factors constant while the chosen variable(s) is (are) examined. Our conclusion can therefore only be stated with limited confidence that it will not be open to attack by those who approach the same problem from a different perspective. Yet I hope sufficient evidence has been presented to claim confirmation of the hypothesis stated at the beginning of this chapter: Elitist leadership assumptions in Marxism-Leninism clash with the egalitarian thrust of popular decision making in populism, the leading ideology in the Third World, and the Grenadian revolution's demise can be traced to this clash. I would welcome constructive dialogue with those who differ.

Looking beyond Grenada, let us return also to the question of how events in that unhappy island should impact the debate concerning the parliamentary road to socialism vs. the path of revolution. If there is merit to the claim to have verified the proposition that Marxist-Leninist elitism came to grief in a contest with populism, it surely must be said to be a victory for the parliamentary roaders. It can also be held out as a modifier to Ionescu and Gellner's claim that until now this recurring mentality of populist egalitarianism usually disappeared in history by absorption into stronger ideologies or movements, such as socialism, nationalism, and peasantism. Finally, we have provided some evidence for Stone's claim that authoritarianism or elitism is the antithesis of populism.

Dead End or Model in Terms of U.S. Motivations for Invasion?

It should be fairly clear by now that the question in this chapter's title can be responded to variously depending on our understanding of *why* it became a dead end (if indeed it did) and *for whom* it might be a model. If it ran into a cul-de-sac of its own making and "imploded" at the end of it, as most commentators have assumed, we need to focus further study on the dynamics of radical social change in small, less developed political systems. I hope I have made the case for including serious analysis of ideology. If the Grenadian revolution's ideology became a dead end because the United States simply would not tolerate it, this may not come as a great surprise to Daniel Ortega, but it should occasion very serious study in U.S. foreign policy and international political circles. A syllabus for such study might include (1) required reading from Thucydides; (2) case studies of destabilization and/or intervention such as, of course, Grenada and Nicaragua, the Dominican Republic in 1963, Chile in 1973, and Angola, The Philippines, Haiti, and Panama in the eighties; (3) a "was it worth it?" analysis of socioeconomic and political conditions in the targeted societies after destabilizataion and/or intervention; and (4) analysis of the extent to which the ideology of the targeted system became a model because of external hostility—the martyr factor.

Is it overly cynical to suggest that one of the chief lessons of this debacle may be for Marxist-Leninist revolutionaries in weak political systems to be a bit more cautious about whom and what they tackle when? They live in glass houses. *The Mouse That Roared* is, unfortunately for them, cruel fiction. The realities of great power "spheres of influence" politics are not hospitable to a tiny Melos taunting mighty Athens, no matter how unfair it might seem.

The Practical Significance of Labels

Was the Grenadian revolution "communist" (Marxist-Leninist), socialist, Black Power–oriented, populist, democratic, authoritarian, totalitarian, all of the above, something else not mentioned, or none of the above? The answer is probably all of the above, both because not all these categories are necessarily mutually exclusive, and because the NJM, as any movement, appears to have contained within it a number of diverse tendencies while retaining a sense of group identity and solidarity, at least up to mid–1983.[71]

There are at least two reasons why we should care about labels. One is that if we can determine with some confidence which *species* of what *genus* the New Jewel revolution represents, our perspective and analysis will benefit. The other is that what one calls oneself and what others call you matters greatly in terms of political response, domestic and external. Witness the hostile U.S. response (the CIA-sponsored 1961 Bay of Pigs invasion by Cuban exiles) when Fidel Castro declared that, contrary to his popular Robin Hood image in the U.S. media, he had always been a Marxist-Leninist.[72] Witness the ease with which Jamaican leaders Alexander Bustamante and Edward Seaga used the red brush to scare an as yet unsophisticated Jamaican electorate into rejecting democratic socialist opponents Norman Washington Manley and Michael Manley, respectively. Witness also the British and U.S. response to Guyanese Marxist Cheddi Jagan and the draconian measures they invoked to make the Guyanese world safe for the somewhat less radical rule of Jagan's opponent, Forbes Burnham. Marx said that "history always repeats itself. The first time is tragedy and the next, farce."[73]

Finally, it is not hard to jump from these examples to the controversy in the late 1980s over U.S. overt and covert aid to the anti-Sandinista "Contras" or "Freedom Fighters" seeking the overthrow of the revolutionary government of Nicaragua that emerged from the 1979 ouster of U.S. ally Anastasio Somoza Debayle. The Reagan administration chose to label Daniel Ortega's successor regime "Communist." The accuracy of the label is not the issue here. The license to act is. In combination with the Monroe Doctrine—the very name of which is often pronounced with awe as if the doctrine is holy or immaculately conceived—the "communist" label was apparently deemed sufficient justification for a policy which not only flouted international law, but which also apparently circumvented U.S. law by supplying the "Contras" through ill-gotten gains from covert arms sales to Iran through "private" channels.

In view of all this, was it literally a fatal mistake for Maurice Bishop to allow it to be known that his movement was Marxist-Leninist? Castro survived his revelation, albeit narrowly. The lucky red star that saved him was the combination of two factors: (1) U.S. intelligence on Cuba and the extent of Castro's support at the time of the ill-fated Bay of Pigs invasion was apparently even worse than the preinvasion information available on Grenada in 1983; and (2) direct participation by U.S. armed forces was limited by President Kennedy to a few bombing sorties over the beaches. The latter "mistake" was not repeated in Grenada, whatever other blunders were committed. The seesaw political battle in the United States over aid to the "Contras" in the late 1980s may demonstrate that Daniel Ortega and the Sandinistas have learned the game sufficiently well to survive. They cannot count on blunders being repeated forever.

Replicability of the Grenada Phenomenon

A mini-state Marxist-Leninist party with substantial support from unionized workers, but without a strong popular base among the peasants and agroproletarians who constituted the backbone of the country's economy, nevertheless succeeded in capturing power from a rather weakly defended government (an Army of 230, and regular police, secret police, and part-time secret police of another 1300). It was a strange spectacle, perhaps sufficiently unique and unlikely to be repeated soon that we should avoid analyzing it to death.

In the beginning of the chapter, I posed the following questions: Did the Grenadian revolution really die? Are embers still smoldering under the ashes, capable of being fanned into flames even after a considerable hiatus? We are in the realm of speculation now. While contemporary Grenada does not come close to matching the prerevolutionary conditions generated by Gairy, it has some characteristics that should make us stop and ponder. U.S. showcasing of postrevolutionary Grenada does not hide the fact that the island's living conditions have changed little since Gairy. I can think of qualifications to Aaron Segal's conclusion, but it appears to have considerable merit, and stands as a warning to all of Anglophone Caribbean: "The roots of the events of 1983 lie in the features of Grenadian society that were detected 20 years earlier and have not basically changed."[74] Four and a half years of raising aspirations for a new Grenada with equal access to resources cannot have failed to leave their mark on the people's consciousness. Finally, the present government's obvious subservience to Washington nurtures the spirit of antiimperialism on which Maurice Bishop and his associates thrived. So while the revolution turned into a cul-de-sac, crashed, and had the coup de grace administered by the invading forces, there is little room for smug assumption that the embers have all been extinguished.

I would enter a further note of caution. Trinidad and Tobago came within a whisker of falling to a radical Black Power—oriented uprising in 1970. The Jamaican government was shaken to the core by the Black Power-oriented Rodney revolt of 1968, and Trevor Munroe, one of the Black Power leaders at that time, has institutionalized the movement's Marxist wing and built it into a political force to be reckoned with. Forbes Burnham of Guyana feared Walter Rodney's radical left political challenge enough to have him assassinated. The four-plus years of the Grenadian revolution inspired similar movements in the area, and drew massive fraternal support and pilgrimages from like-minded people and groups throughout the Caribbean. One may safely assume that the West Indian governments which lent a helping hand in the invasion did so partly because they feared the contagion of the NJM—and perhaps among them the smaller islands such as Dominica more so than the large (Barbados and Jamaica), and partly because their economies needed a shot in the arm from a grateful Uncle Sam. Ironically, some of the invading governments may in fact have contributed to the very resurgence of radical opposition from the New Jewel–like movements in their own back yards which they apparently sought to prevent.

Our final observation about lessons to learn stems from the communiqué of the participants in the Second Conference on Culture and Sovereignty in the Caribbean, held in Trinidad and Tobago January 1984, hard upon the invasion. This was a collection of luminaries who had the modesty to call themselves intellectual workers—a wonderful group of cultural contributors who had celebrated Grenada's progress in the direction of liberating its people from cultural colonialism. This is important to note, for these colleagues were genuinely sympathetic to the "revo," and witnessed in horror the dismantling of the cultural house that Bro. Maurice built. Calling for a careful study of these events from the perspective of Caribbean humanism, they offered the following admonition concerning the internal level of destruction:

[I]n the derailment of the Grenadian Revolution, theory was made an end in itself and divorced from the sensibilities and the struggles of the people, and ... this distortion inevitably resulted in the paramountcy of the Central Committee ... over the party and the people.[75]

Obviously, that point is familiar to the reader by this time. It cannot be overemphasized. Indeed, the same issue of *Caribbean Contact* editorialized on this point, calling it a fundamental flaw of the revolution: "[T]he glaring contradiction between claims that the regime was practising 'grass root' people's participation in government when crucial national issues were being decided by a dozen central committee members, the names of many of whom even party members were unaware."

After all we have waded through, I hope the peoples of the Caribbean and elsewhere, and especially my readers, of whatever ideological persuasion, will agree that the loudest and clearest lesson of the Grenadian tragedy is this: *Any* ideology will be a dead end rather than a model if its mentors and implementors fail to seek the free and informed consent of the people at regular intervals.

Rather than leave the reader with the possibly bitter aftertaste of moralizing by a non-Caribbean, let an indigenous poet have the last word. For as Charles Frye pointed out, the blues tradition demands that "in spite of the assassination of Maurice Bishop and the rape of Grenada, Grenada's peoples and poets ... *still* sing and prophesy.... There is no end. Setbacks, yes. Even death. But no end to the imperative to go on living...."[76] Thus "the protagonist descends into his pain, claims it and whatever lessons it holds, and then ascends to live again." An excerpt from such a Grenadian "song and prophesy" (from the conclusion of the wonderfully titled "Grenada—October 1983—A Work in Progress" by Peggy Anthrobus) carries the thought further:

> Somehow, out of these ashes
> We Caribbean people
> will find truths and strengths
> to forge our own ideology,
> born of our experience and survival
> To rebuild our shattered unity,
> our dignity,
> our faith,
> our dreams.[77]

NOTES

1. Chris Searle, "Interview with Maurice Bishop," Appendix A of Searle's *Grenada: The Struggle Against Destabilization* (London: Writers and Readers, 1983), p. 124.

2. Searle, *Grenada*, pp. 124–25.

3. J. Thomas, *Universal Pronouncing Dictionary of Biography and Mythology* (Philadelphia: J. B. Lippincott, 1885), p. 719.

4. M. G. Smith, *Stratification in Grenada* (Berkeley: University of California Press, 1965), p. 16.

5. Gordon Lewis, "Grenada: The Caribbean Background" and "Grenada: The Island Background." Draft chapters presented at Grenada conference, University of Connecticut, April 1984.

6. Patrick Emmanuel, *Crown Colony Politics in Grenada 1917–1951* (Cave Hill, Barbados: Occasional Papers No. 7, Institute of Social and Economic Research [Eastern Caribbean], University of the West Indies, 1978), pp. 1–2, 5–8.

7. Seymour Martin Lipset, "Some Social Requisites of Democracy: Economic Development and Political Legitimacy," *American Political Science Review* 53 (1959).

8. Emmanuel, *Crown Colony Politics*, pp. 3, 4.

9. Emmanuel, *Crown Colony Politics*, p. 2.

10. Smith, *Stratification in Grenada*, p. 16.

11. Archibald W. Singham, *The Hero and the Crowd in a Colonial Polity* (New Haven, CT: Yale University Press, 1968).

12. George Brizan, *Grenada: Island of Conflict. From Amerindians to People's Revolution 1498–1979* (London: Zed Books, 1984), p. xvi. See also Basil Wilson, "Class, State and Ideology in Pre-Revolutionary Grenada," presented to The National Conference of Black Political Scientists, Washington, DC, April 19–21, 1984.

13. Michael Aberdeen, *Grenada under the P.R.G.: Some Facts and Figures* (Trinidad: People's Popular Movement, n.d. [1984?]), p. 3.

14. We should neither understate nor exaggerate Gairy's contribution. He "was never able...to extend the base of trade union, and therefore political, support beyond rural areas as other unions succeeded in organising the urban

workers." Henry S. Gill, "The Grenada Revolution: Domestic and Foreign Policy Considerations," presented at the Caribbean Studies Association conference, Kingston, Jamaica, 1982.

15. Joel D. Aberbach and Jack L. Walker, *Race in the City: Political Trust and Public Policy in the New Urban System* (Boston: Little, Brown, 1973).

16. Harald M. Sandstrom, "West Indian and Latin American Dependency Theories: A Comparative Study," unpublished doctoral dissertation, University of Pennsylvania, 1975. Compare Walter Rodney, *The Groundings with My Brothers* (London: Bogle-L'ouverture, 1969) and W. Richard Jacobs and Ian Jacobs, *Grenada: The Route to Revolution* (Havana, Cuba: Casa de las Americas, 1980), p. 81, citing B. Meeks, "The Development of the 1970 Revolution in Trinidad and Tobago," unpublished M.Sc. thesis, University of the West Indies, Mona, Jamaica, 1975, ch. 4.

17. Sandstrom, "West Indian and Latin American Dependency Theories," ch. 4, "Dependency Theory in the Caribbean."

18. Anthony Maingot, "Options for Grenada: The Need to Be Cautious, *Caribbean Review* 12, 4 (Fall 1983), p. 26.

19. EPICA Task Force, *Grenada: The Peaceful Revolution* (Washington, DC: EPICA Task Force, 1982), pp. 44–45; Jacobs and Jacobs, *Grenada*, p. 76; Searle, *Grenada*, pp. 14–16.

20. Ibid.

21. D. Sinclair DaBreo, *The Grenada Revolution* (Castries, St. Lucia: M.A.P.S. Publications, 1979), p. 55.

22. Jacobs and Jacobs, *Grenada*, p. 76.

23. Jacobs and Jacobs; *Grenada*, pp. 76–80; Brizan, *Grenada: Island of Conflict*, p. 333.

24. Maingot, "Options for Grenada," p. 26.

25. Brizan, *Grenada: Island of Conflict*, pp. 337–40.

26. Brizan, *Grenada: Island of Conflict*, p. 341; Searle, *Grenada*, pp. 19–21, quoting interview with Selwyn Strachan (at the time Minister of National Mobilization), *The Free West Indian* 17 (November, 1982).

27. EPICA Task Force, *Grenada*, pp. 46–48; Brizan, *Grenada: Island of Conflict*, p. 342.

28. EPICA Task Force, *Grenada*, p. 48; Searle, *Grenada*, pp. 24–31.

29. Interviews with some of the nineteen defendants in the Maurice Bishop murder trial, St. George's, Grenada, March, 1986. See also EPICA Task Force, *Grenada*, pp. 45–55, and *The Daily News*, the U.S. Virgin Islands, October 21, 1983. All references stemming from my discussions with those accused of Bishop's assassination will be to "the nineteen" in order to protect individuals by avoiding specific attribution. As will emerge from the ensuing narrative, among these prisoners were some of the main actors in the drama of the revolution's collapse. I was able to test my understanding of the internal conflict against theirs. I have accepted many of their criticisms. Mindful that these prisoners were on trial for their lives, and have since been sentenced, several of them to death, I appreciate the rejoinder that their interpretations were obviously self-seeking. Perhaps, but no more so than the versions promulgated by the free survivors, such as George Louison and Kenrick Radix, who have had the additional benefit of amplification through U.S. information services.

30. For a representative sampling, see Crane Brinton, *The Anatomy of Revolution* (New York: Vintage Books, 1959 [c. 1952]), Mark N. Hagopian, *The Phenomenon of Revolution* (New York: Dodd, Mead, 1974), Samuel P. Huntington, "Revolution and Political Order" in his *Political Order in Changing Societies* (New Haven: Yale University Press, 1968), Mostafa Rejai, *The Comparative Study of Revolutionary Strategy* (New York: David McKay, 1977), and Ted Robert Gurr, *Why Men Rebel* (Princeton, NJ: Princeton University Press, 1970).

31. Ernest Harsch, "Interview with a Leader of the Grenada Revolution: 'We Will Not Submit or Bow to American Bullying.' " *Intercontinental Press*, Nov. 19, 1979. Reprinted as Appendix I of *Education for Socialists*, Bulletin prepared by the National Education Department, Socialist Workers Party, December, 1980, p. 21.

32. Jacobs and Jacobs, *Grenada*, pp. 80–81.

33. United States, Grenada Documents, Fiche DSI–83–C–002763, #101700. These documents, seized during the invasion and occupation of October 1983, cover activities of the New Jewel Movement and the People's Revolutionary Government of Grenada 1979–83. They are available on microfiche at the U.S. National Archives, Washington, DC. Hereinafter rendered in abbreviated form, with appropriate fiche number, as follows: U.S./Grenada Doc.

34. Embassy of the Republic of Cuba, Grenada, Statement by the Communist Party and Revolutionary Government of Cuba Concerning the Events in Grenada, October 20, pp. 2–3. U.S./Grenada Documents, DSI 83-C–006819, #20049.

35. U.S./Grenada Doc. DSI–83-C–003217 #102069. The word is indeed "rooting," not "footing."

36. U.S./Grenada Doc. DSI–83-C–003066.

37. United States Department of State, "Maurice Bishop's 'Line of March' Speech, September 13,, 1982." Grenada Occasional Papers, No. 1, August, 1984, p. 9.

38. U.S./Grenada Doc. DSI–83-C–003066 ##101964–5; *New Jewel* (August 20, 1983), p. 3.

39. This series of rejoinders stems from my interviews with some of the nineteen defendants in the Maurice Bishop murder trial, March, 1986.

40. J. H. Parry, P. M. Sherlock, and A. P. Maingot, *A Short History of the West Indies* (New York: St. Martin's Press, 1987), p. 289.

41. Michael Massing, "Grenada Before and After," *The Atlantic Monthly*, February 1984, p. 80.

42. U.S./Grenada Doc. DSI 83-C–007323, #3013, pp. 5–9.

43. U.S./Grenada Doc. DSI–83-C–002306 #10039; U.S. Department of State and Department of Defense, *Grenada: A Preliminary Report* (Washington, DC, December 1983), p. 31. Italics in original.

44. U.S./Grenada Doc. DSI–83-C–004619 #103445.

45. U.S./Grenada Doc. DSI–83-C–002019 #00123; U.S. Department of State and Department of Defense, *Grenada: A Preliminary Report* (Washington, DC, December 1983), p. 32.

46. Friends for Jamaica, *The Side You Haven't Heard: Maurice Bishop Murder Trial. Testimony by The Defendants and Analysis by the NJM and Other Grenadians*, Part I (New York: Cathedral Finance Station, Box 20392), p. 33.

47. U.S./Grenada Doc. DSI–83-C–002025 #000181. See also DSI–83-C–

002763 #101700 for a curious reference to a conspiracy theory on a handwritten agenda for the October 12 CC meeting.

48. Bernard Diederich, "Interviewing George Louison: A PRG Minister Talks About the Killings," *Caribbean Review* 12, 4 (1984), p. 18.

49. "The Alienation of Group Therapy: Extraordinary General Meeting of Full Members of the NJM," *Caribbean Review* 12, 4 (1984), p. 54.

50. *The Nation*, Barbados, December 26, 1986, p. 26.

51. Layne court testimony in Friends for Jamaica, *The Side You Haven't Heard*; letter (typescript, verbatim, with some gaps indicating either carelessness in transcribing the handwriting or mental lapses after being beaten all night) postdated Richmond Hill Prisons, St. George's, Grenada, 17/11/83.

52. *The Nation*, Barbados, December 26, 1986, p. 20.

53. U.S./Grenada Doc. DSI–83–C–002019 #000127.

54. U.S./Grenada Doc. DSI–83–C–002019 #000124; DSI–83–C–004619 #103445; DSI–83–C–002025 #0183.

55. Ewart Layne testimony, in Friends for Jamaica, *The Side You Haven't Heard*, pp. 2, 13–15.

56. Maurice Bishop, *Forward Ever! Three Years of the Grenadian Revolution. Speeches of Maurice Bishop* (Sydney: Pathfinder, 1982), p. 18.

57. Massing, "Grenada Before and After," p. 77.

58. Massing, "Grenada Before and After," p. 85.

59. Grenadians for the Truth About 1983, "Grenada 1983: Whose Struggle," in Friends for Jamaica, *The Side You Haven't Heard*, pp. 33–34; compare Diederich, 1984, pp. 17–18.

60. Massing, "Grenada Before and After," p. 85.

61. Grenadians for the Truth About 1983, "Grenada 1983," p. 36, citing interview with Maurice Church, Ministry of National Security, July–August 1985.

62. Massing, "Grenada Before and After, pp. 77, 85.

63. G. Ionescu and E. Gellner, eds., *Populism: Its meanings and National Characteristics* (New York: Macmillan, 1969), pp. 3–4.

64. Edward Shils, *The Torment of Secrecy: The Background and Consequences of American Security Policies* (London: Heineman, 1956), pp. 98–104.

65. Peter Worsley, "The Concept of Populism," in Ionescu and Gellner, *Populism*, pp. 244–46.

66. Gavin Kitching, *Development and Underdevelopment in Historical Perspective: Populism, Nationalism and Industrialization* (London: Methuen, 1982), p. 99.

67. Carl Stone, "Democracy and Socialism in Jamaica: 1972–1979," in *The Newer Caribbean: Decolonization, Democracy, and Development*, ed. Paget Henry and Carl Stone (Philadelphia: Institute for the Study of Human Issues, 1983), pp. 236–37.

68. Hilbourne Watson, "Non-capitalist Path of Development and Contemporary Caribbean Foreign Policy," paper presented to the Fourth Annual Caribbean and Latin American Conference, Hunter College, May 9, 1981.

69. Kitching, *Development and Underdevelopment*, p. 63.

70. Henry and Stone, p. xiv.

71. Rudolph Heberle, *Social Movements: An Introduction to Sociology* (New York: Appleton-Century-Crofts, 1951), pp. 6–8.

72. George Volsky, "Cuba," in The American Assembly, *The United States and the Caribbean* (Englewood Cliffs, NJ: Prentice-Hall, 1971), p. 102.

73. I am indebted to Jan Carew for recalling this witticism in his "History of a Revolution," panel on "The Grenadian Revolution: Accomplishments and Lessons," Tenth Annual Third World Conference, Chicago, March 1984. He repeated it later that year at the end of an uncommonly eloquent and poignant article discussing the destruction by Cortez of pre-Columbian agriculture technologies, especially amaranth cultivation. Five hundred years of colonial rule ensued. The parallel: experimental reintroduction of Amaranth in Bishop's Grenada was destroyed by the October 1983 invasion, leading to reintroduction of neocolonialism. How wonderfully tongue-in-cheek to repeat Marx's dictum in that context. ("Fulcrums of Change," *Race and Class* 26:2 [Autumn 1984]: 1–13.)

74. Aaron Segal, "Background to Grenada: When the Social Scientists Invaded," *Caribbean Review* 12:4 (1984): 44.

75. *Caribbean Contact*, January/February 1984, p. 10.

76. Charles Frye, "Introduction," *Contributions in Black Studies* No. 6 (1983–1984): 2.

77. Cited by Roberto Marquez in "Grenada: History, Neocolonialism, and Culture in the Contemporary Caribbean," *Contributions in Black Studies* No. 8 (1983–1984): 31.

3
From Revolutionary Solidarity to Military Defeat: The Foreign Policy of Grenada, 1979–1983
David E. Lewis

The foreign policy of the New Jewel Movement–led People's Revolutionary Government constituted a critical element in the agenda of social change which followed the successful overthrow in March 1979 of the Gairy regime. As minister of foreign affairs, Unison Whiteman reflected the new orientation: "Any social change would not be worthy of the name—Revolution—if it did not produce the political will to adopt a new and radically different approach to the question of external relations."[1] Given this outlook, the PRG adhered to the five basic principles enunciated by the NJM in its 1973 Manifesto. These were:

1. Antiimperialism and nonalignment;
2. The promotion of a New International Economic Order;
3. To work for world peace and cooperation;
4. The pursuit of regional cooperation and integration; and
5. Constant support of national liberation struggles.[2]

Rather than assess each aspect of this foreign policy orientation, we will attempt to outline and analyze the basic meaning(s) of these commitments and their relationship to the region as a whole and to the eventual demise of the Grenada revolution and the military invasion of October 25, 1983.

It is important to note from the outset that the first and foremost catalyst of the foreign policy tension that characterized the relations between the PRG and the U.S. government resulted from Grenada's conscious policy of challenging American "hegemony" in the region.

Such a policy was the direct and inevitable result of the establishment of close ties between the governments of Grenada and Cuba. As the Carter administration's ambassador to the Eastern Caribbean, Sally A. Shelton, stated,

Our policy toward the Caribbean has traditionally been shaped to a substantial degree by our Cubaphobia. We have generally found it difficult to have friendly and constructive relations with countries which, in turn, have close ties to Cuba. Grenada is a case in point.[3]

The statement is clear evidence that even among more liberal elements of U.S. political leadership the issue of Cuba remained a thorn in the side of the United States.

Within the Caribbean region the most important and revolutionary aspect of the PRG's foreign policy was the ideological and political recognition of the Cuban revolution as both a bonafide member of the Caribbean community, as well as an effective model of political development. This led to Grenada's alignment with what has been referred to as the "core revolutionary community in the Caribbean."[4] The notion of a "core revolutionary community" is used in juxtaposition to that of a "progressive community in the Caribbean." It represents the qualitative distinction between regimes under revolutionary transformation such as Cuba, Nicaragua, and Grenada, on the one hand, and those with certain radical inclinations, such as Guyana and Michael Manley's Jamaica.

The importance of such a distinction cannot be overstated, for in the case of the Grenada revolution it meant that the negative effects which Forbes Burnham's Guyana and Manley's Jamaica had produced for the concept of radical social change in the Caribbean could only now be somewhat redressed through the use of the domestic and foreign policy processes available to the NJM in Grenada. Thus, Grenada was looked upon by many as a beacon of light and a model for those people in the Caribbean who sought societal, political, and economic change. The importance of the Grenada revolution, despite the events of October 1983, will remain as much a part of the Caribbean experience as the slave rebellions of the eighteenth century, the labor riots of the 1930s, the challenges posed to British colonialism during the late 1950s and early 1960s, and the Black Power movement born in the "Rodney riots" of 1968.

As we will see, it was this conscious policy of revolutionary change in both its domestic and foreign relations which put Grenada in direct confrontation with the United States. It was that challenge which provoked the Carter and Reagan administrations to develop economic and military contingency plans against Grenada, and ultimately justified, in the minds of Reagan's political and military advisers, the invasion of

October twenty-fifth. Regardless of the independent internal crisis which the Grenada revolutionaries created for themselves, the U.S. attack conveyed one very clear message to the entire region: that the United States would not tolerate any regime in the area that sought to challenge its hegemony by building close ties with Cuba and the socialist bloc. The invasion of Grenada was a contemporary manifestation of both the Monroe Doctrine and the "Big Stick" policy. It was a logical extension of U.S. policy toward Cuba and Nicaragua, as well as its support of the current government of El Salvador.

In addition to its regional aspect, the PRG's foreign policy embraced the political and ideological rhetoric of antiimperialism and nonalignment (characteristic of many nonrevolutionary Third World governments, such as Mexico). In specific application of this posture, the PRG supported the PLO, recognized the SWAPO forces in Namibia as well as the African National Congress within the Republic of South Africa as legitimate representatives of the peoples of those nations, and extended political support to the USSR and Vietnam regarding their respective involvements in Afghanistan and Cambodia. The latter two, along with the support of Argentine sovereignty over the Falklands/Malvinas, were pursued by the PRG all the way to their respective UN General Assembly votes.[5]

All in all, PRG policies at the level of regional and international relations were a direct manifestation of the national revolutionary process led by a socialist-inclined political movement which was taking place in Grenada. At the international level it never ceased to be a force of antiimperialist and pro–socialist bloc commitment.

Although such a policy drew the challenge and opposition of Washington, the PRG was able to develop excellent relations with many nonsocialist bloc countries, and was likewise accepted by the Western European nations as a legitimate political entity within the capitalist world system. In addition, the new government's administrative efficiency with regard to Grenada's external relations elicited favorable appraisals from important regional and international financial institutions. Indeed, since 1979 Grenada's record with the Caribbean Development Bank, the IMF, and the World Bank earned the government a sound international reputation for efficient and responsible management—a refreshing change from the inefficiency and corruption of the ousted Gairly regime.[6]

Despite the PRG's interest in developing friendly relations with governments in the region, as well as out of it, the regime's domestic political posture had a profound effect on foreign policy and the nature of the relations to be established.[7] Grenada's independent line demanded a certain degree of political tolerance from its neighbors and others if they were to interact in a spirit of cooperation and respect. The latter form is precisely what dominated the relations between Grenada and the majority of the countries of the EEC. In other words, despite certain ideological and political differences, there is greater good to both sides which accrued through establishment of cordial relations.

At the same time it would be dangerous to overlook the imperial presence of the United States in the region, and its inevitable opposition to regimes which challenged the "American way of life" and its notion of a *mare nostrum* in the Caribbean. Castro's Cuba provided a striking example of U.S. reaction to "foreign intervention," that is, communism in the "American lake." That pattern of ostracism and hostility toward Cuba could be repeated for Grenada.

In the long run, then, a key factor that colored Grenada's foreign policy was a pragmatic blend of what best served the national interest in combination with a degree of tolerance for the divergent policies and practices of other nations. True to its unorthodox political behavior since its birth in 1973, the NJM proved in both its domestic and foreign policy the veracity of Burke's statement that the first of political virtues is prudence. Or, as columnist Flora Lewis commented on her interview with Deputy Prime Minister Bernard Coard,

Mr. Coard says that Grenada seriously wants better relations with the U.S., but on its own terms. If national policies were the test, he snaps, "I'd have my own shopping list for the U.S., on things like racism, women's rights, housing, medical service. But we are not so arrogant."[8]

WASHINGTON'S OPPOSITION TO THE CUBAN CONNECTION

As a result of the forceful nature of the overthrow of the Gairy regime and possible repercussions, the top priority of the PRG was militarily to safeguard the existence of the revolution. Needed arms, ammunition, and training for the newly assembled People's Revolutionary Army (PRA) were sought from the United States, Canada, and the United Kingdom, as well as some CARICOM countries. The former three countries indicated their unwillingness to comply with the PRG request, and the latter were of minimal help.[9] The U.S. government, aware of the PRG's need of military assistance, grew apprehensive that the government might approach Cuba, if it had not already done so, to fill the gap. Washington took the decision, therefore, to dissuade the Grenadian government from that course of action and instructed its representatives to this end. The position was conveyed by Ambassador Ortiz (Ms. Shelton's predecessor) in a typewritten statement which he handed to Prime Minister Bishop on April 10, 1979. It stressed that

Although my government recognized your concerns over allegations of a possible counter-coup, it also believes that it would not be in Grenada's best interests to seek such assistance from a country such as Cuba to forestall such an attack. We would view with displeasure any tendency on the part of Grenada to develop closer ties with Cuba.[10]

Grenada responded to the U.S. warning on April thirteenth, when Prime Minister Bishop emphasized at a public rally the government's vehement rejection of such interference in Grenadian affairs, proclaiming that "no one, no matter how mighty and powerful . . . will be permitted to dictate to the government and people of Grenada who we can have friendly relations with and what kind of relations we must have with other countries."[11] In addition, Bishop forcefully protested that "we are not in anybody's backyard and we are definitely not for sale."[12] On the following day, April 14, 1979, diplomatic relations were established with Cuba.

These events gave rise to the initial tensions between Washington and St. Georges, as the Grenada government drew closer to Havana. As relations with the U.S. became further strained, the Grenadan leadership began to view the Carter administration as part of an existing counter-revolutionary security threat to Grenada. Such an assessment was not unrealistic in view of the subsequent revelations that the U.S. government had initially considered establishing a naval blockage of the island.[13]

Cuba-Grenada relations developed rapidly at all levels. In April 1979 the PRG received a shipment of arms for the Army. This was followed by the July ninth signing of a two-year agreement providing generally for technical assistance, training in various fields, and the interchange of scientific and technical programs.[14] As a follow-up, twelve Cuban medical and dental specialists arrived in Grenada to assist in running the country's medical services. In early September 1979, a gift of the first of twelve fishing trawlers was handed over to be used in a training program for Grenadan fishermen directed by Cuban experts. An offer of 38 scholarships for university studies in Cuba was also announced.[15] Trade was also established, and Grenada began to purchase sugar and cement from Cuba. Cuban aid, when compared with the paltry sum of $5,000 Ambassador Ortiz offered to the Grenadan government, made it clear to the PRG that Havana offered significant material as well as ideological support.[16]

In September of 1979, Prime Minister Bishop traveled to Havana for the Nonaligned Summit, which Grenada attended for the first time, and secured Grenada's elections to the Bureau of the Movement. In November, Cuba offered a massive assistance grant to aid in the design and construction of Grenada's proposed new international airport. The airport, which was to cost the U.S. $75 million (E.C. [Eastern Caribbean dollar]

$190 million), had been proposed as a project since 1955 when Grenada was still a British colony. Cuba pledged to contribute "85 pieces of heavy equipment, 250 technical workers, and a substantial part of the project costs."[17] Out of the grand total cost of U.S. $75 million, the Cuban assistance was calculated to be the equivalent of U.S. $33.6 million, with the rest of the aid distributed as follows:

Libya:	U.S. $ 4 million
Syria:	U.S. $ 2 million
Algeria:	U.S. $ 6 million
OPEC:	U.S. $ 2 million
EEC:	U.S. $16 million
Venezuela:	U.S. $ 4 million
Grenada:	U.S. $ 7 million[18]

In addition, the United Kingdom granted a loan of E.C. $33 million to help cover the costs of contracting the British company Plessey Airport Ltd., and Finland loaned E.C. $10.5 million for the work being done by Finland Metex Corp.

The Havana connection had, therefore, been extremely beneficial to Grenada, catering to a number of priority areas identified by the PRG. In exchange, Grenada offered rhetorical and ideological support for Cuba's socialist political economy as a model for regional development and for antihegemonic policies.

These developments, best exemplified in Prime Minister Bishop's visit to Havana for the 1980 May Day rally, found a parallel of sorts in Grenada's growing ties with the Sandinista government in Nicaragua. Revolutionary solidarity between both governments was formally sealed with the visit to Grenada of Junta leader, Commander Daniel Ortega, who was the guest speaker at the first anniversary celebrations of the Grenada revolution in 1980.

With the development of ties with both Cuba and Nicaragua came Grenadan expressions of support for both these regimes, as well as an increased zealousness in condemning U.S. attempts at thwarting such revolutionary processes. On a global level, the PRG also identified its foreign policy with a number of Marxist/socialist-oriented governments in the world, and supported such national liberation movements as the PLO and the Polisario Front. The PRG also sought to broaden its network of diplomatic ties by establishing relations with a number of socialist bloc nations as well as countries with a stated socialist national policy.[19] Bishop felt that this realignment redressed the ideological imbalance in Grenada's foreign relations inherited from the Gairy government.[20]

This new and radical foreign policy orientation, and in particular the closeness to Havana, had an increasingly negative effect on the relations with Washington. After the Ortiz visit, the PRG was particularly sensitive as to its dealings with the U.S. government, but was intent on maintaining its sovereign right to establish relations with any country it deemed as beneficial to Grenada's national interest. Simultaneously, the PRG grew increasingly suspicious that the United States had mounted an anti-Grenadan campaign in the local, regional, and international press.[21]

The Carter plan to set up a Caribbean Military Task Force in June 1979 in the wake of charges that the Soviet Union had combat troops in Cuba was viewed with alarm by the PRG as a potential threat to the revolution. From that point, Grenadan diplomacy attempted to win international condemnation of Carter's plan. In his first address to the UN General Assembly, Prime Minister Bishop condemned the U.S. policy of "using gunboat diplomacy, blockades and destabilization tactics against the peoples of Latin America and the Caribbean."[22] In that speech, Bishop also declared Grenada's support for the independence movement in Puerto Rico and for Cuba's effort to regain control over the U.S. base at Guantanamo.

In the final analysis, it was the continued threat posed by an ever-increasing militarization of the region by the U.S. and Grenadan countermeasures to such policies which dictated the nature of U.S.–Grenadan relations up to the very day of the invasion of October twenty-fifth. Since 1981, many had warned that U.S. military maneuvers in the region were but stage rehearsals for a future eventual invasion of Cuba, Nicaragua, or Grenada.[23] The most ominous scenario was called "Operation Amber and the Amberdines" in October of 1981, in which Americans were taken hostage by "Amber" and then freed by a U.S. invasion after negotiations with the Amber government broke down.

U.S.–Grenada relations were set on a confrontation course. The Carter administration may well have regarded the new PRG foreign policy orientation as part of Soviet-Cuban efforts to penetrate the Caribbean and gain pliable clients. This policy perspective hardened as the Republican administration assumed power in November 1980. The PRG, for its part, worried that the United States would attempt to "roll back" the course of the Revolution and thereby threaten Grenada's independence. It was clear to them that no *modus vivendi* could be reached with the hard-line Reagan administration. Yet, in persistently taking a stance opposed to a number of Washington's key interests and priorities in the Caribbean, the PRG necessarily elicited a hard-line response from the government of a country that had historically had its way in the Caribbean. The Grenada revolutionaries, in their attempt to force the United States to accept Grenada for what it was, failed to understand the real and dangerous geopolitical situation in which it was involved.

The crux of the matter lay in the conflict of interests of a U.S. government seeking to reassert and maintain its political and ideological dominance of the region, and the interests of a revolutionary regime seeking to design an independent, sovereign and socialist bloc–oriented line of action. From the U.S. perspective it is not hard to see what were the major problems with Grenada and the PRG: (1) Grenada's close relationship with Cuba was almost a "mortal sin"; (2) the PRG's virulent antiimperialist/U.S. rhetoric; and (3) Grenada's consistently pro-Cuba and anti–U.S. stance at the UN and the OAS.

THE CARIBBEAN AND GRENADA

In terms of the response of neighboring Caribbean states, Grenada's radically new ideological orientation—as well as the PRG's method of achieving state power—greatly harmed the nation's chance of gaining full reacceptance as a bonafide member of the community and its organizations. Many of the regional governments, led by conservative politicians, such as prime ministers Seaga, Adams, and Charles (Jamaica, Barbados, and Dominica, respectively), had criticized the PRG's delay in holding elections, the detention of alleged counterrevolutionaries without trial, and the severe restrictions on an independent press in Grenada. The coolness of these governments to the Grenada revolution derived in part from the ideological disposition of these government themselves, as well as from their own national domestic considerations. One must also bear in mind that such postures also reflected a deep concern in the region with the effectiveness of the continued constitutionality of the Westminster model of parlimentary politics. As Michael Manley stated,

[t]he Westminster model of democracy really can't survive a Gairy. The Westminster model of democracy survives not only by the restraint of those who are out of power, the opposition, but even more so by the restraint of those who are in power.[24]

What this meant, then, was that other than the close ties of the NJM/PRG with the different Leftist political organizations of the region, the new regime in St. Georges looked upon its relation within the Caribbean with great uncertainty born out of the sensitivity of the critical hostility which had developed in the region. Yet this same government felt that the institutional power and framework of CARICOM, and its commitment to regional cooperation, despite the process of radical change occurring in Grenada, would effectively curtail anything greater than verbal hostility from its neighbor.

The point being that despite their nonacceptance of the revolutionary process in Grenada, the rest of the CARICOM member states were willing at least to respect the new government. The best example of this was in June 1981, when the United States offered a U.S. $4 million grant package to the regional multilateral lending agency, the Caribbean Development Bank, on the condition that none of the money go to Grenada.[25] The CDB's charter specifically states that lending decisions are to be made soley on the basis of economic criteria and not according to political considerations; it also forbids the bank from interfering in the internal affairs of any of its member states. Accordingly, the CDB's board of directors voted unanimously to refuse the grant.[26] This attempt by the United States to use the CDB as an extension of its hegemony in the region drew condemnation from the standing committee of CARICOM foreign ministers, as they viewed the action as "economic aggression" and "gross interference in Grenada's affairs."[27]

The irony of the entire situation is the fact that it was precisely these governments who made the official and legally unsound request for the Reagan administration to invade Grenada. Likewise, it was these very same leaders (Seaga, Adams, and Charles) who, after four years of constant criticism of Mr. Bishop and the Grenada revolution, after his death began to eulogize him as a symbol of democracy in the Caribbean. It is reassuring, nevertheless, to note that Prime Minister Chambers and the government of Trinidad and Tobago are free of guilt in the machinations of Washington and its Caribbean accomplices. Up to the very end of the emergency CARICOM meeting of October 22–23, Mr. Chambers was under the impression that all would be worked out by way of negotiation and was distressed by the U.S. invasion.

Gordon Lewis summed up the situation:

For the Caribbean Left it means that the colonial dependent ideology still remains entrenched in many segments of the regional society. Its characteristic voices— Seaga, Adams, Charles—invented evasive excuses to justify their collaboration with the U.S.–led invasion: that the P.R.G. was engaged in destabilization exercises against their governments (although up to now no concrete evidence has been produced to prove the charge), or that the absence of free elections in Grenada was an affront to "democracy" (although they were ready to sponsor CARICOM membership for the repressive *duvalieriste* regime in Haiti). The real reason is more obvious: for the regional bourgeoisie, Grenada constituted a threat to their own social and economic structures with its message of socialists reconstruction. With that psychotic fear, it is clear that the regional bourgeoisie— or at least its more intransigent elements—will always be prepared to invite outside forces to combat dangerous radical movements, just as in nineteenth century Cuba the *incondicionalista* elements preferred annexation to the U.S. with slavery rather than independence without slavery.[28]

WHERE WAS CUBA?

Despite its strident internationalist policy of the 1970s (which has been nothing but a more passive and diplomatic manifestation of Guevara's notion of "exporting the revolution"), no other instance of the defeat of a progressive and/or revolutionary regime has dealt as serious a blow to Cuban foreign policy as the Grenada tragedy. For beyond its importance as an antiimperialistic, prosocialist ally, Grenada had a meaning for Cuba which transcended all revolutionary bonds. The importance of Cuba to the Grenada revolution was likely matched by the importance of Grenada to the Cuban revolution. Grenada brought Cuba closer to the Caribbean community. It legitimized, via an official government, what many elements of the Left (as well as liberals in the region) have termed "the importance of the Cuban revolution in Caribbean history." By a twist of fate, the Caribbean status quo leaders, for ill or for good, brought the United States back in as the Big Brother of the region.

With Grenada's revolution, Cuba was moving to achieve for its Pan-Caribbean policy what had taken it almost twenty years: to be accepted, regardless of its socialist political economy, as a bonafide cultural, historical, and political sister nation in the Caribbean. All this and more was lost when as Fidel Castro said, the revolution committed suicide. In addition, of course, there are the less critical yet important elements of the friendship and camaraderie between Castro and Bishop. Cultural bonds between Cubans and Grenadans, were developed and Grenada, with Cuba's encouragement, generated the self-consciousness and motivation to change society and replace poverty and underdevelopment with national pride and economic self-improvement.

It is quite clear from many of the documents studied since October 1983 that the new Revolutionary Military Council was under the impression that Cuba would be of support should the Americans invade. Yet such a perception was incredibly naive. Cuba's stance, as early as Castro's first letter to Grenada on October fifteenth, stressed its principled position of noninterference, as well as its realistic assessment of the situation: if the Americans were coming, Cuba could do nothing to stop them.

In his October twentieth statement concerning the killings at Fort Rupert of Bishop and his ministers, Castro is clear and uncompromisingly frank:

The situation is most difficult and complex. Only a miracle of common sense, equanimity, and wisdom on the part of the Grenadian revolutionaries, and of serenity in the reaction and response of the international progressive movement, can still salvage the process.[29]

The bottom line of Havana's stance was that in a situation in which Castro's government was taken totally by surprise, the wisest and safest option would be to stay out of the Grenadan crisis. Regardless of this fact, there had been great speculation among the press that the entire crisis in Grenada was somehow linked to Castro's internal involvements there. Thus, while the Central Committee factions in Grenada were challenging Bishop as to what he had disclosed to Castro concerning the NJM "crisis," foreign presses were speculating as to how Coard and company were acting on behalf of Moscow and Havana. Media misinformation in both the Caribbean and the United States was widespread. As for the effect on Grenada, it means that its people will go through a massive physical and psychological erosion of everything the revolution and Maurice Bishop stood for. As in Orwell's novel, "Who controls the past controls the future; who controls the present controls the past."[30] And it is the U.S. massive information and security agencies who control the present in Grenada.

CONCLUSION

In analyzing the varied aspects of Grenada's foreign relations throughout the tenure of the revolution, I have attempted to spell out the nature and problems confronted by a small island seeking to alter radically its domestic and internal position in the face of the regional policies of Washington and its Caribbean supporters. The Grenada revolutionaries imprudently sought to alter the reality of that balance of power which was held by the "colossus of the North,." They failed to learn from Castro's Cuba what is perhaps the most important factor behind Castro's success: There can be no illusion of regional and international challenge to U.S. hegemony, both until domestic hegemony was under the full control of the party and its leadership, and the government identifies a strong foreign patron. In the Grenada situation, as we now know, the issue of leadership was still being fought out up until the very last moment before the U.S. invasion; and no foreign power intervened with the United States on behalf of Grenada.

Somewhere in time a Caribbean scholar will write the definitive work on the domestic politics of Grenada during its revolutionary years. Only then will we be able fully to grasp and understand what were all the forces that led to the demise of the revolution and the eventual invasion. It has been my intention to shed some light on the complex nature of regional and international politics for a regime seeking to redress the ideological and political balance of power in the Caribbean. In realpolitik terms, it means that the Grenada revolutionaries failed to understand the need to sacrifice some radical rhetoric for a policy of pragmatism to keep the United States at bay. For if in politics we have to balance one actor against another, the PRG failed to realize that it could not simultaneously counterbalance both the Caribbean conservative forces and the Reaganite elements in Washington. Tiny Grenada, like Cuba before it and Nicaragua now, despite their close ties to the Soviet bloc are, for ill or for good, in the U.S. sphere of influence. That, if nothing else, dictates a sober attitude toward the United States, based on mutual respect and the hope of a chance at full autonomous and independent national development. It is as if we have been suddenly awakened from a long dream, and have now to realize, with no time to reflect, that the era of the Monroe Doctrine and its "gunboat diplomacy" is far from over.

NOTES

1. Unison Whiteman, "Birth of a New Foreign Policy." Address given by the Minister of Foreign Affairs at the First International Conference in Solidarity with Grenada, November 1981.

2. The NJM Manifesto for 1973 (St. Georges, Grenada, 1973). Reprinted in Jacobs and Coard, Eds., *Independence for Grenada—Myth or Reality?* (St. Augustine, Trinidad: Institute for International Relations, U.W.I., 1974).

3. Statement by Hon. Ambassador Sally A. Shelton, to the Sub-Committee on Inter-American Affairs of the Committee on Foreign Affairs of the House of Representatives on "U.S. Policy Towards Grenada" (U.S. Government Printing Office, 96–7930, 1982). June 15, 1982, p. 59.

4. Henry S. Gill, "The Grenada Revolution: Foreign Policy and Caribbean Geo-Politics." Paper presented at the Conference on the LDCs of the Caribbean, June 4–7, 1980, Antigua, p. 37.

5. Reference to these is made further on.

6. Respective reports on Grenada by the CDB, IMF, and World Bank, for 1981 and 1982. For further data see Economic Memorandum on Grenada, June 14, 1982. Ministry of Finance and Planning, St. Georges, Grenada.

7. Whiteman, "Birth of a New Foreign Policy."

8. Flora Lewis, "Spice Island Strains." The New York *Times*, Feb. 28, 1983, p. A15.

9. Gill, "The Grenada Revolution."

10. Maurice Bishop, "One Month After the People's Revolution." Address over Radio Free Grenada and Television Free Grenada on April 13, 1979 (T.I.W.U. Printery, Trinidad, 1979), p. 4.

11. Bishop, "One Month After."

12. Bishop, "One Month After."

13. Gill, "The Grenada Revolution," p. 19. Also see The Washington *Post*, July 6, 1979 and the Boston Sunday *Globe*, Feb. 27, 1983, p. 2.

14. Agreement Between the Government of Cuba and the TGovernment of Grenada, July 9, 1979 (Government Printery, St. Georges), pp. 1–3.

15. Ian Jacobs and Richard Jacobs, *Grenada: The Route to Revolution* (Casa de las Americas, Havana, 1979), p. 133.

16. *Maurice Bishop Speaks: The Grenada Revolution, 1979–1983* (New York: Pathfinder Press, 1984), p. 192.

17. Gill, "The Grenada Revolution," p. 20.

18. House of Representatives, "U.S. Policy Towards Grenada," p. 51. Also see Economic Memorandum on Grenada.

19. Diplomatic relations were established with Cuba, North Korea, the USSR, Vietnam, the People's Revolutionary Council of Kampuches, Ethiopia, Algeria, the People's Democratic Republic of Yemen, Nicaragua, Zambia, the German Democratic Republic, Czechoslovakia, Afghanistan, Benin, Laos, São Tomé, Syria, and Iraq. By April 1979, the PRG had severed relations with Pinochet's Chile and Somoza's Nicaragua.

20. Of the 38 countries with which the Gairy regime had diplomatic relations, Hungary, Rumania, and Yugoslavia were the only socialist or socialist-oriented countries.

21. The NJM attended PNP annual congresses, and Bishop gave the feature address at the 1978 congress—at the highpoint of Manley's experiment with "democratic socialism."

22. The Trinidad *Guardian*, October 11, 1979, p. 12.

23. EPICA Task Force, *Grenada: The Peaceful Revolution* (Washington, DC: EPICA Task Force, 1982), p. 122.

24. Michael Manley,"Grenada in the Context of History: Between Neocolonialism and Independence." *Caribbean Review* 12, 4, p. 9.

25. EPICA, p. 119.

26. Latin American Research Review—Caribbean, July 1981.

27. Latin American Research Review—Caribbean, July 1981. Also see the *Free West Indian* (Grenada), June 27, 1981, p. 15.

28. Gordon K. Lewis, "Grenada 1983: The Lessons for the Caribbean Left." Presented at Meeting of Institute of International Relations, U.W.I., St. Augustine, Trinidad, May 24–25, 1984, p. 18.

29. Statement by the Cuban Government and the Cuban Communist Party, in *Maurice Bishop Speaks*, p. 315.

30. George Orwell, *Nineteen Eighty-Four* (New York: Harcourt, Brace and World, 1949), p. 35.

4
False Prophecy and the American Invasion of Grenada
Wendell Bell

Looking back on 1984, future historians may note that it was a good year for George Orwell: His dystopian novel written in 1948, popped up on the best-seller lists.

The key element in Orwell's chilling vision is the ability of a group in power to shape its own and others' view of reality to further some ideological or instrumental objective. One of the most telling examples of Orwellian fiction becoming reality not in 1984 itself but—as if it were a rehearsal—in the last days of 1983 was the American invasion of Grenada. We are not dealing here with simple cases of doubletalk. Rather we are dealing with the ways in which the range of consciousness shrinks, systematic efforts are made to extinguish thought, and the idea begins to grow that the external exists largely, if not entirely, in the mind. It is implied in the Party slogan, "who controls the past controls the future; who controls the present controls the past."[1] It is revealed further in the idea, now going beyond Orwell, that who controls images of the future may control reality itself. By that I mean that those who can invent plausible prophecies and who have power to act *as if* they are true can so change reality by their actions that it is difficult, if not impossible, to know whether prophecies would have turned out to be true or false if no such action had taken place. Yet, if leaders are to be held accountable, some efforts must be made to assess the evidence to see if the action-justifying prophecy was presumptively true or false at the time it was made.

Although the invasion of tiny Grenada will not go down in history as one of the more earthshaking incidents of our troubled age, it is nonetheless significant as a near-perfect illustration of the use of prophecy to justify present action. The Reagan administration gave the people of the world three principal reasons for action, all of them in the form of contingent statements about the future, that is, what would have happened *if* there had been no invasion: (1) U.S. citizens would have been taken hostage or possibly killed; (2) a Soviet-Cuban military bastion would have been established for the export of communism throughout the region, especially the Eastern Caribbean; (3) a modern military airport would have been completed at Point Salines that would have become a threat to the vital interests and national security of the United States. Although we cannot tell now who among the United States' top leaders believed these prophecies at the moment of crisis, we do suspect that none of the three was credible. That is the subject of this essay. Before turning to it, however, I want to summarize the events of the invasion.

OPERATION URGENT FURY[2]

The U.S. invasion of Grenada, code-named "Operation Urgent Fury," began in the early morning hours of October 25, 1983, but not with the roar of violence that would soon follow. Instead, it began with the quiet stealth of a small group of Navy "Seals" who landed north of St. Georges. Their mission was to reach Sir Paul Scoon, governor-general of Grenada. Their purpose was to legitimize the invasion that was about to begin. They probably carried with them for his signature a batch of identical letters, ostensibly from Scoon but written by someone else, addressed to each of the invading countries and dated October twenty-fourth, the day before the invasion, requesting military intervention. (According to Anthony Payne, Paul Sutton, and Tony Thorndike, two batches of such letters were carried by the invading forces, one by U.S. troops and the other by the Caribbean contingent.)[3] It was threadbare legitimacy at best since the governor-generalship was a ceremonial position representing the Crown, a symbolic link to the colonial past and the present British Commonwealth. Yet Scoon certainly could claim more legitimacy than General Hudson Austin and the other members of the Revolutionary Military Council (RMC) who had come to power as a result of the murder of Prime Minister Maurice Bishop.

Some hours after the Seals had landed and were "securing" Sir Paul Scoon, super-modern, postindustrial technowar exploded over Grenada. Eyewitness Hugh O'Shaugnessy describes one of the stupefying death machines: coordinated banks of machine guns carried by the C–130 Hercules "which were able to pour fire into an area the size of a football field from a height of several thousand feet."[4] There were also three hundred soldiers and policemen, mostly the latter, from six Caribbean countries, although they did not actually participate in the fighting.

About four hundred members of the Twenty-second Marine Amphibious Unit transported by helicopters attacked Pearls airport about 5:30 A.M. on October twenty-fifth. They found little resistance and captured it easily. Part of the Marine force then returned to the helicopter carrier, the USS *Guam*, and sailed to the other side of the island. That night they landed and engaged Grenadan troops protecting St. Georges, which had been hit earlier by thundering air strikes. Some eight hundred Army Rangers parachuted into Point Salines about 6:00 A.M. We do not know who fired first, although we do know that the Cubans had been ordered not to fight the Americans unless they were attacked. Members of the People's Revolutionary Army (PRA) of Grenada, of course, were under no such orders and probably fired on the parachuting Rangers. (Payne et al. report that although only two Grenadan soldiers armed with rifles were actually defending the Point Salines airport at the time, they fired and succeeded in shooting down some of the parachutists.)[5] Nonetheless, after the Rangers had landed and regrouped, savage fighting did take place and the Cubans, mostly middle-aged construction workers, resisted energetically. Within a few hours, fighting at Point Salines ended and about six hundred Cubans were captured. Clearing the runway at Point Salines, the Rangers were reinforced by about five thousand men of the Eighty-second Airborne Division.

The medical students at the True Blue campus of the medical school were soon reached. The bulk of students, however, were not there. They were at the Grand Anse campus about two miles away. Inexplicably, they were not reached by U.S. troops until about 4:00 P.M., October twenty-sixth, a day and a half after the invasion began, plenty of time for them to have been captured or murdered several times over if that had been the intention of the Grenadans or the Cubans still at large.

By Friday, October twenty-eighth, the battle was over, except for a few isolated pockets of resistance. Although only a few days long, the operation was not without its blunders and tragic accidents. Robert A. Pastor later reminded members of Congress of some of them: [Four members of the Navy Seals drowned before the invasion started; one U.S. unit called for an air strike on another, wounding over a dozen U.S. soldiers; U.S. Rangers were killed and wounded when two helicopters collided; and U.S. Cobra helicopters, mistaking the former Fort Matther, then a mental hospital, for Fort Frederick, destroyed it, killing between eighteen and thirty inmates (official U.S. sources admit to eighteen). Furthermore, attacking the Cubans at Point Salines instead of moving directly to the medical students may have been a blunder, if it is true that the Cubans only fired to defend themselves.

Although different sources give somewhat different numbers, the best estimates of the casualties are: nineteen Americans killed and 115 wounded; 24 Cubans killed and 57 wounded; sixteen Grenadan soldiers and 37 civilians killed and 357 civilians wounded (60 of whom eventually received treatment in U.S. military hospitals in Bethesda, Maryland, or Puerto Rico) including seventeen-year old Michael Baptiste, who is paralyzed from the wait down and still has a bullet lodged near his spine, and six-year-old Foster Bartholomew who lost his right eye and has severe damage to his mouth, kidneys and liver.[7]

WERE U.S. CITIZENS IN DANGER?

An early justification given by spokesmen for the Reagan administration for the invasion of Grenada was a concern for the welfare of U.S. citizens in Grenada, especially students attending the St. George's University Medical School. U.S. Secretary of State George Schultz, for example, in a special national television broadcast during the afternoon of October twenty-fifth said that the United States had decided to act *before* the Americans were hurt or taken hostage.[8] He said that his "overriding" and "paramount" concern had been "to protect innocent lives, including up to 1,000 Americans,"[9] linking his decision to invade to "the nightmare of our hostages in Iran."[10]

We will never know for certain what would have happened to the medical students *if* the invasion had not taken place, because the invasion intervened in the course of history. But we can ask ourselves: Was the impending danger to U.S. students prophecy and was the allusion to Iran an appropriate image of the past? The answers are "no."

The RMC's General Hudson Austin "sought desperately to negotiate with Washington in the days between Prime Minister Bishop's death and the American-led invasion."[11] During the curfew on Grenada, "General Austin himself called Geoffry Bourne, Vice Chancellor of the Medical School, offering jeeps and transportation and arranging to have the supermarket open just for the students. He also sent one of his officers to check that everything was O.K. and gave Bourne his home phone number if there were any problems"[12] Both Bourne and another administrator of the Medical School, Gary Solin, believed "at the time and in retrospect" that the medical students were "never in danger."[13] Furthermore, Austin guaranteed the safety of U.S. citizens in Grenada and promised the safe evacuation of any of them who wanted to leave. Cuba sent urgent messages to Washington to this effect and joined Grenada in urging that the invasion not take place.[14]

Reacting to the assurances given by Grenada that the United States could evacuate the Americans, Pierre Elliot Trudeau, then prime minister of Canada, was widely reported as saying, "Obviously, if they [the Americans] had the authority to do that, I cannot see any reason for invading to protect your nationals."[15]

There is no indication that the administration made any effort to evacuate Americans peacefully. At first the White House contended that

Pearls airport at Grenada was closed during Monday, October twenty-fourth. Later, U.S. officials admitted that at last four charter planes left that day.[16] Furthermore, as Percy Hintzen has said,

A Canadian plane sent by the Canadian government to get out its own citizens was granted permission to take off from Barbados by that government and the government of the United States. This was two days before the invasion. The reason why no commercial flights were operating in and out of Grenada was because of a ban on air traffic to that country imposed by Caribbean states, and a decision by LIAT [Leeward Island Air Transport], the only commercial airline serving that country, not to fly there. I had nothing to do with any decision by the Grenadian government.[17]

Moreover, as Pastor testified, "two U.S. diplomats flew in and out during the weekend" before the invasion on Tuesday.[18] Why didn't the United States simply arrange to evacuate Americas on Grenada who wanted to leave?

Even the students' parents did not believe that an invasion was necessary. Some parents had been in touch with their children by telephone and a group of parents learned on Sunday that only 10 percent of the students had expressed a desire to leave Grenada in a meeting the students had held earlier that day. The parents, meeting that Sunday evening while the president was on television expressing his concern about the Americans on Grenada, "sent a cable to President Reagan," according to Pastor, "informing him that their children were safe and asking him 'not to move too quickly or to take any precipitous action at this time.' "[19]

Rather than ensuring their safety, the invasion endangered it. The *force majeure* used by the U.S. military was frightening and may have caused more of the emotional displays of those Americans who were eventually evacuated than did the Grenadan situation up until the invasion. Explosions, bullets whistling by, the roar of jet engines and the beat of helicopters, shouts of "Friend or foe?" and the general confusion created by the invasion itself, had some students hiding under their beds and others, no doubt, believing that Death himself had arrived.

A final question can be asked about the prophecy involving the threatened safety of the Americas: Was the invasion carried out in such a way that the safety of the Americans on Grenada was clearly its aim? The answer again is "no." As Michael Manley of Jamaica said, "if an invasion had to take place, just put the Marines around the students and say, 'Look nobody touch these people here or feel the might of U.S. power.' "[20] Moreover, the military intervention was not restricted to securing the safety of the Americans, but "to establish complete control of the island."[21] Most of the students, as stated earlier, were not reached by U.S. troops until a day and a half after the invasion began.[22]

The analogy with the hostages in Iran is equally questionable. The geographical location, size, religions, political structures, language and culture, and prior known threat to Americans in Grenada were totally different from the situation in Iran. In their assessment of the safety of Americans in Grenada, the Reagan administration picked an inappropriate model of the past to follow in the example of Iran.

THE COMING SOVIET-CUBAN "MILITARY BASTION" ON GRENADA

On October twenty-fifth, the Reagan administration justified the invasion by arguments in addition to that of rescuing the medical students. They were to establish law and order and to restore democratic institutions.[23] Neither of these arguments were credible to knowledgeable persons from the start. Before the invasion, order had been restored by General Austin and the PRA. Furthermore, repeated contact and negotiations had taken place between members of the RMC and U.S. officials on the one hand and between the governor-general and representatives of Barbados and Trinidad on the other. The U.S. tolerance of undemocratic regimes, such as Baby Doc's Haiti, for example, mocked the statements about restoring democracy. Both arguments quickly faded away.

In their place, by October twenty-seventh, the U.S. administration claimed that a Soviet fueled "complete takeover by Cuba" and the export of thousands of terrorists spreading out from Grenada to the rest of the Eastern Caribbean had been planned. They introduce ideological arguments of the East-West conflict, the Cold War, and the containment of communism. The specter of a "Soviet-Cuban colony being readied as a major military bastion" was cast before the American people by the president. He and other administration spokesmen pointed to the presence "of heavily armed Cuban troops on the island, as well as advisers from the Soviet Union, East Germany, Bulgaria and North Korea and the discovery of large arms caches." "We got there," President Reagan said, "just in time."[24] Although it was introduced in the media after the fact, the prophecy of advancing Communism had figured in the events leading to the invasion.

Few Western scholars, myself certainly included, have any doubt left about Soviet willingness to exploit opportunity to embarrass, compromise, or undermine the United States and to support anti-U.S. regimes. Yet we must question the official U.S. image of a future Soviet-Cuban takeover and military bastion on Grenada as it was presented to the world in the days following the invasion.

Where were the 1100 "well trained professional" Cuban soldiers that the U.S. admiral, McDonald, had claimed were on Grenada "impersonating construction workers?" The U.S. State Department later acknowledged the accuracy of the detailed roster of the 784 Cubans on Grenada released by Havana which listed only 43 members of the armed forces plus Colonel Pedro Tortolo, chief of the Cuban construction personnel, and twelve members of the crew of aircraft that brought him to Grenada.[25] Although most Cubans in Grenada *were* construction workers, others were working in public health, education, fishing, transport, trade, culture, and communications.

The Soviet presence in Grenada was limited to the usual diplomatic, advisory, and intelligence mix associated with a Soviet Embassy and little more was heard of the handful of East Germans, Bulgarians, and North Koreans who had been said to be on Grenada. Moreover, as Hintzen reminds us, the number of Americans on the island, even during the Bishop period, was always far larger than the number from Cuba, the Soviet Union, and Eastern Europe.[26]

What about the weapons that were found? According to a January 10, 1984, preliminary count submitted to Congress by General George Crist of the U.S. Marine Corps, the total amounted to about 5000 individual infantry weapons plus some crew-operated weapons and ammunition to last two battalions more than 45 days.[27] There were also Grenada-Soviet and Grenada-North Korea agreements found that promised the delivery of several thousand more weapons in the future and the provision of a variety of equipment.[28] All in all, including what was actually on Grenada *and* what was supposed to have been delivered some time in the future according to the agreements, there were between 8000 and 12,000 individual infantry weapons and enough uniforms to outfit 10,800 persons (assuming two uniforms per person).

This is certainly a build-up of arms and a militarization of Grenada compared with the other states of the Eastern Caribbean. This is not in doubt. But did it mean that there was a Soviet-Cuban military bastion aimed at the export of terrorism or armed intervention in other Caribbean states? On several grounds I believe that the answer once more is "no."

First, the military arms and equipment found and planned for Grenada appear to be about the amount needed to provision Grenada's army of roughly 1100 and the People's Militia that was being enlarged to a planned 10,000–person organization, about a third of whom were to be women. Members of the militia were people with regular jobs who were part-time volunteers similar to members of the National Guard in the United States.[29] This militarization of Grenada has as its primary purpose the organization of the people and the motivation and coordination of human effort to develop Grenada. It was an important part of making the revolution itself. As Pastor said,

The armed force of Grenada—as in Cuba, Nicaragua, and other Marxist or quasi-Marxist states—is one of the principal instruments for political mobilization—for educating and convincing the youth of the legitimacy of the revolution. Its second purpose is internal political coercion. To the extent that these regimes have a credible, hostile threat, they can more easily justify the size of their armies. But whether there is a threat or not, the regimes *will* build up their armies to *make* their revolutions and to preclude any political alternative in the country.[30]

Second, Grenada did have a credible hostile threat. There was one prophecy being made prior to the U.S. invasion that turned out to be true. In a speech given on November 3, 1981, Bishop said, "in the last two months alone there have been two major maneuvers carried out upon Caribbean land and sea by warlords of the north: 'Ocean Venture' '81, [which consisted of] 'Operation Amber and the Amberdines' and 'Red X 183' had been shameless rehearsals for eventual invasions of Cuba, Nicaragua, and Grenada and/or preparation for an armed entry into El Salvador on the side of the fascist junta!"[31]

These are strong words and cover a lot of territory, but the prophecy of a U.S. invasion of Grenada also was made by others well before the vent occurred.[32] For example, the Ecumenical Program for Interamerican Communication and Action (EPICA) Task Force gave a "scenario also [that] referred to Ocean Venture '81 which took place from August 1 to October 15, 1981 during which the United States carried out a mock invasion at Viques Island, off Puerto Rico:

The focus of the Caribbean phase of the maneuvers was Cuba—code-named "Red"—and the fictitious island of 'Amber and the Amberdines,' labeled 'our enemy in the Eastern Caribbean.' This barely-disguised reference to Grenada shocked and angered Grenadians, especially since the war game scenario called for 'Amber' to 'seize American hostages' and be invaded by the United States after 'negotiations with the Amber government break down.'[33]

The task force goes on to say that

The hostage scenario represented an ominous turn in U.S. strategy against Grenada. A seizure of American hostages is probably the one event which would be guaranteed to raise emotions high enough in the United States for the U.S. government to justify to the American people an overt military invasion of Grenada.... The Reagan Administration's willingness to use force to overthrow the PRG had become very clear, despite denial of such intentions by Secretary of State Alexander Haig.[34]

Whether or not Bishop and other Grenadan leaders truly believed the prediction of a coming U.S. invasion of Grenada is not clear. Bishop most probably thought that world opinion would prevent a direct landing of the Marines and that the United States would continue to use propaganda destabilization, economic aggression, political and industrial destabilization, and possibly a mercenary army against Grenada, as he said in a speech he gave on July 23, 1981.[35]

Yet the militarization of Grenada probably would have taken place even without the U.S. threat, because putting people in uniform, so the leaders believed, was both symbol and realization of the mass mobilization required to fulfill the Grenadan revolution. It was not basically different, in their view, from other efforts being made, such as promoting the National Women's Organization, the National Youth Organization, and the Workers' Parish Councils.

Ironically, before the U.S. invasion, General Hudson Austin had already neutralized much of Grenada's potential military strength by ordering the disarming of the militia. He was fearful that militia members, angered by Bishop's murder, might take up arms against his own ruling Council. Some of the "Cuban" stockpile of arms around the airport may in fact have been weapons taken from militia members.[36]

THE AIRPORT AT POINT SALINES

No single symbol of the threat contained in the supposed Soviet-Cuban militarization of Grenada seemed as important to the Reagan administration as the 9800-foot international airport nearing completion at Point Salines. In March 1983, as part of his "Star Wars" television announcements, President Reagan displayed aerial reconnaissance photographs of it—as if to say, "Look at this threat to us we've found in the Caribbean from our spy-plane surveillance."[37] A spy plane, however, was hardly necessary, since workers from a Miami, Florida dredging firm were working on the airport, Grenadans were having weekend picnics and flying kites over it, tourists were taking snapshots of it, and the students from the U.S. medical school were regularly jogging on it.[38] But the president proceeded to give the American people another prophecy: The Point Salines airport, he said, was being built to be used in the future for military purposes. Was this, too, a false prophecy?

Here are the facts: The tourist industry has been an important part of the Grenadan economy since the latter part of the 1950s.[39] It has accounted for up to four-fifths of Grenada's foreign exchange earned from commodity exports.[40] After first rejecting tourism because it was not a dignified economic activity and calling it "national cultural prostitution," the PRG took a new initiative on tourism and made a new airport at the "centerpiece of the nation's development plan."[41] There was an obvious need for such an airport if tourism was ever going to grow significantly. It was simply not possible to bring in massive numbers of tourists with the small capacity planes that could land on the short strip at Pearls airport. Modern jets—especially wide-body jets—were needed.

In fact, the idea for the international airport did not originate with Bishop's government. It as an idea that can be traced back to the mid–1950s, and it was recommended by international organizations as an answer to the problem of poverty and underdevelopment in Grenada.[42]

Furthermore, the international airport was not simply a Cuban-aided project. Grenada had requested help from the United States, but it had been denied. Instead, Grenada received help not only from Cuba, but also from as many as fifteen countries, including several Western European countries, Canada, Mexico, Venezuela, and some multilateral agencies such as the Organization of the American States.[43]

The new airport in Grenada is not unusual in the area, and its length is comparable to the airports, among others of Trinidad and Tobago, Barbados, St. Lucia, Guadeloupe, Aruba, and Antigua. It is, in fact, shorter then some, and observers saw no evidence that the airport was being readied as a military base.[44] Canada, for example, planned to build a $16 million hotel near it. More important, a British firm, Plessy, pointed out that a military airbase would have to have a long list of features that the Point Salines international airport did not have, such as protected fuel tanks, antiaircraft defenses, hardened aircraft shelters for protection against a bomb blast, a parallel taxiway, a system of dispersed aircraft parking, radar, underground weapons storage, perimeter security, an operational readiness platform with rapid access, and aircraft engineering workshops.

Though the airport was to be used for tourism, it might have been for military purposes, too. Yet this seems a remote reed on which to hang the justification for the U.S. invasion. Furthermore, it seems unlikely. In his statement before the house committee on Foreign Affairs, Pastor described a conversation that he had had with Maurice Bishop in 1982:

I asked him whether the Grenadian government would permit Soviet or Cuban military planes to land on the airfield, whether it would be used for the transit of Cubans to Africa, or to bring in military equipment. He said that it wouldn't be used for any of those purposes, because to do so would jeopardize it for tourism. I communicated these points to the State Department when I returned and noted that whether he was telling the truth or not, it would make sense for our diplomats to confirm these points privately and then try to elicit a public statement to that effect . . . I do not know whether the State Department followed up my conversion. What should one conclude from the fact that the administration made no attempt to pursue this serious security concern by conversations or negotiations?[45]

What has become of the airport at Point Salines that the Reagan administration claimed was to be used for military purposes and to export terrorism? One of the first acts of the Interim Governing Council in Grenada, installed after the U.S. invasion, was to decide to complete the airport in the interest of economic development in Grenada. The council said that the completion of the project "would give Grenada large jet capability and night landing facilities for the first time which is considered vital to developing tourism here."[46]

Guess who paid for it? In April 1984, the Reagan administration announced that it was seeking U.S. $40 million in new aid for Grenada, the latest single item being $19 million of the $24 million needed to complete Grenada's international airport.[47] President Reagan, himself, in a four and a half hour visit to the island on February 20, 1986, dedicated a plaque for the newly completed Point Salines airport.[48]

Finally, we must note two additional things. First, if the Soviet Union and Cuba had been intent on attempting coups on the other islands, there is very little that couldn't have been done directly in and from Cuba itself without any staging area in Grenada. Revolutionaries from various islands could have been trained and equipped in Cuba and returned to their home islands in Cuban ships. The truth is that, despite the close ties that had developed *after* Bishop and his revolutionary government came to power, there is no evidence that Cuba had anything to do with the coup carried out by the New Jewel movement in Grenada.

Second, taking an anti-Soviet Union position, Fidel Castro vociferously condemned the ultra-leftists in Grenada and what he said was the "brutal assassination" of Bishop and others. Referring to Bishop's murderers as "hyenas" and Coard's group as the "Pol Pot Group," Castro accused them of destroying the Grenadan revolution. He called them "conspirators" and their short-lived government "morally indefensible."[49]

HOW DID IT HAPPEN?

How was the decision to invade made? Was it simply a decision to excise the perceived long-festering sore of the Cubans and Marxists from Grenada? No doubt there is some truth in that. On many fronts and in many ways, the United States had been trying to destroy Grenada's economy in a series of acts beginning shortly after Bishop's coup in 1979.[50] The invasion was a continuation of a war already underway, a logical progression from economic to military battle. A military rehearsal had even been staged at Vieques Island.

Was it also to show that the United States is no helpless giant, but can and will take effective military action? Was it to build credibility worldwide in demonstrating America's firm control of "its own backyard" and, thus, its freedom to maneuver without worries wherever it deem necessary? Was it simply a therapeutic and cathartic act born of the general frustration with the "Vietnam syndrome" that had led many Americans to believe that the use of force led to failure, not success?[51] All of the above may have entered into the picture, many decisions and interpretations of reality over several years (some stretching back for generations) leading tragically toward a particular end encouraged by the distorted images of reality and false images of the future given to us by our leaders and conveyed to us through the national news media.

There is little doubt that a precipitating factor was the tragic news of the 241 marines killed in the barracks bombing in Lebanon on October 23, 1983. Unfortunately for Grenada, that news reached the administration during the final stages of decision making regarding the possibility of an invasion. A U.S. task force had been diverted to Grenada after Bishop's murder as a precautionary measure. Having joined up with the additional naval units, it was now, like a loaded gun, pointed at Grenada.

Without the precipitating event of the bombing in Lebanon, the U.S. invasion of Grenada might not have occurred. Yet the tensions between the United States and Grenada, beginning with Bishop's rise to power in 1979, were the underlying causes of the action. These tensions, however, cannot be laid solely at the door of the Americans. Bishop and his fellow leaders of the People's Revolutionary Government must shoulder some of the blame for their own destruction. Their own revolutionary utopianism, to use a term aptly applied by Anthony P. Maignot,[52] led to actions based on dogmatic realism rather than pragmatic realism: "The voice of the people must be heard," the Marxist-Leninists said, as they removed the popular Bishop in the name of an abstraction, knowing full well that the real, live, breathing Grenadan people out there on the street admired Bishop and would disapprove of their action.[53]

Since 1979, Bishop and the PRG had led Grenada down a path of development with a socialist tendency. But they pursued pragmatic social reforms that could have been achieved under a democratic system, encouraged a mixed economy, cooperated with the bourgeoisie, and made important gains, especially in education and literacy, internal policies with which the United States easily could have lived.[54] In fact, leftist critics accused Bishop of being a petit bourgeois and not getting on with the true socialist revolution.[55]

But no elections were held, freedom of the press was abrogated, political prisoners were taken and civil rights were violated. Even so, the United States has tolerated worse violations by its presumed friends, in Haiti or the Dominican Republic, for example, not to mention El Salvador.

What fueled the hostility of the United States was the inflammatory radical rhetoric and antiimperialist foreign policy of the PRG, particularly the attacks, sometimes totally unfair, on the United States.[56] Bishop's speeches and actions show that he was committed to the public welfare of Grenadans, to social justice, and to economic betterment, yet they also show that he had a tendency to yield to demagoguery, to the temptation to overdramatize and exaggerate, and to engage in overblown empty rhetoric. While his radical rhetoric was a cause of concern in the United States, it was also more extreme and radical than his own policies in Grenada. It was partly self-indulgent posturing. At a June 1983 meeting in Washington with Judge Clark and Deputy Secretary of State Dam in the latter's office, Bishop "expressed an interest in better relations with the United States." Bishop was told that "we hoped he could demonstrate his true desire for better relations by lowering the level of rhetorical attacks on the United States; and if he was prepared to do that, we were prepared to entertain some of the specific suggestions he had as to intermediate ways to get back to a regular relationship."[57] But by then it was too late. The Marxist-Leninists of the PRG acted on a different image of the future.

CONCLUSION: PROPHECIES AND REALITY

In this essay, I have used Grenada as a case study—meaning, of course, that it is a specimen of a larger genus. Although there is insufficient space here to elaborate, I suggest that a careful analysis of similar incidents will reveal parallels, such as the thought mechanisms that led Britain's battle in the Falklands, U.S. air strikes in Libya based on the assumption that they would reduce Libya's future support of terrorist activities, U.S. proposals to escalate the fighting in Central America, the official betrayal of truth and trust during the U.S. military buildup in Vietnam, and, to take an example from domestic politics, David A. Stockman's revelations about the deliberate use of false economic forecasts to justify tax and spending policies and President Reagan promising, "as it were, to alter the laws of arithmetic."[58]

At the time they are made, of course, prophecies may be sincerely believed to be true or they may be disbelieved, even by their makers. In either case they can be used to rationalize present behavior and to control the course of future history.

Whether believed or not, prophecies, at the time they are made, cannot be proven absolutely to be true or false. For they concern the future which by its very nature remains uncertain until it becomes the present. Predictions also may have self-altering aspects, as Robert K. Merton told us years ago, fostering action that fulfills or negates the predictions themselves, no matter how presumptively true or false they may have been when they were made.[59]

Recognizing these limitations, however, I've tried to show that at least three of the major prophecies made by the Reagan administration to justify its invasion of Grenada were probably false. Cubans on Grenada were *not* intended as a means to export terrorism or revolution to Grenada's Caribbean neighbors, but primarily as an effort to mobilize people in Grenada as part of revolutionary changes at home. The international airport at Point Salines was *not* intended to be a Soviet-Cuban military base, but was intended to be a major facility in Grenada's economic development. Furthermore, analogy between the hostages in Iran and the medical students in Grenada was inappropriate and not a good guide to action, while the bombing in Lebanon and events in Grenada were connected only by national needs and the thread of timing. Yet both added to the erroneous conceptions of reality that brought death, mayhem, and destruction to Grenada.

Next time around, why don't we pause and question before we act? Why don't we ask what violence we are doing truth before we do violence to people? Why don't we critically appraise pronouncements? Any group of fools or madmen can distort objective realities and send the truth down the memory hole. If that is to be our national choice, then we might as well join Orwell's defeated character, Winston Smith, drinking victory gin at the Chestnut Tree Café writing with his finger in the dust on the table, "2 + 2 = 5."

NOTES

This is a revised version of a paper first published in *The Yale Review* 75 (Summer 1986): 564–86, copyright Yale University. I thank Professor C. Hintzen, University of California, Berkeley for sharing with me an early article he wrote on Grenada from which I have occasionally drawn. Also, I thank my Yale colleagues Michael G. Cook, Kai T. Ericson, and M. G. Smith for their comments on a draft of this paper.

1. George Orwell, *Nineteen Eighty-Four* (New York: Harcourt, Brace & World, 1949), p. 35.

2. In this section, I rely heavily on the informed and balanced account of the invasion given by Hugh O'Shaughnessy, *Grenada: An Eyewitness Account of the U.S. Invasion and the Caribbean History That Provoked It* (New York: Dodd, Mead, 1984); and Anthony Payne, Paul Sutton, and Tony Thorndike, *Grenada: Revolution and Invasion* (London & Sydney: Croom Helm, 1984).

3. Payne et al., *Grenada: Revolution and Invasion*, p. 157.

4. O'Shaughnessy, *Grenada: an Eyewitness Account*, pp. 7–8.

5. Payne et al., *Grenada: Revolution and Invasion*, p. 159.

6. Robert A. Pastor, statement before the Committee on Foreign Affairs, U.S. House of Representatives (November 3, 1983), p. 19. Page numbers here and elsewhere from Pastor's testimony, unless otherwise noted, are from his original manuscript.

7. The New York *Times* (February 5, 1984), p. A6.

8. Personal observation.

9. Pastor, statement before the Committee on Foreign Affairs, p. 4; and personal observation.

10. Personal observation.

11. Barbara Crossette, "The Caribbean after Grenada," The New York *Times Magazine* (March 18, 1984), p. 66.

12. Pastor, statement before the Committee on Foreign Affairs, pp. 5–6.

13. Pastor, statement before the Committee on Foreign Affairs, p. 7.

14. The New York *Times* (October 30, 1983), p. 20.

15. The New Haven *Register* (October 26, 1983), p. A2.

16. The New York *Times* (October 30, 1983), p. A20; O'Shaughnessy, *Grenada: An Eyewitmess Account*, p. 207.

17. Percy Hintzen, untitled news release for Pacific News Service, p. 8 (quotatins are from manuscript pages).

18. Pastor, statement before the Committee on Foreign Affairs, p. 5.

19. Pastor, statement before the Committee on Foreign Affairs, p. 5.

20. "Grenada in the Context of History: Between Neocolonialism and Independence," *Caribbean Review*, 12, 4 (Fall 1983), p. 46.

21. *Caribbean Review*, 12, 4 (Fall 1983), p. 46.

22. *Time* (November 21, 1983), p. 17. The Cubans, however, had shown concern for the safety of U. S. students, The "told the Grenadians that it would be better if soldiers were kept away from St. George's University Medical School so that it should not become a battle ground and justify any invasion." O'Shaughnessy, *Grenada: An Eyewitness Acccount of the U.S. Invasion*, p. 152.

23. President Reagan said, "to *restore* democratic institutions" [emphasis added], but its not clear what exactly he planned to "restore" because he certainly would not define the government established by Maurice Bishop and other leaders of the New Jewel Movement as "democratic." After all, they had overthrown the government headed by Eric Gairy by force on March 13, 1979 and had ruled as People's Revolutionary Government (PRG) without elections until the murder of Bishop and others on October 19, 1983. Futhermore, the PRG had violated a number of public liberties such as freedom of the press. If the president was referring to "restoring" the political system as it was, before the PRG, under Gairy, he was equally inexact, because Gairy's rule increasingly had depended on interfering with free and fair elections, intimidation of opposition leaders and followers, and other corruptions of the democratic process.

24. The New York *Times*, (October 30, 1983), p. A20, and personal observation.

25. Ibid., p. 211, The New York *Times* (November 6, 1983).

26. Hintzen, untitled news release for Pacific News Service, p. 12. Secretary of Defense Casper W. Weinberger was asked about the Bulgarians, East Germans, and North Koreans at a congressional hearing on November 8, 1983. He answered, "They were not specifically armed military personnel. They were more like defense attachés and spies and the normal type of thing." Subcommittee of the Committee on Appropriations, House of Representatives, Hearing on the "Situation in Lebanon and Grenada," November 8, 1983 (Washington, DC: U.S. Government Printing Office, 1983), p. 39.

27. Subcommittee of International Security and Scientific Affairs and on Western Hemisphere Affairs of the Committee on Foreign Affairs, House of Representatives, Hearing on "U.S. Military Actions in Grenada: Implications for U.S. Policy in the Eastern Caribbean," November 2, 3, and 16, 1983 (Washington DC: U.S. Government Printing Office, 1984), pp. 17–18.

28. Nestor D. Sanchez, "What Was Uncovered in Grenada: The Weapons and Documents," *Caribbean Review*, 12, 4 (Fall 1983), pp. 22–23, 59. Sanchez, who is U.S. deputy assistant secretary of Defense for Inter-American Affairs, overestimates the number of rifles in his report if General Crist's account is correct (pp. 21–22).

29. Ecumenical Program for Interamerican Communication and Action (EPICA) Task Force, *Grenada: The Peaceful Revolution* (Washington DC, 1982), p. 92.

30. Pastor, statement before the Committee on Foreign Affairs, p. 16.

31. Maurice Bishop, *Forward Ever! Speeches of Maurice Bishop* (Sydney, Australia: Pathfinder Press, 1982), p. 241.

32. EPICA, *Grenada: The Peaceful Revolution*, pp. 122–124.

33. EPICA, *Grenada: The Peaceful Revolution*, p. 122. The single quotes within the quotation are from an Associated Press release, August 11, 1981.

34. EPICA, *Grenada: The Peaceful Revolution*, p. 122.

35. Bishop, *Forward Ever!*, p. 214.

36. Ecumenical Program for Interamerican Communication and Action (EPICA), *Death of a Revolution: An Analysis of the Grenada Tragedy and the U.S. Invasion*, (Washington, DC, January, 1984), p. 17. How much of the stockpile of arms found at the airport was from the militia is problematic, but there is little question about the militia having been "virtually disarmed." See O'Shaughnessy, *Grenada: an Eyewitness Account of the U.S. Invasion*, p. 222.

37. The president referred to the Point Salines airport twice in March; Pastor, statement before the Committee on Foreign Affairs, p. 12.

38,. Chris Searle, *Grenada: The Struggle Against Destabilization* (London: Writers and Readers Publishing Cooperative Society, no date, probably 1984), pp. 1–2.

39. A. W. Singham, *The Hero and the Crowd in a Colonial Polity* (New Haven: Yale University Press, 1968), p. 59.

40. Selwyn Ryan, "Grenada: Balance Sheet of the Revolution," unpublished paper read at the annual meeting of the Caribbean Studies Association, St. Kitts (May 30–June 2, 1984), p. 12.

41. Anthony P. Maingot, "Options for Grenada: The Need to Be Cautious," *Caribbean Review*, 12, 4 (Fall 1983), p. 27.

42. EPICA (1984), *Death of a Revolution*, p. 16.

43. Hintzen, untitled news release for Pacific News Services, p. 6.

44. Hintzen, pp. 5–6; and EPICA (1984) *Death of Revolution*, p. 16.

45. Pastor, statement before The Committee on Foreign Affairs, p. 13.

46. *The Jamaican Weekly Gleaner* (December 19, 1983), p. 9.

47. *The Jamaican Weekly Gleaner* (April 2, 1984), p. 17; and The New York *Times* (April 15, 1984), p. A11.

48. The New Haven *Register* (February 21, 1986), p. A17.

49. See the text of Fidel Castro's speech of November 14, 1983, reprinted in O'Shaughnessy, *Grenada: an Eyewitness to Revolution*, pp. 229–45.

50. See Jim Percy, "Introduction," in *Forward Ever! Speeches of Maurice Bishop* (Sydney, Australia: Pathfinder Press, 1982), p. 10; Bishop, *Forward Ever!*, pp. 50, 213; and Searle, *Grenada: The Struggle Against Destabilization*.

51. *Newsweek* (November 11, 1983), p. 42.

52. O'Shaughnessy, *Grenada: An Eyewitness Account*, p. 26.

53. "The Alienation of Lenisnist Group Therapy: Extraordinary General Meeting of Full Members of the NJM," *Caribbean Review*, 12, 4 (Fall, 1983), pp. 14–15, 48–58.

54. Ryan, "The Balance Sheet of the Revolution"; Thorndike, "Revolutional Political Culture: The Case of Grenada"; and Hilborne A. Watson, "Grenada: Non-Capitalist Path and the Derailment of a Populist Revolution," unpublished papers read at the annual meeting of the Caribbean Studies Association, St. Kitts (May 30–June 2, 1984).

55. Watson, "Grenada: Non-Capitalist Path"; Fitzroy Ambursley, "Grenada: The New Jewel Revolution," in Fitzroy Ambursley and Robin Cohen (eds.), *Crisis in the Caribbean* (Kingston, Port of Spain, London: Heinemann, 1983), pp. 191–222.

56. Sally Shelton-Colby, for example, says that Grenadan leaders "consistently castigated the U.S. Government in public for refusing to aid Grenada and for refusing to cooperate in extraditing Gairy," when they knew that these allegations were not true. Subcommittees of International Security and Scientific Affairs and on Western Hemisphere Affairs (November 2, 3, and 16, 1983), "U.S. Military Actions in Grenada", p. 57. Of course, some of their allegations were true as well, especially concerning aid.

57. Subcommittee of International Security and Scientific Affairs and on Western Hemisphere Affairs (November 2, 3, and 16, 1983), "U. S. Military Actions in Grenada", p. 23.

58. The New York *Times* (April 13, 1984), pp. A1, 36.

59. Wendell Bell, "An Introduction to Futuristics: Assumptions, Theories, Methods, and Research Topics," *Social and Economic Studies*, 32, 2 (June 1983); and Wendell Bell, *The Foundations of Futuristics: An Introduction to Social Change and Futures Research* (New York: Random House, 1988).

5
The Invasion of Grenada: A Pre- and Post-Mortem
Robert A. Pastor

INTRODUCTION

The invasion of Grenada by the United States and six Caribbean governments on October 25, 1983 raised numerous significant questions. Was the action legal? Were U.S. medical students in Grenada in danger after the murder of Prime Minister Bishop? Were there alternatives to intervention, and were these seriously considered by the United States? Did the Grenadan revolutionary government constitute a strategic threat—"a Soviet beachhead"—to U.S. interests? These questions surfaced at the beginning of the invasion, but like a submarine after it spotted a destroyer, the questions descended again to the depths.

The administration answered these questions either openly or in background briefings to the press, but there was little information at the time to judge whether their answers were accurate. Nonetheless, nine days after the invasion, the House Foreign Affairs Committee asked me to judge the credibility of the administration's answers. With the information available, I concluded tentatively that the administration's answers were either misleading or wrong.[1]

During the invasion, U.S. troops captured and sent to Washington roughly 35,000 pounds of documents of the New Jewel Movement (NJM) and the People's Revolutionary Government of Grenada.[2] These documents and other information permit firmer answers to the central questions about the justification for the invasion, and the principal purpose of this chapter is to reexamine those questions. At the end of the chapter, I will also evaluate the costs and the benefits of the invasion, and assess whether the benefits might have been attainable at less cost.

International Law

On October 31, 1983, shortly after U.S. troops landed in Grenada, Ambassador Sol M. Linowitz posed what he called the "threshold" question: Is there a sound legal basis for U.S. action?[3]

While the Reagan administration was correct in its assumption that none of the mini-states in the Eastern Caribbean were signatories to the Rio Pact (the Inter-American Treaty of Reciprocal Assistance signed in Rio, August 15–September 2, 1947), the United States was a party to that agreement, and U.S. action appeared to have violated the nonintervention principle (Articles 15 and 17), which is the heart of that treaty as well as the charters of the United Nations and Organization of American States. The administration based its action in part on the request for assistance from the Organization of Eastern Caribbean States, but article 8 of the 1981 Treaty establishing that organization required that collective action only be undertaken by unanimous decision of all seven parties and only in response to external aggression against one of the member states. Neither condition was met. Only four countries (Dominica, St. Vincent, St. Lucia, and Antigua) voted to request intervention; St. Kitts–Nevis and Montserrat abstained, and of course Grenada did not participate. Moreover, the United States was not a party to the treaty, and indeed, the Treaty itself was not registered with the United Nations, which would have given it the status of international law.

There remains the question as to whether the request for assistance by Grenada's governor-general, Sir Paul Scoon preceded or followed the decision to invade Grenada? Why did President Reagan not refer to the request in his address on October twenty-seventh, even though Dominica's Prime Minister Eugenia Charles had already mentioned it and Sir Paul Scoon was already safe? The confusion concerning this point deepened when in March 1984, the British House of Commons released a report which included an analysis of Scoon's alleged request. According to the report, "Both the timing and the nature of the request, which is said by the U.S. government to have been a critical factor in providing a legal justification for their decision to act, remain shrouded in some mystery, and it is evidently the intention of the parties directly involved that the mystery should not be displaced." The written request was obtained *after* the invasion; the only question that remains is whether an oral request preceded it.

Safety of U.S. Citizens

Even if the legal grounds were tenuous, the action might be justified if there were extenuating circumstances. Were U.S. citizens in danger on the island of Grenada?

In his speech to the nation on October 27, 1983, President Reagan stated that his "overriding" and "paramount" concern was "to protect innocent lives, including up to 1,000 Americans." Prior to his decision on Sunday, October twenty-third, the president said that he had "received reports that a large number of our citizens were seeking to escape the island, thereby exposing themselves to great danger." In his press conference on October twenty-fifth, the day of the invasion, Secretary of State George Shultz said that the president had made a "tentative decision" that previous Sunday night (October twenty-third) because of a "violent situation threatening our citizens." On November second, Deputy Secretary Kenneth Dam confirmed an earlier State Department report that the administration's concern over the safety of U.S. citizens was due in part to its belief that the Grenadan airport was closed.

Thirty hours after the invasion, some of the Americans said that they were frightened. However, there was considerable evidence that the vast majority of the Americans were not fearful before the invasion, and that they were not at risk. The only regular contact between U.S. citizens on the island and the United States was a telex at the Medical School, but many students also communicated with their parents by telephone. That Sunday evening when the president indicated his concern about the safety of the Americans, parents of five hundred students were meeting in New York. Though the meeting had been scheduled months before for another reason, the discussion shifted to the recent events in Grenada—the murder of Prime Minister Maurice Bishop and several other Cabinet officials and the takeover of the government by the Revolutionary Military Council (RMC). The group heard from parents who had been in touch with their children, and they discussed a telex, which had just arrived, summarizing a meeting that day at the school where only 10 percent of the students expressed a desire to leave.[4] The parents then sent a cable to President Reagan informing him that their children were safe and asking him "not to move too quickly or to take any precipitous actions at this time."[5] Did the president receive this cable, part of which was published in the New York *Times* the next day, and did he weigh it against other evidence?

Before the meeting, Charles Modica, the chancellor of the university, had received a phone call from U.S. Ambassador to Barbados Milan Bish, as well as from others in the State Department. The call was designed to elicit a statement from him that the students were in danger. Based on his own contacts, he knew this was not the case, and he refused to make the statement. Were these calls aimed at obtaining pretext for intervention?[6]

What led the United States to believe that its citizens were in special danger? In answer to questions from the U.S. House of Representatives Foreign Affairs Committee on November 2, 1983, Deputy Secretary of

State Kenneth Dam admitted that he had "no information" that any Americans were harmed or threatened after the murder of Maurice Bishop. (Later, the State Department confirmed that no American was harmed or threatened by the Grenadan military government.)

During the emergency, the Grenadan government went out of its way to assure both the U.S. citizens and the U.S. government. Two U.S. diplomats flew in and out during the weekend, and there were four or five flights (which included several Americans) on Monday, October twenty-fourth. Moreover, both the British and the Canadians had arranged evacuation flights, which were prevented not by the Grenadan authorities but by the other Caribbean governments. Moreover, General Hudson Austin himself called Geoffrey Bourne, vice chancellor of the Medical School, offering jeeps and transportation and arranging to have the supermarket open just for the students. He also sent one of his officers to check that everything was in order and gave Bourne his home number if there were any problems.[7]

One of the most effective points made by Secretary of State Shultz in his press conference on October twenty-fifth, the day of the invasion, was that one of the concerns of the administration was to anticipate and preclude a hostage-taking situation like that of Iran. The U.S. government later suggested that it had obtained secret documents purporting to show that the Grenadan government considered taking U.S. citizens as hostages. That evidence was never provided. None of the Grenadan documents captured by the U.S. government after the invasion provide any substantiation of the charge the Grenadans were planning to take hostages at that time. Common sense would suggest that the Grenadan government knew that the United States was eager to find a pretext for an invasion, and taking hostages would have provided a reasons, not a pretext.

The Grenadan government would be more likely to take hostages if there was an imminent or probable invasion than if the U.S. government was in direct contact trying to gain assurances of safety for U.S. citizens. In that sense, an invasion would have endangered the lives of U.S. citizens rather than have protected them. Actually, the Grenadan government and the Cubans had literally hundreds of opportunities to take U.S. citizens hostage *after* the Marines landed, and especially during the fighting at the Medical School; this never happened. Of course, hostages *could* have been taken—just as it is possible in El Salvador by either leftist or rightist thugs, Iran, Turkey, Colombia, and a dozen other countries.

Was there an "atmosphere of violent uncertainty" much different from other countries experiencing a violent change in government? If one looks at military takeovers in Latin America over the last two decades, the Grenadan coup was not nearly as violent, uncertain, or dangerous to U.S. citizens as most others. The military coup in Chile and the revolution in Nicaragua were much more violent, and indeed Americans were killed in both. Moreover, as of November 2, 1983, Deputy Secretary Dam still did know whether anybody—Grenadans or Americans—had been shot or killed in the period after the murder of Bishop on October nineteenth and before the invasion. There were none.

If events were so uncertain, why then did the United States not try to seek out General Hudson Austin and others on the RMC to find out what was happening and to further increase the safety of U.S. citizens?[8] Two administrators of the Medical School, Dr. Geoffrey Bourne and Gary Solin, both agreed at the time and in retrospect that the safety of the medical students, in Solin's words, "was never in danger." In Bourne's words, "From the point of view of saving our students, the invasion was unnecessary,"[9] Indeed, with the fighting near the Medical School, and the fear that hostages could be taken, one could argue that their safety was endangered, not protected, by the invasion. And, of course, as a result of the invasion, eighteen Americans did die and 116 were wounded; 24 Cubans were killed and 59 were wounded; and 45 Grenadians were killed and 337 were wounded.

It almost appears as if the United States did not want to receive any information about the students from their parents, or from the Grenadan government unless that information reinforced their own assessment that they were in danger. The U.S. government, incredibly, did not seek assurances from the RMC that the safety of U.S. citizens would be protected.

If the invasion had occurred a day later, British and Canadian citizens would probably have been evacuated. Is it possible that the "Marines got there just in time," in President Reagan's phrase, before the new Grenadan government could prove to the international community that it was a government, and that it could assure the safety of U.S. citizens?

Unquestionably, there were some U.S. citizens on the island who were afraid, and others who were not. But the question for U.S. policymakers was whether the "atmosphere of violent uncertainty" in Grenada from October nineteenth was worse than in El Salvador during the last decade, or in Guatemala in 1981, or in Bolivia for two-thirds of the last decades? Did U.S. citizens have more or less to fear from the Grenadan government than they had from an invasion? The available evidence suggests that U.S. citizens had less to fear from the RMC than from the invasion.

U.S. consular officials did try to negotiate an evacuation of the students and initially received some cooperation from the Grenadans for evacuating several hundred medical students by commercial aircraft. However, over the weekend before the invasion, Barbadian radio reports were received in Grenada about the possibility of an invasion. These heightened fears among the medical students, and a much larger number requested evacuation. At the same time, the Caribbean governments decided to stop commercial flights into Grenada.

When the consular officials approached the Grenadans again to ask to evacuate 2000 Americans by U.S. military aircraft, the Grenadans changed their tone, fearing that the U.S. Air Force flights were intended to bring in Marines rather than take out medical students. They therefore stalled, and tried to get the Americans to talk about fewer numbers and commercial rather than military flights. The consular officers, seemingly unaware of the preparations by the United States, viewed the Grenadan response as uncooperative, whether for a specific purpose or not.

The congressional delegation that flew to Grenada after the intervention was told of the stalling by the Revolutionary Military Council, but not the reason why. Without the entire story, several congressmen concluded that the lack of cooperation by the RMC was deliberate, that it put the U.S. students in danger, and that it justified the action.

First Option or Last Resort?

If one considers military intervention a grave act with considerable human and political risks and costs, then the presumption ought to be that all other alternatives should be explored and exhausted before turning to the military option as a last resort. Was military intervention a first option or a last resort? What was the nature of the relationship between the Reagan administration and the OECS governments? Did the United States stimulate a request from these governments or respond to one?

Two points seem pertinent. A New York *Times* report on October 30, 1983, indicated that the OECS request was drafted in Washington and conveyed to the Caribbean leaders by special U.S. emissaries. Secondly, U.S. ships were diverted to the region on October twentieth, even before the Caribbean leaders met. The administration said that it was a "precautionary measure," and Prime Minister Tom Adams of Barbados said that he had already had conversations with the United States about the possibility of intervention.

In considering these questions, it is important to recognize that *the nations of the Eastern Caribbean are democracies with strong and articulate leaders. They are no one's "puppets."* All of the governments were unsettled by the Bishop coup in March 1979, but they were prepared to live with that government provided Bishop did not interfere in their internal affairs. After that coup, the leaders of these nations met in Barbados, and after obtaining assurances from Bishop that he would hold early elections, they recognized his government. Over time, as it became clear that he did not intend to fulfill his initial pledge, the governments increased their pressure on Bishop, and it may be that these countries were the most important source of influence on Grenada.

The murders on October nineteenth horrified the entire English-speaking Caribbean, and several of the OECS governments met in emergency session to condemn the killing and break relations. The leaders probably came to an independent judgment that a Marxist military government in the Eastern Caribbean was unacceptable. It would appear that the United States had come to that judgment long before, but had recognized that it could not take action without the acquiescence or support of the Eastern Caribbean nations. *The massacre in Grenada on October nineteenth led to a convergence of thinking.* It is unlikely that the United States forced the OECS to make the request, but the diversion of the U.S. fleet provided a dramatic demonstration of U.S. seriousness and of the availability of a military option.

Did the United States discourage consideration of other options? Right after the establishment of the RMC, Milton Cato, the prime minister of St. Vincent, offered to meet with Hudson Austin, and Austin immediately accepted, but the meeting was never held. Cato was discouraged from holding the meeting with Austin by almost everyone—by Vincentians primarily, by his Caribbean colleagues secondly, and lastly, by the United States. His constituents had the greatest influence on him.[10]

What were the other alternatives, and did they stand a chance of restoring peace to Grenada? The killing of Bishop left the RMC weakened, divided, and totally isolated from the rest of the Caribbean. In an unprecedented move, both the OECS and CARICOM decided during the weekend before the invasion to condemn the new government, break relations, suspend Grenada from CARICOM, and impose trade sanctions. Even Fidel Castro issued a strong condemnation of the regime, and Michael Manley pledged publicly to seek the expulsion of the New Jewel Movement from the Socialist International. The Grenadan regime was totally isolated.

CARICOM also decided to contact Grenada's governor-general in order to have him: (1) establish a broadly based civilian government of national reconciliation which would hold elections "at the earliest possible date"; (2) receive "a factfinding mission comprising eminent citizens of CARICOM states"; (3) put in place evacuation measures for foreign nationals; and (4) accept the deployment in Grenada of a peace-keeping force from Caribbean countries. According to George Chambers, the prime minister of Trinidad and Tobago, who summarized the results of the CARICOM meeting, there was complete agreement on these measures; the only differences within CARICOM were when and how to use force if the Grenadan regime rejected these steps.[11]

The Grenadan leadership realized that it was in an impossible position and tried through a number of channels to find an exit. Austin spoke with Geoffrey Bourne from the Medical School, who, in Bourne's words, "looked as though he wanted" advice. Bourne spoke with his son, Dr. Peter Bourne, who was an adviser on health issues to President Carter. Peter Bourne (who consulted briefly with the author and several others) suggested that an approach to Austin should be premised on skepticism and should aim to test Austin's sincerity. Bishop had promised elections, but reneged. Austin should break with the past and announce his intention to serve as a transition figure toward reestablishing parliamentary democracy. But even those steps would not be sufficient. In order to regain the confidence of CARICOM, he would have to prove his sincerity with clear actions.

More importantly, Austin called Trinidad's president, Ellis Clarke on Friday before the CARICOM meeting to say that his government was prepared to accept a visit by an international group from CARICOM to discuss elections and other items. Clarke informed Prime Minister Chambers, who then began contacting senior statesmen in the region.[12] The CARICOM decisions listed above would have provided such a test of Austin's intentions.

It is not known whether Austin was sincerely seeking an exist or just trying to buy time, because the Marines landed before Bourne even received the message from his son let alone conveyed it to Austin. The Marines also landed before the CARICOM decisions could be implemented.

If one believes that the killing of Bishop was a premeditated effort to seize control by an extreme leftist group tied even more tightly than Bishop to the Soviets and Cubans, then one would properly judge Austin's effort as a ploy, and conclude he was not worth dealing with. If, on the other hand, the events surrounding the murder of Bishop were not premeditated, that Bishop forced the hand of the military by going to Fort Rupert with his supporters, and that the military reacted with fear as well as anger, then one might conclude that events had overtaken the RMC. If this latter scenario is more probable, then one might conclude that the quick reaction by CARICOM must have shocked the RMC, and that they might seek some exit.

The evidence is by no means clear on which of these two scenarios is more probable, but if it is the latter, that the killings were not planned and events overtook the Grenadan government, then it is possible that Austin was seeking an exit, and, at the least, his purported interest should have been tested. It is worth noting that the Trinidadian government opposed military action *before* the Grenadan regime would have an opportunity to respond to CARICOM.

Was the invasion an attempt to forestall further violence or an attempt to dislodge a group that might be prepared to consider alternatives? Did the U.S. forces arrive "just in time" before negotiations between CAR-

ICOM and the Austin regime might have produced a peaceful, nego-tiated outcome? It seems clear that alternatives to military action were quickly ruled out, if they were even considered.

The Grenadan documents reveal significant divisions within the New Jewel Movement, but there is nothing at all that suggests that the Coard faction was planning to kill Bishop or the others. Indeed, the weight of the evidence thus far confirms the author's second scenario, that the Austin regime was overtaken by events. The documents show a high level of tension and confusion among the NJM leadership in the days preceding the killing. In the words of one of the leaders, "the Central Committee was suffering from an overdose of paranoia."[13]

Strategic Threat

President Reagan said on October 25, 1983, that "we got there just in time" as Grenada was "a Soviet-Cuban colony being readied as a major military bastion." While the U.S. government did not publicly use this strategic concern as a justification for the invasion, it clearly played a central role in its view of Grenada from the beginning. In 1982, President Reagan publicly accused Grenada of attempting "to spread the [Com-munist] virus among its neighbors." On March 10 and 23, 1983, he displayed aerial reconnaissance photographs of the construction of Grenada's new airfield and said it represented "the Soviet-Cuban mili-tarization of Grenada" which "can only be seen as a power projection into the region."

At the time of the invasion, the administration claimed it had docu-ments proving that the Soviets and Cubans were in the process of taking over the country and converting it into a base for subversion. But the documents that it later released do not prove either assertion. To the contrary, the documents show that the Cubans and the Soviets were at least as confused and upset by the events of October 1983 as the United States. Indeed, in a letter to the Central Committee of the NJM on October 15, 1983, the day after the house arrest of Bishop, Fidel Castro himself admitted that "everything which happened [the divisions within the Grenadian government and the arrest of Bishop] was for us a surprise and disagreeable."[14] The documents also show that Castro tried hard to preclude, not promote the coup against Bishop, whom he later described as having "very close and affectionate links with our [Cuban Communist] party's leadership."[15] It was a considerable embarrassment for Castro to admit that he was so uninformed about such critical developments in the affairs of such a close friend, but all available evidence suggests that his admission was accurate.

On the other hand, the documents do make clear that the NJM lead-ership held the Soviet Union and Cuba in the highest regard and endeavored to prove their revolutionary credentials and solidarity with both. The Cubans were clearly more helpful and closer to the Grenadans. The Embassy of Grenada in Moscow reported that "the Caribbean—as they [the Soviets] repeatedly state . . . is very distant from them. It is quite frankly, not one of their priorities."[16] The NJM considered themselves a Communist party, and it tried hard to impress the Soviets and Cubans. Indeed, the vote by Grenada to support the Soviet Union on Afghanistan is one indication of this. (Even the Sandinistas abstained.)

In summary, the direction of influence appears the opposite of what President Reagan alleged. Instead of the Soviets and Cubans trying to take over Grenada covertly, the problem—for the United States—was that the Grenadan regime invited the Soviets and Cubans to play a larger role in helping them to transform Grenada. Ironically, the Soviets were reluctant to do that.

The Airport. Grenada's 9000-foot airfield is not large by Caribbean standards. Antigua, Aruba, the Bahamas, Curaçao, the Dominican Republic, Guadeloupe, Jamaica, Martinique, Puerto Rico, St. Lucia, Trinidad, and Barbados all have airports that are about the same size or larger. There is little question that Grenada needed a new airport for tourism as the other was old, run-down, and small. The project was supported by many countries, including Venezuela, Canada, and the Europeans, and the British government guaranteed a loan for the project. If it were intended for military use, according to the British contractor, it would have had protected fuel dumps, antiaircraft defenses, and hardened shelter for warplanes, which was not the case. The airport was open for viewing, and Canada reportedly intended to build a sixteen million dollar hotel within sight of it.

Though the airport's principal purpose was for tourism, that does not mean that it could not have been used for military purposes as well. In a conversation with Bishop in October 1982, this writer asked whether the Grenadan government would permit Soviet or Cuban military planes to land on the airfield, whether it would be used for transit of Cubans to Africa, or to bring in military equipment. The Grenadan leader said that it would not be used for any of those purposes, because to do so would jeopardize it for tourism. This information was conveyed to a high-level official of the State Department. Whether or not Bishop was telling the truth, it would have made sense for our diplomats to confirm these points privately and then try to elicit a public statement to that effect. Such statements could not guarantee that Bishop was not lying or would not change his mind, but it would make it more costly for him to do so. The State Department did not follow up any of these points.

If one did not want to negotiate a serious security concern like the use of Grenada's airfield, what were the alternatives for the United States—other than military force? Since the airfield is so open, verifying

Bishop's assurance did not appear an insurmountable obstacle. What should one conclude from his failure to pursue this serious security concern by conversations or negotiations?

After the invasion, the U.S. government discovered the airport's importance to tourism and pledged $21 million to its completion. The airport was open one year after the invasion and a week or so before the 1984 presidential elections in the United States.

Although the documents disclosed a number of military agreements with the Soviet Union and Cuba, there are no references in those documents to possible military use of the airport. A barely legible, hand-written page from the notebook of Liam James, a member of the Political Bureau, indicated: "The Revo has been able to crush counter-revolution internationally. Airport will be used for Cuban and Soviet military."[17] This note, however, is not confirmed in any of the secret military agreements between Grenada and the Soviet Union or Cuba, or in any of the minutes of the Political Bureau or the Central Committee. However, the minutes of a Political Bureau meeting on December 19, 1982, in which Bishop, Austin, and a number of other leaders were present, discussed a specific request from Cuba for special refueling concessions to be granted after the completion of the airport. The decision was to tell the Cubans that "the request is to be studied." No further response was given to the Cubans.[18]

In short, there is substantial evidence that the Grenadan regime wanted to use the airport for tourist purposes, and a single, comparatively weak and questionable suggestion to the contrary. More importantly, if the Grenadan regime had already secretly arranged for the Soviets and Cubans to use the airport for military purposes, it is impossible to explain why they would put off the Cuban request, and secondly, why they would permit a Canadian company to build a hotel adjacent to the airport where U.S. agents could have monitored the air traffic.

The Size of the Cuban Presence. U.S. estimates of the size of the Cuban presence varied enormously. U.S. Navy Admiral McDonald first stated that captured documents showed there were more than 1100 Cubans and that they were preparing a massive buildup. Subsequently, the number was revised to 1000. Later, State Department officials said that they would not quarrel with Cuba's own number of 784, having accused them of being completely untrustworthy a few days before.

It was subsequently confirmed by the U.S. government, and by the documents themselves, that the Cuban numbers were accurate; there were about 784 Cubans in Grenada, of which more than 600 were construction workers. A military agreement between Cuba and Grenada provided for a maximum of 42 Cuban military advisors to go to Grenada to train and organize the military, of which twelve or thirteen would be stationed for a two or four month period, and 29 would be stationed for longer periods.[19] None of the documents released suggests that these advisers were either "occupying the country" or intending to occupy it. Nor is there any evidence that these advisers gave instructions to the Grenadan government.

These are large numbers for such a small country as Grenada, and a legitimate source of concern for the United States and the neighboring states in the Eastern Caribbean. The Cubans, of course, export labor abroad, and this was their principal contribution to the construction of the airport—an ironic form of aid in a country of such high unemployment. But the fact that the Grenadan regime needed over 150 Cuban military advisers—more than all U.S. military advisers in South America and the Caribbean—is an indication perhaps that they were not as popular as they repeatedly claimed they were.

Platform for Insurgency. The various military agreements with the Soviet Union, Cuba, North Korea, and Czechoslovakia indicate that Grenada would have received by 1986 a very large quantity of military hardware, including approximately 10,000 rifles, 4500 machine guns, and 15,000 hand grenades. The U.S. Defense Department estimated that this arsenal could equip a fighting force of roughly 10,000 men.[20] Alternatively, it could represent a five-year or longer stockpile for an armed force of about 2000–3000.

None of the documents released since the intervention show any evidence that the Grenadans, the Soviets, or the Cubans intended that any part of this arsenal would be transferred to subversives in a third country. Quite the opposite. The secret military agreements between Grenada, Cuba, and the Soviet Union, which the Defense and State Departments repeatedly cited to justify the invasion, explicitly prohibited any arms transfers to third countries or to groups outside of Grenada. There is no evidence that any of the arms were sent outside of Grenada. There is substantial evidence of contacts with Communists and "progressives" from throughout the world for purposes of solidarity, and consultation, but nothing between Grenada and guerrilla groups, with one ironic exception. The M-19 guerrilla group from Colombia wrote to the New Jewel Movement expressing greetings and a desire to establish links with the party. However, the Political Bureau of the NJM decided not to reply to the request.[21]

Instead of a source of "infection," Grenada had proved to be the opposite, inoculating the region to Marxism. Since the revolution in 1979, democratic institutions in the English-speaking Caribbean grew stronger; moderates won in almost a dozen elections.[22] Grenada's capacity to influence, let alone subvert its neighbors, declined during the revolution's four years. After the death of Bishop, it turned negative.

During the short duration of New Jewel Movement's revolution, the rest of the Caribbean was on guard to find any evidence of Grenadan support for subversion. If any evidence were found, it would have provoked collective action, which would have been legal and justifiable. And the United States would have been on much firmer footing in responding to a request to counter aggression or subversion than it was in undertaking a preemptive strike. Bishop understood this, and was sensitive to it. He told the writer that after the incident in 1980 involving the training of bodyguards of George Oldum, who was then deputy prime minister of St. Lucia, he would never again permit any training of Caribbean security officials in Grenada without the express permission of the appropriate head of state.[23] Bishop also quickly extradited Bumba Charles, the leader of a group that had tried to seize neighboring Union Island (St. Vincent), but fled to Grenada after he failed.

The United States knew that the Soviets were supplying arms. There were grounds for concern about the ties of Grenada to the Soviet Union and Cuba. The U.S. government knew within one month of the coup of March 1979 that Cuban advisers and arms had arrived in Grenada, although there is still no evidence of Cuban involvement in the 1979 coup.[24] Since 1979, the rest of the Caribbean was very wary of Grenada, and any sign that the Grenadans were trying to subvert their neighbors would have brought a quick response.

After Bishop's murder, the Grenadan government lost all credibility in the Caribbean. Rather than being a threat to the region, it had become a threat only to itself. Indeed, the armed forces, which Bishop created, devoured him in the end. That is really the Cuban-Soviet legacy in the Third World—militarized revolution—and that point is clearly understood in the region.

Why did the Grenadan regime need so many arms and such a large armed force? In a region where most nations did not have defense forces, and police forces were quite small, Grenada's was disproportionately large. Of course, as the invasion demonstrated, the Grenadan regime may have had more reason to fear its neighbors than the other way around. But it is unlikely that the Grenadan Armed Forces were large either to attack or to defend their revolution. The armed forces in Grenada—as in Cuba, Nicaragua, and other Marxist or quasi-Marxist states— is one of the principal instruments for political mobilization—for education and convincing the youth of the legitimacy of the revolution. Its second purpose is internal political coercion. The regimes build up their armies to *make* their revolutions and to preclude any political alternative in the country.

The question for U.S. policy was whether to intervene because of fears rather than facts that Grenada was subverting its neighbors. The distinction between fears and facts is everything. International law permits collective action after aggression, not before. If the United States sanctioned preemptive strikes, it would become prisoner to its worst fears; it would draw up worst case scenarios and then implement them.

This is, of course, the line of reasoning that brought U.S. forces into Grenada.

A Question of Intelligence

How good was the collection and analysis of political intelligence on Grenada during the 1980s and especially during the weeks before and after the invasion?

An analysis of U.S. background briefings to the press during the time of the invasion would suggest that the United States interpreted events in the following way: the Soviets and Cubans manipulated Bernard Coard and several other extreme Marxist-Leninists to launch a coup against Bishop, who was too moderate for their taste. One of the reasons suggested by U.S. government sources as to why Bishop was overthrown was because he was interested in better relations with the United States.

There is considerable evidence that would impugn this interpretation. Rather than trying to overthrow Bishop, Cuban Ambassador Julian Torres Rizo was instructed to meet with Coard and express Castro's strong views that Bishop should be released from confinement. Coard, who was supposed to be close to Cuba, refused to see Torres. Although Coard was perceived to be more communist than Bishop, he had actually been criticized a few months before by many, reportedly including Bishop, for drawing too liberal a code for foreign investment. Though the Cubans were alleged to be behind the coup against Bishop, they took the unprecedented step of condemning it in the strongest terms. Finally, the entire Grenadian leadership wanted—or rather said it wanted—good relations with the United States; the question was, on what terms? No evidence has been presented that Bishop and Coard differed on the answer to the question.

Based on conversations with Bishop and Coard, this writer does not believe that there were any important differences ideologically between them. However, they differed greatly in style, and Coard was jealous of Bishop's popularity and power. As a rule, attempts to impose ideological prisms on petty personality politics in the Caribbean obscures more than it illuminates, and the case of the Bishop-Coard rivalry seems to fit the rule. It is conceivable that there were differences between the Cuban and Soviet strategies, but that also remains to be proven.

This is just one of many examples of where the administration's ideology forced disparate information into an ill-fitting compartment in order to try to justify the invasion. The administration's assertions suggested a massive intelligence failure at the analytic level, or alternatively, a deliberate effort to misinform the American people. The Reagan administration contended that their problem was the lack of CIA operatives in the region, and they blamed previous administrations for reducing assets. However, this transparent attempt to shift the blame is wrong on two counts. First, President Reagan's statements about Grenada in 1981 and 1982 suggest that the administration gave the highest strategic priority to the island. Why, nearly three years later, had intelligence capabilities not been increased? Secondly, the administration's response reflects a bias toward covert action, which is inappropriate and frankly unnecessary in the Caribbean, which is remarkably open. Simple, open conversation can achieve what operatives cannot. The administration did not know anything about Coard when the conflict started simply because it had never bothered to talk to him; officials probably read intelligence reports with a host of labels that missed the man and the point. This was the cost of the administration's policy not to communicate with the Grenadan regime.

CONCLUSION

Benefits and Costs

Advocates of the intervention have tended to underestimate or not see the costs, while opponents naturally tend to stress the costs and downplay the benefits. Any judgment of the invasion requires a systematic and dispassionate evaluation of both the costs and the benefits.

On the benefits, Grenada restored democracy and elections were held in November 1984. Second, the Eastern Caribbean returned to being a group of democratic states. Third, the United States demonstrated that it was responsive to a serious request by them. Fourth, the use of force by the United States lent credibility to U.S. threats. Fifth, Cuba lost a Marxist ally in the Caribbean and found itself more isolated from the rest of the Caribbean. These benefits are significant.

What of the costs, and is there any evidence they were weighed carefully? First, the human cost—eighteen Americans killed and 116 wounded; 45 Grenadians dead and 337 wounded; and 24 Cubans killed and 59 wounded. The U.S. bombing of the mental hospital was particularly tragic. Secondly, there were heavy international political costs. The day after the invasion, fifteen O.A.S. members joined Grenada for a severe condemnation of the United States. The United States had to veto (11–1) a UN Security Council resolution condemning the action. The UN General Assembly also condemned the United States by a vote of 108–9—declaring the action "a flagrant violation of international law." Finally, Cuba gained a powerful talking point about "U.S. imperialism" and a temporary alliance with many Latin American governments.

The United States' closest friends and allies not only criticized the action, but questioned the judgment of the United States for taking it. The deployment of missiles in Europe was made more difficult by this action and the lack of consultation. The United States had, once again, helped its adversaries in Western Europe by giving them good arguments for why Europe should not trust the United States.

To Latin America, the invasion connoted a return to the Big Stick, harming efforts to demonstrate that U.S. interventionism was a thing of the past, not the present, or the future. It is not just that Cubans and leftists condemn U.S. imperialism and intervention, but that some of Latin America's youth would find their arguments compelling. This makes it harder for the United States to gain the cooperation of its friends in the region.

When the United States acts with scant legal basis it reduces the credibility of the rule of law internationally. Ambassador Sol Linowitz put it so well: "The United States is not just a superpower; it is also a democracy that must hold itself up to higher standards than the Soviet Union."

Finally, there was a large economic cost of rebuilding Grenada and helping to develop the rest of the Caribbean. In effect, the United States replaced the British in the region, and this meant a larger economic obligation than the United States had shouldered before.

In assessing the costs and benefits, the key question from the U.S. perspective is not whether they sum to a net benefit or a net cost; that will depend on the values attached to each of the costs or benefits. The key questions are, first, whether there is agreement on the list of what constitutes costs and benefits, and secondly, whether the benefits might have been attainable with a less costly strategy.

With the important exception of those who died as a result of the invasion, most of the costs are intangible. Were these costs weighed in making the decision? On "Meet the Press" on October 30, 1983, then U.S. Ambassador to the United Nations Jeane Kirkpatrick said: "I'm telling you that I don't think there's any moral cost to that action." This insensitivity to international public opinion—especially when so many of the United States' closest friends condemned the action—is ill-suited to the United States.

In comparison to the almost casual way U.S. leaders dismissed international criticism, the late Prime Minister Tom Adams of Barbados, with much more at stake in the invasion, described the views of the world with much more detachment and perceptiveness. In a debate in the Barbados House of Assembly, Adams figuratively toured the world, trying to explain the positions of various countries that opposed the action. Pausing at Latin America, he said:

Geography brings us together, and we are partners in many international institutions. But we in the English-speaking Caribbean are a different people, with a different history and different traditions.... The English-speaking Caribbean has never been threatened by the military power of the U.S. There has never been any occasion where the U.S. has had a military occupation against our will in an English-speaking island.... We have never had any historical reason to fear the U.S. This is not so in Latin America and, therefore, I understand their vote (condemning the invasion).[25]

What are the lessons of the action in Grenada? It should be stressed that the available evidence still does not permit a definitive conclusion, but here are some tentative conclusions. First, there is good reason to question whether there is any legal basis for the action. Second, the safety of U.S. citizens was endangered more by the invasion than by the political situation that preceded it. Third, the administration turned to the military option as a first step rather than a last resort. It showed no inclination to negotiate or even communicate with members of the new Revolutionary Military Council.

The Eastern Caribbean leaders came to a similar, though independent judgment. The United States chose to respond to the request for military action by the OECS rather than to the diplomatic-political strategy agreed to by the larger, thirteen-nation CARICOM. Since the United States would bear the more significant military cost, it was wholly appropriate for it to question whether military action was the only or the most appropriate means for dealing with the new political situation in Grenada. Instead of asking such a question, the U.S. government seemed delighted with the opportunity to change the Grenadan government by force.

There were good reasons to be concerned with the Grenadan relationship with the Soviet Union and Cuba, but the Grenadan capacity to influence developments in the rest of the Caribbean had been reduced in the four years since the coup, and indeed, the rest of the Caribbean had apparently increased its influence on Grenada. After Bishop's murder, Cuban, Soviet, and Grenadan influence sank to an unprecedented low level in the region; under those circumstances, it was hard to conceive of Grenada as a Soviet-Cuban platform for insurgency. Any effort at subversion by the Grenadans would have easily elicited a collective security response, which would have been clearer in its legality and justification than the "preemptive action" that occurred. The United States would have been on much firmer ground responding to such a request than to the one that led to the invasion.

If U.S. citizens had been put in danger by the new government, if the legal basis for intervention had existed, if Grenada was a "Soviet-Cuban colony" and a "bastion" of arms to be used to subvert or overrun democracies in the area, and if other alternatives were explored or the administration could make a convincing case why they were not, then the action would have been justified. But none of these conditions existed.

An important factor arguing for help—though not necessarily, the Marines—is the regional community of the OECS; this is indeed a unique community of nations, which requires support. Ironically, the Reagan administration had pursued a strategy from 1981–1983 of undermining that unity, thus undermining one of its alleged reasons for intervention. Nonetheless, supporting those small, vulnerable democracies is an important U.S. interest.

In examining the action and its relationship with the rest of the administration's foreign policy, what was most disturbing was its apparent proclivity to think and act in military or covert terms. The administration left no room for diplomacy—for negotiations—for pursuing U.S. interests in anything but a military or clandestine manner. In this case, as in many others, the administration never pursued its interests through sincere negotiations. Ideological barriers based on twin premises that the Cubans and Soviets are behind all the instability in the region and the world, and that Marxists are inherently untrustworthy, prevented the United States from seeing opportunities or reducing uncertainties to its citizens or its interests. This left the United States in a position where there was no alternative but to send in the Marines.

There were other alternatives.

NOTES

1. For my original testimony, see House Committee on Foreign Affairs, *Hearings: U.S. Military Actions in Grenada: Implications for U.S. Policy in the Eastern Caribbean*, November 2, 3, and 16, 1983, pp. 72–102 [henceforth, *Hearings*]. This chapter represents an update of that original testimony.

2. For the documents, see The Department of State and the Department of Defense, *Grenada: A Preliminary Report* (Washington, DC: December 16, 1983); The Department of State and the Department of Defense, *Grenada Documents: An Overview and Selection* (Washington, DC: September 1984) [henceforth "State/Defense"]; and Paul Seabury and Walter A. McDougall, *The Grenada Papers* (San Francisco: Institute for Contemporary Studies, 1984) [henceforth Seabury and McDougall].

3. Washington *Post*, October 31, 1983, p. A1.

4. New York *Times*, October 24, 1983, p. A1.

5. New York *Times*, October 24, 1983, p. A1. Geoffrey Bourne, the head of the Medical School, later confirmed in testimony to Congress that only 10 percent of the medical students wanted to leave the island during the crisis. Only after students heard an outside broadcast "saying that the CARICOM countries were going to invade," a couple of days before the actual invasion, did the students become afraid. A vote after that broadcast showed 50 percent of the students wanting to leave. *Hearings*, p. 193.

6. In several conversations at the time Modica told me of his talks with Bish, and he suspected that the purpose was to elicit an excuse for intervention.

7. See *Hearings*, pp. 188–96.

8. Interview with State Department official on Caribbean desk, July 1, 1985. The official confirmed that no Americans were threatened or harmed during the period from the murder of Bishop to the invasion, and that the State Department had not approached Austin directly.

9. Cited in Edward Cody, "Medical School Director Says He Backs Invasion," Washington *Post*, November 1, 1983, p. A23. Bourne said he supported the invasion for political reasons, but in this interview, he acknowledged it wasn't necessary to rescue the students.

10. Author's interview with Hon. Milton Cato and others on St. Vincent, February 1984.

11. The CARICOM decisions and a statement by Prime Minister George Chambers can be found in Appendix 2 of *Hearings*, pp. 218–30.

12. Author's interview with one of the statesmen who were contacted by Chambers. January 28, 1987, Atlanta, Georgia.

13. Seabury and McDougall, *The Grenada Papers*, p. 333.

14. Seabury and McDougall, p. 327.

15. "Farewell Address to the Funeral of the 24 Cubans Killed in Grenada," November 14, 1983. Published by the Center for Cuban Studies, *Cuba Update*.

16. Seabury and McDougall, *The Grenada Papers*, pp. 198–216.

17. The Department of State and of Defense, *Grenada Documents* #23.

18. *Grenada Documents* #87–4.

19. *Grenada Documents* #16.

20. *Grenada Documents* #16, p. 6.

21. *Grenada Documents* #87–3.

22. For further discussion, see chapter 1 on the Eastern Caribbean by Sally Shelton-Colby and Chapter 10, "Heading Toward a New Instability in the Caribbean's Eastern Tier?" by Scott B. MacDonald, Erik Kopp and Victor Bonilla.

23. Author's interview with Maurice Bishop, St. George's, Grenada, October 25–27, 1982. Bishop also publicly signed a CARICOM Communiqué in November 1982 which noted that "where any member state considers that its nationals are being trained without its consent for the purpose of pursuing acts of aggression or destabilization against it, it may consult with other member states with a view to deciding what coordinated diplomatic action may be taken by them." (Text of CARICOM 16–18 November 1982 Summit Communiqué, Ocho Rios, Jamaica, reprinted in Foreign Broadcasting Information Service, Caribbean, November 22, 1982, p. S3.)

24. For a discussion of this period and U.S.–Grenadian relations, see Robert Pastor, "Does the United States Push Revolutions to Cuba: The Case of Grenada," *Journal of Interamerican Studies and World Affairs* (Spring 1986): 1–34.

25. Barbados, *House of Assembly Debate*, November 15, 1983, pp. 56–57, cited in Robert Pastor, "The Impact of Grenada on the Caribbean: Ripples from a Revolution," in Jack W. Hopkins (ed.) *Latin America and the Caribbean Contemporary Record*, Vol. III, 1983–84. (New York: Holmes and Meier, 1985). This chapter analyses the short-, medium-, and longer-term impact of Grenada on the wider Caribbean area. It was written in July 1984.

PART II
REVOLUTION, CONFLICT, AND
DEMOCRACY IN THE CARIBBEAN

6
The Jamaican Models: The United States and Democracy in the Caribbean
Georges Fauriol

INTRODUCTION

Winston Churchill is said to have remarked that democracies are the worst form of government except for all those other forms that have been tried over several centuries. Despite this admittedly timid endorsement, democracies remain the exception, not the rule in the Third World. The odds have in fact been against the survival of regimes with democratic foundations. Conspicuous exceptions that probably confirm the validity of the above statement are to be found in the Caribbean region. Jamaica is one of those countries.

This is of considerable relevance since the 1980s have been operating under an acute resurgence of democracy as a belief and governing system. It has also been a philosophical underpinning of America's projection of itself in the international community under Ronald Reagan. This has found its most spectacular expressions in the U.S. policy of support for Nicaraguan "freedom fighters" or in the case of military operations against the Marxist government of Grenada. Quite apart from the rhetoric, demands for democracy have indeed been on the rise throughout the Third World, and particularly in in Latin America. In the face of military, authoritarian, and at times simply archaic forms of governance, political democracy has made a remarkable comeback in some countries, in South America in particular. In the other regions, for example Central America, it has had to be built from the ground up. This has involved a distribution of political authority in society and some attention to economic and social issues.

Much of this experimentation with political democracy in the region

has operated in tandem with the difficult search for economic democracy, and as Irving Louis Horowitz has perceptively noted, social democracy.[1] In all three areas, Third World societies have been lured by—
to borrow liberally from Jean-François Revel—the totalitarian tempta-
tions. Somewhat erroneously believing that forced redistributive economic programs were preconditions to an upgraded level of social
welfare, much of this experimentation has instead generated a paralyzing
narrowing of economic rights and political choices.

THE JAMAICAN EXPERIENCE

In Jamaica, the government's attempt under Michael Manley to obtain
control of the commanding heights of society led instead to economic
stagnation and social chaos. The failure of the above impulse to generate
satisfactory results was replaced by an equally ambitious attempt to revert
to purer or liberal forms of economic democracy. Pursuing a free market
strategy under Edward Seaga after 1980 has proven to be as challenging
a task as that of Michael Manley's dismal experience with democratic
socialism.

Thus, after 25 years of independent life, Jamaican democracy has
generated an intriguing sequence of paths to development and stability.
For the first ten years after 1962 the island nation experienced rapid
economic growth with a decaying social environment alongside it; unemployment grew, as did visible signs of poverty, crime rates, and an
overall sense of political violence. The next decade was essentially that
of a turn to the left in ideological terms and idealistic pursuit of a major
program of social transformation. In turn, the 1980s brought the previous eight-year experimentation to a halt and introduced private sector–
oriented development, itself marked with enormous pitfalls in its implementation. With the nation facing another possible political transition
through election before the end of the 1980s, the cycles and twists in
Jamaica developments and their regional salience deserve continued
careful attention.

The relevance of these Jamaican twists and turns lie in two interrelated
spheres. One aspect of this is directly associated with the character of
Jamaican politics and economics and their impact on the viability of the
nation itself. Since the early 1970s, there have been recurring battles
regarding the outlook on progress in Jamaica. A second relevant aspect
lies in the regional or international arena, to the degree that Jamaica is
viewed as a model or harbinger of things to come—or to avoid.

Although the Caribbean constitutes one of the oldest spheres of Western colonial enterprise, the region also represents one of the more concentrated experiments in constitutional government. British rule
produced in Jamaica an intangible and fragile effect, translated into an

appreciation for the rule of law and the maintenance of representative political institutions. That this modern political development was the product of rather disinterested colonial management and more recently of a period of strikes, riots, and general unease in the 1930s and 1940s, is quite extraordinary. It did generate an unquestionable philosophical affinity for a liberal value system and related political rules of conduct. In the years immediately following independence in 1962, Jamaicans at the United Nations were known as the 'Afro-Saxons.'

In contrast to other end-products of the colonial experience, Jamaica has in the last 40 years seen fit only to tinker with its governmental structure. The latter was modeled on the British administrative and party system. Despite difficulties, and some attempts at modernizing this environment, the latter has essentially remained constant. This occasionally violent Jamaican version of parliamentary rule and electoral competition deserves emphasis, and even an accolade or two. Halfway through Michael Manley's turbulent tenure, Carl Stone, one of Jamaica's foremost political analysts, could in 1976 write with little pretension that there were only a few "Third World countries where parliamentary and competitive party politics continue to flourish under social environments not qualitatively different from those where such governmental institutions have either collapsed or have been modified beyond recognition."[2]

The political transition that occurred in 1980, from Manley to Seaga, was so traumatic as to suggest the possible unraveling of the entire political system. With all the elements of conspiracy, bloodshed, economic chaos, and external interest, the ability of Jamaican democracy to achieve a viable political synthesis appeared at an impossible end. But the political system did survive. And in the process it sustained its ability as a role model of sorts in the region.

It has ironically maintained this tentative role despite drastic changes in the form of socio-economic management. The democratic socialism of the 1970s was an articulation of the hopes of the progressive element of Caribbean politics—ultimately outflanked by its own more radical variant, internally and regionally, as the Grenadan case demonstrated. By contrast, the free market rhetoric of the 1980s meshed in very well and encouraged soul mates elsewhere in the English-speaking Caribbean. The latter, in turn, all come together with the remnants of the region's 1970s socialist experimentation, in the context of the Grenadan crisis of 1983.

For Jamaicans, a certain pride, insular nationalism, and sense of regional leadership has ensued from these experiences. Deferring to Jamaica's relevance to regional political unity in the 1960s, the late Prime Minister of Trinidad and Tobago Eric Williams noted with a touch of irritation, that without Kingston's involvement, not much was possible— "ten minus one equals zero."[3] In the 1970s, this reached grander proportions to the extent that Jamaica's international visibility was out of proportion with its domestic capabilities. This measurable involvement can largely be credited to the prime minister's active maneuvering towards not only a regional role but a special Jamaican 'niche' in world politics. Michael Manley, more than other Jamaican leaders, formulated a grand view of the role of a small state and its ability to make change and generate a following.

Edward Seaga's landslide victory in 1980 coincided with Ronald Reagan's own electoral victory. Seaga's leadership pretensions have been more restrained, yet in the economic domain he was from the beginning the prime Caribbean force behind a realignment of regional diplomacy more sympathetic to the United States. In tandem, the economic development strategy of the incoming Jamaican Labour Party (JLP)—the Seaga Model—quickly generated a regional momentun, with similar rhetoric and policies becoming more visible in other governments (Dominica, Barbados, St. Lucia, for example). Seaga's bold Marshall-type program for the Caribbean reinforced at a critical time the new U.S. administration's development of an effort that ultimately turned into a Caribbean Basin Initiative (CBI). And when in October 1983 the Eastern Caribbean states consulted with Jamaica in the aftermath of Maurice Bishop's murder, Edward Seaga was able to add his own political weight to the invitation that Washington received to restore order in Grenada.

On a regional and more global scale, Jamaica has viewed itself and in fact acted as a spokesman for the Caribbean. Michael Manley did it in an expansive fashion, and Edward Seaga has to a narrower degree sustained this impulse. Both have sought to bring the problems of Jamaica and the region to the attention of more affluent nations and the community of international institutions.

Jamaica's high profile has had a considerable impact on the character of U.S. policy in the region. Since the 1960s, Kingston has been perceived by Washington as a potential model for the region to emulate or alternatively as a dangerous experiment the influence of which was to be eradicated. Jamaica went from being a Caribbean ally to being a fellow traveler conspiring with the enemy. The election of the PNP government in 1972, and the mid–1980s uncertainty regarding Jamaica's free market development, have become salient parameters for U.S. policy thinking toward the Caribbean Basin as a whole. The important interaction of Jamaican developments and U.S. policy in the region can be analyzed by focusing on the following thresholds: 1972, 1979, 1980, 1983, and 1989.

1972

From independence in 1962 through the late 1960s, Jamaica largely concentrated on domestic development issues. From this ensued conventional economic policy objectives. Close relations were maintained with the United Kingdom, while ties with the United States were formalized. Within this framework, Jamaica enjoyed ten years of moderate politics and relative (and uneven) economic growth. This placid facade began to come undone with an eroding confidence of the electorate in the government's economic policies. In 1972, the country swung sharply to the left on the basis of Michael Manley's electoral slogan: "Better must come".

In retrospect, 1972 marks two critical developments. First, it introduces a new leadership to Jamaican politics, not only because of Manley's election but because of the passing from the scene in the immediately preceding years of the nation's senior political figures, Norman Manley (Michael's father) and Alexander Bustamante. But, secondly, with this transition also disappears Jamaican politics' relative consensus that had brought the nation from the 1930s and 1940s through independence and the first decade of nationhood. The political leadership that came to lead Jamaica in the 1970s and 1980s—Manley and Seaga—have not had a common conception of the nation, except perhaps to their credit an ultimately strong commitment to democratic politics.

Manley proceeded to initiate a broad process of social change, increasing state ownership, introducing job programs, and engaging the foreign corporate sector in a battle of wills. This ambitious program of social reforms, tinted with economic nationalism and forceful challenges to traditional economic interests, led by 1974 to several years of increasing social polarization, economic decline, and rising violence. Indicative of where things were going, Manley provided hints of the ideological definition of his program in *The Politics of Change*, written in 1973.[4] In it, he suggested much of his subsequent policy thrust: nationalization of the "commanding heights of the economy," increased economic self-reliance, a nonaligned foreign policy, restructuring of social policy (education, mass media, etc.), and promotion of constitutional changes to expand 'popular' control of the system.[5]

In 1974, this was formally given a political label, democratic socialism, in a series of speeches by Manley and related press reviews. The tone of the "thirteen principles" were perhaps to a degree a desperate move suggestive of Jamaica's dire straits by late 1974, and the slippery slope Manley was by then undertaking in the international arena. In early 1975 Edward Seaga, now JLP leader, launched his campaign against economic mismanagement and the government's increasingly close international ties with the left. The latter sent alarms ringing in Washington.

Manley radicalized Jamaica's foreign policy and deliberately sought Third World ties. He took advantage of, and eventually helped widen, the shift in the international system toward South-South cooperation.

Implied by this changing environment was a sharply new vision of an "open" foreign policy, one involving ties with countries whose ideological and political systems were not always directly compatible with Jamaica's existing relationships. In politically overt actions, relations were established with the PRC and Cuba in late 1972. The warming of relations with Cuba blossomed very quickly with Manley's trip with Castro to the Algiers Nonalignment summit in 1973. It further intensified with a number of cultural and technical assistance exchanges, particularly after 1975. At Castro's invitation, Manley visited Cuba in 1975.

At the Algier's summit, Manley hammered away at his main themes—Third World economic unity and political cooperation. With an economic impasse at home and irked by what it viewed as an unresponsive global environment, Jamaica embarked upon a radicalization of its own initiatives. The negotiations with the nation's foreign-owned bauxite sector were the leadoff for several years of undisguised economic warfare. In tandem, Kingston took the lead in "cartelizing" bauxite and the formation of an ultimately weak clone of OPEC: The International Bauxite Association (IBA).

Not surprisingly, between late 1975 and 1977 relations with Washington hit their low point. There were good reasons for that. Kingston sided with Cuba's military intervention in Africa. It gave vocal support to the Popular Movement for the Liberation of Angola (MPLA), and in March 1976 officially recognized it. Four months earlier, U.S. Secretary of State Henry Kissinger had visited Jamaica, ostensibly on vacation. Subsequent development suggest that he failed to distance Kingston from Cuba's Angolan policy. He also failed to reassure Manley of U.S. noninterference in Jamaica's increasingly turbulent domestic politics and complex Cuban linkages. By the spring of 1976 cries of CIA activities began to appear in public statements and the media. Some linked external actors with the increasing tempo of domestic violence. In turn, the Manley government declared emergency rule and charged Washington with instigating a policy of "destabilization." Relations with the United States went into a tailspin and had to wait out the bitter and violent December 1976 elections and the change of administrations in Washington to improve.

The Carter administration's definition of a "pluralistic" Caribbean region enabled Washington and Kingston to resume a more constructive dialogue. On the economic front, much attention was paid to Jamaica's trade and balance of payments problems. Discussions shifted to serious negotiations at the multilateral level. Initiated in late 1976, discussions with the IMF led to one loan agreement—the terms of which subsequently Jamaica could not (or would not) live up to. Several protracted negotiation phases ensued, resulting in a hardening of the Jamaican government posture, but unfortunately leading to an intransigent no-win political contest. Under pressure from Washington, few viable financing alternatives were found (the USSR was approached in 1977 but showed little enthusiasm about acquiring another Caribbean expense account). This further eroded invester confidence and deepened Jamaica's negative economic growth rate. As the country's financial structure teetered on the brink of bankruptcy, increasingly restrictive emergency measures were instituted. This essentially continued until 1980 and the loss of the PNP at the polls in November of that year.

On the political front, Kingston's signals were increasingly perceived in Washington as evolving not only toward the institutionalization of Jamaican socialism but also the "Cubanization" of society. The former was perceived as destructive but the latter was simply dangerous. By then regional events began to dovetail with U.S.–Jamaican problems. As the Carter administration focused greater attention on the Caribbean Basin, a coup in Grenada and a revolution in Nicaragua gave Jamaica–U.S. relations an altogether different security dimension. Concerns regarding possible Cuban military intervention began to surface as the Jamaican elections neared. It also became obvious that Michael Manley's own PNP party structure was being stretched further and further to the left. Until the outcome of the 1980 elections (both in Jamaica and the United States) could be determined, Kingston and Washington settled back into a slow boil and generally unproductive relationship. In stark contrasts, the new Seaga and Reagan administrations developed a warm and generally productive tie.[6]

1979

With Carter's accession to power in early 1977, United States policy was influenced by the Linowitz Commission Report and its suggested need to respect regional diversity and ideology, and the interdependent role of the region in global relations. With a global economic crisis in full swing, this encouraged the development of a number of well-intentioned efforts, such as the World Bank's Group for Cooperation in Economic Development, responding to economic depression in the Caribbean. But it was in the political domain that the real impact of policy was to be measured. Hints of a United States initiative toward Cuba appeared in the air and expressions of a redefinition of the basis of regional U.S. security interests began to focus on economic justice and social development. In philosophical terms, the thinking of important members of the Carter administration, Andrew Young, for example, and the development of human rights as the cutting edge of U.S. policy, were visible expressions of a new approach.

Because of the administration's slow grasp of events, the coup in Grenada in March 1979 caught Washington policymakers by surprise and did not lead to an immediate reappraisal of U.S. policy. Maurice Bishop's arrival to power broke the rule of constitutional transfer of power, although that turned out to be the least significant element. The real issues were made apparent by the very rapid response of the Cuban government to the People's Revolutionary Government's (PRG) friendly approach for close ties and the subsequent institutionalization of a government with Marxist structure and ideology. The internal dynamics of the Grenadan revolution were immediately relevant to political trends in the Caribbean as a whole, and Jamaica in particular.

The bases of modern Caribbean political culture are anchored in Fabian politics and the advances of the area's trade union movement. To a certain extent, Maurice Bishop was representative of a highly politicized and cultured generation of leaders that succeeded the aging political aristocracy of Norman Manley of Jamaica, even his son Michael, Forbes Burnham of Guyana, and many others. It could be argued that Marxist undercurrents have been part of the political scenery of this newer generation of which Bishop was a lead actor.[7]

Unlike Bishop's Grenada, Manley's loose operational definition of social democracy ultimately generated weak rather than flexible governance. This constituted flexibility by political design, a compromising and probably only possible approach for Manley. But even for Bishop, in addition to Manley, or another socialist leader of the region, the late Forbes Burnham of Guyana, political pragmatism was in the final analysis considered a sign of weakness. It ultimately represented an inability to articulate a meaningful ideology relevant to domestic needs or the strategic reality of the nation.

Indeed, Michael Manley had since 1977 been under pressure to move his PNP party toward more draconian economic and political measures to face a clearly worsening national situation. Behind the rhetoric of the negotiations with the IMF and other financial policy issues, it became quite clear that, while resisting, Manley had let the PNP structure and the government slip under the influence of the party's left, and Marxist intellectuals such as Trevor Munroe. Manley succeeded in emerging from these confrontations within the party stronger but more radical. He effectively reasserted the West Indian tradition of "one leader," which the electorate believed was being challenged by radicals. Not deviating from this, Manley did not attempt something as risky as "collective leadership."

For the region's radicals and the Grenadans in particular, Manley represented a degree of respectability, ironically very much because of the fact that he was a democratically elected leader. This gave him visibility before the Socialist International (Manley was its regional vice president) and popularity among Latin American and North American democratic "progressives." The latter's support and sympathy was not affected by his support for the Marxist Grenadan regime, the reported secret meetings in Managua on ways to influence the Socialist International, and his close friendship with Castro and Cuba. But these contradictions were bound to catch up with one even so skillful as Manley. And ultimately they did for Manley in late 1980 and Bishop in late 1983.[8]

Beyond Grenada, two other developments also marked 1979–1980 in a way very relevant to Jamaica. The first was the decisive success of the Nicaraguan revolution. Initially supported by Washington, subsequent developments in Nicaragua demonstrated the basic strains in the Carter administration's logic to U.S. regional interests. The second element was the 1980 spring and summer spectacle of the Cuban refugee crisis. Turning the tables on the United States, Cuba was able to translate a human rights policy defeat into a political cleansing of its own society. Nicaragua and the refugee crisis further sharpened the pressures that Manley's socialist experiment was feeling from Washington.

1980–1981

The fall of the PNP brought to an abrupt end the Socialist International's most important experience in the Caribbean, if not even the Third World. Edward Seaga's arrival on the scene provided the equally new and vigorous Reagan administration with an invaluable ally to pursue a new policy designed to reverse the challenges generated by the events of 1979–1980. One of Seaga's first political moves on taking office was to expel the Cuban ambassador in Kingston, a senior member of Cuba's intelligence services, the DGI.

The situation Seaga inherited in late 1980 was hardly pleasant. The economy was in shambles and the social situation electric. The nation's best managerial talent had left, along with their capital. Political violence during the fall 1980 elections had finished off what was already a frightened tourist industry. Unemployment was up, as were the numbers of guns in private hands, and the nation's marijuana production.[9]

In going about resurrecting the economy, Seaga combined public with private sector initiatives. But things did not go smoothly. Although often viewed as a Caribbean Ronald Reagan, Seaga's model has ultimately not been a clean sweep of government involvement in the economy. The latter's bad shape, coupled with a demoralized entrepreneurial class, made an easy use of private sector mechanisms difficult. And to the chagrin of U.S. conservatives who discovered Seaga in the late 1970s, he himself was in his younger days very much a proponent of some form of state intervention in economic affairs. He did have a change of heart after witnessing Michael Manley's dismal performance. Meanwhile, the international economic environment has not always cooperated with

Seaga, as was the case in the case of the collapse of the bauxite market in the early 1980s.

The Seaga administration placed foreign investment at the heart of its policy of recovery, and promoted the introduction of new technology in Jamaica's limited manufacturing and export portfolio. It was hoped that this would open up new industries and alternative export sectors. The invitation to foreign investment was developed in tandem with a significant expansion of major loan and aid programs from foreign governments (primarily the United States) and international organizations. To make this work, the government early on set about streamlining the bloated bureaucracy, then increasing its efficiency, and forcing protected domestic manufacturers and markets to become more competitive. Slowly, a policy of divesture of public enterprises was pursued. To round out the program, from the beginning Seaga accepted the World Bank–IMF structural adjustment policies, the stabilization component of which led to politically unpopular budget cuts, wage restraints, and currency devaluation. The overall result was an upswing in Jamaica's self-confidence, even if immediate improvements in daily living conditions did not materialize. A by-product of the above was that tourism shot back up to respectable levels with a widely publicized "come back to Jamaica" campaign.

Seaga was the first head of state to visit Washington and meet President Reagan after his inauguration. In fact, he had already come on a private visit in the wake of the latter's election. Seaga's visits established very warm relations between the two men and set in motion several initiatives. The first of these was the U.S. Economic Committee of Jamaica, whose task it was to promote U.S. investment in the island. At Reagan's personal request, Chase Manhattan Chairman David Rockefeller headed the committee. The Committee ended up having more of a promotional value than a concrete economic impact. Seaga's visits also reinforced the idea of a U.S.–backed Marshall plan–like program for the Caribbean region. This suggestion eventually evolved into the Caribbean Basin Initiative (CBI). A third result of Seaga's meetings with the new U.S. administration was more immediate and visible. The United States increased aid to Jamaica massively, making it a lead recipient in the region. Jamaica also benefited from other aspects of discussions with the United States, such as income from the agreement for the sale of 1.6m tons of bauxite for its strategic stockpile in 1982 and again in 1983.

In February 1982 the CBI program was unveiled. The centerpiece of the program was duty-free entry into the United States for twelve years of all goods produced in the Caribbean Basin, with meaningful exceptions, such as textiles. Sugar, which was already regulated by U.S. agricultural policy, was also left out. The CBI did include tax and insurance incentives for investment in the area; a one-time $350 million balance-of-payments aid package, with Jamaica joining El Salvador as the largest beneficiaries. After much negotiation in the U.S. Congress, the CBI was passed in a modified form in the fall of 1983.

The election of the Seaga administration was therefore a timely development enabling Washington to reverse a dangerous expansion of Cuban influence in the English-speaking Caribbean. By pushing aside the Cuban-backed PNP, the Seaga administration was in effect also eliminating what Washington saw as the emergence of left-wing influence in the government of Jamaica. With trouble in Central America, the United States was overjoyed with this development. During his April 1982 working holiday in Jamaica, Reagan noted that Seaga had "rescued" Jamaica from a government which had almost fallen under "communist control." Significantly, Seaga's attacks on socialist influence in the PNP government extended to the PNP's support for the Bishop government of Grenada. This further tied Seaga to Reagan administration diplomacy of regionally isolating the Cuban-backed leftist government of Maurice Bishop.[10]

1983

The Seaga government has been one of the staunchest supporters of U.S. policy in the Caribbean Basin region. Any by 1983 Jamaica was able to play a key role in the undoing of the Grenadan experiment. To get there, Seaga had in the elections of 1980 committed his Jamaican Labour Party to an anti-communist and anti-Cuban policy. When in power, his first foreign policy statements were therefore directed at Cuba and Grenada.

A year after throwing out the Cuban ambassador, in 1981 Seaga severed diplomatic relations with Cuba. His most likely correct excuse for this action was continued Cuban interference in Jamaica's internal affairs. Seaga also waged a campaign within the Caribbean Community (CARICOM) against the membership of Bishop's Grenada. In pursuing this line of attack, Seaga was simply following up on a political strategy that had proven highly successful in the election defeat of the PNP government in 1980. Michael Manley had been particularly vulnerable to criticism of Cuban interference and even subversion of Jamaica based upon the PNP's close party ties with the Cuban Communist party and New Jewel Movement of Grenada.

There were good reasons for Seaga's tough policy thrust. The fraternal cooperation between the left wing of the PNP, the Cuban Communist party, and the NJM had become a fact. On the Cuba-Jamaica front alone, the 1975–1979 period had seen a considerable increase in exchanges. Viewed with particular concern was the Brigadista program of interparty exchanges with Cuba involving the training of between three and four hundred young Jamaican men and women in Cuba and the presence of an estimated two hundred Cubans in Jamaica. Likewise, the formation of the Jamaica Home Guard as a local community adjunct to the police in combating growing incidents of criminal violence was patterned after the Cuban model and was indicative of the potential for radicalization of the PNP. These were serious concerns during the last year of the Carter administration. The possibility of a left-wing coup in Jamaica brought nightmares of a bigger, more dangerous, NJM struggle in Grenada.

Relations between the PNP and the NJM before Bishop came to power were translated into active promotion of Bishop by Manley after 1979. The PNP had already adopted the NJM as a fraternal socialist party despite the tension this produced with the Grenadan government of Eric Gairy. After the NJM's seizure of power, the PNP played an instrumental role in persuading Caribbean states to accept Grenada's participation as a full-fledged partner in regional activities, despite some misgivings on the part of several CARICOM governments. Manley himself maintained a close personal relationship with Bishop and sponsored the recognition of Bishop's government at the Non-Aligned Movement meeting in Havana. He went further and became the People's Revolutionary Government's most ardent spokesman for recognition by the United States, suggesting in fact that the NJM was like his own PNP.[11]

The situation was altered dramatically with the change of leadership in Jamaica. At the first CARICOM Heads of Government Conference to be held after the PRG came to power (Ocho Rios, Jamaica, November 1982), Seaga actively worked with Prime Minister Tom Adams of Barbados to isolate Grenada. Without naming Grenada, the suggestion was made to change the CARICOM treaty to exclude member countries which deviated from the norms of parliamentary democracy and violated human rights.

When the situation unraveled in Grenada in the fall of 1983, Jamaica played a politically mobilizing role. Seaga attended an extraordinary meeting of the Organization of Eastern Caribbean States (OECS), of which Jamaica was not a member; Grenada was absent. The only other non-OECS country represented at this meeting, held in Barbados, was Tom Adams. The timing of this session was such that it was held two days after "Bloody Wednesday" in which Maurice Bishop, three cabinet members and two Labour leaders were killed, and four days before the U.S.–led operation began in Grenada on October twenty-fifth. The conclusion of the OECS and its two outside participants was to request U.S. assistance to restore order by disbanding the interim military government (the Revolutionary Military Council, RMC) nominally led by General Hudson Austin. The outcome would be to set up a civilian interim government, leading to elections and the restoration of a democratic government.

In addition to mobilizing Commonwealth Caribbean support for United States policy and becoming an articulate spokesman of the Grenada operation, Seaga took a direct hand in fostering the restoration of a new government in Grenada. He played a role in helping to merge various political factions into the New National Party (NNP) led by Herbert Blaize, who ultimately won the 1984 elections. Jamaica provided the NNP financial and technical assistance that included seconding JLP Member of Parliament Cliff Stone and others to help with election campaigning.

An extension of the JLP's efforts toward the Grenada affairs was evident in his decision to call general elections two years before it was constitutionally required. The Jamaican electorate appeared very supportive of the nation's involvement and appreciated the defeat Cuban influence had suffered in the Caribbean. The timing of the general election in December 1983, and the PNP's refusal to contest the elections for self-serving political reasons, resulted in the JLP winning all 60 parliamentary seats by default. Seaga's quick capitalization of the Grenada operation played upon a popular 1980 election theme (Cuban subversion), but most importantly simply took advantage of popular enthusiasm for his shrewd sense of leadership and action.[12]

Looking at 1989

The swings in Jamaican politics have been matched by the deep interest of Washington in the fate of the Caribbean as a whole. More than any other nation in the region, Jamaica has either been viewed as a close ally or a crisis in the making. Certainly, since 1981 Edward Seaga has redirected his nation toward being the most strategic of friends for the United States in the region. But domestically, in the aftermath of the snap 1983 elections, and an unresponsive economy, Seaga has fought an uphill battle to keep the government out of increasingly rough seas. Could Washington's close friend turn into a crisis point?

Part of the answer lies in the electoral uncertainties in both Jamaica and the United States in the 1988–1989 period. As has been the case previously, the results of almost simultaneous elections have had enormous impact on the character of the subsequent diplomatic relationship between the two nations. In 1972, the two nations ended up at the opposite sides of the political spectrum, although the PNP's radical character was only latent in the 1972–1976 Nixon-Ford administration. Despite the responsiveness of the Carter administration, after 1976 the countries began to clash openly. In 1980, the electoral results produced harmonious ideological outcomes. Seaga faces an election in the 1988–1989 period, the results of which will help define U.S. policy toward the Caribbean regardless of the party in power at the White House.

The reason for this lies partly in the psychological arena. Jamaica and Edward Seaga have represented something important for the region, as well as the United States. This has involved not only a certain approach toward economic development, and a common search for the region's long-term viability—as exemplified by the CBI—but it has also involved a common political approach, in which Edward Seaga has acted as an anchor not only to U.S. policy, but Ronald Reagan's personal relationship with the region. If the latter had not been side-tracked by events in Central America, the almost inherent spiritual quality of this relationship would have become even more open.

By extension, Edward Seaga has become to a degree a "CBI prime minister," or CBI government. It has been replicated elsewhere in the region, with Eugenia Charles of Dominica and John Campton being the most visible examples. They and others all came together most notably in the context of the Grenadan operation in late 1983. But the favorable situation since then has changed. These changes have occurred in three overlapping arenas: first, alterations in the Caribbean's political landscape; second, complications in the strategic picture of the Caribbean Basin as a whole; and third, a changing framework for Edward Seaga's personal standing back home.

In the years since the collapse of the Bishop government in 1983, the governments of Barbados and Trinidad and Tobago have undergone significant changes. The Barbadian elections of 1986 replaced the government that had, through the late Tom Adams, played such a crucial role in 1983. The Democratic Labour party's Errol Barrow indicated upon taking office that he was going to pursue a foreign policy more independent from Washington, and somewhat by implication, distance himself from the latter's favorite policy subject matter, Grenada and Jamaica. For Seaga, the salience of the Barbadian election also lay in the fact that the DLP's electoral success was due to its economic policy plank (a fundamental issue for the Jamaican electorate) rather than any friction over foreign and defense policy. Economic policy was also what ultimately unseated the People's National Movement (PNM) from three decades of continuous rule in Trinidad and Tobago in late 1986.

As for Grenada itself, the original post–1983 enthusiasm began to rub off when the economic situation did not show dramatic improvements. As in the case of Jamaica, CBI induced foreign investments have in the early years been slow to materialize. Unemployment remains high. By early 1987, the government was facing not only those continuing economic problems but political challenges as well.

These Caribbean challenges have been competing with Central American developments for attention in Washington. The latter's complicated strategic picture has not only drawn off energy and resources but has also affected the visibility of Edward Seaga's own policies. Although clearly philosophically anticommunist, and strongly suggestive of the value of democratic government, Jamaica's most salient policy campaigns have been fought on the economic front. That has meshed very well with such regional efforts as the Caribbean Basin Initiative, or after the 1984 and 1986 CARICOM Heads of State meetings, the reversing of the downward spiral in regional trade. Although these economic policies have received enthusiastic endorsements and material support from Washington, the latter's primary focus shifted to the political and security front on Central America.

While regional political and security issues are likely to remain, which also happen to be concerns of the Jamaican leadership, the real issue at hand upon which Edward Seaga is likely to be judged is the Jamaican quality of life. As painful as it has been for governing circles to admit it, Carl Stone's suggestion of a Jamaica "running out of options" is indicative of a very frustrating situation.[13] Seaga's predicament was made even more apparent when attacks on the very heart of his program—economic policy—began to come in from traditionally sympathetic voices in the United States. The Heritage Foundation's *Backgrounder* Report, issued just prior to Seaga's visit to Washington in the fall of 1986, contained a friendly but sharp reminder that he had deviated from the original free market program.[14]

As suggested earlier in this article, Seaga's program was predicated on foreign investment providing the basis for economic growth—as opposed to Manley's state ownership. In fact, while much has been attempted, the free market model has continued to collide with a state sector that still controls large chunks of the sugar industry, tourism sector, bauxite lands, telecommunication companies, the national airline, banking, and other miscellaneous activities. Borrowing from external sources was expanded on such a scale that by 1987, debt payments were consuming about 40 percent of export earnings. While the government endorsed World Bank–IMF structural adjustment policies early on, in 1986 it attempted to deviate from it by promoting a reflationary policy. The decision to distance itself from IMF-mandated austerity policies was ultimately partially reversed in 1987 with Paris Club foreign debt rescheduling talks and a new IMF agreement. But unless hard currency earnings rise dramatically, capacity to repay debts will be hampered, and Jamaican credit worthiness will be dependent on political support in Washington.

The government's hopes have to a degree been pinned on the fact that economically just about everything has been tried. Thus, after several years of austerity, economic policies should be able to bear some fruits. In macroeconomic terms, and providing a psychological lift to Jamaica's leaders, the traditional GDP declines of the 1970s have been replaced by moderate growth rates. Unemployment did decline during the first three years of Seaga's tenure. There is no doubt that while the overall investment levels did not hit their expected targets, they have been on the upswing. While the bauxite sector has been hit very hard, agricultural, and, more recently, textile exports have shown dramatic increases. Tourism rebounded.

Whether Seaga's frustrations are due to deviations from free market economics remains a debatable point. A number of issues have in any event conspired against him. Most notable among these has been the collapse of the aluminum industry in the mid–1980s. That took away a major traditional foundation of the economy and sources of export earnings. Secondly, Seaga inherited a sick economy, one showing negative growth and a burdensome foreign debt. And thirdly, the government also inherited a dispirited, if not simply uncommitted private sector. The latter was to a degree the linchpin of the Seaga plan, and its less than vigorous response has most likely caused considerable frustration for Edward Seaga personally. The Jamaican private sector, already frightened away by the Manley years, has remained in great part a U.S.–based community. One Jamaican source has noted that 80 percent of Jamaica's businessmen are holders of U.S. permanent residency green cards.[15] In the original thinking, Jamaica's investment rise was to have been supported by the established and large Jamaican and U.S. investor community. In fact, much of the private sector inflow has been generated— not by the blue-chip corporate sector of either country—but by small scale investors.

CONCLUSION

It is unclear whether Jamaica has indeed run out of options. However, there is no doubt that the maneuvering room made available to Jamaica through Seaga's arrival on the scene in 1980 has eroded. If there are any flaws, they appear to be as much the fault of any possible weakness in Seaga's policies as they are the result of Jamaica's limited ability to entirely control its destiny in the modern world. If there is any salient feature in a future political change in Jamaican leadership, it is that any incoming administration is likely to inherit a nation on the verge of total collapse as it was in 1980.

Some of Seaga's moves on the domestic economic front have been the result of a rejuvenated Michael Manley and PNP. With Grenada, the snap elections of 1983 and the 1970s' dismal PNP tenure fading into history, the opposition has swung back into action and taken advantage of the Achilles' heel of any democratically elected government: popular frustrations over, not the grand designs of policy, but simply daily living conditions.

By 1987, with public opinion polls indicating a positive PNP rating, Michael Manley could safely travel to Washington and meet with U.S. government officials. Kingston's *Daily Gleaner*, never a friend of the PNP, could also vote him the "outstanding politician of 1986." Manley, who had withdrawn his party from the 1983 elections, was now reborn, regarded by some as having moderated some of his views, and ready for a new round of battle if he felt confident of winning.

Manley has downplayed his association with Cuba and other "progressives." And the anti-American rhetoric has been toned down. Yet, the degree to which the PNP program remains decidedly distant from Reagan or Seaga administration policy is to suggest potentially turbulent moments ahead. The call for a decreased reliance on the United States across the board has, however, rung a bell in the region, as reflected most notably in the post–1986 government in Barbados. Likewise, Manley's emphasis on intraregional trade concerns has echoed CARICOM talks in this area. And thirdly, a shifting of institutional emphasis away from the CBI framework toward CARICOM, the Caribbean Development Bank, and other regional institutions, has reflected a certain impatience of Caribbean governments with U.S. policy.

Obviously, there are no indications that the above emphasis would work any better than Manley's previous initiatives—or even Seaga's. Nor does it appear to appreciate the fact that Jamaica (and the Caribbean as a whole) has received a degree of positive U.S. attention and even presidential passion not likely to be sustained if the region began to retreat from a warm cooperative spirit with Washington. One does suspect that the cool heads that have prevailed under the JLP tenure have moderated the entire Jamaican political system. However, this has not destroyed some of the nefarious aspects of the nation's polity, particularly its violent local political character, and the presence in its midst of constituencies that do not abide by democratic rules of conduct. Ideologically motivated groups, and a drug underworld, provide dangerous competition for any elected government. The Jamaican development experience will therefore continue to be a salient issue for the Caribbean as a whole as well as the United States.

NOTES

1. See his excellent conceptual article, "Democracy and Development: Policy Perspectives in a Post-Colonial Context," in the *New Caribbean*, Paget Henry and Carl Stone, eds. (Philadelphia: Institute for the Study of Human Issues, 1983), pp. 221–233.

2. Carl Stone, "Class and the Institutionalization of Two-Party Politics in Jamaica," *Journal of Commonwealth and Comparative Politics* 14 (July 1976), p. 177.

3. Sir John Mordecai, *The West Indies: The Federal Negotiations* (Evanston: Northwestern University Press, 1968), pp. 376–77.

4. Michael Manley, *The Politics of Change: A Jamaican Testament* (Washington, DC: Howard University Press, 1975).

5. *The Politics of Change: A Jamaican Testament* (Washington, DC: Howard University Press, 1975). There are numerous government documents and also analytical pieces of the Manley government platforms; the shortest and most coherent exposé is Carl Stone's 1983 summary in "Democracy and Socialism in Jamaica," in Henry and Stone (1983), pp. 243–44.

6. Georges Fauriol, *Foreign Policy Behavior of Caribbean States: Guyana, Haiti, and Jamaica* (Lanham, Maryland: University Press of America, 1984), chapter 6, provides an assessment of Jamaica's foreign relations in the 1970s.

7. See Georges Fauriol, "Comments," in Jiri Valenta and Herbert Ellison (Eds.), *Grenada and Soviet/Cuban Policy* (Boulder, CO: Westview Press, 1986), pp. 148–51.

8. On the Manley-Grenada political relationship, see Anthony P. Maingot, "Grenada and the Caribbean: Mutual Lineages and Influences," Valenta and Ellison (1986), pp. 130–47.

9. The Manley administration of 1972–1980 has attracted numerous analyses, none of which are definitive. One point of reference is Manley's own interpretation, *Jamaica: Struggle in the Periphery* (London: 3rd World Media, 1982); two sympathetic assessments are, Michael Kaufman, *Jamaica Under Manley*, (Westport, CT: Lawrence Hill, 1985); and the somewhat more scholarly but politically oriented volume by Evelyne Huber Stephens and John D. Stephens, *Democratic Socialism in Jamaica*, (Princeton, NJ: Princeton University Press, 1986).

10. For a treatment of policy under both Jamaican administrations, see John D. Forbes, *Jamaica: Managing Political and Economic Change*, (Washington, DC: American Enterprise Institute, 1985).

11. A useful summary of these developments is provided in Timothy Ashby's *The Bear in the Back Yard* (Lexington, KY: Lexington Books, 1987), chapters 4 and 7.

12. For the complex Jamaica-Grenada interaction, the Grenada Documents captured in 1983 are helpful; for a sample, see Michael Ledeen and Herbert Romerstein, eds., *Grenada Documents: An Overview and Selection* (Washington, DC: U.S. Departments of State and Defense, Sept. 1984), especially documents 33–44. For Jamaican assessments of the 1983 events, see Michael Manley, "Grenada in the Context of History," and Carl Stone, "The Jamaican Reaction," both in *Caribbean Review* 12 (Fall 1983): 7–9, 31–32, 45–47, 60–63.

13. See Stone's splendid comparative review of the Seaga and Manley government records, "Running Out of Options in Jamaica," *Caribbean Review* 20 (Winter 1987): 10–12, 29–32.

14. "The U.S. Message for Jamaica's Seaga: It's Time to Keep Your Promise," *Backgrounder* 531 (Washington, DC: Heritage Foundation, Sept. 2, 1986).

15. Stone (1987): 31.

7
Apanjaht and Revolution in Caribbean Politics: The Case of Suriname
Edward Dew

INTRODUCTION

All societies in the Caribbean are plural societies. Gordon K. Lewis has lamented the focus of so many of us on the concept of cultural pluralism,[1] and I sympathize strongly with his position. Looking at what divides societies—their cultural, racial, religious, or other primordial attachments—is done at the expense of those emerging phenomena that unite them. Cultural pluralists like myself should hope, one day, to work ourselves out of a job. Or, better yet, cultural pluralism should work itself out of political science and into the hands of those in the humanities who celebrate a society's cultural riches.

But for the time being, at least, pluralism with its political plagues on society is very much in evidence in most parts of the Caribbean and the Third World. I want to draw a quick parallel between Grenada and the Southern Caribbean, and then focus on Suriname, as what happened in the Eastern Caribbean in October 1983 has a degree of significance in that country.

Of particular interest is the problem of "received political structures" in the Caribbean—a problem that began to undergo very close examination in the 1970s in the explosively polarized atmosphere that followed the Black Power movement's emergence in the late 1960s. The question was whether the received forms of European parliamentary government were applicable to the needs of small, troubled, developing societies. In Jamaica, Michael Manley seemed to stretch the constitution to its very limits, dramatically transforming the political economy in the process;[2] and in Trinidad a constitutional advisory committee was instituted to make proposals for revision of the existing document.[3] Such reforms were, in fact, instituted in Guyana under the less democratically inclined government of the late Forbes Burnham.[4] But in all cases the debate went on. Thus, it was with some considerable excitement throughout the Caribbean when Maurice Bishop and the New Jewel Movement came to power in Grenada. If ever an apparent travesty had been made of parliamentary democracy, it was in the Grenada of Eric Gairy, the brutal, populist demagogue.[5] Bishop carried out his coup in 1979, yet by the time he was murdered in 1983 he had still not put anything definitive in the place of the Gairy constitution.[6] Nevertheless, new structures were a central concern, and bold experimentation was under way.

These cases have been used as a kind of backdrop to the focus of this study and will be referred to from time to time. Grenada is especially important because of the similarity—in certain respects—between this society and that of Suriname.

Suriname, located on the northeast shoulder of South America and also known as Dutch Guiana, has a population which is only equal to that of Hartford, Connecticut although it is spread across a territory the size of Wisconsin. It is the central one of the Guianas, with French Guiana on the east, Guyana (or old British Guiana) on the west, Brazil to the south, and the Atlantic on the north. In this sense, the three Guianas are real incongruities. They are spoken of as being Caribbean, but they are not on the Caribbean. The Guianas are seen as Caribbean—and Central America is not—for socioeconomic and historical reasons: they were possessions, for the most part, of non-Iberian societies, and their social dynamics were focused on plantation economies and the related exploitation of imported slave populations. In this regard the Guianas are as Caribbean as any of the islands.

Like Grenada, and all the others, Suriname is now a plural society—a culturally plural society—defined loosely as a society composed of two or more distinct ethnic segments.[7] In Grenada's case, M.G. Smith, a social anthropologist, talks of two major groups: a very Westernized generally light-skinned elite in St. George's together with a large, racially darker, traditional folk society in the hinterland and the shanties. They are (or were) traditional in a host of ways identifiable to the ethnographer: family structure, belief system, customary behavior and so on.[8]

In Suriname, there is a much more complicated social mosaic—one that fascinates the rare visitor there because of its incredible diversity. There is, for starters, an amazingly wide variety of racial groups, and within each of these there are the subcultural cleavages already mentioned for Grenada.[9]

In the 1971 census (the last one available) 31 percent of the population is black or Creole. The equivalent of the majority of Grenadans, these are the descendants of slaves, culturally oriented to traditional beliefs or to the West, or spread-eagled somewhere in between. They speak Sranantongo and/or Dutch—mostly both. A slightly larger group, 37 percent, is East Indian or Hindustani, descendants of contract laborers imported from India in the period after slavery was abolished. They are religiously divided between Moslems and Hindus, while the Hindus are further divided between orthodox and reform Hinduism. Some of the Hindustanis have also become Christians. Some blacks have become Moslems. They speak Sarnami Hindustani, Sranantongo, and/or Dutch.

Fifteen percent of the Surinamers are Indonesian (Javanese). Though all of them are Moslem, they are still deeply divided between those traditionally praying to the West and those more modern ones who pray to the East. They speak an archaic form of Malayan (dating from the time that they were brought to Suriname as contract laborers, from the 1880s through the Great Depression). Most also speak Sranantongo and Dutch.

Eleven percent of the population is Bush Negro—descendants of escaped slaves who fought several bitter wars of independence against the Dutch in the seventeenth and eighteenth centuries and, with ultimate victory, established a number of virtual states-within-a-state in the interior. Large numbers are reportedly moving into the margins of the town for "push" as well as "pull" reasons—that is, their conditions in the interior have worsened somewhat, and the present government has taken advantage of this to provide at least some employment for them in the urban area, generating further migration and straining the retention of their social institutions.

Three percent of Surinamers are Amerindians, descendants of the original Carib and Arawak peoples who originally peopled the Caribbean islands and the Guyana coast. These, like the Bush Negroes, live in tribal groups, preserving their own languages, and dealing with the Westernized society with great caution. Despite inevitable borrowing and attrition, they remain culturally distinct, reminding us of what is was like before the conquerors arrived to set up these artificial societies.

Finally, 4 percent comprise the four other ethnic groups: the Europeans (including Americans), the Brazilian Jews, the Syrians, and the Chinese. Most, but not all of these people have achieved fairly comfortable lives. A large percentage of the Creoles and Hindustanis have also made it. It is possible that Suriname has the largest middle class in the region. In 1980, it enjoyed a GNP per capita of $2,946, putting it behind only the overseas departments of France and the United States and the oil-rich territories of Trinidad and the Netherlands Antilles.[10] But there are pockets of poverty—big pockets in the countryside and the city and the 10 percent index of unemployment masks more than it reveals in terms of underemployment, marginal income, and so on.[11]

Given its small population of roughly 350,000, Suriname is fairly well-endowed economically and capable of considerable self-sufficiency. Nevertheless, the cultural impact of Dutch colonialism has brought it a degree of consumerism and dependency and the need to husband one's foreign exchange reserves for capital goods expenditures. Suriname draws about 80 percent of its foreign exchange from the export of bauxite and its refined products of alumina and aluminum.[12] Most of the rest of her foreign exchange comes from exports of rice, lumber, shrimp, and various tropical fruits. The involvement of foreign corporations in the economy is high, and remains high even after four years of radical-sounding military government.

THE POLITICAL EVOLUTION OF APANJAHT POLITICS

Suriname had an advisory legislative council for some one hundred years before she became independent in 1975. In 1948 the Dutch extended universal suffrage to Suriname after a popular multiethnic campaign, and shortly thereafter home rule was established—that is, a fullfledged system of parliamentary government—complete with cabinet and prime minister—a few years after Jamaica, but before Grenada, Guyana, and Trinidad and Tobago. The ultimate sovereign powers, defense and foreign policy, were shared with the motherland.[13] But the Surinamers got a type of government that was quite the same as in the Netherlands. At the time, it was a matter of great pride.

Another feature of Surinamese politics, which can only be termed indigenous, regardless of its parallels in many other countries, is the practice known as *apanjaht*. In the Caribbean, this is the practice of voting for your own race, your own kind. This phenomenon was observed in Guyana with Cheddi Jagan and Forbes Burnham, and in Trinidad with Eric Williams and a string of opposition East Indian leaders.[14] It could even be argued that Sir Eric Gairy's rise to power in Grenada, as well as his prolonged stay there, might be credited to ethnic, traditional cultural appeals to the marginalized masses of his country.[15]

Apanjaht politics is generally condemned for pandering to the meanest suspicions and biases of the group vis-à-vis its ethnic and cultural rivals. It feeds a "we-versus-they" set of group identifications that is counterproductive to national identity and national development. Yet it can also be said that *apanjahtism* rests on positive foundations. At the time in which it made its entrance to the Caribbean in the 1940s and 1950s, it served not only as a means of political mobilization but also as a source of social liberation. It asserted an identity that usually had been scorned or abused by the earlier elites—the elites that now were being displaced.[16] It is hardly a dysfunctional phenomenon to see the downtrodden finding new ways to make a fist, even if the end result was a new kind of elitism.

As Surinamers sorted themselves out by means of *apanjaht* into viable ethnic political parties, they developed another indigenous institution—inventing another internationally familiar wheel from a local and authentic need. This one bears the dreadfully cumbersome name of "consociationalism" or "consociational democracy."[17] When a multiethnic population, in which no group constitutes anything near a majority, is combined in an open and fair electoral system with *apanjaht* politics, electoral outcomes in which no party has a majority is the result. Thus multiethnic coalitions become essential. That, in short, is what consociational democracy is—a form of government for culturally plural societies in which the ethnic issue is addressed by means of proportionality and power sharing.[18] Surveying the wreckage of multiethnic democracies around the world—from Lebanon to Nigeria—one may wonder if there is any point in trying. How do they do it in Switzerland? In fact, how is it done in the United States? The answer, probably, is that in these societies there is enough wealth to go around. In the Third World's plural societies, there usually is not.

APANJAHT AND REVOLUTION IN SURINAME

In Suriname there seemed to be enough to go around, and for twenty years *apanjaht* consociationalism worked.[19] Nevertheless, *apanjaht* breeds alienation, especially among the young. Successful political socialization toward the symbols of national unity inevitably starts to cut into the bases for *apanjaht*. Study abroad, a common phenomenon for Surinamese students, has led them into alien circumstances where their Surinamese national identity was deepened, and their exposure to other forms of politics—ideological, programmatic politics—gave them the inspiration to return home and take on the system, to overhaul it, make it serve the people's needs. And there should be no doubt about it: Consociational democracy, even where it does work does not work well.[20] It is an *ad hoc*, incrementalist, deal-striking kind of politics which, if not immobilized by its very mechanics, certainly looks like it is.

It is probable that that is the way politics look in any *apanjaht* society and there is a possibility that that is the way Gairy's Grenada looked to Maurice Bishop. And that is certainly the way Burnham's Guyana looked to Walter Rodney.[21] In Suriname, that is the way *apanjaht* consociationalism looked to the vast majority. Thus, it was a matter of considerable excitement when, in February 1980, a group of young noncommissioned officers, led by a sports instructor named Desi Bouterse, took over the government. Most likely, the coup was the accidental capstone of a chain of events that history just dropped on Suriname. The events were not entirely random, yet their sequence was so easily alterable that the end product was like a bolt from the blue for everyone—the NCOs included.[22]

What happens with a government that has suddenly fallen into your hands? If all along you had been out to get power, you probably reveal your interests fairly rapidly. But Bouterse and his colleagues did not have many interests to reveal. One of their first acts was to put a big suggestion box on the gates of the military base. They did successfully articulate the public's discontent with the old regime, arresting most of the old leaders and subjecting them, unsuccessfully, to scrutiny for possible acts of corruption. They did try in the beginning to clean up the waste and low productivity of the civil service, they cracked down on street crime, and they purged the military of those officers that had given them the worst trouble.[23] And they did condemn the *apanjaht* character of the old order, promising a wholly new system—one that still has not seen the light of day.[24]

With the big *apanjaht* parties licking their wounds, a few of the radical parties of reimmigrating former students moved in on Bouterse. Thus, after a year or so in which he tried to govern with civilian partners representing only an anti-*apanjaht* general reformism, Bouterse and his men began to talk in a more radical vein.[25] It should be added that Bishop and Bouterse became fast friends in this period.[26]

There are two puzzling ironies in this gradual movement to the left. At each stage, from the first nonaligned government through the three governments that followed, there has been a fairly careful adherence to the principles of consociationalism. Of course, that might be expected given the random draw of talented professionals out of the society. But when one considers that the military itself is heavily Creole, the impulse to display at least token representation must respond to a deep instinct toward consociationalism that cannot be repudiated, even where *apanjaht* politics is abandoned. The second, more puzzling irony is the failure of the small leftist parties to either amalgamate or to build followings among the people. Betty Sedoc Dahlberg, former chancellor of the University of Suriname and now a professor at the University of Florida, has described these groups as having their origins in the Dutch universities. For whatever reason—the influence of their professors, or the intellectual orientation of their leaders—they each acquired somewhat different ideological directions, modeling their vision of an ideal Suriname after such widely different experiments as the Chinese, the Cuban, the Albanian, and the Tanzanian.[27] Like Latin American *caudillos* and their personalist politics, these little bands came back, running separate party lists in elections, getting virtually no popular support, each brilliantly dissecting the society and its ills, but devoting greater attention to dissecting each other.[28] It is probable that Bouterse was in a quandary with all of these small groups coming at him on every side. But he has since learned how to use them to his own advantage, giving them each their turn at the controls and avoiding personal accountability by letting them sink themselves.

By 1982, the public's patience had worn thin. Although the leftist groups had made some headway in awakening class consciousness of some of the poorest elements in the society and bouterse's government had helped them mostly by printing currency and creating work in the military, the popular militias, the secret police, and so on, neither Bouterse nor they were ever able to draw large crowds to their rallies.[29] In both the lower and middle classes loyalty and dependence on the old *apanjaht* parties remained strong. In the fall of 1982 a series of disturbing rallies and marches took place, accompanied by published declarations by a host of Suriname's long-established newspapers, unions, religious and civic groups, calling for a return to democracy. What was especially irritating to Bouterse was that a government rally to greet Maurice Bishop drew far less people than an anti-government demonstration on the same day. Furthermore, Bishop's brief stopover in Suriname was marred by widespread strikes. This campaign aimed at a return to democracy ended December 8, 1982 in the murder of some fifteen of its leaders by Bouterse and his associates.[30] As one of the leaders of the radical parties is reported to have said, "for every execution we ought to have a year of peace." Well, 1983 was a very quiet year in Suriname . . . though only until December.

The Tanzanian-oriented group took the reins from the Cuban-oriented group after the murders, and with Bouterse's apparent blessing it turned to Brazil for economic assistance. But because the Dutch cut all aid to Suriname after the murders, Suriname has been exhausting its supply of foreign exchange. Brazil is in no position to make up for the massive programs the Dutch had going, and thus Suriname's leaders have been scavenging desperately for ways to keep their heads above water. Efforts in the spring of 1983 to woo aid from Cuba while simultaneously courting Brazil were not appreciated by the latter, and Suriname was forced into at least a token repudiation of this flirtation, exiling their best-known Cuba-liners in the military elite.[31]

Thus it was not surprising, even if it was puzzling for the coincidence, that on the very day U.S. troops landed in Grenada, Desi Bouterse appeared on Surinamese television to announce the ouster of most Cuban aid and diplomatic personnel. Was there a tie-in to Grenada? Bouterse may have believed the early rumors alleging that the Cubans were behind the overthrow of Maurice Bishop, and that they may have planned a similar fate for Bouterse, replacing him with an exiled leader.[32] He told his television audience on October twenty-fifth that Suriname's relations with Cuba had become "increasingly unmanageable" in recent

months, "a result both of the turbulent development of these relations...and more especially of the somewhat individual style of the
Cuban Ambassador...."[33]

After the ouster of the Cubans, Bouterse completed his swing to
the right by sending his civilian Tanzanianists to Washington in October for talks with the World Bank and IMF. In December, to try to
balance the budget and win favor at the IMF, Suriname imposed new
taxes on the bauxite workers. The workers went out on a five-week
strike that cost the nation over 25 million dollars in foreign exchange.[34] As strikes go, this was a rather amazing one in that it was,
to all appearances, leaderless. But it was effective in bringing the government to some major concessions. The Tanzanianists were ousted
and blamed by Bouterse for all the problems. In their place is a government composed of promilitary independents and representatives
of the business community and labor unions. Among their responsibilities through the balance of 1984 was the formation of a new constitution. They were also pledged to support the restoration of a free
press and other fundamental freedoms.[35] While the questionable
movement toward a new constitution and some form of democratic
process were activated in mid-1984, and ran, with fits and starts,
through 1985 and into 1986, a civil war began in July 1986. Anti-
Bouterse forces, centering round Corporal Ronnie Brunswijk's "Jungle Commando," challenged the government militarily in the field.
The government responded with force, yet the insurrection has continued. Elections were set for November 1987, but the government
remains as it was—under Bouterse's control.

What about the "received political forms," the Western institutions
that have caused so much concern throughout the Third World? In
many culturally plural societies, like that of Tanzania, a single mass-
based party is seen as a very attractive alternative to Westminister-type,
government-and-opposition systems. As one author has put it, "The
Caribbean has learned how easily men of ability are excluded from the
governing process by the multi-party system in small societies short of
skills.... It has seen how easily the electoral process can be interfered
with, how easily independent newspapers or unions can be undermined,
Parliaments manipulated, dissent ignored."[36] Although it has seen all
this, the Caribbean has also seen more. It has seen how the alternatives,
in Grenada and Suriname, have been stillborn or aborted. What is
viewed, romantically, as the sense of efficiency and solidarity within a
single mass-based party turns out, on closer examination, to be either a
deeply divided and potentially murderous exercise in Leninist debate as
was observed in Grenada, or it is an equally murderous game of musical
chairs as in Suriname that is shamefully wasteful of a small society's
precious skills.

CONCLUSION

What it all comes down to is the fact that the "received political forms," while certainly not above constant adjustment to local needs, are not the central problems in these societies. What are the central problems are trust, tolerance, and cooperation. In short, political civility is what is most needed. This is the failing not only of radical groups that have been seen in recent years, but also the failure of the old elites and their publics. In culturally plural societies civility is not an easy thing to come by. Moreover, it is more demanding there, perhaps, than in more homogenous and well-endowed societies. Furthermore, *apanjaht* machine politics does not especially build solid foundations for it. Yet, the practice of consociationalism has, built within it, the means of its own transcendence. To the extent that party coalitions change from postelection to preelection and then transmutate into internal party balanced-ticketism, the population groups in a plural society overcome their suspicions and alienation, ultimately looking at issues from interests other than ethnic ones. Such a society, obviously, is not "home free" as a result; but it will have come to the point that its cultural inheritance may be a source of strength rather than foreboding.

In the meantime Suriname's radical experiment has run aground, moving inexorably through the familiar cycle of repression, relaxation, unrest, and repression. The November 1987 elections did bring some relief, although there will still be the question of the "Jungle Commando" insurrection. The new civilian government entered 1988 based on the power of the traditional parties and cautious of the military's behind-the-scenes, yet obvious influence. The economy, moreover, was in a serious state of disequilibrium because of the insurrection. Suriname's dialectic, like Grenada's, should be more familiar to readers of Dante than of Marx.

NOTES

1. Gordon K. Lewis, review of Eric Williams, *History of the People of Trinidad and Tobago, Caribbean Studies* 3, 1 (April 1963), p. 104.

2. *The New York Times*, May 16, 1975, p. A4; also J. Daniel O'Flaherty, "Finding Jamaica's Way," *Foreign Policy* 31 (Summer 1978), p. 149; and Irving Kaplan et al., *Area Handbook for Jamaica* (Washington, DC: U.S. Government Printing Office, 1976), pp. 200, 218–21.

3. Jan Knippers Black et al., *Area Handbook for Trinidad and Tobago* (Washington, DC: U.S. Government Printing Office, 1976), pp. 186, 197–98; and Anthony Maingot (member of the commission), personal communication.

4. See Clive Y. Thomas, "State Capitalism in Guyana: An Assessment of Burnham's Cooperative Socialist Republic," in Fitzroy Ambursley and Robin

Cohen, eds., *Crisis in the Caribbean* (New York: Monthly Review, 1983), pp. 40–42.

5. Anthony Payne, Paul Sutton, and Tony Thorndike, *Grenada: Revolution and Invasion* (New York: St. Martins, 1984), pp. 2–16.

6. Payne et al. *Grenada*, pp. 34–39.

7. See M. G. Smith's classic statement in "Social and Cultural Pluralism," *Annals of the New York Academy of Sciences* 83 (1960), reprinted in his collection, *The Plural Society in the British West Indies* (Berkeley, CA: University of California Press, 1965), pp. 75–91.

8. M. G. Smith, "Structure and Crisis in Grenada, 1950–1954," in his *The Plural Society in the British West Indies* (The Hague: Martinus Nijhoff, 1978), pp. 276–79.

9. Edward Dew, *The Difficult Flowering of Surinam: Ethnicity and Politics in a Plural Society* (The Hague: Martinus Nijhoff, 1978), pp. 4–20.

10. *Almanaque Mundial 1983* (Panama: Editorial America, 1982), pp. 295, 308, 360.

11. *Time*, May 30, 1983, p. 17. J. Brandsma estimated at the time of Suriname's independence (1975) that unemployment and underemployment together came to 52 percent of the economically active population (J. Brandsma, "Werkgelegenheid in een Plantagemaatschappij," *Beleid en Maatschappij* [September 1975], p. 239).

12. "Surinam: Between Self-Interest and Development," *Antillan Review* 3, 1 (December 1982/January 1983), p. 35.

13. Albert Gastmann reviews the constitution of the Kingdom of The Netherlands in *The Politics of Suriname and the Netherlands Antilles* (Rio Piedras: University of Puerto Rico, 1968), pp. 109–14.

14. Leo A. Despres, *Cultural Pluralism and Nationalist Politics in British Guiana* (Chicago: Rand McNally, 1967); J. E. Greene, *Race vs. Politics in Guyana: Political Cleavages and Political Mobilization in the 1968 General Election* (Mona, Jamaica: ISER, University of the West Indies, 1974); and Paul Singh, *Guyana: Socialism in a Plural Society* (London: Fabian Society, 1972); all offer detailed accounts of this phenomenon for Guyana. Selwyn Ryan, *Race and Nationalism in Trinidad and Tobago* (Toronto: University of Toronto Press, 1972) and Krishna Bahadoorsingh, *Trinidad Electoral Politics: The Persistence of the Race Factor* (London: Institute of Race Relations, 1968) offer useful illustrations from Trinidad.

15. Payne et al., *Grenada*, pp. 7–8.

16. Dew, *The Difficult Flowering of Surinam*, pp. 59–64.

17. Arend Lijphart, "Consociational Democracy," *World Politics* 21 (January 1969), pp. 207–25.

18. Lijphart, *Democracy in Plural Societies: A Comparative Exploration* (New Haven, CT: Yale University Press, 1977).

19. Dew, chs. 5 and 6.

20. Dew, "Surinam: The Test of Consociationalism," *Plural Societies* 3, 4 (Autumn 1972), pp. 35–36.

21. Percy C. Hintzen and Ralph R. Premdas, "Guyana: Coercion and Control in Political Change," *Journal of Interamerican Studies and World Affairs* 24, 3 (August 1982), pp. 347–50; and Thomas, "State Capitalism," pp. 27–48.

22. Henk Boom, *Staatsgreep in Suriname: De Opstand van de Sergeanten op de Voet Gevolgd* (Utrecht: Veen, 1982).

23. Dew, "Suriname," in Jack W. Hopkins, ed., *Latin America and Caribbean Contemporary Record*, Vol I: 1981–82 (New York: Holmes & Meier, 1983), pp. 355–56.

24. Dew, "Suriname Tar Baby: The Signature of Terror," *Caribbean Review* 12, 1 (Winter 1983), p. 4.

25. Dew, "Suriname Tar Baby."

26. Dew, "Suriname Tar Baby," p. 6.

27. Betty Sedoc-Dahlberg, *Surinaamse Studenten in Nederland: Een Onderzoek Rond de Problematiek van de Toekomstige Intellectueel Kadervorming in Suriname* (Amsterdam: University of Amsterdam, 1971), pp. 121–25; and "Refugees from Suriname," *Refuge* 3, 3 (March 1984), pp. 5–10.

28. Dew, "The Year of the Sergants," *Caribbean Review* 9, 2 (Spring 1980), pp. 7, 46. See also Sandew Hira, "Class Formation and Class Struggle in Suriname," in Ambursley and Cohen, *Crisis in the Caribbean*, 181–83.

29. Dew, "Suriname–1982," in Hopkins, *Latin America* Vol II: 1982–83.

30. Dew, "Suriname Tar Baby," pp. 4–6.

31. *Algemeen Dagblad* (Amsterdam), June 11, 1983. On the Brazilian tie, see *Latin American Weekly Report*, October 21, 1983, p. 4.

32. *Miami Herald*, November 29, 1983, p. A3; *NRC Handelsblad* (Rotterdam), October 26, 1983; and *Latin American Regional Reports-Caribbean*, November 4, 1983, p. 6.

33. *Miami Herald*, November 29, 1983, p. A5.

34. *NRC-Handelsblad*, December 22, 23, 28, 30, 1983, and January 7, 1984.

35. *NRC-Handelsblad*, January 20, 23, 24, 25, 27, 30; and February 1, 3, 1984.

36. "In Defense of Democracy," *Caribbean and West Indies Chronicle* 99 (April/May 1983), p. 3.

8
Haiti: The Duvaliers and Beyond
Aaron Segal

INTRODUCTION

The 29-year Duvalier family dynasty (1957–1986) ruled Haiti longer than any other regime in its troubled history.[1] Through massive coercion and cooptation, the Duvaliers imposed a heavy-handed form of stability on a nation known for its political and social unrest.

Haiti, since the Grenadan invasion in 1983, has undergone profound political changes, which in part will be examined in this chapter. This essay also reflects what the Duvaliers, father and son, have meant to Haiti and what impact this will have on the nation's future development. Although there were important differences in political styles between "Papa Doc" François Duvalier (1907–1971) and his son Jean-Claude (1952–), or "Baby Doc," the continuities were more important. While the definitive history of this period remains to be written and will require historical distance, it is nevertheless possible to examine the impact of the Duvaliers on Haiti.

THE HAITIAN ECONOMY UNDER THE DUVALIERS

During the Duvalier reign the economic situation of most Haitians deteriorated by most acceptable standards—per capita income, nutrition, infant mortality, literacy, and access to health care.[2] Haitians experienced what Clifford Geertz in his study of Indonesia has called "immiseration" or steadily eroding or falling standards of living.[3] The primary cause was an economy with a rate of per capita economic growth (1.1 percent from 1965 to 1983) nearly equal to net annual population increase (1.6

percent 1975–1984). The economic pie got small for most Haitians during the Duvalier reign and its allocation was largely determined by politics, cronyism and nepotism. What little economic growth that occurred was appropriated by the regime and its friends.

How did Haitians cope with immiseration in all its various forms? Rural Haitians continued to divide plots of land which were already too small. They also postponed their first marital or consensual union, stripped the eroded hills of firewood, and, to survive, switched from cash to food crops. Another form of rural adaptation was out-migration directed principally at the primary city of Port-au-Prince. Between 1960 and 1980 the percentage of urban Haitians living in the capital rose from 42 to 56 percent as the Duvaliers concentrated jobs, favors, and investment in a single city. During the period 1965–1984 the urban population as a percentage of the Haitian total increased from 18 to 27 percent.[4] An estimated 800,000 emigrated to the United States, Canada, the Bahamas, the Dominican Republic, France, Africa, French Guiana, and Venezuela.[5] Remittances from Haitians working abroad were estimated at $100 million a year during the 1980s. Put another way, each Haitian employed overseas who sent money home supported four persons on the island.[6]

Urbanization and massive internal migration had similar roots. Urbanization as a result of a strong current of internal migration had as its mirror image an exodus of skilled professionals who fled Haiti to escape the violence of a regime that resented their status, wealth, position and, under Papa Doc, their race (i.e., mulatto). Throughout the Duvalier years Haiti saw many of its most talented people leave for new lives in Canada, the United States, and France.[7]

Internal migration and much of the illegal emigration cut across all sectors of Haitian society. It was prompted by a combination of immiseration, political intimidation by Duvalier-appointed rural bosses and their thugs (the Tonton Macoute), and informal networks that facilitated travel. Thus peasants from the periodically drought-stricken Northeast set sail for the Bahamas and Florida; peasants from Central Haiti walked to sugarcane harvesting jobs in the Dominican Republic; and peasants in the South and throughout the country moved to Port-au-Prince.[8]

Population movement, which was triggered by negative economic and political realities, nevertheless prompted a significant development in Haiti's social structure. The Haitian diaspora with its social mobility, remittances, exile politics and use of Creole, the language of dissent, became a new dynamic force in society and began to alter values and beliefs. The historic dominance of the brown elite (i.e., mulatto) at the expense of blacks, was altered by Duvalier Sr. who promoted blacks. The son, however, married into a prominent brown family, and race relations on the surface became less tense. There was also extensive black-brown mixing among the diaspora.[9] Massive urbanization and emigration for the first time mixed Haitians from all parts of the country and regional differences began to diminish among the expatriates. At the same time, however, the Duvalier practice of concentrating resources in the capital and discriminating against the other major cities and towns *increased* regional sentiment, especially in Cap Haitien and the North.

Why did the economy fail to develop during the Duvalier dynasty? One factor was the amassing by the Duvaliers of a personal family fortune banked overseas and never invested in Haiti. They used a variety of special taxes—cement, sugar, tobacco—to enrich themselves and to take capital out of Haiti. While not as ostentatious as former Philippine President Ferdinand Marcos, the Duvalier family's total assets abroad have been estimated at perhaps $200 million.[10] Unlike former dictator Rafael Trujillo of the Dominican Republic (1930–1962) the Duvaliers were reluctant to invest at home, whether in hotels, sugar estates, casinos, or other enterprises. Instead they effectively skimmed an annual 1–2 percent from the Haitian Gross Domestic Product (GDP). The net effect was to suppress domestic savings and investment.

Lack of economic growth has more basic causes than Duvalier family corruption. Between 1965 and 1973 agricultural production fell –0.3 percent; between 1973 and 1983 it increased by 0.7 percent. Haitian farmers experienced relentless soil erosion and deforestation, a deterioration of roads and all other rural services, regressive taxation and harsh local authority, and arbitrarily set coffee prices. Some reacted by migrating to Port-au-Prince or the Dominican Republic; others endured while their output stagnated. The most detrimental aspect of Duvalier rule was the massive disincentive for rural output. These more than offset the symbolic changes that encouraged *Voudon* religious practices and sought to identify Papa Doc, a one-time student of ethnography, with Haitian folk beliefs.

Why were the Duvaliers, father and son, so insensitive to the plight of peasants who provided their economic wherewithal and some of their political support? Almost certainly they believed that the peasants would and could endure great suffering as they have throughout Haitian history. The manipulation of resources for urban elites was essential to the retention of power and required the redirection of both public services and revenue. Patronage, too, had its price and the Tonton Macoutes, who ensured rural order, had to be rewarded for service rendered.

Loyalty to the regime was based on personalism. There was no ideological commitment and the government's legitimacy rested on force, not consent. Papa Doc was a masterful manipulator of folk beliefs and symbols but his son, city-raised and foreign-bred, was never at ease with his countrymen. Exploitation of the peasantry was consistent with Haitian history and political culture and there were few who dared to tell the Duvaliers that enough could become too much.

Despite the Duvaliers, the tiny economy grew from a GDP of $350 million in 1965 to $1,630 million in 1983. The dynamic element was industry, primarily assembly plants producing items such as baseballs and garments for export. Industrial production grew by 4.8 percent from 1965 to 1973 and by 4.5 percent from 1973 to 1984. Assembly plants generated 65,000 new jobs in Port-au-Prince, salvaged the balance of payments from rising oil prices and coffee slumps, and produced a new Haitian managerial group.[11] Not surprisingly, the traditionally minded Duvaliers demonstrated little interest in assembly plants in which they did not invest. Their primary concerns were the more established import-substitution industries of tobacco, cement, and beer, which they regarded as part of their patrimony.

There was little else to provide economic hope. Bauxite mining by Reynolds Aluminum proved uneconomic because of the slump in world market prices during the 1970s. While Haitian crafts and especially primitive painting began to find markets abroad, tourists and travel agencies neglected a country with a reputation for *Acquired Immune Deficiency Syndrome* (AIDS), dictatorship, and hard-to-reach beaches. The Duvaliers throughout their reign refused to diversify the economy, create a favorable climate for domestic and foreign private sector investment, or halt the degradation of a crumbling infrastructure. They were content to skim the economy and allow their cronies to do the same. The Duvalier income was stolen primarily from earnings generated by export crops grown by peasants and the cigarettes, matches, beer, and other basic products sold by monopolistic local industries. Attempts to skim the assembly plants were thwarted by stern warnings that this would result in their leaving and relocating elsewhere. The Haitian-American Chamber of Commerce proved a more effective lobbyist than fragmented rural interests.

The figures clearly reveal the persistent neglect of agriculture. A contributing factor was the emigration of Haiti's most qualified agronomists, the absence of meaningful agricultural research, and the nonexistence of agricultural extension services. Cereal imports rose from 83,000 metric tons in 1974 to 209,000 metric tons in 1983 of which 90,000 tons were provided through food aid. The average index of food production per capita fell from 100 in 1974–1976 to 90 in 1981–1983. More and more Haitians had less and less to eat. Imported food aid kept hundreds of thousands of people alive while more and more foreign exchange in the 1970s was diverted to pay for higher-cost imports of fuel. Daily calorie intake per capita in 1983 was estimated at 1,887 or 83 percent of normal requirements. Marginal malnutrition became a fact of life and death.

CORRUPTION AND A DEPENDENT ECONOMY

The Duvaliers ran the government as a "kleptocracy." Except for the Central Bank, which struggled to maintain a minimum of integrity and kept the Haitian currency tied to the U.S. dollar, most government and parastatal agencies were patronage driven. Total government spending as a percentage of GDP rose from 14.5 percent in 1972 to 18.5 percent in 1982, but most of this went into salaries and kickbacks. Frequent changes of ministers and senior civil servants was a favorite device of Duvalier father and son to ensure control. The price in terms of viable economic planning or ministerial continuity was high. The government had little inclination to provide any services in rural areas and was adept only at tax collection. The Duvaliers neglected secondary cities and towns, and chose to use government revenues to reward supporters in the capital. Although official figures show increases in primary and secondary school enrollment from 1965 to 1982 such advances were achieved largely through the growing network of Catholic and Protestant schools. External donors, often in combination with local groups, provided health, education, and other services which the Haitian government failed to offer. Those donors who attempted to work with the government experienced intense frustration at its lack of organization and the propensity to use funds for its own purposes.[12]

An unexpected by-product of this reign of immiseration was forced responsibility. Papa Doc practiced an isolationist foreign policy and lost interest in foreign aid after it was no longer available on his terms. Baby Doc allowed his entourage to solicit external public and private capital but on a short leash. Although Haiti during the 1980s encountered serious balance of payments problems it did not resort to extensive external borrowing, nor was it particularly attractive to lenders. Haiti in 1984 owed $494 million, and was paying 5.6 percent of its exports in the form of long-term debt service, a modest figure. A trickle of foreign private investment and about $130 million a year in official development aid during the 1980s, mostly from the United States, Canada, France, and the World Bank, kept the economy afloat. External capital flows were the primary source of investment, allowed hundreds and thousands of Haitians to be fed and funded most development projects. Official aid was calculated at 7.5 percent of GNP in 1984.

This story of a largely stagnant economy with a highly skewed distribution of income and a repressed peasant majority does not explain how the Duvaliers were able to stay in power. Moreover, it misses the nature of the political system which they created and is their most enduring legacy.

PAPA DOC TO BABY DOC

Papa Doc combined Black Power populism with a ruthless monopoly of power to break the hold of the brown elites. He organized and mobilized available power groups—taxi drivers, Voudon priests and priestesses, Black Power intellectuals, and others. He disarmed the army, switched senior officers, and created a rural-urban personal militia—the Tonton Macoutes. He cultivated local notables, guaranteed their tax-collecting authority, and relied on massive personal patronage to gain support.[13]

The external world for Papa Doc was implacably hostile and to be kept at a distance so that Haiti would not be vulnerable. He provided sanctuary for opponents of the government of the Dominican Republic and denounced Fidel Castro. Foreign policy was isolationist. External aid from bilateral and multilateral sources largely evaporated during his tenure. The shrinking economy became a principal tool of intimidation in Papa Doc's pursuit of power. Supporters prospered while others languished.

His most lasting contribution was to promote his own generation of educated black professionals to positions of power and influence. While the black-brown divisions persisted, Papa Doc espoused Black Power, symbolically changed the colors of the national flag, and confirmed that blacks were preferred for positions of authority.

Papa Doc clashed with the Catholic church, the decimated trade union movement, the U.S. government, and the remnants of an internal opposition. His tactics of defiance, coercion, prearranged and "populist" demonstrations cowed much of the internal opposition. The alternatives were torture and prison or voluntary exile. The decision of the dying father to designate his son as "President for Life" at age nineteen was hailed by sycophants and denounced by exiles. The internal opposition by 1971 was largely intimidated or coopted.

Although Papa Doc established an official mass party it was little more than a parade of paid followers. Lacking in personal charisma Papa Doc excelled in palace intrigue, aided by his wife Simone and their respective families. The proposed "new city" of Duvalierville proved an expensive fiasco. The regime had no economic ideology nor competence. It was dependent on a private sector of urban merchants which it could intimidate but not eliminate. Government became a giant patronage mechanism controlled directly from the Presidential Palace. Most government employees were converted into courtiers.

The strength of Papa Doc was his understanding of rural attitudes and practices based on his study of ethnography and his experience as a physician.[14] He embraced some of the symbols of rural life (although not the official use of Creole), confronted the unpopular brown businessmen, named "sons" of the people to prominent jobs, and defied ungrateful foreign devils. It was showmanship in the midst of poverty but it did produce followers.

Jean-Claude became president at age nineteen; his playboy image, a penchant for fast cars and expensive toys, an erratic education provided mostly by tutors, and very little experience did not present a solid foundation for the country's future. During his first years in office his mother Simone and a palace cabal tried to run the country in the style and spirit of his father. His marriage to Michele Bennett, divorcee and scion of a wealthy mulatto business family of Jamaican origins, prompted an intense palace wife versus daughter-in-law struggle for power and influence. The lavish marriage was to symbolize a new black-brown reconciliation at the highest level but it alienated many of the Black Power disciples of Papa Doc. The Bennett marriage offended as many mulattoes as it pleased and revived fears of mulatto domination among black urban workers and slum dwellers. Jean-Claude Duvalier was never able to construct a stable and legitimate power base during his fourteen years in office. He gave the impression of indecisiveness and was uninterested in public affairs. He lived in seclusion, failed to cultivate the rural notables who had supported his father and was clearly uncomfortable in public settings and rural milieus. He was no man of the people. His sporadic efforts to nominate technocrats to senior posts were followed by quick dismissals and reshuffles when they raised issues of corruption and accountability. Jean-Claude also neglected the army, cut its budget, dismissed senior officers, and kept it partly disarmed.[15] The Tonton Macoute, however, were not strengthened as an alternative to the military.

While Papa Doc wielded many sticks and a few carrots, Baby Doc lacked a consistent presidential style. There were periods of openness, with encouragement for foreign investment and foreign aid and officially tolerated internal dissent followed by periods of external isolation and internal crackdowns. The handling of Creole language policy is an example.[16] Although Creole was allowed on private radio stations, these same stations were periodically closed for alleged dissent. Creole was authorized at the presidential level for use in the elementary schools but promoters of its use were then dismissed from government posts. It was alleged that brown elites close to the presidential family insisted that Creole be discouraged but it was never clear what were the views of the president.

Lacking a firm military, political party, social class or other power base the regime came to rely on personal manipulation and the alternation of periods of repression and openness. Ostentation substituted for meaningful politics. A color television channel and Miss Haiti beauty contests constantly reminded Haitians of a presidential style that was increasingly intolerable. This ostentation was centered on Port-au-Prince with its wealthy neighborhoods surrounded by growing squalor and destitution. Fearing political unrest in provincial cities where regional sentiments continued, the regime concentrated what little development that took place in the capital. It even allowed oil supplied by Mexico and Venezuela at discount prices during the 1970s to be resold at higher prices to South Africa with the revenue going back into presidential coffers.

The pluralistic forces and institutions that had been so ruthlessly suppressed or brutally coopted by Papa Doc reemerged to challenge his son. The Catholic church stripped of many of its foreign senior clergy who were expelled by Papa Doc, became eventually a stronger indigenous body. Strengthened by support from Rome, the spread of new social doctrines such as liberation theology, and a Papal visit in 1983 which indirectly chastised the Duvaliers, the Catholic church used its radio, its printing presses, and its schools and seminaries to pressure the regime. The loosely organized National Council of Protestant Churches promoted the use of Creole on the radio and in the schools and used its growing numbers to press for change. Trade unions both coopted and repressed in the 1960s, began to organize during the late 1970s in assembly plants and other industries. Unions were again repressed but resisted cooptation. The active voice of the Haitian diaspora community with its newspapers and radio stations abroad began to serve as a restraint on total repression.

THE FALL OF THE DUVALIERS

The story of the decline and fall of the Duvaliers remains to be told in detail. However it has many precedents in 180 years of Haitian history. Despotic Haitian leaders surrounded by their sycophants, have periodically lost legitimacy, authority, and finally control. As in February 1987, the end has often been marked by "mobocracy" with the urban masses taking to the streets and to the Palace to overthrow a hated ruler. Some despots have been lynched by the mobs while others have been saved by foreign intervention and sent into exile, as was Baby Doc. Again in 1987 the military and the hired thugs refused to risk their lives against the enraged mob in order to defend the fallen leader. History had in form if not in substance repeated itself in Haiti.

The decline of the Duvaliers had many causal factors. Economic decline combined with the conspicuous consumption and corruption among the ruling elite were important. The courting of well-known brown elites served to destroy what little legitimacy remained among the black population. The corruption, mishandling of and profiteering from imported food supplies enraged many city dwellers, especially on the margins of Port-au-Prince where food distribution often broke down. An eruption of swine fever resulted in the required destruction of the favorite animal protein of most Haitians and was interpreted as an evil omen. The military were underpaid, underarmed, ridiculed, and neglected. The Tonton Macoutes were arbitrary, brutal, hated, ill-disciplined, and loyal to no one. The churches, the radio stations, the battered trade unions, had shown that the government could be attacked.

The external factor was significant but not vital in the decline and fall. Foreign aid from all sources had stabilized in the early 1980s and was insufficient to restore economic growth. The Reagan administration in 1981–1982 had pressured Haiti to allow the U.S. Navy to patrol close to Haitian waters to reduce the outflow of boat people. Prior to 1985–1986 the consensus was that Washington preferred a "stable" Haiti under the Duvaliers rather than risk turmoil. Canada and France, the other major bilateral donors, appeared to agree. A hardcore of mostly liberal Democrat congressmen challenged U.S. aid to Haiti on the grounds of human rights' violations, but made little headway. The nonviolent removal of President Marcos in the Philippines in January 1986 encouraged Haitian exiles, U.S., and other foreign opponents of the Duvaliers, as well as internal opposition to resist and prompted the Reagan administration to reconsider its Haitian policy. In the fall of 1986 Washington publicly denounced Haitian human rights violations, made further economic aid to Haiti conditional on internal changes, and indicated that the United States would not act to keep Duvalier in power. The final step was to intercede as mediator to arrange with France a safe exile. External actors served to accelerate the decline and fall but it was essentially brought about from within.

AFTER THE FALL

Two Duvaliers and 29 years of a family dynasty brought many changes in Haiti. The future of Haiti will in large measure be determined by changes already set in motion. Internationally, Haiti has become part of the U.S. sphere of influence in the Caribbean. French language, culture, business, and trade have declined and no longer represent a major force. Quebec has provided aid, tourists, and a home for Haitian émigrés, but is not an alternative to the U.S. influence. Ironically the Duvaliers' defiance of the United States served only to increase the size of the diaspora there. Haitians remain passionately devoted to independence but in the post-Duvalier period they have again become effectively dependent on the United States for trade, aid, and, most importantly, external culture.

A second major international trend is the permanent impact of the diaspora. Unlikely to return permanently to Haiti in large numbers, the diaspora, including the first generation born abroad, are a source of remittances, visitors, investment capital, skills, criticism, and contacts. New bonds are being formed between post-Duvalier Haiti and the diaspora which are likely to characterize all future Haitian regimes. The Duvaliers sought to isolate the diaspora and taxed Haitians who traveled abroad, squeezed remittances, and exploited family ties. Future Haitian regimes will need to learn how to cultivate the diaspora by building reciprocal ties.

Internally, the most important trend for the future is the depth and spread of pluralism. The Catholic and Protestant churches, the trade unions, and other organizations learned how to express dissent during those 29 years. The enormous number of sycophants and camp followers did not overwhelm the few courageous voices who risked prison and exile. The radio stations in Creole became vital sources of dissent in a society where literacy is a luxury. Future prospects for a nonauthoritarian Haiti depend more on these channels being kept open than on formal political parties, parliaments, or constitutions. Should the pluralist, religious, and other elements in Haitian society develop their contacts with diaspora sympathizers, the social basis for dissent will be strengthened. Any Haitian government that arrests a journalist in Port-au-Prince will be aware that within a few hours this news will be broadcast in New York and Miami.

Related to the emergence and consolidation of political pluralism is the development of a national social conscience. Historian Jean-Price Mars in this writings and teaching instilled in Haitians a sense of their Africanness and its embodiment in Haitian culture and values.[17] He helped them to recognize that rather than being "Black Frenchmen" they were Haitians proud of their African origins. Papa Doc distorted those teachings to promote a racially based black power nationalism which served to divide. What is gradually emerging, with the churches taking the lead, is a social doctrine which emphasizes Africanness in a Haitian context that recognizes responsibility for the welfare of all members of the society. Relying on Creole which is spoken and understood by all Haitians, the emphasis is on grassroots activities that will harness popular initiative and the profound Haitian values of social cooperation. The corollary is that the resources of the Haitian government are extremely limited and that much development will have to come from below rather than the capital.

The initial post-Duvalier period has been understandably confusing. A triumvirate headed by General Henri Namphy has ruled with a promise to hand over power to elected politicians. The Tonton Macoutes have been dissolved with some violence while demands to try Duvalier supporters persist. There has been a proliferation of political parties, independent newspapers and radio stations, and public dissent. The economy continues to deteriorate. The poorly equipped army maintains an uneasy peace. Capital flees, foreign investors are wary, tourists stay away, and poverty deepens. The Duvaliers enjoy a comfortable exile in the South of France while the Haitian government hopes to go to court to repatriate the family fortune.[18]

The interim government has done little to confront the two most serious threats to Haiti: population increase and soil erosion. The modest family planning program begun with external aid under Baby Doc does not reach most rural Haitians.[19] The need is imperative for a rural combined maternal health-family planning program to help to further slow down a birthrate that has begun to decline. Massive emigration in the 1990s as a partial solution to problems is dependent on the policies of the Dominican Republic, the United States, Bahamian, and other governments and cannot be relied on. Slowing down the birthrate while improving health services is currently beyond the resources and organizational capabilities of this or future Haitian governments. Failure to slow down the birthrate means malnutrition, hunger, and possibly famine.

Several centuries of deforestation has converted much of Haiti into gullies and ravines and permanently destroyed much of its arable land.[20] The Duvaliers were uninterested in the problem, fearing perhaps that a resort to rural forced labor to halt deforestation would be extremely unpopular. Historically, Haitian governments have preferred to avoid imposing forced labor in the rural areas so as not to evoke memories of slavery. Although the government agreed to small-scale experiments in recent years with fast-growing leucania and other trees, these projects were undertaken by nonprofit groups with external aid.[21] A national reforestation campaign, perhaps with external aid for cash wages, is imperative if what remains of arable Haiti is to be saved. It is difficult to see where the internal or external initiative will come from or the organization.

The economic future of Haiti is daunting at best and grim if nothing is done about population increase and soil erosion. There is scope for expansion of assembly plants based on the cheapest labor in the Caribbean, for increased agricultural production and export diversification, and for a revival of the tourist industry, particularly cruise ships. The prerequisites include political stability, capital inflows, and administrative improvement among others.

The political future is perhaps less uncertain. Historically Haiti has gravitated towards personalist, authoritarian rule based on coercive power and cooption. Lacking an electoral role, electoral process, or national political institutions, it is doubtful that a fragmentary, inconclusive election will produce a government capable of governing. Strongman rule need not be despotic if the churches, trade unions, technocrats, politicized diaspora, and other elements insist on pluralism and opposition. The alternatives need not be dictatorship or mobocracy; semiauthoritarianism with effective constraints may be the best to which Haiti can realistically aspire. Haiti has never been able to harness its deep national cultural identity to working, accepted political institutions. The post-Duvalier era provides another chance to bridge the gap between elite and masses. Rather than political elites and multiple parties and elections to bridge the gap it may be a combination of a strongman leader constrained by the Catholic and Protestant churches, the radio stations, the vocal diaspora, and other countervailing forces.

NOTES

1. Robert Debs Heinl, Jr. and Nancy Gordon Heinl, *Written in Blood: The Story of the Haitian People 1792–1971* (Boston: Houghton Mifflin, 1978).

2. All economic data in this chapter are from the World Bank, *World Development Report 1986* (Washington, DC, 1986). The Haitian Institute of Statistics and the Central Bank have struggled over the years against enormous obstacles to provide economic data which is subject to a high margin of error.

3. Clifford Geertz, *Interpretation of Cultures* (New York: Basic Books, 1973).

4. Uli Locher, "Migration in Haiti," in Charles R. Foster and Albert Valdman, eds., *Haiti—Today and Tomorrow: An Interdisciplinary Study*, (Lanham, MD: University Press of America, 1984). This volume is an excellent social science survey of contemporary Haiti.

5. Alex Stepick, "The Haitian Exodus," in *The Caribbean Exodus*, ed. Barry B. Levine (New York: Praeger, 1986), pp. 131–52. Figures on Haitian emigration vary considerably. An excellent source is Robert Lawless, *Bibliography on Haiti: English and Creole Items*, Paper No. 6, Center for Latin American Studies, University of Florida, Gainesville, 1985.

6. Aaron Segal and Brian Weinstein, *Haiti: Political Failures, Cultural Successes* (New York: Praeger, 1984), p. 124.

7. Stepick, "The Haitian Exodus." See also Michel Laguerre, *American Odyssey: Haitians in New York City* (Ithaca, NY: Cornell, 1984).

8. Locher, "Migration in Haiti"; Stepick, "The Haitian Exodus."

9. David Nicholls, *From Dessalines to Duvalier: Race, Color and National Independence in Haiti* (Cambridge: Cambridge University Press, 1979). This is the definitive historical study of race relations in Haiti.

10. Segal and Weinstein, *Haiti: Political Failures*, p. 84.

11. Joseph Grunwald and Kenneth Flamm, *The Global Factory: Foreign Assembly in International Trade* (Washington, DC: Brookings Institution, 1985), pp. 180–205.

12. Segal and Weinstein, *Haiti: Political Failures*, pp. 116–23.

13. The political style of President François Duvalier is discussed in Heinl and Heinl, *Written in Blood*, and Segal and Weinstein, *Haiti: Political Failures*.

14. Remy Bastien and Harold Courlander, *Religion and Politics in Haiti* (Washington, DC: Institute for Cross-Cultural Research, 1966).

15. Kern Delince, *Armeé et politique en Haiti* (Paris: L'Harmattan, 1979), is an

informed account by an ex-officer. Heinl and Heinl, *Written in Blood* has a detailed analysis of the military up to 1971.

16. Albert Valdman, "The Linguistic Situation of Haiti," in Foster and Valdman, eds., *Haiti—Today and Tomorrow*, pp. 77–100.

17. Jean Price-Mars, *So Spoke the Uncle* (Washington, DC: Three Continents, 1983). English translation of the highly influential study first published in French in 1928.

18. New York *Times*, February 7, 1987, p. A5 carries an analysis of the first year after the overthrow of Duvalier.

19. James Allman and John May, "Fertility, Mortality, Migration and Family Planning in Haiti," *Population Studies* 33 (1982):505–21.

20. Georges Anglade, *L'espace Haitien* (Montreal: Edition des Alizes, 1981).

21. Gerald F. Murray, "The Wood Tree as a Peasant Cash-Crop: An Anthropological Strategy for the Domestication of Energy," in Foster and Valdman, eds., *Haiti—Today and Tomorrow*, pp. 141–60.

9
The April 1986 Elections in the Dominican Republic
G. Pope Atkins

On May 16, 1986, some 2.2 million Dominican voters went to the polls to select their elective officials for president, vice president and both houses of congress. Following an unsuccessful challenge by one of the major candidates to the validity of the elections, the preliminary vote count was completed. Seventy-eight-year-old Joaquín Balaguer, active in Dominican politics since the 1920s and president of the republic from 1966 to 1978, won the presidency and was inaugurated on August 16, 1986.

The elections were notable for a number of reasons. They were the sixth to be held in an unbroken quadrennial series that began in 1966 and served to reinforce the Dominican Republic's evolving democracy. While some violence occurred during the campaign and on election day, the general political atmosphere was peaceful given the intense nature of the process. Despite serious national problems, the campaign emphasized personalities rather than issues. A new "unitary ballot" discouraged voter fraud, encouraged party alliances, and deemphasized the need for many candidates to campaign. Of particular importance, the appointment of a distinguished citizens' Advisory Commission to oversee the elections had the salutary consequence of ensuring an honest and peaceful outcome. In more general terms, the elections signaled a political transition period as the parties and their leaders were open to realignment, possibly in fundamental ways.[1]

THE POLITICAL SYSTEM

The May 1986 elections indicated that the democratic process was alive and well in the Dominican Republic—an important factor in the

Caribbean, especially in the aftermath of Grenada in October 1983. Though problems related to debt management existed in the Dominican Republic from 1983 to 1986, the country was not wracked by revolutionary upheaval, nor was there a military coup, reflecting a growing maturity on the part of democratic institutions. The Dominican Republic, in certain respects, has already gone through many of the trials and tribulations of revolution and counterrevolution confronting many states in the region. In this light, it can be held up as an example of democratic evolution.

The Dominican Republic has established a representative democratic system despite a tumultuous history, the poverty of most of its people, and difficult international economic relationships. Dominican democracy is even more remarkable when one considers that it followed a long sequence of alternating dictatorships, internal chaos, and foreign interventions. Politics today remain noninstitutionalized and personalist, although evidence suggests the possibility of changes in these dimensions. In sum, Dominican democracy is impressive because it seems to have developed against serious odds; but the system as a whole is under stress.

The entire Dominican experience prior to 1966 ran counter to any kind of open and freely competitive political tradition.[2] Spain's first American colony served as a base for subsequent expansion, but by the mid-sixteenth century had become a poverty-ridden and neglected appendage of the Spanish-American empire. Spanish rule was based on harsh political authoritarianism, African slavery, economic exploitation, and a rigid social structure. Dominican nationalists ousted Spain in 1821 after almost 330 years of colonialism; but the following year, neighboring Haiti—independent since 1804 when black slaves successfully revolted against their French masters—invaded the Dominican Republic and ruled for 22 years. Dominicans ejected the Haitians in 1844 and proclaimed a Republic for a second time.

For the remainder of the nineteenth century and into the twentieth, Dominican presidents by and large were a succession of military men presiding over corrupt and violent regimes. This hardly generated a viable sense of purpose among competing strongmen, ultimately resulting in foreign involvement. While the Haitians attempted numerous unsuccessful invasions, Spain accepted a Dominican government's invitation to resume a short-lived colonial rule in the 1860s. A treaty of annexation was negotiated with the United States in 1870, but the U.S. Senate refused to consent. Ultimately, internal chaos led to direct U.S. administration of the most important aspects of the Dominican economy, beginning in 1905; and in 1914 to direct U.S. supervision of elections. Further political strife culminated with U.S. military intervention from 1916 to 1924.

United States occupation of the Dominican Republic under a military government resulted in numerous infrastructure improvements, but little was achieved in the way of enforced political development. The United States organized and trained a centralized force that was later converted into the Dominican Army. Then in 1924, after supervising national elections and overseeing the inauguration of a civilian president, U.S. military forces departed. U.S. intentions that the Dominican armed service would protect constitutional government, however, were frustrated six years later when, in the context of the 1930 elections, General Rafaél Leónidas Trujillo Molina used his position as head of the Army to overthrow the president and maneuver himself into power.

Trujillo established an absolute dictatorship and ruled for 31 years. He dominated all political and economic aspects of the country and built a thoroughgoing political and financial empire. His personalist leadership involved astuteness and skill, combined with megalomania, greed, and brutality. Trujillo controlled the armed forces (which were his primary basis of power), the church, and communications media. His official political party was the only one allowed for most of his dictatorship and interest associations were beholden to him. Trujillo's power waned in the late 1950s as he faced a declining economy, domestic dissatisfaction, exile invasions, and worsening relations with the United States. This was not helped by his complicity in an unsuccessful attempt in 1960 to assassinate the president of Venezuela and the subsequent Organization of American States (OAS) sanctions. On May 31, 1961, a group of Trujillo's countrymen, with varying motives, assassinated the dictator.

The Dominican Republic passed through a difficult five-year post-Trujillo period from 1961 to 1966 as it moved from dictatorship to nascent democracy. During this time, the United States and the OAS were active in guiding the nation's political direction. Dominicans were governed by an interim president who was forced to resign, a Council of State, an elected president who was overthrown by the armed forces, and another Council of State that evolved into a government whose overthrow precipitated civil war. The United States intervened militarily in April 1965, with a force that was converted into the Inter-American Peace Force. Subsequently a provisional government was established and elections held in 1966. In that year, a president was inaugurated and foreign troops withdrawn.

Politics during the two decades beginning in 1966 may be viewed as a single evolving period directly leading to the situation in which the 1986 campaign and elections took place. Many of the leading political personalities and issues have remained relatively constant, even as the Dominican political system has changed.[3]

Joaquin Balaguer was president of the Dominican Republic for twelve years, from 1966 to 1978. Governing imperiously behind a democratic facade, Balaguer presided over a period of increasing peace and prosperity. He coopted the political opposition as well as repressed it. The state-run sector of the economy expanded, and patronage and corruption reached new heights. Particularly notable was the fact that Balaguer maintained control over the armed forces through a combined process of patronage and power balancing. In the 1978 elections, a military faction attempted a coup on election night when it became apparent that Balaguer was losing. The combined outrage of the Dominican electorate, the Venezuelan government, and the Carter administration in Washington forced a continuation of the vote counting; Balaguer's presidency thus came to an end.

Two successive presidents were elected carrying the standard of the Dominican Revolutionary party (PRD). President Silvestre Antonio Guzmán (1978–1982) was sensitive to questions of social justice and his government was respectful of civil rights. He sought to revitalize agriculture and diversify the economy into light industry while encouraging foreign investment and tourism and expanding exports. A number of important infrastructure projects were realized. But economic difficulties, especially falling commodity export prices and high imported petroleum costs, disallowed as forceful an approach to social reform as Guzmán had promised, and the general economic growth rate declined. The president kept the armed forces under control through regular reassignments, forced retirements, and promotion of officers loyal to him and the PRD.

In a surprise development, President Guzmán committed suicide toward the end of his term in July 1982. Vice President Jacobo Majluta served as interim president until newly elected Salvador Jorge Blanco was inaugurated.

President Jorge Blanco, elected in 1982 for a four-year term, campaigned on the theme of "economic democracy"; but in his inaugural address he declared the country to be "financially bankrupt." Like Guzmán, he governed democratically. Economic conditions, however, became even more severe until the president finally adopted an austerity program that further delayed the long-promised reforms. Austerity led to "food riots" in spring 1984. The situation stabilized and by early 1986 the country appeared calm. International Monetary Fund (IMF) requirements had been met for a standby agreement and the external debt had been renegotiated with international commercial banks. A high political cost, however, had been paid. Jorge Blanco continued Guzmán's techniques for controlling the armed forces, applying them even more intensely. He retired dozens of generals and promoted loyalists; budget denials decreased their political power, as well as their military efficiency. By the election of 1986, Blanco had helped further democratize the country, though personalism remained an important force.

THE POLITICAL PARTIES

Thirteen of the fifteen officially recognized political parties competed in the 1986 elections.[4] However, the presidential race was between two men and their primary party organizations: Jacobo Majluta, age 52, of the broadly based Dominican Revolutionary party (PRD) as well as his personalist Structural party (LE); and conservative former president, Joaquin Balaguer, age 78, of the Christian Social Reformist party (PRSC). A strong third-party challenge came from the Dominican Liberation party (PLD) led by leftist former president Juan Bosch, age 76. Seven of the remaining ten parties aligned with one or the other principal candidates (Majluta or Balaguer).

The Dominican Revolutionary party (PRD) entered the campaign with the broadest popular base. As the majority party, it had elected its presidential candidates in the last two elections and held a majority in both houses of Congress. But its popularity had declined since the last election and it went through a badly divisive nomination struggle. Ideology and issues were secondary to personal ambitions, animosities, and alliances among party leaders. The PRD was not assured of again capturing the presidency or gaining a congressional majority.

The combination of shifting ideology, personalism, and fracturing have long characterized the PRD. The party was founded in Havana in 1939 by a group of anti-Trujillo exiles led by Juan Bosch, who remained a national political figure into the 1986 elections. The PRD operated outside the country until 1961. Bosch was elected president in 1963, but was overthrown by a military coup after only seven months in office. Returning from exile in 1965, he pursued a limited presidential campaign, advocating populist democratic socialism, and in 1966 lost to Joaquín Balaguer by a margin of 2-to-1.

Bosch went into self-exile, during which he abandoned social democracy, advocated "popular dictatorship," and expressed bitter hostility toward the United States. Meanwhile, the PRD was taken over by José Francisco Peña Gómez, a young radical lawyer and Bosch protégé left with the impossible task of reconciling social democracy and popular dictatorship. The Party was also suffering from pressure from other quarters, especially during 1966–1971, as the main target for sustained attacks from the army and police. The PRD abstained from participation in the 1970 elections, claiming with good reason the lack of a proper climate for free and fair voting; personal infighting also prohibited agreement on a candidate.

Bosch returned to the Dominican Republic in 1970, but he and Peña Gómez split irrevocably over the nature of party doctrine; in 1973 Bosch resigned from the PRD and formed his own new party. In the 1974 elections, the PRD initially led a coalition of six parties called the *Acuerdo de Santiago*; but the coalition withdrew from the elections, charging "colossal fraud."

Official PRD ideology returned to social democracy and in 1976 the party became a member of the Socialist International. (In this regard, the PRD has had a particularly close relationship with its counterpart *Acción Democrática* party in Venezuela.) In 1978 it won the presidency for Antonio Guzman and repeated its victory in 1982 with Salvador Jorge Blanco. The two presidents after 1978 moved the Party to the center while reflecting commitments to civil liberties and rights, social justice and reform, and democratic processes. Despite its many problems, the PRD remained broadly based under older members and newly recruited younger politicians. While affiliated with the Socialist International, the Party had a conservative business-oriented wing, a Marxist left wing, and a dominant center.

The PRD traditionally drew its core support from the urban poor, the lower middle class, students, intellectuals, and some of the upper class. In the 1978 and 1982 elections it acquired new voters from the business community, other middle-class elements, and the rural sector (prior to 1978 the rural poor had strongly supported Balaguer). The PRD won an impressive 47 percent of the vote in the multiparty elections of 1982. But by 1986 this constituency had eroded following continued economic decline under both President Guzmán and President Jorge Blanco and unseemly public infighting among Party rivals.

The PRD entered the 1986 electoral period on the heels of a particularly divisive nomination struggle. Conflict and long-standing animosities centered on three competing personalities: outgoing President Jorge Salvador Blanco, Senator Jacobo Majluta, and Santo Domingo Mayor José Francisco Peña Gómez, the three principal Party leaders. In coming to the nomination, each one brought a complex political history dating roughly to the PRD convention of 1977.

The PRD had nominated Guzmán for the presidency at its 1977 convention only after Majluta had offered his support in exchange for the vice presidency. Guzman was a landowner and a businessman representing the more conservative elements in the PRD. Majluta, a former businessman of Lebanese extraction, had been a party activist since the early 1960s and was inclined toward Guzmán's positions. Jorge Blanco, the other leading contender for the presidential nomination at the convention, was elected to the Senate. Positioned to the left of Guzmán, and popular with the Party's urban and rural poor and younger elements, Jorge Blanco subsequently used his office as president of the Senate to obstruct Guzmán's legislative proposals as if he were an opposition leader.

Peña Gómez had supported Jorge Blanco at the convention; he continued to dominate the Party machinery as secretary general, a post he had held for many years. As the leader of the PRD left wing, Peña Gómez had held the Party together during the difficult years following the election loss in 1966, and then after Bosch's defection in 1973. He helped to keep the Party in line during the relatively conservative Guzmán presidency, although strained relations between the two men were evident.

Guzmán had been expected to seek a second term in 1982, but his announcement in June 1981 that he would not left open the PRD nomination. He chose Majluta as his successor, but was defied by this party's nominating convention. Peña Gómez and others wanted the government to address the reform issues that Guzmán had neglected and were able to gain the Party nomination for Jorge Blanco. In turn, Majluta was elected to the Senate and, as president of that body, sharply criticized Jorge Blanco just as the latter, from the same position, had opposed Guzmán. Peña Gómez, who had deferred to and supported Jorge Blanco, was elected major of Santo Domingo, but indicated future presidential aspirations of his own. In 1983 he gave up the post of party secretary general in order to concentrate on his campaign to secure the presidential nomination for 1986.

PRD leadership competition turned to crisis in the wake of the Party's primary election campaign. The national Party convention in November 1985 deteriorated into violence; fighting occurred and gunshots left at least one delegate dead. Peña Gómez apparently thought he had the nomination, but with almost all primary votes counted, Majluta claimed to have 54 percent to Peña's 46 percent. The latter's supporters claimed fraud and a stolen election, which may have had a basis in fact. Yet Peña Gómez had neglected his duties as Santo Domingo major, where his core constituency resided, and probably allowed his popular base to wither. Meanwhile, Jorge Blanco's support for Peña vacillated; the president was apparently tempted to seek reelection. Majluta's grass roots organization was excellent in both the cities and countryside; he had out-organized and outmaneuvered the competition.

After the convention the two rivals launched separate presidential campaigns with their personal intraparty *tendéncias*, in existence since 1984, and seemed to be moving toward a formal split. Majluta had organized his "tendency" as *La Estructura* (LE) and, after the Party convention, successfully petitioned for official recognition as a separate political party; it then affiliated with the Liberal International in competition with the Socialist International. Peña Gómez had organized his *Bloque Institucional* around the Party's left wing. Jorge Blanco also organized his element, but with no particular label attached to it (it was sometimes informally referred to as the *tendéncia jorgeblanquista*). The three tendencies were essentially parties within the Party, with the LE having a separately independent character as well. Jorge Blanco and Peña Gómez had a vacillating off-and-on alliance; Jorge Blanco was apparently still considering the possibility of reelection. In December 1985, Peña Gómez's supporters forcibly (with arms) seized the PRD national headquarters in Santo Domingo and some local offices around the country; in January, Peña Gómez himself announced that he unilaterally had dismissed his successor as PRD secretary general and had reassumed the position. Shortly, thereafter, the crisis cooled.

After months of public squabbling, the PRD rivals finally managed to come to an agreement about the presidential nomination and other matters. The agreement at least temporarily papered over factional divisions, but bitter feelings remained. On January 27, 1986, President Jorge Blanco announced a *pacto de unión* that gave the presidential nomination to Majluta and that for vice president to Peña Gómez. Peña Gómez also became Party president, and one of Jorge Blanco's allies, Hatuey de Camps, was named secretary general.

Literally within hours of the announcement, however, Peña Gómez's infuriated supporters convinced him to withdraw his name from the ticket on the continuing grounds that the primary election had been stolen from them. In withdrawing, Peña Gómez also gave up all claims to the presidential nomination. Majluta accepted the nomination and, in accordance with *el pacto*, dropped his harsh criticism of the Jorge Blanco government.

With the top spot on the ticket settled, the PRD met again in late March to decide the rest of the slate and named candidates for Congress, municipal government, and district officials. Majluta named Nicolás Vargas as his vice presidential running mate. Vargas, a wealthy 74-year-old business administrator from Santiago, was closely associated with the Guzmán and Bermudez families and their financial interests. Vargas was primarily not a politician and probably had little voter appeal, but he was neutral enough not to divide the Party even further. Furthermore, his nomination signaled Majluta's reassurance to voters in the north (he hailed from Santo Domingo in the south) that their interests would not be ignored—the last three presidents had been from that region. President Jorge Blanco's wife, Asela Mera de Jorge Blanco, was named candidate for the Senate from Santo Domingo, a move widely interpreted to mean that the president was already maneuvering for a reelection run to 1990. Peña Gómez was less subtle—he publicly stated that the 1990 nomination should be his and warned the Party of dire consequences if he were again pushed aside.

Five parties aligned with Majluta in a somewhat complicated way. One of them was his personal Structural party (LE). Even after obtaining the nomination, Majluta and his supporters decided not to disband the independent LE party and to campaign under two banners. Other parties decided to join forces with Majluta in exchange for a number of ballot positions reserved for their own members. One of them was the National Conciliation movement (MCN), but in agreement with the LE, not the PRD. The MCN has been founded for the 1970 elections by the former provisional president (1965–1966) Héctor García-Godóy; he died a month before the elections and was replaced by Jaime Manuél Fernández. Balaguer then named Fernández his foreign minister and the MCN temporarily disappeared. But the party reappeared for the 1978 elections and participated in the 1982 elections as well, under Fernández's leadership, who continued to head the Party in 1986.

Three more parties aligned with the PRD and presented Majluta as their presidential candidate: the Constitutional Action party (PAC), the Democratic Unity (UD), and the Christian Popular party (PPC). PAC was founded in 1980 and received only a handful of votes on the national level. UD was a new party. The PPC was also a new party, on the left, and initially fielded its own candidates; but it later withdrew them to align with the PRD and to present Majluta as its candidate.

Majluta, the PRD, and their allies faced a strong challenge from Joaquín Balaguer and his Christian Social Reformist party (PRSC). Balaguer founded the Reformist party (PR) in 1963 while in exile in New York. It served as his campaign vehicle in 1965–1966 and more broadly as a patronage organization until the end of his presidency in 1978. On that basis, the PR had little philosophical or program content beyond loyalty to Balaguer and the patronage opportunities, although an undercurrent of conservatism and anticommunism was an ideological theme. Throughout his presidency, Balaguer enjoyed the support of most conservative sectors of Dominican society, including middle- and upper-class voters and most business interests. He was also popular in rural areas, which he frequently visited and where he pursued a highly publicized agrarian reform program. By 1978, things were changing and the PR was voted out. The PR's apathy and ineptitude, Balaguer's poor health and failing eyesight, declining rural support because of faltering land reform, and public knowledge of massive corruption in high places (but not, apparently, to include Balaguer himself) were key factors in the defeat.

Despite health problems, Balaguer returned as the PR presidential candidate in 1982. He reminded the electorate of the economic gains made under his administration and argued that the PRD was again becoming a party of the extreme left. Despite little campaign effort on his part, Balaguer won 37 percent of the vote to the PRD's 47 percent.

In 1984 Balaguer agreed to amalgamate his Reformist party with the Christian Social Revolutionary party (PRSC) and form a new Christian Social Reformist party (which, coincidentally, had the same abbreviation of PRSC). The original PRSC was Christian Democratic in orientation and programmatic in nature, a multiclass party advocating nonviolent social reform. But it was small and factionalized, unable to achieve a consensus on many specific issues. Founded in exile in 1961, it ran its first electoral campaign in 1970 and refused to adhere to the general opposition boycott. In 1974 it joined the PRD-led *Acuerdo de Santiago* and ran independent campaigns in 1978 and 1982. The party saw an opportunity to broaden its base when it eventually inherited Balaguer's personalist organization. Balaguer himself cared little about ideology, but valued the technical and financial help that would come from the Christian Democratic World Union, with which the PRSC became affiliated. COPEI, the Christian Democratic party in Venezuela, was instrumental in bringing together the two Dominican parties.

Balaguer named as his vice presidential candidate Carlos Morales Troncosco. Morales was 45 years old and highly respected in several important sectors. He was president of the country's largest sugar-milling company, the Central Romana Corporation; he had been head of Gulf & Western in the Dominican Republic for several years. Not only was Morales well-regarded for his high-level administrative skills; he was not a political figure and was therefore less objectionable to active PRSC political figures who had sought the nomination. Morales was from a political family, however. His grandfather, Manuél de Jesús Troncosco, was president for two years (1940–1942) in the Trujillo era; and his brother, Pedro Morales Troncosco, was a minister in the Balaguer government.

Two parties were aligned with Balaguer and the PRSC. Both were personalist groupings led by former military men. General Elias Wessin y Wessin, loyalist commander in the 1965 civil war, had led the extreme right-wing Democratic Quisqueyan party (PQD) since the 1970 elections. The general had originally filed his own presidential candidacy because numerous Christian Democratic members of Balaguer's party were leery of accepting his alliance; but Balaguer was in favor of Wessin's formal support and had his way. General Luis Ney Tejada Alvarez also joined his Civilian Veterans National party (PNVC) to Balaguer's efforts. The PNVC contained a dissident element, however, the publicly endorsed Majluta.

Juan Bosch formed his own political organization when he left the PRD in 1973 and thereafter bitterly opposed his former colleagues. Beginning in 1974, Bosch ran for president in each election as candidate of his Dominican Liberation party (PLD). He won 10 percent of the vote in 1982, and some polls in April 1986 gave him as high as 20 percent of the 1986 vote. His increased support came primarily from disillusioned voters from the PRD left wing. Bosch referred to himself as "a Marxist but not a Leninist." The PLD was well-organized. While Bosch could not win the presidency, his party aimed at taking enough seats in the Chamber of Deputies to allow him to be something of a power broker.

Three small parties also ran their own slates. They had no chance of winning the presidency and few opportunities for other offices. Two of them were new parties: the Nationalist Democratic party (PDN) on the left and the Progressive National Forces (FNP) on the right. The Dominican Communist party (PDC), founded in 1944, outlawed in 1962, and recognized in 1977, also presented its own candidates.

Finally, the other officially recognized groupings of the left decided not to field slates—the Communist party of the Dominican Republic (PACOREDO) and the Socialist bloc (BS). The latter group informally "endorsed" Bosch.

THE CAMPAIGN AND ELECTION

While the electoral campaign officially began on March 31, 1986, it was not in full swing until mid-April, little more than a month prior to the polling date. Until then, attention had been focused on the selection of candidates, accommodation of intraparty competitions, and arrangement of interparty alliances. The campaign itself centered on personalities rather than issues. National problems could not be ignored, however, and as election day neared some issues began to surface. To be sure, national conditions were difficult. The economy continued to suffer serious dislocations, social conditions were making slow progress at best, and other situations begged for solutions. Yet issues were secondary and, by and large, addressed in highly general terms.

None of the candidates took specific programmatic positions that excited the electorate or offered concrete solutions. The three principal candidates all promised to rectify the errors of the past eight years. Majluta distanced himself from his own party's two previous administrations and talked of increased public expenditures. Balaguer reminded Dominicans of the relative prosperity during his presidency from 1966 to 1978 and argued for more foreign investment. Bosch appealed to the radical left with an antiimperialist theme and called for widespread nationalizations. All three men promised to reduce fuel and food costs if elected.

Personalist politics remained prevalent. Mutual *ad hominem* attacks were made, involving charges of corruption, cronyism, propensities for violence, and other personal aspects. In addition, many congressional candidates felt no need to mount serious campaigns since interparty alliances virtually assured their election under any circumstances, further eroding the public debate. In sum, the election revolved around a small and highly visible cast of characters—Balaguer, Majluta, Bosch, and their key colleagues.

While the elections were controversial and intense, they occurred in a relatively calm atmosphere. Nevertheless, certain fragile aspects of the political environment were spotlighted by sporadic clashes between supporters of opposing political groups and serious charges of impending vote fraud. Five people died during the six-week campaign period and numerous others were injured around the country. Two incidents of violence stood out. In early April, Comandante Bayardo Arce of Nicaragua visited Santo Domingo to attend a Socialist International meeting; he made an impassioned antiimperialist speech at the Autonomous University of Santo Domingo (USAD) that was followed by violent student demonstrations and a strong police response. President Blanco denounced the speech, noting that the Nicaraguan leader's presence had seriously hurt relations between the two countries. University authorities suspended classes, later extending the suspension until after May sixteenth because of the "agitated" election campaign.

The most serious incident occurred on May fourth in the town of Boca Chica with a shootout between PRD and PRSC supporters. Majluta was present and charged the opposition with an assassination attempt. On the next day, May fifth, outgoing President Jorge Blanco visited the three principal presidential contenders. He, Majluta, and Balaguer signed a pact pledging to take measures to reduce tension and to accept the results of the elections. Bosch refused to sign the document because, he said, his followers had been involved in no violence; however, he expressed support for the spirit of the agreement.

Only two days after the election pact was signed, the PRD filed documents with the Central Election Commission charging that the PRSC and the PLD were conspiring to rig the elections by tampering with the computerized vote-counting programs that would give the opposition an incrementally increasing number of phantom votes. A few days later, the PRD informed the commission of its concern that further fraud could be perpetrated because of irregularities in the electoral register—that there were "displacement lists" of PRD voters that would cause them to report to incorrect polling places.

While violence did not generally characterize the campaign, and fraud was a possibility rather than actuality, they injected a worrisome element into the electoral process. President Jorge Blanco feared that violence might increase and charges of fraud assume credibility. To preempt these threats, the president acted to ensure a peaceful and honest election. He invited prominent international figures to observe the elections so that they could, in the president's words, "perceive personally the exemplary manner of our elections." The Dominican government invited six people to form a commission of international observers during the elections. Three of them represented the Organization of American States (OAS); the others were Galo Plaza Lasso, expresident of Ecuador and former secretary general of the OAS; Sonia Picado, president of the Inter-American Institute of Human Rights headquartered in Costa Rica; and a representative of former Costa Rican president Daniel Oduber. Other international observers representing various entities from eight different countries also accepted the government's invitations; among them were former Venezuelan presidents Carlos Andrés Pérez and Luís Herrera Campíns.

On May thirteenth, President Jorge Blanco appointed a nine-member panel of distinguished Dominicans to oversee the electoral process. The Electoral Advisory Commission (*Comision de Asesores Electorales*) was made up of the Archbishop of Santo Domingo, Msgr. Nicolás de Jesús López Rodríguez, as president; the country's leading historian, Dr. Frank Moya Pons, as secretary and principal spokesman; and seven other prominent figures as members. As it turned out, the commission played a crucial role in ensuring a free and fair outcome.

The elections were held on May sixteenth. Some violence occurred during the day. In the afternoon, two men serving as party observers were shot dead in an argument with a soldier at a *mesa* near the town of Barahona. That evening, after the polls had closed, a third man was killed during a political argument in Santo Domingo. In general, however, proceedings were orderly and the country peaceful.

POST-ELECTION CRISIS

A ten-day post-election crisis, involving a complex series of events, commenced over the weekend following the election. On the afternoon of Sunday May eighteenth, the JCE announced that vote counting had been suspended and would re resumed the following morning. It was by then apparent that Balaguer was winning the election—according to the latest Junta Central electoral bulletin (no. 23) issued at 7:30 that morning, Balaguer enjoyed an almost two-percentage-point lead over Majluta, 41.5 percent to 39.6 percent, with 92 percent of the polling places reporting. As it turned out, the reasons for stopping the count were innocent enough: most of the remaining ballots had not arrived from the countryside because bad weather prevented helicopter deliveries, so the JCE staff was sent home to rest. But the JCE did not explain this at the time, arousing public suspicions that some conspiracy was afoot. At about 5:00 P.M., the chairman of the Advisory Commission addressed the nation in an attempt to allay public fears and preempt charges of fraud. He said that the commission was in a position to assure voters that the elections had been free and clean and that the results were being computed in an entirely professional and objective manner. Charges of fraud, however, were soon made.

Within two hours of the commission's statement, Majluta was on national television and radio to announce that the political parties endorsing his candidacy had decided to challenge the competence of (*recusar*) two JCE officials. This concept is similar to that of "recuse" in the Anglo-American legal tradition—to challenge or reject a judge or juror as disqualified or incompetent to act. In the instance of the Dominican JCE, political parties had the right to challenge electoral officials who were exercising judicial functions. The JCE itself was then required to hear the charges and render a decision.

Majluta charged that JCE President Caonabo Fernández Naránjo and member Rubéns Suro were biased in favor of the PRSC and, therefore, not competent to serve as election officials. Majluta said that, according to calculations made by his own counting center, he had won the elections. He also accused the JCE's computer center director of bias. Majluta further charged that suffrage had been denied thousands of voters and that the JCE had failed to take into account, as required by law, complaints lodged at polling places by his supporting parties. He demanded a recount. Formal recuse documents were filed with the JCE that night.

As Majluta spoke, the Election Police Force increased its presence on the streets of Santo Domingo, but the city remained quiet. At the same time, top military leaders issued a communiqué supporting the Advisory Commission's position that the elections were free, fair, and honest, and that the public should remain calm. The brief statement, signed by the secretary of the Armed Forces, the chiefs of staff of the Army, Navy, and Air Force, and the chief of National Police, was prominently published the next day in Monday morning newspapers.

Fernández and Suro disqualified themselves from continuing official functions in view of the challenges filed against them, but without the charges being heard or formal JCE judgments rendered. They were replaced by their designated alternates (*suplentes*). Under the circumstances, the vote counting was not resumed. The PRSC then retaliated by recusing the new JCE president, Ponciano Rondón Sánchez, who also disqualified himself and was replaced by another alternate. (The PRSC charged only one official because a single prior-appointed alternate remained; otherwise, the JCE would have effectively dissolved and the crisis deepened for a prolonged period—not in Balaguer's interest since he was ahead in the polling.) President Jorge Blanco sent a public letter to Majluta saying that he had been precipitate and unfair; Peña Gómez later said the interruption of the vote counting had created a dangerous situation for the country.

The new JCE moved to resume the counting, but it was unclear whether a recount would be ordered and, if so, on what basis it would be made. In a dramatic move, the Advisory Commission withdrew from JCE headquarters. It said that the counting should not be resumed until the challenges had been heard and decided upon as required by law. The commission also bluntly stated that under the circumstances the accuracy of any further vote counting was suspect and could not be relied upon.

With these considerable pressures brought to bear, Majluta and Balaguer held a lengthy meeting on the evening of Thursday May twenty-second. They agreed that the Senate should designate an entirely new JCE, composed of persons without political ties, so that the electoral outcome could be concluded as soon as possible. The Senate held a special session the next day, presided over by Majluta. It approved a resolution asking all three recused JCE officials to tender their resignations so that a new body could be appointed. In a surprise development, however, the Senate request was ignored.

On Saturday May twenty-fourth, the Advisory Commission met with President Jorge Blanco and recommended that the original JCE membership be restored. The president in turn consulted with the Attorney General and Chief of Electoral Police, who supported the recommendation. At 6:30 P.M. on Sunday evening, Fernández and Suro returned to the JCE, joining the remaining unrecused third member, Juan Rolando Ramos Pimentál. They rejected the charges against themselves as without foundation. The Advisory Commission returned to the JCE building and counting resumed. Majluta protested, but to no avail. In fact, on Tuesday May twenty-seventh, he acknowledged Balaguer's victory.

Majluta apparently had been surprised by the early election returns solidly in Balaguer's favor and seemed to be trying to discredit and confuse the electoral process through legalistic recourses at his disposal as a desperate last resort. The credibility of his charges was eroded by the fact that the JCE officials whom he accused were appointed by a PRD-dominated Senate presided over by Majluta himself. President Blanco's interest in the elections was tied to neither of the principal candidates; rather, he wanted to ensure the clear election of his successor and emerge with a statesmanlike image. The Advisory Commission was the most important factor in keeping the affair within peaceful and legal bounds. While its public statement on May eighteenth had not preempted the charges of fraud as it was intended to do, its subsequent actions, along with the public perception of its absolute integrity, was crucial to ensuring that the election outcome was an accurate reflection of the popular vote. The JCE, on the other hand, brought public discredit upon itself, coming to be perceived as timid and confused, with its intended function as electoral guarantor actually being carried out by the Advisory Commission.

Election Results

With JCE Bulletin #26 issued on May twenty-sixth, the preliminary vote count was completed and most election results were known. Joaquín Balaguer won the presidency and his running mate, Carlos Morales Troncoso, the vice presidency. Their Christian Social Reformist party won a comfortable majority in the Senate, but took less than half the seats in the Chamber of Deputies.

Of the 2,177,258 votes counted 2,064,503 were valid, 84,210 had been declared invalid (*nulos*), and 28,545 had been challenged (*observados*) and were under investigation. The three principal presidential candidates—Balaguer, Majluta, and Bosch—garnered more than 99 percent of the vote. The other three candidates split about 0.6 percent. Since the elections were by direct universal vote with no requirement or provision for a runoff, Balaguer was elected with a 41 percent plurality.

Public opinion polls taken during the campaign in April held up well on election day. They had indicated a virtual tie between Majluta and Balaguer at about the 40 percent level for each, with Majluta enjoying a slight lead. Bosch had 18–20 percent of the vote, about half of his share attributed to defections from the disillusioned or protesting PRD left wing. But many voters, perhaps as high as 20 percent, were uncommitted and remained so until just prior to election day. As it turned out, they decided in favor of Balaguer in enough numbers to overcome Majluta's lead at the same time that the defecting PRD-left remained in Bosch's camp.

President-elect Balaguer's PRSC representation in Congress was a majority in the Senate but shy of half the seats in the Chamber of Deputies. In the 30-member Senate, the PRSC won seventeen, the PRD eleven, and the PLD two. Thus, Balaguer had a comfortable working majority in the Senate, which, it should be noted, controls judicial appointments. In the 120-member Chamber of Deputies, the PRSC won 58 seats, the PRD 44 seats (but representing intraparty *tendéncias*—28 for Jorge Blanco, twelve for Peña Gómez, and only four for Majluta), and Bosch's PLD some eighteen seats. We may anticipate that considerable maneuvering and shifting alliances will be an important element in the Chamber's proceedings, with Bosch and Blanco enjoying influence with the presidential party.

Voting abstentions turned out to be only marginally more important than in past elections. About 29 percent of the votes listed in the Electoral Register did not appear at the polls. The seemingly high abstention rate was deceptive since the register had not been corrected for deaths or duplications since 1978, and included a very large number of eligible voters who lived outside the country (the Dominican Republic had no provision for absentee voting). A more realistic abstention rate of eligible in-country votes was probably no more than 15 percent.

THE OUTLOOK FOR POLITICS AND DEMOCRACY

The new Balaguer government faced serious problems, especially economic and social, and its first year performance loomed as a crucial one. Dominicans were expecting results after weathering the problems of the past few years and in the wake of national elections. Balaguer's post-election statements indicated that he had an eye on his place in Dominican history and that he realized he would enjoy considerable freedom to govern as he chose. Depending on the public policies he pursued, the success he had in resolving national problems, and the methods he employed, he could go down in history as either a great leader or another *caudillo*.

The electoral contest had important consequences for the future of the party system. Activists in the major parties seemed to be more interested, beyond lip service, in party institutionalization. Scenarios, however, were difficult to visualize; many permutations were possible with changing leadership and alliance possibilities. Nevertheless, the 1986 elections signaled a period of political change for the following four years. Several prominent leaders were expected to vie for the presidency in 1990, but others would probably retire from active participation, including aging politicians Balaguer and Bosch. It was an open question as to what sort of party realignments might occur or about which new personalities would emerge into prominence.

Balaguer's PRSC was a 1984 amalgamation of his Reformist party with the Christian Democratic World Union. Yet Balaguer himself cared little about ideology, and without his leadership the party could easily fracture among several ambitious younger party members. To continue as a major party, the PRSC probably needed a successful government under Balaguer, a disciplined leadership selection process, and the building of the basic gross roots structure that it lacked. It was highly possible that Vice President Morales Troncoso would transform into a politician and assume party leadership.

For its part the PRD went through a badly divisive nomination struggle and losing election effort. It was less institutionalized, less ideological, more personalist, and more divided than when it won the 1978 elections. The important question was whether the party would reunify or fragment. *Personalism* was the PRD's problem—specifically, the strong personality conflicts reflected in its three *tendéncias*. Majluta and Peña Gómez declared they would seek the presidency in the next election and it was widely assumed that Jorge Blanco would try for a second term at that time. Majluta and Peña Gómez exchanged harsh words soon after the 1986 elections about why the PRD lost. The PRD was picking up the pieces and its future was impossible to predict.

When Juan Bosch leaves the political scene, his personalist PLD will entirely lack leadership. It seemed unlikely that Peña Gómez and Bosch would formally ally, as predicted by the radical right. Yet PLD membership was a relatively heterogeneous reflection of the political left and provided a natural constituency for Peña Gómez; the problem for Peña was devising a strategy for mobilizing that sector.

In a more general vein, a positive note may be struck about the future of democracy in the Dominican Republic. The country faced very serious national problems in 1986 and politics remained an intense enterprise. A sense of crisis, however, was lacking; no guerrilla insurgency was active and the armed forces did not threaten to intervene. It was true that Dominican democracy was defined by special national values and characteristics; yet that democracy, however defined, was increasingly well-established. Twenty-five years had passed since the end of the Trujillo dictatorship and twenty years since the civil war and foreign intervention of 1965–1966. The successful elections of 1986 were the sixth in an unbroken two-decade series. While the severity of national economic and social problems placed Dominican democracy under stress, it was encouraging to realize that a new generation approached middle age and leadership positions having matured in an increasingly peaceful and open society and socialized with dominant values rejecting any form of dictatorship. They had enjoyed considerably more freedom than had their parents; they accepted democratic values and, in a practical way, felt their interests best served in a democratic system.[5]

The larger Caribbean implications of domestic Dominican politics are to be found in the ongoing and functional nature of the country's democratic institutions. Though Dominican democracy is far from perfect, it has allowed an increasing amount of civil rights and political expression on the part of the population. In that light, the Dominican Republic's transition from an authoritarian regime in the first half of the century to a democratic state in the second half offers hope for nations in the wider Caribbean region, like El Salvador and Nicaragua.

NOTES

1. This chapter is a revised version of G. Pope Atkins, "Dominican Republic Election Study Report," Georgetown University Center for Strategic and International Studies; Report #1: May 2, 1986; Report #2: June 19, 1986. A survey of *Listín Diario, El Caribe*, and *El Nacional* from October 1, 1985 through June 10, 1986, served as a basis for sequences of events. Two visits were made to Santo Domingo in 1986, one during the campaign and the other as election

results became known, in order to observe events, conduct interviews, and review other sources of information. Appreciation is expressed to Jonathan Hartlyn for sharing his special knowledge of the Dominican electoral process, and to Georges Fauriol for his commentary and assistance.

2. See G. Pope Atkins, *Arms and Politics in the Dominican Republic* (Boulder, CO: Westview Press, 1981), pp. 5–17.

3. See Atkins, *Arms and Politics in the Dominican Republic*, pp. 5–17, chaps. 4 and 5; and two essays by Howard J. Wiarda and Michael J. Kryzanek, "The Dominican Republic," in Jack W. Hopkins (ed.), *Latin America and Caribbean Contemporary Record*, vol. I: 1981–82, pp. 544–54; and vol. II: 1982–83, pp. 667–76 (New York: Holmes & Meier, 1983, 1984).

4. Important sources for information and analysis about the electoral system are Julio Brea Franco, *Introducción al Processo Electoral Dominicano* (Santo Domingo: Licorería Siboney, 1984); and Brea Franco, *El Sistema Constitucional Dominicano, 2 vols.* (Santo Domingo: Editorial CENEPAC, 1986). See also Julio Brea Franco, Nelson Buttén Varona, Julio Campillo Pérez, José A. Silié Gatón, *Legislación Electoral de la República Dominicana* (San José, Costa Rica: Instituto Interamericano de Derechos Humanos, 1986).

5. See Frank Moya Pon's insightful comments about the recent course of Dominican party politics and the socialization process, "La Politica Dominicana: Agosto 1984," *LASA Forum* 15, 2 (Fall 1984), pp. 19–21. Moya expressed an earlier pessimistic view about the prospects for the Dominican Republic in his *El futuro dominicano* (Santo Domingo: 1980). Also of interest are Dominican views expressed in *Los Problemas de la Institucionalización y Preservación de la Democracia en la República Dominicana* (Santo Domingo: Forum, 1982), the published results of thoughtful conference papers and commentaries.

10
Heading Toward a New Instability in the Caribbean's Eastern Tier?
Scott B. MacDonald,
Erik Kopp,
and Victor J. Bonilla

INTRODUCTION

The Caribbean's eastern tier is a largely understudied region.[1] Although it occupies a strategic location in the Caribbean, in proximity to North American communication and supply lines to South America, the Atlantic, and the Pacific through the Panama Canal, it has been forced upon the "movers and shakers" of United States foreign policy only in a fleeting fashion. Obviously, the New Jewel Movement revolution of 1979–1983 and the invasion of Grenada in 1983 reflected, for the moment, United States' concern. With the passing of the crisis and the revolution it is appropriate to surmise if Washington, otherwise distracted, will again ignore the Caribbean's eastern tier.

It is the purpose of this chapter to examine and project the state of the Caribbean's eastern tier from the mid to the late 1980s. It is likely that the region with its English, French, and Dutch subregions, will present new problems and possible crises. Such developments could precipitate a new wave of revolutions and coup attempts, possible anti-Americanism and the advance of alternative poles of global power. It might also lead to progressive economic development, equitable distributions of national wealth and positive economic integration with responsive regional standing mechanisms. Much hinges, however, on regional leadership and responses from the United States, its European allies, and Canada, and to a lesser extent, Mexico, Venezuela, and Brazil.

This essay is divided into five sections, each covering a particular subregion of the Caribbean's eastern tier: the French islands of Martinique and Guadeloupe and French Guiana on the northeastern shoulder of the South American mainland; the smaller English-speaking states in the Eastern Caribbean; the larger English-speaking states of Barbados, Trinidad and Tobago, and Guyana; the Dutch Caribbean of the Netherlands Antilles and independent Suriname; and a brief discussion over whether or not the region's problems will lead to a new round of instability. The geographic definition of the Caribbean's eastern tier has been stretched to include the Netherlands Antilles islands of Aruba, Bonaire and Curaçao. The fact that their political and economic development has been in part related and linked to the rest of the nations and overseas holdings in the Eastern Caribbean, makes a discussion of their problems and future pertinent.

THE FRENCH CARIBBEAN

While it has been said that the sun has set on the British Empire, it still continues to shine, in a fashion, on the French. The *tricolore* still waves over a number of far-flung islands in the Indian Ocean, the South Pacific, off the coast of Canada, and in the Caribbean.[2] These former colonies, however, have been transformed either into overseas departments or overseas territories. In 1946, the predominantly black populations of the eastern Caribbean islands of Martinique and Guadeloupe, along with French Guiana, voted to become overseas departments (*départements d'outre-mer* or DOMs) of France. As Richard D.E. Burton noted,

The transformation of Martinique (along with Guadeloupe, Guyane and Reunion) into a department of France, theoretically indistinguishable from Tarn-et-Garonne, Lozère or Ardèche, was in no sense an abrupt or unexpected modification of the island-colony's status but rather the logical culmination of a century-long process of progressive incorporation into the Metropole beginning with the abolition of slavery in 1848, or even with the revolutionary constitution of Year III with its epoch-making declaration that French colonies are an integral part of the territory (of France) and are subject to the same constitutional law.[3]

The French islands and Guiana are integral administrative, political and economic parts of the French nation, similar to Hawaii's relationship with the United States. Citizens from these overseas departments have the right to vote and stand for local and national government. Each region is represented in the French Chamber of Deputies and the Senate in Paris and their citizens are entitled to all the socioeconomic benefits of the French state. This overseas departmental status has had an enormous impact on the French Caribbean's standard of living. Social security benefits, unemployment compensation and pensions are quite high, while levels of education, welfare and health are relatively well advanced. In French Guiana, the Ariane Space Program has created additional employment opportunities and has gained considerable attention by those watching the space race.[4]

Primary education, free since 1889, is only one example of the comparatively high level of development related to the massive infusion of French funds. The official literacy rate is above 90 percent and the reported average school attendance for the three departments is 97 percent. Each island department contains more that three hundred primary schools and secondary school enrollment amounted to more than forty thousand. A university education is also available on both island departments, while students, including those from French Guiana, regularly attend universities in Europe.

Despite France's substantial investment in the two Eastern Caribbean islands and Guiana, serious problems exist within the context of identity for many Caribbean inhabitants. The European influence in each department is overwhelming: Fort-de-France and Pointe-à-Pitre (Martinique's and Guadeloupe's departmental capitals, respectively) abound with French boutiques and cafés, audio and video shops, while Peugeots and Mercedes clog the streets. Beyond the city centers, the outlines of ultramodern tourist hotels are evident as are numbers of Europeans and North Americans on vacation, enjoying the beaches or wandering through the shopping districts. French is taught in school, is the language of commerce, and dominates almost all facets of the media. Moreover, there has been a quiet, gradual "white invasion" of retirees and mainlanders seeking a better life in the sun, especially in the islands. Although French Guiana has missed the tourist invasion, it has instead become a destination for illegal immigrants from Brazil, Haiti, and elsewhere, attracted by higher wages and the trickle-down of the French state's social benefits. In addition, much of the food consumed by the populations of the Caribbean departments is imported daily from France and local industries, such as sugar and rum production, have been deliberately run down by the French government for the benefit of French sugar beet farmers and cognac distilleries. Nothing has replaced sugar, the traditional economic backbone of the French Caribbean and the departments import far more than they export. The disequilibrium of the Martinican, Guadeloupean, and Guianese economies has grown worse since the late–1960s and is reflected by high unemployment of between 20 and 40 percent and, in some quarters, a questioning of the alleged benefits of departmentalization.

From the French viewpoint, assimilation of these departments in 1946 was a form of decolonization.[5] The populations of these islands and South American enclave had a choice: they could become a constitutional and equal part of the French state or join the community of sovereign nations as did the majority of the English colonies in the Eastern Caribbean or former French colonies in Africa, such as Senegal. By voting to remain in the French fold, the Caribbean departments guaranteed themselves artificially higher standards of living than many of their independent neighbors and avoided, according to some, the developmental cul-de-sac of another former French colony, Haiti. At the same time, departmentalization created a distance between the French-speaking islands and their English-speaking neighbors. On the Eastern Caribbean's southern flank, French Guiana remained even more isolated due to the jungle terrain and coastal swamps and rivers.

A substantial majority of Martinicans, Guadeloupeans, and Guianese have repeatedly voted in the French elections, indicating their commitment to remaining what Arvin Murch has called "black Frenchmen".[6] Despite that, proindependence groups have emerged. They are largely divided between those who believe in the parliamentary process, such as the Guianese Workers Union, and those, such as the outlawed Caribbean Révolutionary Alliance (*Alliance Révolutionaire Caraïbe* or ARC), who have opted for terrorism in pursuit of their goals. The ARC was particularly active in the early 1980s, and conducted bombing campaigns in the Caribbean and in Paris that took several lives, injured many, cost thousands of dollars in damages, hurt Guadeloupe's tourist industry, and raised concerns in France and the DOMS about Libyan and Cuban involvement. Both the governments of Giscard d'Estaing and his Socialist successor, François Mitterand, have been unable to eradicate entirely proindependence terrorist activities.

The Mitterand government has found the independence movement in Guadeloupe especially troublesome as the cause there was given considerable impetus by the Kanaka rebellion in New Caledonia in late 1984. That rebellion occurred on the South Pacific island territory when the native population of Kanakas, who constitute some 42 percent of the population, decided to create an independent Kanaka nation. Though the rebellion was quickly suppressed with a minimum of violence, it had an impact on other independence groups in overseas France. In April 1984, one of the major independence parties, the Popular Union for the Liberation of Guadeloupe (ULPG), hosted a conference for "the last French colonies."[7] Representatives came from independence groups in other Caribbean departments, Reunion and Mayotte in the Indian Ocean, and New Caledonia. Anti-French declarations were made and a number of disturbances occurred on the island. Despite these disturbances, there was little public outpouring in support of the conference or its objectives. Furthermore, those organizations that attended, such as the rival groups from Martinique, reflected disunity even on a local level. In addition the majority of Caribbean proindependence groups, such as the Popular Union for the Liberation of Guadeloupe, have a vision which is limited solely to their particular location, in a sense preempting a possibility of a sovereign French Caribbean nation composed of Martinique, Guadeloupe, and French Guiana. As the English-speaking nations around them found it difficult to create an enduring political union in the form of the West Indies Federation, the French DOMs appear to be afflicted with the same perceptualization and the seeds for a possible independent future have already been sown with disunity.

The March 19, 1986, National Assembly and Regional Council elections mirrored the current state of the French Caribbean. Electoral reforms, allowing greater proportional representation, created new parliamentary seats which were evenly divided between the forces of the left and right. The left, composed of local Socialists, the Martinican Progressive party (PPM), and communists narrowly held control of the regional council in Martinique, while similar coalitions won in Guadeloupe and French Guiana.

There were three disturbing elements evident in the aftermath of the elections. While voter turnout was relatively high in Martinique and Guiana, averaging 56 percent, it was noticeably lower (40 percent) in Guadeloupe.[8] This perhaps reflected a growing disenchantment with the status quo and the political system in general. A second related factor was election-connected violence in Guadeloupe: Arson was twice attempted and some of the major roads were barricaded by independence militants. This perhaps indicated that the problem of *la contagion* (that is, the spread of proindependence violence as occurred in New Caledonia in 1985 and 1986), remains. A third factor was that the extreme rightist National Front (FN) ran candidates in both islands. Although unable to gain any seats on either the regional councils or to the National Assembly, the FN's presence contributes to the narrowing of the region's political center, which is already cramped by the proindependence radicals. A polarization in the political process appears to be developing, especially in Guadeloupe. The elections for president in April and May 1988, in which Mitterand won in the Caribbean Overseas Department, reflected little change in this process.

In the mid–1980s, the French Caribbean, an important and often overlooked subregion within the Caribbean's eastern tier, is reaching an important crossroads in its development. There is some apprehension about the turmoil in Guadeloupe: If the department does gain independence, it is probable that its political orientation, based on the ideological slant of the current proindependence forces, would be pro-Cuban.

France, with some seven thousand troops and a substantial air and naval presence in the Eastern Caribbean, has conducted joint manuevers with both U.S. and Dutch forces, and has opened up French Guiana to jungle training for U.S. soldiers.[9] It would appear that Paris has no intention of leaving the region, and that the majority of French Antilleans and Guianese favor maintaining the relationship. At the same time, change is needed, especially in the economic field. Something must be done to move the island and Guianese economies from their states of disequilibrium to balanced growth. As the answers have yet to appear, future prospects remain troubled.

THE SMALLER STATES OF THE EASTERN CARIBBEAN

The smaller Commonwealth states of the Eastern Caribbean consist of Antigua and Barbuda, Dominica, Grenada, St. Kitts–Nevis, St. Lucia, and St. Vincent and the Grenadines. English-speaking Anguilla and Montserrat, though still "colonies" of the United Kingdom, are self-governing and have extensive cultural and commercial linkages to their neighbors. Along these lines, Montserrat is a member of both the Caribbean Common Market (CARICOM) and the Organization of Eastern Caribbean States (OECS).

With predominantly African-descended populations and long histories of British colonialism, the smaller English-speaking Eastern Caribbean nations share many characteristics and problems. Productive activities directed at local markets are restricted due to the size of the populations, ranging from Anguilla's 7,019 inhabitants to St. Vincent's 127,883. The geographical dispersion of the islands adds to transportation costs, and some islands, like Dominica and St. Vincent, lack adequate international airports and associated facilities. These factors narrow opportunities for production based on exports. As one World Bank official noted, "A limited resource base in most countries restricts opportunities for productive investment and creates a dependence on single exports, such as sugar . . . or tourism, which have been subject, particularly recently, to the vagaries of international prices and demand.[10]

All the nations of the Eastern Caribbean rely heavily on international trade: The region's import bill, which averages about 50 percent of their gross domestic product annually, is concentrated in food, petroleum, and manufactured goods.[11] To improve their position in the global economy these states are confronted by the similar problems of crop diversification, industrialization, and, above all, infrastructure development. Reflecting this, Dr. Joseph E. Edmunds, ambassador of St. Lucia to the United States and to the Organization of American States, who identified his country's needs as new financing for improved infrastructural development, labor-intensive industries to reduce unemployment and assistance in capital funding and private sector construction works.[12]

While the 1960s and early 1970s were a period of growth, the oil shocks in 1973/1974 and 1979 caused considerable problems for Eastern

Caribbean states. Fluctuating sugar, banana, and citrus prices also hurt the economies of St. Kitts–Nevis, Dominica, St. Lucia, and Grenada. Hurricanes devastated more than one economy. Compounding the economic difficulties, that included a slump in the tourist industry, were political problems: While Sir Eric Gairy's quasi-authoritarian regime in Grenada was toppled in a coup on March 13, 1979, St. Lucia and Dominica underwent crises that challenged the tradition of parliamentary government. A succession of short-lived left-of-center governments, marked by instability convulsed St. Lucia while the situation in Dominica was even more tenuous as the government of Prime Minister Eugenia Charles weathered more that one coup attempt.

Since the U.S. intervention in 1983 and the implementation of the United States' twelve-year duty-free trade program for the Caribbean and Central America, the Caribbean Basin Initiative (CBI), the Eastern Caribbean states have settled into a period of relative political calm with moderate or conservative governments that were democratically elected. Though many development problems remain and results have not always matched expectations (i.e. the CBI), a majority of states have been able to achieve economic growth. In 1985, St. Lucia's economy expanded 5.8 percent, a rate not matched since 1978.[13] The strategy of targeting agriculture, tourism, and construction has clearly benefitted from the renewed growth of the U.S. economy and the solid management of the Compton government.

Antigua and Barbuda has also experienced growth in the mid–1980s after difficulties at the beginning of the decade. Acknowledging tourism as its major growth industry, the government of Prime Minister Vere Bird created a favorable climate for foreign investment. Although tourism accounts for 80 percent of foreign exchange, other sectors have not been entirely neglected. Using molasses from St. Kitts, Antigua produces and exports rum (Cavalier Antigua Rum) and has attracted several electronics companies. Cottage industries, such as the production of sea island cotton, have also been encouraged. Antigua has also benefitted from its close ties to the United States which has a satellite tracking facility on the island as well as a station that broadcasts the Voice of America.

Antigua and Barbuda's political development in the 1980s has not been entirely smooth as friction has existed between the two islands. Barbuda, as the smaller island with a population of 1,200, has often vocalized its discontent about what it considers an unequal relationship. Antigua, with 80,000 people and a more diversified economy, has often found the relationship frustrating. At the same time, Antigua has no intention of allowing any further fragmentation of the English-speaking region. An earlier attempt before independence on the part of the Barbudians to come under the wing of the United States and Canada failed. The 1983 Grenada affair, moreover, reinforced doubts about the viability of Barbuda becoming another microstate.

St. Lucia's political development since Grenada has been dominated by Prime Minister George Compton, who was reelected in 1982. His conservative United Workers party (UWP) held fourteen seats in parliament to the opposition's three. However, the centrist St. Lucia Labour party (SLP), led by Julian Hunt, regained a degree of political cohesiveness which it had earlier lost because of infighting. Hunt emerged as a strong leader and managed to oust radical elements from the Party. The SLP's new face, that of pragmatism as opposed to its earlier socialist leanings, made it a stronger challenger in the 1987 elections. Though Compton's government presided over positive economic growth in 1985 and 1986, the SLP won eight seats to the UMP's nine. Compton's party won, but its majority was diminished. The left-of-center Progressive Labour party, which had split from the SLP, lost both of its seats. In many respects, the St. Lucian elections reflected that democracy was "alive and well."

Since the 1983 intervention in Grenada elections have been held in both St. Vincent and the Grenadines and Dominica. In July 1984, the pragmatic left-center National Democratic party led by James "Sonny" Mitchell, won a resounding victory over the incumbent St. Vincent Labour party government of Prime Minister Milton Cato. While Cato was a strong supporter of the United States in the region, Mitchell was representative of a more nationalistic and regionalistic line of thinking. Dominica's political development since 1983 continued to be dominated by the English-speaking Caribbean's first woman chief executive, Eugenia Charles. Charles gained international renown for her role as the chairperson of the Organization of Eastern Caribbean States who requested U.S. intervention. On the domestic front, Charles' conservative Dominica Freedom party (DFP) first came to office in 1980. The new prime minister presided over a nation marked by political turbulence linked to the quasi-authoritarian nature of the Patrick John administration. Charles government was confronted by both manmade and natural problems. In 1981, Hurricane Frederick struck the island and three armed coup attempts were launched, two by members of the Dominican Defense Force (DDF) which had been created by John. Despite the many obstacles faced by Charles, she led her party to victory again in 1985, winning fifteen of the twenty-one seats. The underlying reason for her success was the government's solid economic management and its ability to implement meaningful development programs. These ranged from substantial road building to housing and were funded by the United States, France, the United Kingdom, and Canada. While the economic situation helped the government, the opposition's lack of unity also helped Charles in her reelection bid. Alleged linkages to the Soviet Union and Libya, the Marxist-Leninism of certain individuals and personal differences combined to hurt the Labour party of Dominica (which won five seats in 1985) and the leftist United Dominica Labour party (which won one seat). The Labour party, moreover, proved to be a poor opposition leader as it boycotted parliament for a year and a half (ended December 29, 1986) to protest a government decision to eliminate live radio broadcasts of parliamentary debates. In addition, the Freedom party won a majority of seats in two village council elections at the end of 1986. The DFP's victory was significant in that the area had been regarded as an opposition stronghold.

Grenada since the intervention has witnessed elections, the establishment of a new government, the protracted tiral of former New Jewel Movement leaders, and the gradual withdrawal of the United States military presence. Probably the most severe problem facing the government of Grenada in the aftermath of the invasion has been its search for legitimacy. While the majority of Grenadans supported the U.S.–led intervention, the ability of the New National party (NNP) to maintain internal unity and lead the nation were increasingly questioned in 1986 and 1987. The NNP was formed in 1984 and was a merger of Grenada National party (GNP), the Grenada Democratic Movement (GDM), the National Democratic party (NDP), and Christian Democratic Labour party (CDLP). The NNP's founding was, in part, because of outside influence. The United States, Barbados, St. Vincent, and St. Lucia strongly suggested that these largely centrist parties unite. The main concern of the other Caribbean nations and the United States was that if the electorate was faced with a plethora of centrist parties, Eric Gairy's Grenada United Labour party (GULP) stood a chance of winning. The thought of Gairy making a political comeback decidedly chilled the United States and the surrounding Eastern Caribbean states. It also put considerable pressure on the centrist politicians to pull together.

On December 5, 1984, the NNP won the national elections and replaced the interim government that had been established in the aftermath of the invasion. Though the new party won every seat except one, the NNP brought into office a number of schisms. Even before the election, the small CDLP had left the party. Norman Blaize, the leader of the GNP and a former prime minister, became the new head of state. Though the opposition held only one seat (GULP), the NNP's lack of cohesiveness gradually became evident. Blaize, 69-years-old at the time and in poor health, proved to be an inflexible leader who often refused to discuss policy issues. Due to illness, he was often absent from the country. As resentment grew within the party, Francis Alexis and George Brizan, leaders of two other parties that formed the merger, emerged as possible successors to Blaize. The prime minister, however, despite his illnesses refused to relinquish control. By early 1988, the somewhat divided NNP was still in office and waiting on the political periphery was Gairy.

In the aftermath of the intervention, Grenada's political left was in serious disarray. Part of the New Jewel Movement's leadership was put on trial, a process that continued through 1986 and into early 1987. Among those on trial were General Hudson Austin, Bernard and Phyliss Coard, and most of those in the short-lived Revolutionary Military Council. Another group of former New Jewel Movement members, led by ex-Peoples Revolutionary Government (PRG) ministers George Louison and Kendrick Radix, formed the Maurice Bishop Patriotic Movement (MBPM). They participated in the 1984 elections and fared poorly because of their linkage with a difficult time in the nation's history. There have also been at least two other strands of the New Jewel Movement period, being the loose development of a social democratic wing led by ex-PRG high commissioner in the United Kingdom, Fennis Augustine, and the development of a small, hardline, pro-Coard faction around Ian St. Bernard, who was released from custody for lack of evidence.

Grenada, in many respects, represents a serious challenge for the United States in the Caribbean's eastern tier. Considerable economic aid has been provided, almost to the point of creating a dependency on the United States by Grenada. Moreover, expectations in the aftermath of the invasion and occupation did not match reality. Simply stated, U.S. taxpayers were not going to fund Grenada's development and at some point, there would be a reduction in the high levels of assistance . The political situation has also left much to be desired. There has been a growing feeling of resentment on the Grenadian side over what is perceived as heavy-handedness on the part of certain U.S. officials on the island. On the U.S. side there has been frustration over the seeming inability of the NNP rank and file to form a cohesive political organization, especially as the popularity of Gairy increased in 1986 and 1987. A political comeback for Gairy would create a highly charged situation for the United States as well as the surrounding Caribbean nations. Grenada adrift in 1988 opens to door to renewed political instability in the Eastern tier.

On an overall basis, the Commonwealth Eastern Caribbean islands advance into the late–1980s with fragile economies. Close links to metropolitan nations and to each other through CARICOM and the Eastern Caribbean Common Market have not produced significant changes. Development concerns remain focused on infrastructure and the need to diversify to those nontraditional products which can find access to the U.S. market under the CBI and to the Canadian market under CARI-CAB, Ottawa's version of the U.S. trade program. As Lionel Hurst, first secretary at the Embassy of Antigua and Barbuda stated, "These programs are long term and consequently their results will not occur over-night."[14]

A shorter-term consideration for these nations is their inclusion with the larger and culturally different Central American states under the CBI. While many Central American countries have a history of author-itarian governments, most Commonwealth Caribbean nations have fol-lowed the Westminster parliamentary tradition. Moreover, the lion's share of economic aid has consistently been given to Central America; something that many in the Eastern Caribbean find disconcerting. Though rarely said, there is sometimes the feeling that Washington has made little effort to understand the region.

The United States is not the only nation projecting its influence into the Eastern Caribbean, despite the fact that it is the predominant power. Venezuela, Brazil, Canada, Cuba, Libya, South Korea, Taiwan, the Peo-ple's Republic of China, Japan, and a number of European nations have been involved in the region's affairs. The British, French, and Dutch have armed forces in the area, while a small number of leftist parties have maintained relations or received military training and funding from Libya and Cuba. Taiwan and the People's Republic of China have also found the smaller states of the Eastern Caribbean an arena in which diplomatic recognition, a long-standing issue between the two Far East-ern states, can be obtained by developmental assistance. For the Japanese and South Koreans, the region has the potential of becoming another entry into the U.S. market, which has partially been closed to direct access by protectionist measures. Furthermore, it is probable that if an-other Grenada-style revolutionary regime were to emerge, the Soviet Union would have few qualms about exploiting a new target of oppor-tunity.

THE LARGER ENGLISH-SPEAKING STATES

Of the larger eastern tier states there is a considerable difference between the island-nations of Barbados and Trinidad and Tobago and Guyana on the mainland. On the islands, the standard of living is rel-atively advanced, the political systems are parliamentary democracies, and development strategies have largely been market-oriented and suc-cessful. Guyana under Forbes Burham from 1964 to 1985 followed a radically different developmental path from its northern island neigh-bors. While Barbados and Trinidad have had consistently meaningful elections that have usually provided a legitimate role for a democratic opposition and guarantees for civil liberties, Guyana's political system under Burnham was leftist-leaning authoritarian regime, operating be-hind a facade of empty democratic procedures and supported and main-tained for the Afro-Creole segment of the population.

The Afro-Creoles constitute 43 percent of Guyana's population and have consistently sought to exclude East Indians (51 percent of the nation's citizenry) from the nation's political life. Both major ethnic groups, Afro-Creoles as slaves and East Indians as indentured workers, were brought to Guyana, then a British colony, to labor on the sugar plantations. Ethnic cleavages divided Guyanese politics and society. Forbes Burnham's largely Afro-Creole People's National Congress played on ethnic differences to achieve power.

The alternative to Burnham had been the openly Marxist leader of the People's Progressive party (PPP), the East Indian Cheddi Jagan. Jagan, who had been the nation's first chief minister, was eased from power after riots in the early 1960s, which had been partially inspired by the United States. The United States, apprehensive about the spread of leftist groups in the Caribbean and Central America after the Cuban Revolution, put pressure on the British to oust Jagan and sought to cultivate Burnham as a non-Communist alternative. The British suspended the constitution and held new elections which Burnham, in a coalition with the small United Front party, won.

During Burnham's 21-year reign Guyana moved steadily leftward, developed ties to Cuba and became increasingly authoritarian. Grandiose projects were undertaken, socialist rhetoric flowed, and the nation was proclaimed the Cooperative Republic in 1970. By 1980, 80 percent of the economy had been nationalized and most foreign investment had been driven away. Economic mismanagement and widespread corruption left many development projects unfinished, and by the early 1980s the Guyanese economy was in serious disequilibrium. In 1983 the economy contracted 7.2 percent, there was reduced production of bauxite and sugar (the nation's two major exports), and the external debt was $1.3 billion.[15]

The development cul-de-sac of the Guyanese government was also manifest in a thriving black market and shortages of fuel and certain foods. Guyana also lost its right to draw money from the International Monetary Fund because it was in arrears, and the U.S. Agency for International Development closed its mission in July 1985, as it was owed $12 million. Economic malaise was accompanied by political corruption and elections became increasingly fraudulent.

Burnham's death on August 6, 1985, due to complications during surgery, initially brought no changes in the nation's condition. Desmond Hoyte, the new chief executive easily "won" elections in December 1985, overriding well-founded opposition claims of fraud. The economy remained in poor health, relations with the nation's international creditors and trade partners were troubled, and the backbone of the regime continued to be the predominantly Afro-Creole 17,000-man Guyana Defense Force and other police and paramilitary organizations.[16] Despite the relatively depressing nature of the economy and serious questions concerning the nation's future political direction, relations with the United States improved somewhat in early 1986 and 1987 as the Hoyte administration quietly downplayed anti-American rhetoric. At the same time, Guyana remained one of five nations in the world that lost the right to borrow from the International Monetary Fund because of arrears in payment on its debt.

While Guyana's politics and economy appear to have gone from bad to worse in the 1970s and 1980s, Barbados and Trinidad and Tobago have advanced along distinctively different paths. Trinidad and Tobago, in many respects, are a mirror image of Guyana in terms of ethnic composition, with a parity of roughly 42 percent for both Afro-Creoles and East Indians; the remainder consists of a mixed group (those of mixed Afro-Creole and East Indian or European or Chinese blood) of 14 percent and small groups of whites (Portuguese) and Chinese. Though tensions have existed between the two major ethnic groups in Trinidad, there was never the deterioration of the parliamentary system as occurred in Guyana or, for that matter, Grenada. Moreover, in the aftermath of the 1973–1974 oil price rise, the two-island state underwent an oil-led export boom resulting in an average GDP growth rate of 5.1 percent from 1970 to 1980.[17] By 1980, the per capita income was $2,654 compared to Guyana's $665.

There has, however, been a cost to heavy dependence on oil. Despite the government's efforts to diversify, 80 percent of total exports are oil related, down 10 percent from 1978. The agricultural sector has only gradually made inroads into the substantial food import bill. Moreover, the few successful initiatives in developing a broader manufacturing base have not been enough to make the necessary headway against its dependence on oil exports. Trinidad's foreign exchange earnings declined with the fall in oil prices in 1985–1986 and the government turned to foreign borrowing as a possible short-term cushion, especially as elections were to be held no later than March 1987. A projected 40 percent decline in foreign exchange earnings due to depressed oil prices meant the burdens of economic adjustment during the rest of the decade will be heavier than those that resulted from Prime Minister George Chambers' austerity measures from 1982 to 1985. With an external debt of $1.9 billion in 1986, borrowing also appears to have its limitations.

Despite the gloomy economic picture of −6.8 GDP growth in 1985 and flat or marginal growth through the end of the decade, the parliamentary system has proven to be enduring in Trinidad and Tobago.[18] In the December 10, 1986, elections, the 30-year-old reign of the People's National Movement (PNM), was ended. The high costs of the adjustment program fueled discontent with the PNM while confidence in the government was eroded by corruption and scandal allegations. This was earlier reflected in the municipal elections in August 1983, when the opposition National Alliance for Reconstruction (NAR) won more than half of the contested seats and in November 1984, when it captured eleven of twelve seats in the Tobago House of Assembly.

Under the leadership of A.N.R. Robinson the NAR began its campaign in early 1986, waiting for Chambers to announce the date for the elections, which he did in November. The desire for change was strong as the NAR captured an overwhelming 33 of 36 parliamentary seats, leaving the PNM with the remainder. Even Chambers, the former prime minister, lost his seat. Though the incoming NAR government inherited a number of economic problems, its victory clearly indicated that Trinidad and Tobago has a democratic tradition which has been upheld.

In Barbados in May, 1986, parliament was dissolved and general elections were set for May twenty-seventh. The island-state's political parties embarked upon their respective campaigns, demonstrating that democratic practices and traditions of a meaningful nature were very much evident. The culmination of the parliamentary contest was a crushing defeat for the government Barbados Labour party (BLP). The opposition Democratic Labour party (DLP), led by Errol Barrow, won 24 of 27 seats. The BLP won only three seats, losing its majority of seventeen seats in the House of Assembly (the parliament). Adding insult to injury, outgoing BLP Prime Minister Bernard St. John lost in his own constituency by a narrow 252 votes.[19] The small, Marxist-leaning Workers party of Barbados (WPB) fielded only two candidates and failed to capture any seats. A number of independents also ran, but were equally unsuccessful.

In the light of the landslide DLP victory and a substantial 83.3 percent voter turnout, up 11.8 percent from the 1981 elections, the opposition's victory was largely due to two factors. Although BLP Prime Minister Tom Adams had demonstrated strong leadership from 1976 to his death in February 1985, the economy suffered serious problems. Adam's successor, St. John, though regarded as a capable leader, lacked the presence of his predecessor. The loss of Adams and the inability of St. John to fill his political shoes, combined with concern over the economy, resulted in a large voter turnout that favored the DLP. In turn, the opposition party, out of power since its loss in 1976, was perceived as offering new solutions to the nation's economic difficulties.

Beyond the differences over economic issues, the DLP and BLP have few ideological contrasts; both favor democratic pluralism, the Westminster parliamentary tradition, free enterprise and foreign investment. The change of the government from the BLP to the DLP brought few changes in Barbados' relations with its neighbors, the Caribbean Common Market states, or the United States and the United Kingdom. The change in government in Barbados underlined the depth of democratic institutions in the English-speaking Caribbean and a long tradition often overlooked in the discussion about redemocratization in Latin America.

The economic challenge has remained a constant for Barbados despite the change in government. While Prime Minister Adams had been an outspoken supporter of the United States in the Eastern Caribbean, spoke in favor of the Caribbean Basin Initiative, a regional military force backed by U.S. military and economic aid, and was strongly opposed to the New Jewel Movement in Grenada, the nation's economy had its difficulties. Like many other Eastern Caribbean nations, the combined effects of the second oil price hike in 1979, the slowdown of the U.S. economy, which meant fewer tourists, and swings, usually downward, in its major export commodities (especially sugar) were reflected in economic contractions. There was a clear linkage between the aspirations of foreign policy, that is, an alliance with the United States in regional affairs, and a failure of economic revitalization linked, in large part, to increasing protectionism in the United States and the inability of the CBI to live up to expectations. Consequently, the mixture of politics and economics in small nation-state actors, such as Barbados, had been an interrelated fact of existence to which most regional leaders must accommodate. The oftentimes difficult task of reaching such accommodation has been defeat at the polls.

In 1984, Barbados recorded 2.4 percent growth in its GDP after several years of stagnation.[20] This was largely the result of a bumper sugarcane crop and a substantial increase in tourism. In addition, the production of electronic components for export to the United States increased by 30 percent. That growth spurt, however, was not easily duplicated in 1985 and 1986. Tourism—one of the mainstays of the economy—fell off, U.S. reductions in sugar quotas hurt that sector, and a number of foreign firms, such as Intel, left the island, claiming that labor costs were no longer competitive to those of certain Asian states. With a meager 1.0 percent GDP growth in 1985, unemployment rose to an official rate of 15.6 percent.[21]

In response to his nation's economic problems, St. John sought to implement "employment-generating" programs such as the construction of a new road system. The failure of the CBI and protectionist sugar policy were discussed with Washington. There was concern, however, that foreign loans were being used to finance job-creating projects, all of which add to the country's growing external debt of $470 million. Although St. John benefitted from increased sugar sales to the British company Tate & Lyle, which provided the government with some additional revenue to spend on the campaign, the opposition DLP won the elections. Barrows campaign message apparently hit a responsive chord: "It is a matter of top priority that the DLP take urgent effective measures to set the people to work again."[22] As the DLP victory was indeed convincing, the people of Barbados demonstrated their ability to vote and change their government as they so desired. Though Barrows died of a heart attack in May 1987, there was no succession crisis and Erskine Sandiford became the country's next prime minister.

Both Trinidad and Barbados look to futures in which the democratic system is likely to continue to function, following the Eastern Caribbean's largely pluralistic tradition. Though there are economic problems, the political systems are healthy and maintain legitimacy in the eyes of their population. There remains a fundamental belief that despite the inadequacies of the parliamentary system, it is the best possible system for the region and is capable of solving the nation's economic problems.

In contrast to Trinidad and Tobago and Barbados, Guyana's political system is a democratic sham, representative of an ethnic group reluctant to share the decision-making process about the nation's future development. Even the regime's support from the Afro-Creole segment of the population has eroded as the economy has stagnated in the 1980s. The change of leadership from Burnham to Hoyte offers some hope, but actual improvements have yet to be observed.

The larger nations of the Eastern Caribbean offer alternative paths to development. Democratic capitalism, though far from being perfect, has provided the island-states with a relatively stable and representative model of development usually overlooked in the lengthy discourses about democracy in the Third World. Guyana's cooperative socialism, driven by ethnic and political divisions and an economy in serious disequilibrium, offers a stark contrast. It would be difficult to hold Guyana under Burham up as a model for any nation; except as nations in the Eastern Caribbean are important examples for any discussion on political and economic development, they remain sadly understudied. Perhaps, in the cases of Barbados and Trinidad, more scrutiny should be given two successful examples of democracy in the developing world, especially in the Latin American redemocratization debate in the 1980s.

THE DUTCH CARIBBEAN: ARUBA, THE NETHERLANDS ANTILLES, AND SURINAME

The Dutch Caribbean consists of Suriname on the northeast shoulder of South America and the Netherlands Antilles of the Five—Bonaire, Curaçao, Saba, Sint Maarten, and Sint Eustatius—and Aruba, which left the federation on January 1, 1986. Aruba, Bonaire and Curaçao, referred to as the ABCs are located north of South America and the three Ss, the other three smaller islands are situated in the Eastern Caribbean. These islands and Suriname have long colonial linkages to the Netherlands, dating back to the seventeenth century. Through the Dutch colonial system, both areas developed populations that are ethnically diverse. Suriname's population is divided into communities of African, East Indian, Javanese, and Portuguese descent, while the islands share an equally diverse composition.[23]

In 1975 Suriname was jettisoned by the Dutch into independence despite substantial local opposition. Suriname's development as an independent nation has been characterized by the breakdown of parliamentary democracy in 1980, followed by the dictatorial rule of Lt. Col. Desi Bouterse and an attempt to forge a democratic path in late 1987 with elections. The Surinamese economy, dependent on bauxite and Dutch aid, progressively deteriorated from December 1982, when the Dutch and U.S. governments terminated financial assistance following a massacre of leading opposition figures.[24] The economic slide continued in 1983 and the long slump in bauxite prices greatly reduced the inflow of foreign exchange throughout 1984–1985. Suriname, having once enjoyed one of the highest regional standards of living in the Caribbean, had embarked upon a path to counterdevelopment akin to Guyana under Burnham.

The search for financial solvency, necessitated by the loss of Western aid, brought Suriname into contact with Cuba, Libya, the Soviet Union, and other Eastern European nations. As these nations were unable to provide the same high level of assistance that the Dutch had, and considering the dismal state of Suriname's economy, Bouterse also sought assistance from Brazil. A limited amount of Brazilian aid was provided at a political price. Brazil asked for and got a significant reduction of the Cuban presence in Suriname late in 1983.

In July 1986, a sustained effort to overthrow Bouterse's government began. Corporal Ronnie Brunswijk, a former bodyguard to Bouterse, defected from the government and established what was to become the Surinam National Liberation Army (SNLA). The SNLA was also know as the "Jungle Commando". The SNLA expanded its scope of operations from the border area into the interior.[25] By April 1987, the war was a stalemate with the SNLA in control of at least half the nation and the government holding the coast and the capital, which has the majority of the population. The November 26, 1987, elections presented a new and complicating element: the democratic opposition won 40 of the available 51 seats, while the government's National Democratic party won only two seats. How much authority will this new government, headed by President Ramsewak Shankar, actually have vis-à-vis Bouterse? This has become a particularly thorny problem as the new government's major task is the revitalization of the economy, something that cannot be done without making peace with the Jungle Commando which controls a substantial part of the country and can sabotage any number of projects. Simply stated, the road to democratic development in Suriname will be exceedingly difficult as the middle ground for democratic parties has been narrowed by the deeds of the past.

In contrast to Suriname's political turmoil since independence, the Netherlands Antilles' political history was relatively peaceful. When the Dutch government suggested that the six-island federation—which was self-governing in 1954—become independent after Suriname, the then prime minister of the Netherlands Antilles, Juan Evertsz, stated that although it was certainly the right of any former colony to obtain independence that same colony had the right to decide when and under what conditions it would achieve it. The Dutch Socialist government clearly felt that any "imperialistic baggage," such as the surviving colonial linkages in the Caribbean, was bad. However, those who were "colonized" felt differently, preferring to remain under a loosened form of Dutch sovereignty provided by the 1954 self-government ruling.

The Dutch government was not entirely deterred and established a mixed Dutch/Antilles Commission in 1976 with the intent of preparing the Netherlands Antilles for independence. In 1983, after several years of talks, it was agreed Aruba would be granted *status aparte*, which went into effect on January 1, 1986. At that time, Aruba officially left the Netherlands Antilles federation and became a separate self-governing political unit under the Dutch, who maintained their responsibility for foreign affairs and defense. Under this arrangement, Aruba became the third part of the tripartite Kingdom of the Netherlands, assuming the position vacated by Suriname upon its independence. The other two members of this constitutional arrangement are the Netherlands Antilles of the Five and Holland.

Aruba's move out of the federation was due to its perception of its relationship with Curaçao, the largest Dutch island, to which it had long been attached administratively. As one native of Curaçao commented, "Three hundred years of Dutch administration from Curaçao until self-government in 1954, made many Arubans feel as though they had been governed like a plantation."[26] This friction between the federation's two largest islands also had a racial dimension. Curaçao's population is largely of African descent. In contrast, that of Aruba's is partially Amerindian. Though on the surface, this may not appear to be a significant factor, it has become a part of the socio-political mythology of the region.

While the Aruba-Curaçao friction dominated the politics of the islands, the region's economy underwent several changes in response to major transformations in the international economic system. The three pillars of the Netherlands Antilles' economy were the processing of crude oil (largely from Venezuela), tourism, and service industries related to the financial sector. Venezuela and the United States as well as the EEC have been and remain the most important trading partners.

Throughout most of the 1970s, the Netherlands Antilles economy grew and benefitted from the two oil shocks in 1974 and 1979. At the same time, the upsurge in oil prices stimulated a wave of tourism from Venezuela. Duty-free shopping facilities and free trade zones, in particular, underwent a boom. In addition, there was a substantial increase in the number of offshore finance companies making use of the favorable provisions in the tax treaty between the Netherlands Antilles and the United States.

Buoyant economic growth from 1979 to 1982, upon which Aruban separatists based their hopes, gave way to the economic contraction of 1983–1986. GDP growth fell from 5.0 percent in 1981 to a −6.5 percent in 1984.[27] Venezuela's debt problems resulted in a drastic decline in tourist arrivals after the Bolivar's devaluation in 1982. In 1984, the United States repealed a withholding tax on investment income accruing to nonresidents, which hurt the financial sector. And the Lago Oil refinery on Aruba ceased operations in 1985. Although the refinery on Curaçao was maintained, the Venezuelan government was brought in as a new majority partner. Unemployment in Aruba and the Netherlands Antilles of the Five correspondingly rose. There was also apprehension that the international drug trade could make inroads into the populations of both Aruba and Curaçao as unemployed people are attracted to the possibly lucrative rewards of this illegal activity.[28] Moreover, the Caribbean Basin Initiative brought the Dutch islands few benefits. According to one Antillean official, "The CBI threatens to neutralize the advantages that the islands already have: a well-developed infrastructure and a highly educated and skilled work force."[29]

The Netherlands Antilles has traditionally been pro–United States, but the withdrawal of U.S. corporations, U.S. protectionist legislation that barred oil by-products, and the termination of the tax treaty hurt the islands' economies. Added to the economic uncertainties are the political questions: Can Aruba eventually achieve independence in 1996 as was charted with the Dutch and, in the short term, will the coalition governments of Prime Minister Don Martina in the federal capital of Willemstad and Prime Minister Henry Eman in Aruba survive rising unemployment? If these islands do become independent and there is no massive support for that development, will they travel the path of Suriname?

It is likely that the Netherlands Antilles of the Five will remain within the Dutch orbit. There has not been a dramatic groundswell of support for independence. Even in Aruba, which pushed for separation from Curaçao, there is not well-organized, powerful anticolonial movement. As George J. Cvenjanovich commented, "[m]ost of the electorate (78 percent) wants little or no formal cooperation with Curaçao. At the same time, however, most (68 percent) want to keep their Dutch passports."[30]

Aruba's departure has caused a shift of power to the smaller islands of St. Maarten, Saba, and St. Eustatius, which hold five of the 22 seats in the *Staten* (parliament). As the future development of the French and Dutch regions (regarding independence for the remaining British possessions and what to do about the nagging problem of external debt in Guyana) threaten, in a collective sense, to overwhelm policymakers and local governments, the Caribbean's eastern tier has also drifted from the mainstream of U.S. consciousness and the results have the potential to be most damaging in terms of a lack of response to the region's expressed needs. The nations of the region are, moreover, unique in themselves and are very different from the Central American nations with which they have been bunched within the framework of the Caribbean Basin Initiative.

CONCLUSION

What is called for in the Caribbean's eastern tier in the future is greater economic integration in the form of such organizations as the Caribbean Common Market (CARICOM) or the Eastern Caribbean Common Market. In addition, the CBI should be restructured on a longer time frame beyond its current twelve years, provisions should be made for a higher quota of sugar allowed into the U.S. market, and new integrative economic mechanisms, covering macroeconomic issues, should be established. The United States should also invest more in the education of the region's younger generation as they will provide the leadership for the next generation. The states of the Caribbean's eastern tier should also pool their resources, examine nonparallel productive paths to development, and coordinate their policies in the international organizations to which they belong, such as the Organization of American states.

In the Caribbean's eastern tier there is a strong possibility that the region will avoid future instability. High unemployment, a frustrated generation of youth who have time on their hands, and the lure of those who advocate quick and simple solutions to complex problems threaten to introduce a new round of revolutions, interventions and big power rivalry. While the norm has been democratic governments, with nondemocratic experiments being the exception, there can be no preclusion of the possibility of authoritarian developments. The responsibility for the future rests both with local leadership elites and, to a lesser extent, with the United States, its European allies, and Canada. Coordination of policies and maintaining an ability to communicate are essential for avoiding a conflictual 1990s. If the past is any teacher about the future, it is doubtful that the historical lessons have not been learned. It will take a new wave of political instability to draw attention to an important and strategic region.

NOTES

1. The literature on the Caribbean's eastern tier is not substantial beyond the material on Trinidad and Tobago, Guyana, and Barbados, especially in English. Grenada, the focus of international attention for several years, has finally developed a substantial literature. The rest of the region, however, is somewhat lacking and the following list is only a brief menu: Paget Henry, *Peripheral Capitalism and Underdevelopment in Antigua* (New Brunswick, NJ: Transaction Books, 1985); Willie James, *St. Lucia's Turmoil* (Castries, St. Lucia: Voice Press, 1982); George Black, "Mare Nostrum: US Security Policy in the English-speaking Caribbean," *NACLA* 19, 4 (July/August 1985); Patrick A. M. Emmannuel, "Revolutionary Theory and Political Reality in the Eastern Caribbean," *Journal of Interamerican Studies and World Affairs* 25, 2 (May 1983): 193–228; J. Hartog, *Curaçao: From Colonial Dependence to Autonomy* (Aruba: de Witt Inc., N.V. 1968); Edward Dew, *The Difficult Flowering of Surinam* (The Hague: Martinus Nijhoff, 1978); William A. Anderson and Russell R. Dynes, *Social Movements, Violence and Change: The May Movement in Curaçao* (Columbus, OH: Ohio State University Press, 1975); Albert L. Gastmann, *The Politics of Surinam and the Netherlands Antilles* (Rio Piedras, PR: Institute of Caribbean Studies, University of Puerto Rico, 1968); by the same author, *Historical Dictionary of the French and Dutch Caribbean* (Metuchen, NJ: The Scarecrow Press, 1978); Cornelis C. Goslings, *A Short History of the Netherlands Antilles and Surinam* (The Hague: Martinus Nijhoff, 1979); Jean Pouquet, *Les Antilles Françaises* (Paris: Presses Universitaires de France, 1976); and Scott B. MacDonald and Albert L. Gastmann, "Mitterand's Headache: The French Antilles in the 1980s," *Caribbean Review* 13, 2 (Spring 1984).

2. These distant islands are Reunion and Mayotte in the Indian Ocean, New Caledonia and French Polynesia in the South Pacific, and two islands off the coast of Canada, Miquelon and St. Pierre.

3. Richard D. E. Burton, *Assimilation or Independence?: Prospects for Martinique* (Montreal: Occasional Papers Series, No. 13, Centre for Developing-Area Studies, 1978), p. 1.

4. For a discussion of the French space program see Gerhard Drekonja-Kornat, "On the Edge of Civilization: Paris in the Jungle," *Caribbean Review* 13, 2 (Spring 1984): 26–27.

5. M. E. Chamberlain, *Decolonization: The Fall of the European Empires* (London: Basil Blackwell, Ltd., 1985), chapter 5.

6. See Arvin Murch, *Black Frenchman: The Political Integration of the French Antilles* (Cambridge, MA.: Schenkman Publishing Company, 1971).

7. Jerome Marchand, "Antilles: au-dessous des volcans," *L'Express*, July 26, 1985, pp. 54–59.

8. Marchand, "Antilles," July 26, 1985, pp. 54–59.

9. *Le Monde*, March 19, 1986, p. 14.

10. Robert Kanchuger, "The Caribbean Group: Its Evolution and Role," *Finance and Development*, September 1984, p. 44. Also see William Demas, "Consolidating Our Independence" *Caribbean Contact*, August 1986, pp. 8–9.

11. Kanchuger, "The Caribbean Group", *Finance and Development*.

12. Interview conducted by MacDonald, Kopp, and Bonilla with Dr. Joseph

E. Edmunds, ambassador of St. Lucia to the United States and Organization of American States, Washington, DC, June 10, 1986.

13. Prime Minister John Compton, "Budget Address," Address to St. Lucian Parliament, March 25, 1986, p. 4.

14. Interview conducted by MacDonald, Kopp, and Bonilla, with Lionel Hurst, trade and investment promotion officer, Embassy of Antigua and Barbuda, Washington, DC, June 18, 1986.

15. International Monetary Fund, *International Financial Statistics September 1986* (Washington, DC: International Monetary Fund, 1986), p. 240.

16. See George K. Danns, *Domination and Power in Guyana: A Study of the Police in a Third World Context* (New Brunswick, NJ: Transaction Press, 1982).

17. World Bank, *World Development Report 1982* (New York: Oxford University Press, 1982), p. 113.

18. The Royal Bank of Trinidad and Tobago Limited, *Quarterly Economic Report, Quarter Ending March 1986* 56, 14, pp. 1–2.

19. Election results provided by the Embassy of Barbados in Washington, DC.

20. Canute James, "Barbados," in *Latin American and Caribbean 1986* (Saffron Walden, Essex, United Kingdom: World of Information, 1985).

21. Central Bank of Barbados, *Economic Review* 13, 1 (June 1986), p. 1.

22. *FBIS*, May 13, 1986, p. S2. Also see editorial, "The People's Responsibility," *Barbados Advocate (News)*, May 8, 1986, p. 4.

23. See Vera Green, *Migrants in Aruba: Interethnic Integration* (Assen, The Netherlands: Van Gorcum and Camp, B.V., 1974).

24. See Greg Chamberlain, "Seventeen Die in Suriname Purge," *The Guardian*, December 19, 1982, p. 14.

25. "Euro-parlement zal politieke situatie in Suriname onderzoeken," *NRC Handelsblad*, February 18, 1987, p. 1; and Frans van Klaveren, "Bouterse zou zich ontdoen van Kibiers," *NRC Handelsblad*, December 23, 1986, p. 1.

26. MacDonald interview with unnamed Dutch official in Washington, DC, June 1986.

27. Barclays Bank Report on the Netherlands Antilles, November 1985, p. 1.

28. Expressed by several shopkeepers interviewed in Aruba by MacDonald during a visit to that island in June 1986.

29. Herald Henriquez, plenipotentiary and minister of Netherlands Antilles Affairs, Embassy of the Netherlands, Washington, DC made this comment in an interview with MacDonald in July 1986.

30. George J. Cvenjanovich, "Future Aruba: Can It Make It Alone?," *Caribbean Review* 14, 3 (Summer 1985), p. 42.

PART III
ISSUES ON THE PERIPHERY

11
Contadora and the Central American Republics: A Slide Down a Slippery Slope
Jonathan Lemco

The long-standing effort to find a peaceful solution to the myriad of disputes in Central America continues to prove terribly frustrating. The most recent attempt to resolve the very serious problem there, which has come to be known as the Contadora Peace Process, has been stymied. The points of dispute in the region concern civil war in El Salvador and insurgency in Nicaragua, abject poverty in five of the republics, social dislocation in the region and the interventions of outside powers pursuing their own interest—often to the detriment of the Central American nations themselves. Clearly, it should be no surprise that peace remains elusive.

This essay will provide an overview of the Contadora Peace Process. After a brief historical discussion, the interests and concerns of Nicaragua, El Salvador, Honduras, Guatemala, and Costa Rica will be examined. The United States is a prominent actor in the region and its view of Contadora will then be discussed. Canada, too, may have an important, although indirect, role to play and its efforts to contribute to the peace process will be summarized. Finally the likely prospects for peace in the region, such as they are, will be explored.

The Contadora Peace talks were initiated by Mexico on January 8–9, 1983 and named for the island off the coast of Panama where the foreign ministers of Mexico, Venezuela, Colombia, and Panama met to discuss strategies for arriving at peace and social justice in Central America. (This group was referred to as the Contadora members or support group.) Of prime importance was their determination to find a regional resolution to Central America's problems, rather than having outside

powers imposing their solutions, as had been the traditional practice.[1]
The basic goals of Contadora, both in 1983 and currently, include:

1. The removal of foreign military advisers from Central America. The Contadora ministers share a distaste both for previous unilateral U.S. interventions in the region, e.g., Guatemala in 1954, Cuba in 1961, the Dominican Republic in 1965. In addition, they share a desire to moderate and contain the Sandinista regime in Nicaragua and the FMLN revolutionaries in El Salvador, and to avoid the expansion of a Soviet-bloc presence in Nicaragua. The Contadora ministers fear any repetition of these activities and they want to avoid the conversion of the region into an epicenter of East-West tensions.

2. The end to arms imports and arms smuggling.

3. The end to international military maneuvers.

4. The closing of all foreign military bases.

5. The end of support for guerrilla movements.

6. Comprehensive control and verification procedures.

7. The institution of democratic, pluralistic governments with major socio-economic reconstruction.

The Foreign ministers pledged to find "Latin American solutions to Latin American problems" by seeking negotiated settlements of the rapidly intensifying armed conflicts in Nicaragua and El Salvador.[2] To this end, the United States would have to be convinced that Central American socioeconomic development was crucial.

From the outset the Contadora negotiators recognized that the United States did have legitimate security concerns in the region and and they worked to reduce Soviet and Cuban influence there. Nevertheless they disagreed fundamentally with the Reagan administration about the underlying cause of the turmoil in Central America. If the United States saw the problems as caused by Soviet-Cuban expansionism, the Contadora countries saw the basic causes of civil strife to be internal (i.e., poverty and social injustice). Moreover, they blamed the United States for having tolerted repressive right wing regimes for decades, thereby contributing to instability.

The solution of the Contadora ministers was to seek a regional solution to their problems, thereby challenging U.S. hegemony in the region. In addition, they felt that negotiation and dialogue would have to become standard devices in restoring political stability and social peace to Central America. There was also a consensus that negotiations with Cuba to limit Soviet-Cuban influence in the region was mandatory. Above all, the threat of regional wars had to be ended.

At first the United States ignored the Contadora Group. Later it publicly professed support, while repeatedly undermining the process. For example, in July 1983, just as the Contadora countries were producing their first comprehensive proposals, President Reagan dispatched navel vessels to the Pacific and Caribbean coasts of Nicaragua and announced that the largest U.S. military exercises to dat, Big Pine II, would take place in Honduras during the fall.

In September of 1983, the Contadora support group of Mexico, Colombia, Panama, and Venezuela presented a 21-point proposal as the basis for peace. This document was then signed by the five Central American nations and supported, in principle, by the United States. The proposals provided guidelines for mutually agreed upon measures to eliminate or reduce any foreign military presence in the region. In fact, the Reagan administration simultaneously attempted to revive Condeca (the Central American Defense Council), a body for regional military cooperation, which had ceased to function after the downfall of President Somoza in Nicaragua. The United States hoped to unite the Salvadorean, Honduran, and Guatemalan armed forces to use them against the Sandinistas or the Salvadorean guerrillas. The plan failed when the Guatamalan army balked at the idea.

In spite of the U.S. efforts to sabotage the Contadora effort, the 21 points were put into treaty form. At one time, over one hundred regional advisers and diplomats were involved. Finally on September 7, 1984, the four Contadora countries agreed on a compromise version and submitted it to the Central American governments, which had been consulted extensively during its preparation.

If implemented, the proposed treaty would have reversed the thrust toward militarization in several ways. The countries of the region would agree to submit inventories of their present arms, suspend new arms acquisitions, and establish limits on certain types of equipment, particularly offensive weapons. Nicaraguan and El Salvadorean arms buildups, in particular, would be halted. Next they would establish limits on personnel. A commission on verification and control would assure complience. Moreover, the governments would agree not to authorize foreign military bases, and to eliminate existing ones within six months of signing the treaty. International military maneuvers would be forbidden and external support for insurgents fighting against El Salvador or Nicaragua would be ended. Furthermore, Cuban and Soviet military advisers would be withdrawn from Nicaragua and U.S. advisors taken out of El Salvador. In addition, there would be freedom of movement for a verification commission. The holding of free elections in the region's nations was also promised.

Nicaragua agreed to the draft version on September twenty-first. Although it had frequently voiced its verbal support, the Reagan administration was caught off guard. Administration spokespersons called the treaty proposals unfair, citing for example the fact that foreign military advisers engaged in training and operations (such as U.S. personnel in

El Salvador) would have to leave while those involved in maintenance (such as the Cubans and Soviets in Nicaragua) would not. They stated further that it was one-sided to end U.S. military exercises and close U.S. military bases without exacting anything from Nicagagua. That objection, however, only underscored the one-sidedness of the U.S. military involvement: No other foreign power was constructing bases or holding maneuvers. The Reagan administration also feared that Nicaragua would be allowed to retain large miltiary forces. A neutral commission from the perspective of the White House, might well have accepted Nicaragua's argument that it needed a large military force to deter a U.S. invasion.

By October 19, 1984, there began a series of counter proposals formultated by U.S. allies Costa Rica, El Salvador and Honduras.[3] These three are members of the "Central American Democratic Community"— a euphemism for nations heavily influenced by the United States. A leaked United States National Security Council document, discussed in press reports on November 6, 1984, indicated that the Reagan administration had "effectively blocked" the adoption of the draft treaty.[4]

While Contadora was undercut, the U.S. initiated a more aggressive policy against Nicaragua. On January 17, 1985, the United States ended bilateral talks with Nicaragua which it had initiated in mid-1984 at the urging of the Contadora nations. On the next day the United States suspended for two years its recognition of the International Court of Justice's jurisdiction on matters related to Central America. This followed the Court's calling on the United States to desist from mining Nicaraguan harbors or engaging in threatening military activities directed at that country.

On February 21, 1985, President Reagan stated that the United States wanted to "remove the present structure" of the Nicaraguan government. He added that the Sandinistas would be acceptable only if "they'd say uncle."

On May 1, 1985, the United States announced the imposition of a trade embargo against Nicaragua. Soon after, relations were further strained when Nicaraguan President Daniel Ortega visited the Soviet Union and the U.S. Congress subsequently approved "humanitarian assistance" to the contras.

Amidst this climate of exacerbated tension and conflict, the Contadora countries initiated efforts to iron out a second draft treaty. Border clases on the Costa Rican–Nicaraguan frontier were more frequent.

In December 1985 the Contadora Group announced the suspension of its activities until May 1986. A Contadora foreign minister noted that the suspension was caused by the "deep confrontation" between the United States and Nicaragua. The decision to postpone furhter negotiations reflected a serious impasse in the Contadora process, but it also created the conditions that led to the elections and changes in government which took place in Costa Rica, Guatemala, and Honduras in late 1985 and early 1986.

The Contadora Group met with the so-called Lima Group of countries (Argentina, Brazil, Peru, and Uruguay) on January 11–12, 1986, and produced the Carabelleda message which reaffirmed the original Contadora principles as a basis for peace in Central America and outlined a plan for immediate action. Subsequently, the Guatemala Declaration, signed on January seventeenth by the Contadora and Lima Groups as well as the five Central American countries, reaffirmed the Caraballeda message. A month later, on February tneth, the foreign ministers of the Contadora and Lima groups held their first combined talks in Washington with Secretary of State George Schultz.

It appeared, however, that after four years of talks and multiple draft treaties, the negotiations were deadlocked. Behind the stalemate, the key issues were regional arms limitations, democratization in Nicaragua, and U.S. support for the contras. Each of these issues, in turn, touched directly upon the principles of nonintervention, self-determination, and respect for national sovereignty upon which the Contadora Group's basic consensus rested. The United States and its closest Central American allies—Costa Rica, Honduras, and El Salvador—demanded that the Sandinistas reduce the size of their armed forces and install a "democratic"political system before they would halt support for the contras. The Sandinistas, in turn, refused to "disarm" or to negotiate with their political opposition until the United States and neighboring Central American goverments halted aid to the contras.

By June 1986, the Contadora Group was unable to produce an acceptable treaty to the five Central American countries or the United States. At this point, on June fifteenth, the U.S. House of Representatives reversed its two-year ban on military assistance to the contras and approved the Reagan administration's request for a $100 million U.S. aid package in military and "humanitarian" assistance to the rebel forces. In August, President Reagan publicly acknowledged for the first time that it might ultimately be necessary for the contras to overthrow the Sandinista government militarily.

The Contadora process is still a reality, although it is clearly moribund. If the United States does not intervene directly, then the contras alone will not be able to defeat the Sandinistas. The Nicaraguan government will continue to rely on Soviet and Cuban aid, thus permitting an external presence in that country as well. The Sandinistas will not be able to completely defeat the contras so long as the latter can continue to retreat to sanctuaries in Honduras and El Salvador. The prospects, then, are for protracted war in Nicaragua accompanied by inevitable spillover effects in Costa Rica, Honduras, and El Salvador.

NICARAGUA AND CONTADORA

Nicaragua's priority is to consolidate its revolution and protect its borders. To that end, any attempt to braoden peaceful ties with its neighbors is, on the surface at least, welcomed. As a result, Nicaragua appears to look quite favorably upon the Contadora process as a possible vehicle for arriving at peace in the region. Until recently however, Nicaragua claimed that it could not be a signatory to the agreement until all parties were subject to its provisions. By this it meant that the United States would have to cease its support of the contras, end the CIA mining of Nicaraguan harbors, and terminate its attempts to destablize the Sandinista regime.

Furthermore, Nicaragua insisted that it would sign the Contadora Act, reduce its military buildup, and withdraw Soviet and Cuban advisers only if the United States simultaneously ceased hostilities directed at the Sandinista regime and signed a protocol committing itself to respect the provisions of the Contadora agreement. As far as Nicaragua was concerned, this would effectively prohibit support for the contra forces.[5]

When the Contadora process was first discussed, Nicaragua favored bilateral nonaggression pacts with its Central American neighbors and joint border patrols with Honduras and Costa Rica.[6] When the talks appeared to be ready to collapse soon after, Nicaragua agreed to accept a multilateral negotiating framework.

In October 1983, Nicaragua resumed its attempt to negotiate bilateral treaties with the United States and Honduras. The United States immediately rejected this approach, stressing instead that a peace accord could be achieved only through the Contadora process in the ensuing three years. Nicaragua resisted pressure by the United States and the other Central American countries to reduce its military forces and continued to maintain that its large standing army and heavy military expenditures were necessary to resist the U.S. threat. In addition, it stressed that its military preparedness would remain at a high level until the United States signed the Contadora treaty and thereby stopped supporting the Contra insurgents. The United States, in turn, accused the Sandinista government of resisting the peace initiatives and, in fact, of ostensibly supporting Contadora only in an effort to maximize its public relations potential. At about this time, the Reagan administration was flush from its success in Grenada and was taking a particularly aggressive stance against what it labeled the Marxist-Leninist regime of Nicaragua. Indeed, there were suspicions in many circles that having defeated the communist regime in the Caribbean, Nicaragua would be a prime target for U.S. military intervention.

In September of 1984, a circulation draft of the Contadora peace treaty was signed by Nicaragua. The document banned international military maneuvers, restricted the buildup of military forces and outlawed support for insurgent forces aginst other nations in Central America. As mentioned, the United States was caught off guard by this Nicaraguan action.

The United States immediately denounced Nicaragua's support for Contadora and called it a publicity stunt. In fact, the United States was put in an uncomfortable position, for it could not now legitimately accuse the Sandanista regime of taking every opportunity to create unrest in the region. In addition, Washington was stifled in its efforts to isolate Nicaragua internationally. Finally, the United States could not easily justify its hostility to Nicaragua so long as Nicaragua appeared to be making a peaceful gesture.

The United States then pressured Honduras, El Salvador, and Costa Rica to reverse their acceptance of the Contadora draft and insist upon revisions. In addition, the United States accused Nicaragua of agreeing to the draft in its early stages only if no further changes occurred. The Reagan administration, in other words, attempted to portray Nicaragua as inflexible. Soon after the United States successfully encouraged its Central American allies to block acceptance of the treaty.

In the next two years, no unanimous agreement was reached on the Contadora treaty. Nicaragua continued to insist that although it supported the peace process in principle, it could not reduce its military establishment until its borders were secure and the U.S.–Contra threat was ended. The United States also claimed to support Contadora in principle, yet could not sign the treaty until Nicaragua reduced its military commitment. Indeed, U.S. officials began to call for a new regime in Nicaragua. Of course, underneath all of this was the U.S. desire to avoid anything that would serve to "legitimize" the Sandinistas. The situation was then, and remains today, a diplomatic stalemate.

By November of 1985, the negotiating process had produced few concrete solutions and discussions were postponed until April 1986. At that time, the talks resumed with the parties again soon deadlocked. Only recently has some movement been evident.

EL SALVADOR AND CONTADORA

El Salvador is a country that has been torn apart by civil war, poverty and social injustice. The Duarte government has expressed support for the Contador peace process but it is absolutely dependent upon U.S. economic aid and military assistance in its attempt to develop economically and provide political stability. These goals are especially difficult to reach given the high costs of the struggle against the FMLN guerrillas. President Duarte is forced therefore to adopt positions within the Contadora negotiations that are consistent with the U.S. position. El Salvador is not alone in this regard. Costa Rica and Honduras have also found it advantageous to support the U.S. position when required. As a result, it is conventional widsom that Washington's close relations with the governments of El Salvador, Honduras, and Costa Rica give the Reagan administration veto power over any agreement drafted by the Contadora nations, since no agreement can take effect until all five of the Central American nations sign.

HONDURAS AND CONTADORA

Like El Salvador, Honduran interests are closely tied to the United States. This precludes any strong support for the Contadora peace process unless the U.S. position on Nicaragua and Contadora is tempered. Honduras' foreign policy initiatives are further circumscribed because it is the poorest of the Central American republics and one of the poorest countries in the hemisphere.

In 1982, following a decade of military government, Honduras returned to civilian rule and formal democratic political institutions. The United States continues to support the government militarily and provides developmental aid in exchange for U.S. military use of Honduran territory and unofficial sanctuary for the contras.

Honduras is concerned about the Nicaraguan military buildup on its border and the possibility of Nicaraguan reprisals for contra attacks launched from Honduras. As a result, it would be reluctant to alienate its U.S. ally and demonstrate greater enthusiasm for Contadora than is already the case. Indeed, Honduras regularly takes the lead in promoting the U.S. position at Contadora-related meetings and has repeatedly accused Nicaragua of obstructing the peace process and worked to increase the Sandinistas' diplomatic isolation. Furthermore, when the United States feels that the negotiations have proceeded too rapidly, Honduras has predictably slowed down the negotiations by raising technical objections or presenting new proposals.[7]

GUATEMALA AND CONTADORA

Guatemala is the largest and most industrialized Central American country. In the 1970s and 1980s its military rulers had a grim record of human rights violations which prompted the United States (and other Western countries) to donate little economic or military aid. Ironically, on the one hand, Guatemala's leaders were fervently anti-communist, while on the other it received little support from that bastion of anti-communism—the United States. This is particularly interesting given the constant threat of armed insurgency within Guatemala and the terrible economic problems faced by that country in the form of a burgeoning debt and severe recession.

Because of its strained relations with the United States, its lesser degree of economic dependence on U.S. aid, and the apparent capacity of the Guatemalan military to contain domestic insurgents, Guatemala has maintained foreign policy positions more independent of the United States than any other Central American nation except Nicaragua. The current Christian Democratic government of President Vinicio Cerezo (inaugurated in Janaury 1986) has been particularly interested in promoting the Contadora process. Guatemala fears a direct confrontation with Nicaragua and seeks to distance itself from its anti-Sandinista neighbors and the United States.

This point must be quialified, however, for Guatemala continues to face an economic crisis, its military is still a potent force and always a threat to overthrow the government, and U.S. aid has recently increased. How long Guatemala can continue its policy of "active neutrality" is anyone's guess.[8]

COSTA RICA AND CONTADORA

Costa Rica is the only Central American country, indeed it is one of the few countries in Latin America, to retain a civilian government and democratic institutions for most of its history. It is also unique in that it retains no standing army. Like many of its neighbors, Costa Rica has modeled its constitution on that of the United States, but it is almost alone in its ability to practice the principles that the constitution embodies.

There are a number of reasons that one could cite to explain Costa Rica's free society, but for our purposes a particularly notable one is the strong tie that has alwyas existed between that country and the United States. Costa Rica, like Honduras and El Salvador, is reluctant to diverge too sharply from the United States on foreign policy issues. Accordingly, Costa Rica's position on Contadora is hesitant. Although it is in its interest to support the peace process as a means of preserving its democratic stability, Cost Rica will not go so far as to undermine U.S. interests. It shares President Reagan's concerns about the Sandinista threat and depends heavily on U.S. markets and economic assistance to sustain its fragile economy.

Nevertheless, the Costa Rican government officially opposed its territory as a base for contra operations or U.S. military maneuvers. It is reluctant to provoke open conflict with Nicaragua. In practice, however, the contras do operate out of Costa Rican territory. Along with Honduras and El Salvador, Costa Rica remains a member of what has been called the "Central American Democratic Community" and continues to support the isolation of the Sandinista regime in Nicaragua. Costa Rica's tie to the United States is still of primary concern, and it will support the United States even if that country continues to demonstrate its doubts about the Contadora initiatives.[9]

UNITED STATES AND CONTADORA

The United States is a major political actor in Central America. It has a myriad of strategic, political, and investment interests in the region, and as a result all efforts to find a peaceful solution to the strife in Central America must take U.S. concerns into account. Indeed, one motivation for the formation of the Contadora peace talks was to demonstrate that the countries of Latin America could reach peaceful agreements without the intervention of external powers. Intervention is one thing, however, and concerns quite another, for U.S. interests are always a factor in the Central American peace process. The United States and the Soviet Union are the most prominent external powers and their involvements in Central American affairs have had enormous repercussions for the region. The United States, in particular, has been able to marshall vast political, economic and military resources, reward cooperative nations in the region, would not sanction any attempt to challenge its hegemony, or intervene when it considers such an action necessary.

President Reagan supports the removal of the Sandinista regime from power, the strengthening of the Duarte government in El Salvador, and the containment of radical or revolutionary movements in the rest of Central America. He has managed to convince most members of Congress and much of the public that the Sandinista regime constitutes a threat to its neighbors and the United States. President Reagan, however, has not been able to generate a national consensus in support of the overthrow of the Nicaraguan government or for the use of overt military force against Nicaragua. As a result, Washington has not been in a position to apply the full range of U.S. power resources in Central America and has been forced to rely on "second-best" strategies, such as covert support for the contras.[10]

This support may end in the near future, however, as the House and Senate are likely to oppose the president's contra policy by approving a special resolution to withhold $40 million of military aid still due the contras. The revelations that U.S. officials secretly diverted Iranian arms payments to the contras have alienated Congress across ideological lines and have jeopardized further votes on contra aid.

With regard to the Contadora process, the United States is in an awkward position. The U.S. government supports a peaceful solution to the problems of the region. President Reagan has declared that the Contadora process is the best tool available to resolve difficulties there. However many analysts argue that the president in only paying lip service to Contadora and that his real goals are military, that is, to undermine the Sandinista government, to support the Duarte regime, and to safe-guard the United States' strategic interests. To these ends the United States discourages Nicaraguan participation in Contadora, supports the contra forces and encourages El Salvador, Costa Rica, and Honduras to protect U.S. interests.

If a successful Contador agreement is reached, then some U.S. analysts feel that this could be a useful vehicle for the survival and consolidation of the Nicaraguan revolution.[11] This might well be another reason for President Reagan's less than wholehearted support for the Contradora process. Indeed, Undersecretary of State Elliot Abrams has stated that the U.S. government would prefer no treaty at all to a "bad" agreement, by which he means that the United States would prefer no agreement to one that would permit the retention of the Sandinista regime. Fur-thermore, on May 20, 1986 the U.S. Defense Department released its study of the Contadora peace plan in which the peace effort was severely criticized as giving Nicaragua "a shield from behind which they could continue their use of subersive aggression." This would require sending 100,000 U.S. troops to Central America within several years.[12]

Although this is a Defense Department view and not necessarily a State Department one, it is clear that there is a great deal of U.S. gov-ernment concern over the possible repercussions of Contadora.

As far as the United States is concerned, Contadora's efforts to ne-gotiate a verifiable treaty that neutralizes Nicaragua as a security threat via agreements on the withdrawal of foreign bases and advisers, limits on the size of military establishments, and controls on arms buildups and mutual nonaggression pacts, are inadequate because communists simply cannot be trusted.[13]

As a result the best U.S. strategy for the region is to promote the contra forces rather than the Contadora process. The United States, then, will continue to demand that the Contadora draft include two provisions with which the Nicaraguans cannot live. These include the continuation of U.S. military maneuvers in Honduras, which Nicaragua wants eliminated, and a provision to set limits on the size of each Central American country's arms, which would require Nicaragua to make sharp reductions in troop levels, scrap some of its arsenal, and repatriate its Cuban advisers (if any exist). It should also be acknowledged that strict compliance with the provisions of the Contadora treaty would require an end to Nicaraguan press censorship and harassment of the Catholic church and political parties. The provision for internal reconciliation would require negotiation with the U.S.-backed contras. Finally, the ban on cross-border subversion would rule out Sandinista aid to the Salva-dorean rebels.

The main explanation which President Ortega offers for his resistance to the treaty is that his government needs all the arms it can obtain in order to keep the U.S. imperialists at bay. One might argue, however, that this is a curious rationale since the terms of Contadora provide his best opportunity to evict U.S. military power from the region.

Costa Rica and Honduras, the two Central American states which have harbored the contras, would be bound by the treaty to deny such sanctuary. Honduras and El Salvador would have to completely restrict the presence of U.S. military advisers on their soil. Contradora, then, has the potentioal to dismantle most of the anticommunist infrastructure which the United States has so elaborately built up in Central America in recent years.

On the other hand, one could make the credible argument that by supporting Contadora, the Reagan administration would gain a solid base of support in both domestic and international public opinion for a tough policy toward Nicaragua, should the Sandinistas violate the treaty. Richard Bloomfield, for example, argues that Contadora could put the United States on the side of principle and put the onus of violating principle on Nicaragua.[14] In signing the agreement the United States would gain the Contadora governments—Colombia, Mexico, Panama, and Venezuela—as allies. These countries represent the major democracies of the region and a significant percentage of Latin America's population. Further, one might argue that by joining such allies in supporting Contadora, the United States would then be in a stronger position to demand that allies abroad join it in sanctions against a Nicaragua that was breaking its commitments.

This is not a likely scenario for the foreseeable future, however. There is an enormous climate of mistrust between the United States and Nicaragua and neither country will demonstrate strong support for Contadora in its present form.

CANADA AND CONTADORA

Canada is not a country that is normally thought of as having a strong interest in Central American affairs.[15] Indeed, it is true that for much of its history, Canada's closest links in the region were to those Caribbean countries where Canada had banking and investment ties. (At first, Canada expressed reservations about the U.S. invasion of Grenada. This was more a reflection of Canada feeling slighted for not being consulted by the United States prior to the invasion rather than any sharp divergence from U.S. policy, however. The Grenada invasion plays no significant role in Canadian foreign policy decisions in Central America.) Nevertheless, successive Canadian governments in the 1970s and 1980s have expressed their strong support for Central American peace in general, and the contadora peace process in particular. Canada's room to maneuver in Central America is limited, however, by the fact that it will go to great lengths not to embarrass its closest ally, the United States. As a result, Canada will not publicly diverge too sharply from the U.S. position.

Canada has bestowed good wishes, advice, and economic support on Contadora without involving itself directly in the process. Prime Minister Mulroney maintains that the Central American countries and the Contadora group will have to resolve their problems on their own. He stresses that regional problems must have regional solutions. Like his predecessors in the prime minister's office, Mulroney believes that there is a place for multilateral dialogue and cooperation, but peace is an international matter best reserved for organizations like the UN or the Contadora countries. External powers, particularly the United States and the Soviet Union, should stay out or they will amost certainly aggravate tensions.

Canada's greatest contribution to the Contadora peace process at this time is its offered comments on the control and verification commission portion of the Contadora drafts. This is a natural contribution, for it has had years of experience as a peacekeeper in Vietnam, the Sinai, and elsewhere.

Canada's Contadora comments have been universal in scope rather than specific to Central America. They have related to the funding, composition, communications, and structure of the verification commission. Many of the details of these comments have not been made public, although it is known that Canada suggested that a controlling authority, like the UN, be established to coordinate and supervise the work of all commissions formed to implement the Contadora act. Other points discussed included "time limits on the Control and Verification Commission (CVC) mandate, the need for specific guarantees relating to freedom of movement, access by the CVC, their physical security, definition of size, logistic and communications support, and recommendations with respect to financial operations."[16]

Canadian government officials also emphasized that the mass media should be granted detailed knowledge of the CVC. They retain important reservations about the prospects for Contadora, but understand that it is the only effort that stands a chance of arriving at peaceful solutions to the problems of the region.[17] Government officials also recognize that although Canada's views carry weight and are respected in Central America, it does not exercise a vital influence. Indeed, what influence it has would probably deteriorate should it take sides or become vocal in its criticism of political actors in the region.

CONCLUSION

At the present time it is difficult to be optimistic about the prospects for a successful agreement on the Contadora peace process. The United States remains hostile to Nicaragua, Nicaragua is perceived as a threat by its neighbors, El Salvador continues to be engulfed in a civil war and the parties to the proposed agreement are no longer demonstrating the required degree of enthusiasm.

One can take an opposite tack, of course, and stress that whether or not the Contadora act is signed, it has still had a considerable significance for Latin America, an indication of a new willingness to coordinate policies in the face of the region's problems and a symbol of Latin America's greater independence from U.S. influence.

This is putting the best face on a bleak situation, however, for the Contadora process has failed to attain its primary objectives thus far. It has not been able to ensure peace and stability in the region. There has been no reconciliation between the United States and Nicaragua, or between the Duarte government in El Salvador and the FMLN. Although it is true that Contadora was the most significant display of Central American unity since the long-expired Central American Federation of 1824–1839, it has failed to accomplish its central purpose.

This is not to say that the talks are over. From time to time, political analysts proclaim Contadora dead, and then like a phoenix reemerging from the ashes it reappers. At this writing, eight Latin American foreign ministers, the UN, and the OAS heads have just concluded another unsuccessful attempt to reach a compromise. The effort continues, however, for not only does the possibility of peace remain, but in Contadora the Latin American countries can continue to demonstrate that they have the means to solve their own problems, no longer reliant on outside powers. One should not underemphasize this powerful rationale for an accord.

NOTES

1. For a good overview of the root causes of Central America's problems, see Howard J. Wiarda (ed.) *Rift and Revolution: The Central American Imbroglio* (Washington, DC: AEI, 1984); and Morris Blachman, William LeoGrande and Kennth Sharpe (eds.) *Confronting Revolution: Security Through Diplomacy in Central America* (New York: Pantheon, 1986).

2. For a comprehensive review of these points, see Bruce Michael Bagley, "Contadora: The Failure of Diplomacy," in Abraham Lowenthal (ed.), *Latin America and Caribbean Contemporary Record* (New York: Holmes and Meier Publishers, 1987).

3. For a comprehensive discussion of these proposals, see Everett A. Bauman, *The Strengths and Weaknesses of Contadora as Regional Diplomacy in the Caribbean Basin* (unpublished working paper for the Latin American program, Woodrow Wilson International Center for Scholars, 1985).

4. This last point is reported in Lisa North, *Negotiations for Peace in Central America: A Conference Report* No. 1 (Ottawa: Canadian Instutute for International Peace and Security, 1985.

5. For a detailed discussion of this point, see the "Press Comuniqué from the Office of the Presidency," Republic of Nicaragua, Managua (April 12, 1986).

6. See William LeoGrande, "Rollback or Containment? The United States, Nicaragua, and the Search for Peace in Central America" in *International Security* 11, 2 (Fall 1986): 89–120.

7. For a detailed discussion of this point, see Bruce Bagley (ed.), *Contadora and the Diplomacy of Peace in Central America* (Boulder, Co: Westview Press, 1987).

8. For a good discussion of Guatemala's foreign affairs interests, see Robert Trudeau and Lars Schoultz, "Guatemala" in Morris Blachman, et al. (eds), *Confronting Revolution*, pp. 23–49.

9. For an excellent discussion of current Costa Rican policy initiatives, see Cahlmers Rumbaugh, "Costa Rica: The Making of a Livable Society" (unpublished Ph.D. dissertation: The University of Wisconsin, 1985).

10. For a good overview of U.S. policy toward Central America, see Morris J. Blachman et al. (eds.), *Confronting Revolution*, pp. 295–386.

11. For a good discussion of this point, see William M. LeoGrande, "Cuba," in Blachman et al. (eds.), *Confronting Revolution*, pp. 229–55.

12. This statement is quoted from "Latin America: Chronology 1986," in *Foreign Affairs* 65, 3 (Winter 1987): 687.

13. For a comprehensive discussion of this point, see Bruce Michael Bagley and Juan Gabriel Tokatlian, "Contadora: The Limits of Negotiation," unpublished paper for the Latin American Studies Program of the School of Advanced International Studies, The Johns Hopkins University, Washington, DC, 1986.

14. Richard J. Bloomfield, "Using the Contadora Solution," in The New York *Times*, February 17, 1987, p. A23.

15. For a fuller discussion of Canadian interests in the Contadora peace process, see Jonathan Lemco, "Canadian Foreign Policy Interests in Central America: Some Current Issues," in *The Journal of Interamerican Studies and World Affairs* 28, 2 (Summer 1986): 119–46.

16. John Graham, "Canada and Contadora," speech delivered to the Canadian Institute of Strategic Studies, Toronto, Canada (November 8, 1985), p. 7.

17. For a discussion of these reservations, see Jonathan Lemco, "Canadian Foreign Policy Interests in Central America: Some Current Issues," pp. 136–38.

12
Panama: Lurching Toward Democracy?
Eva Loser

INTRODUCTION

Since the late 1970s, in a search for socioeconomic and political development, many of the nations of the Caribbean basin proper (geographically defined as Central America and the Caribbean Islands) have attempted to seek such advances through either a transition to democratic rule, or have sought to sustain a democratic tradition. With regard to the former, much documentation of the region's transitions from authoritarian to democratic rule has been carried out, demonstrating there is not set prescription to establish civilian rule: Rather, each nation has forged a political opening in its own manner, often following a circuitous route. Furthermore, underlying each transition has been an implicit assumption relating to the belief that the goal of democratic rule is a normative theme—or in other words, that political democracy is, unto itself, a desirable goal.[1]

In 1984, Panama, one of the United States' most important strategic allies in the Caribbean basin region followed this trend. Recent events in Panama's emerging civilian democracy have suggested that progress toward emocratic rule has been tenuous: specifically, that the nation has not constructed a viable civilian political arena, free from the intrusion of military influence in affairs of governance. It is argued that since 1984, instead of creating a framework for the institutionalization of democratic rule, the nation has created a democratic veneer of constitutional mechanisms designed to cover a continued pattern of authoritarian rule.

Since President Ardito Barletta's resignation in 1985 and subsequent replacement by Eric del Valle, the U.S. foreign policymaking community has, once again, focused increased attention on the Panamanian situation. In tandem, the Reagan administration, despite its emphasis on addressing the Central American imbroglio, has appeared to be relatively helpless in inducing any changes in Panama's domestic environment; in this context, Washington has cast around for policies of leverage/influence, but has emerged empty-handed.

But in this search for policy options, there has perhaps been a tendency to "put the cart before the horse." Indeed it would seem appropirate that before policy options are selected, there exists the need to have a clear vision of the current situation in Panama. While it has been easy to assign the blame of Panama's current predicament to the Panamanian Defense Forces (PDF) and the role of General Manuel Noriega, there are other ills that exist in Panama (for example, relating to the actions of the civilian political community) which have not received the attention they deserve. This essay therefore, will attempt to provide an analysis in historical perspective of Panama's contemporary experience in the construction of a democratic polity, as well as to examine Panama's potential for affecting trends within the Caribbean basin and implications for bilateral relations with Washington.

BACKGROUND

Societal development can occur in the absence of democracy. In the aftermath of the 1968 coup which removed Arnulfo Arias Madrid from the presidency and catapulted General Omar Torrijos Herrera into power, the Panamanian environment did undergo substantial change.[2]

Previously governed by a small group of urban-based elites who demonstrated difficulty in addressing even the most basic needs of the populace, the goals of the new left-leaning military government were threefold: (1) to gain control of the Panama Canal and attendant Canal Zone; (2) to meet the socioeconomic needs of the population; and (3) to create a broader base of political representation. The first was accomplished through long and arduous negotiations culminating in the 1978 Panama Canal Treaty, granting full territorial sovereignty of the Canal Zone to Panama, although transit activities associated with the Canal and the latter's maintenance will be administered by the United States until the year 2000. With regard to the second goal, although the economic infrastructure of the nation was to remain essentially unaltered, the resources were to become more equitably distributed. And finally, through the creation of the Democratic Revolutionary Party (PRD) the Defense Forces have obtained the means by which to control events within the political arena.

PANAMA'S NEW SOVEREIGNTY AND THE 1978 CANAL TREATIES

From the turn of the twentieth century, the United States' principal interest in Panama has related to the Canal. Although construction of the latter was not completed until 1914, since 1903 Washington had not only retained control of the Canal, but held direct territorial sovereignty over the Canal Zone.[3] As a direct result, the spirit of Panamanian nationalism has easily been aroused in efforts to "recover" control of the territory.

In fact, nationalistic sentiment has been so strong on this issue that in the 1950s and early 1960s a series of riots broke out, taking place not only in the Canal Zone but spreading to Panama City as well. Such violence led to a fairly swift U.S. response: The Johnson administration attempted to negotiate a new set of treaties in the mid–1960s which recognized Panamanian sovereignty in the Zone and alluded to a termination of U.S. control (defense and operation) of the Canal. But Panamanian disaffection with the draft treaties, relating to the lack of Panamanian control over the waterway's administration, led to a breakdown in negotiations.

The underlying importance of defense and operation of the Canal continued to be a critical issue in domestic Panamanian politics; efforts to regain control over the land mass were subsequently utilized by the Torrijos regime as a means to arouse nationalistic sentiment. In this context, despite Washington's temporary lapse of attention to this issue, the military government continued to press for the negotiation of new treaties. Throughout the 1970s, the Torrijos government continued its skillful politicking, but this time with a new focus on not only rallying domestic support, but on an international level as well. Drawing on support in the United Nations, as well as flirting with radical Third World regimes, including Libya's Muammar Khadaffi and Cuba's Fidel Castro, the Torrijos regime managed to rally renewed international support against Washington's "imperialist" tendencies. In addition, raising the haunting specter of "another Vietnam" in U.S. foreign policy virtually assured a U.S. policy response. In fact, by 1974 a formal bilateral agreement between Washington and Panama City was reached through the "Joint Statement of Principles" to renegotiate the treaties. Through 1976, negotiations continued at a snails's pace, but gained momentum under the Carter administration.

By 1978, following substantial and difficult congressional debate, two new treaties were ratified by the U.S. Congress.[4] The first of the two treaties which remains in effect to the year 2000 permits the United States to continue operation and administration of the Canal through the means of a new commission. The second treaty calls for Panamanian participation in this commission, although the United States retains de factor control of this group through a voting majority. In addition, the administration of the Canal will be presided over by a U.S. citizen until 1990; at that time, a Panamanian citizen will assume control. The second treaty is to take effect in the year 2000, granting Panama operating control of the Canal, but at the same time guarantees continued U.S. access to the waterway. Finally, it is important to note that the Canal, since its inception, has remained physically unaltered with few exceptions; the key to its continued successful operation has rested upon high levels of maintenance-related work. Thus, as Panama readies itself to assume full control of operations, the nation must generate a domestic capacity to assure continued maintenance.

TOWARD A POLITICAL OPENING

Negotiation of the 1978 Canal treaties was the central component of the Torrijos regime's foreign policy objectives; on a domestic level, the regime had broad goals to change the structure of national representation. Prior to 1968, Panama's electoral system had a strong bias toward representation of urban elites, excluding meaningful representation of rural constituencies. The regime attempted to expand the latter group's input through elaborate mechanisms of electoral manipulation. One such mechanism was the creation of the Democratic Revolutionary party (PRD), formed by Torrijos in 1978 to create a political party which would provide electoral support to the regime's goals. Incorporating elements of organized labor, peasants, and public employees, among other groups, the PRD's platform was to forcefully continue the political direction implemented by the Defense Forces, through drawing upon a broader constituency of support.

Conceived in the early/mid–1970s, by 1978, the Torrijos regime was ready to move toward a political opening, to be initiated over a six-year period. The principle aim of this process was to create a stable atmosphere for the maintenance of current policy and leadership. To begin the process of moving toward direct civilian rule and to replenish the vacuum created by Torrijos' withdrawal from the national executive, Aristedes Royo, a former minister of education, was "elevated" to the presidency in 1978; the climax of this opening was to occur in 1984 with direct presidential elections.

While societal stability was the overarching concern of this process, in fact, the domestic environment failed to stabilize. In July 1981, Torrijos was killed in a mysterious plane crash, creating a vacuum of immense proportions in the political area. With Torrijos "jefe maximo" of the nation, the nation became doomed to a period of instablity without his guidance. In this context, Royo resigned from the presidency in late

July 1982 under pressure from the military; his replacement, Ricardo de la Espriella was forced to do the same by February 1984. A third candidate, Jorge Illueca served in 1984, overseeing the 1984 electoral sequence.

By early 1984, a deteriorating economic and political climate within Panama converged to create a troubled environment in advance of the scheduled 1984 presidential elections. Nevertheless, Panama continued to move toward a preliminary political opening, in the hopes that the nation's ills could be more effectively addressed through civilian rule. Thus, on May 6, 1984, Panama held direct popular elections for president, and as part of the presidential ticket, newly constituted first and second vice president positions.[5] At the same time, voters chose approximately 67 legislators to fill a substantially more powerful Assembly created under earlier constitutional reforms. Finally, on June tenth, municipal elections followed the presidential and Assembly contests.

For the presidential contest, Nicolas Ardito Barletta, the candidate of the National Democratic Union coalition (UNADE) and representing a direct link to policies of the post–1968 period, squared off against Arnulfo Arias Madrid, the candidate of the Democratic Opposition Alliance (ADO), one of the nation's leading politicians, removed from presidential office by the 1968 coup. Although voting procedures were reputed to have been implemented in a fair fashion, it has been widely rumored that vote-counting was carried out in a less than reputable fashion.[6] Barletta's candidacy prevailed over Arias' by a slim margin of approximately 2000 votes. And in the legislature, the PRD, as part of the UNADE coalition won a majority of seats when allied with their coalition partners.

One of Barletta's first tasks was to bring the national economy under control. Selected as UNADE's candidate primarily because of his tenure and attendant economic expertise gained as president of the World Bank, Panama watched and waited for Barletta to perform magic tricks on the economy. In essence, the desired magic trick was to implement fiscal responsibility without inflicting the attendant social costs associated with policies of economic austerity. And by 1984, as Barletta assumed power, the entire economy was in complete disarray and in desperate need of such magic tricks: The national bureaucracy had become tremendously overgrown; leading economic indicators were down; inflationary pressures were building; national industries had become uncompetitive due to high tariff walls; and because Panama employs the U.S. dollar as its currency (only coinage is domestically minted), government-sponsored growth was financed through international borrowing, leading to an enormous external debt valued at approximately U.S. $3.65 billion.[7]

Drawing on his links to international lending institutions, Barletta entered negotiations over the external debt issue with the latter. But the radical austerity measures which were called for to readjust the national economy, such as reducing the size of the governmental bureaucracy, were to earn him the enmity of his opposition, as well as his own political allies. Perhaps the most damaging aspect of Barletta's plans were intended changes in labor and industrial legislation. Labor's leadership, long-associated with the PRD, remained concerned that the gains made in the 1970s and early 1980s would be unilaterally removed by contemplated changes in the labor code. Furthermore, the industrial/business groups grew anxious that changes in the tariff structure would leave the business community exposed and unable to compete on the international market.

Resistance to Barletta's proposed policies began early in his term as president, triggering sentiment within the UNADE coalition (principally within the PRD) that Barletta's magic tricks on the economy were simply not going to work: there was no rabbit to be pulled out of a hat which would resolve Panama's economic ills without triggering political backlash. And it was this very backlash which most concerned the PRD. The overriding concern which came to the fore during this period was that dissatisfaction with economic policies of structural readjustment would create further instabilities within the political arena, which the country could ill afford. By July 1985, the situation degenerated even further: the National Council of Organized Workers (CONATO) expressed their disaffection with governmental policy through a 48-hour strike.

If the handling of the economic domain was the underlying current which forced Barletta's resignation, the straw which broke the PRD's back was the brutal murder of Dr. Hugo Spadafora and subsequent political backlash triggered by Barletta. The former, having served in the Torrijos government as vice minister of health, in addition to later exploits stretching from Guinea-Bissau to Nicaragua, earned him a reputation as an eclectic supporter of revolutionary movements. Beginning in 1984, his dispute with General Noriega over the issue of the latter's alleged personal involvement with governmental corruption became well-publicized; thus, in conjunction with circumstances surrounding his death, Noriega, and more broadly, agents of the Panamanian G–2 intelligence became likely suspects.

President Barletta's call for an independent counsel to investigate the Spadafora affair broke the ties which remained between himself and the PRD. An uneasy alliance of necessity which had resulted from Panama's pressing national problems could no longer be resurrected through the person of Barletta: Neither side of the alliance was willing to negotiate to save the current government.

But in retrospect, it is unlikely that at any point in Barletta's term had he been able to consolidate his position, suggesting a failure of political leadership. Indicative of this situation was Barletta's inability not only to garner support from opposition groups, but to maintain the support of his own constituencies, reaching down to the Cabinet level. Rumors have since surfaced that he was personally disliked by members of his Cabinet, not for his economic policies, but rather for the manner in which he dealt with subordinates. One particular incident indicates that Cabinet meetings were held in a classroom-like environment, with a blackboard available for demonstration. Overall, despite attempts to the contrary, Barletta was, and remained in office, an economist—not a politican who clearly understood the need for negotiation and consensus building within his ruling coalition.

THE VIEW FROM WASHINGTON

Another variable that came to play in the Panamanian political arena was that of U.S. policy. While relations with Washington remained strong through 1984 and early 1985, relations took a nosedive with Barletta's fall from power. In an alliance of unusual political bedfellows, Washington's attention was drawn to the turn of events within Panama. On the one side, the conservative community, represented by Senator Jesse Helms, attempted to draw attention to the deteriorating domestic situation through a series of hearings held on Capitol Hill in mid–1986—focusing on the alleged involvement of th Defense Forces in illicit activities. And the liberal community, represented by Seymour Hersh, although preceding Helms' congressional actions, addressed the same issues through the publication of several articles in The New York *Times*.[8]

Within the Washington policymaking community, two major strains of thought seemed to emerge. The first, perhaps relating to a version of realpolitik, viewed the PRD's influence in domestic politics as part of the status quo. Furthermore, in light of the latter organization's tacit support, and by extension, the UNADE coalition, for the Reagan administration's goals in Central America, many were willing to accept such an outcome as the price to be paid for continued support. In contrast, others demonstrated concern not only with the Defense Force's continued intrusion in the civilian political arena and attendant impact on the nation's political development, but with the notorious activities of the latter.

And while Washington was unable to solve its current policy conundrum, the vocal nature of the debate only served to push Panama into an increasingly defensive posture. The U.S. debate not only served to stir up nationalistic, anti-U.S. sentiment within Panama, but perhaps in a more ominous tone, rally support and thereby strengthen the hand of General Noriega in governance.

Taking a turn to the bizarre, Noriega and del Valle attempted to draw national attention to a "seditious plot" designed not only to topple the current government, but the entire political infrastructure, from power. This "plot" was reputed to involve not only members of the U.S. policymaking community (i.e., Senator Jesse Helms) but political elements within Panama who stood in opposition to the UNADE coalition and style of governance implanted in Panama. Furthermore, by capitalizing on the publicity associated with such a plot, the government (and ruling coalition) was able to accomplish two key short term goals: (1) as indicated earlier, bring chauvinistic sentiment to the fore; and (2) direct public attention away from domestic political and economic ills, focusing instead on acts of external "aggression."

THE DEL VALLE PERIOD

Following Barletta's resignation in September 1985, his first vice president, Eric del Valle assumed the presidency. Reinforcing the interpretation that Barletta resigned from office an isolated political figure unable to generate support from his coalition. Only a minor reshuffling of Cabinet chairs accompanied the change in the presidential office—in fact, many of the principal players in the two Cabinets have remained the same.

It has been widely recognized that as del Valle assumed power, more severe limitations on his "maneuvering space" with regard to the formulation and implementation of national policy was exerted upon him by the PRD. But to date, del Valle has been able not only to implement a majority of suggested policies/legislation, but there have been tentative signs that he has been able ever so slightly to expand his leverage within the ruling UNADE coalition.

In this context, del Valle has shown himself to be more closely attuned to the political winds in Panama. For example, in early 1986, del Valle was able to muster PRD support for a series of new economic laws relating to the industial, labor, and agricultural sectors, which were subsequently passed through the National Assembly. While the passage of such legislation unto itself is far from spectacular, the fact that this legislation virtually mirrored legislation which Barletta had unsuccessfully sought to enact during his tenure demonstrates, in part, the political savy of del Valle.

But if del Valle has been able nominally to strengthen his position within the ruling coalition, other trends have emerged that would appear to suggest the continued intrusion of the PRD. For example, in Fall 1986 a shake-up occurred in the Cabinet, in which three ministers representing PALA and the PRD were replaced, albeit with officials from the same party; this episode was viewed as an attempt by the PRD to flex its political muscle.

Furthermore, in 1985, General Noriega made a clear attempt to increase his influence in the political arena. A general staff was created within the Defense Forces with capabilities in both domestic and international affairs which was to operate in conjunction with the Defense Forces' general staff. In turn, this staff was to work with civilian elements in the formulating and implementing policy.

And finally, despite the legislation which del Valle succeeded in passing relating to the labor, industrial, and agricultural sectors, the economic picture has changed little. The national economy is essentially composed of two broad sectors: (1) a service sector, relating to Canal services, trade in the Colon Free Zone, and international banking; and (2) a sector reliant upon agriculture, construction, and manufacturing. While the former has shown low rates of growth in 1985 and 1986, the latter has been stagnant relating to depressed international commodity prices, cutbacks in government spending for public housing, and a changing domestic tariff structure. Thus, while modest growth rates have been registered, it has been principally due to gains wrought by the service sector.

LOOKING TOWARD THE 1989 ELECTONS

In 1989, Panama is scheduled to hold another series of presidential, legislative, and municipal elections. The key outcome to be determined by this electoral exercise will be whether Panama has the ability to construct a viable civilian political arena, through which the nation's pressing domestic problems may be resolved. Restated in a perhaps simpler fashion, the 1989 elections will be interpreted as a litmus test by which the current potential for a valid transition to democratic rule may be measured.

And clearly Washington is concerned with the turn of events within Panama: As preparations are made to formally cede control of the Canal in the year 2000, perhaps there are concerns that the domestic climate could become increasingly unstable, which presumably could bring more toward a more radical solution to the nation's ills. Short-term interests are also at stake: Panama is viewed as a likely barrier to the extension of radical regimes throughout Central America. And finally, the impli cations of continued alleged illicit activities remain a key concern.

The issue remains: In which direction is Panama headed? Cyncial observers of the Panamanian scene would suggest that the status quo will be maintained, and furthermore that the current political and socioeconomic difficlties will snowball to the point of no return. But perhaps such a view of Panama's internal situation is not entirely unwarranted; indeed, the current situation may contain some elements of hope.

To begin with, since 1983 the nation has been able to construct a seriesof constitutional mechanisms by which the beginnings of a civilian, democratic government may be managed. In this context, although there

are undoubtedly segments of Panamanian society who would prefer that
the executive (and legislative) branch be occupied by elements of the
Defense Forces, civilian leadership has dominated these posts. And while
the importance of such a feat may be easily minimized, for the past
several years public perceptions have been slowly altered to come to
expect civilian political leadership, at the very least, physically to dominate these offices. In addition, over the past few years, Panama's middle-
income sector has grown in size, reflecting increased levels of education
and living standards. And in keeping with such developments, public
demands for the creation of modern, civilian political institutions are
less than surprising.

But in contrast, the Defense Forces, through the person of General
Noriega, and perhaps more importantly, the PRD has been able to keep
a close watch over events in affairs of governance. Furthermore, these
elements have also proven themselves capable of manipulating the mechanisms of the civilian political arena not only to further their personal
ends, but more importantly, to play a pivotal role in the direction of
national policy. And it is this very fact, in combination with alleged
continued illicit activities, which has both opposition domestic political
groups as well as the U.S. policymaking community concerned for the
future prospects of the institutionalization of democratic rule within
Panama.

At present, it remains highly unlikely that either the PRD or the Defense Forces will take on any constructive measures of their own by
which to minimize their political leverage. Thus, it would seem clear that
if such a scenario were to prevail, elements outside of these two groups
would need in some manner to take the necessary action.

While opposition elements do currently exist within Panama, principally within the ADO coalition, such elements represent minority factions—and therefore do not have the capabilities to either institute or
legislate appropriate changes. From this equation, it could perhaps be in-
ferred that one of the key obstacles to the construction of democratic rule
within Panama is represented by civilian political groups which remain
allied to the PRD. In this context, since the early 1980s there has not been
any substantial realignment of political forces; such an equilibrium has
only served to perpetuate the current governing balance. And yet, there
is cause for a glimmer of hope within Panama: Continued activity by the
nation's various political parties could be viewed as a necessary prereq-
uisite to the formation of a stable, multiparty system. But at present, the
verdict is out as to whether or not this will in fact transpire.

In examining political systems with authoritarian tendencies within
Latin America, ruling political groups have alternately used tactics of
both cooptation and repression to maintain themselves in power: cooptation to enlarge their base of support, and repression to quell voices of

opposition. In the Panamanian case, the PRD has in fact retained its current status predominantly through methods of cooptation. Thus, it remains probable that if the PRD were to beome a politically isolated segment, implying a withdrawal of support by its current coalition partners within the Panamanian polity, their leverage over the political arena could be substantially weakened.

Furthermore, the PRD has maintained itself as a viable political force through the cooptation of several segments of society within its ranks. In the early years of the Torrijos regime, overtures were made toward groups which had little voice in the formulation of national policy: namely, left-wing groups and the labor force. Once accomplished, the regime moved toward a successful incorporation of private sector interests into the PRD as well. Thus, the latter's foundation of support remains firm with the support of several key constituencies: The Defense Forces; private sector/business interests; left-wing groups; and the labor sector.

As a result, it remains unlikely that the PRD's status could be diminished solely in a direct manner. But there remains a distinct possibility that should an "acceptable" candidate for the presidential office be fielded by the opposition, a switch in the reins of power could occur. If the 1984 elections are to be used as a yardstick for measure, it is apparent that Arnulfo Arias Madrid is not a viable candidate. Representing the policy line which was decimated by the 1968 coup and being of poor health, despite his broad-based appeal to the population at large, it is clear that civilian political elements closely tied to the national policy of the pre-Torrijos era is viewed with disdain by the PRD. Thus, resurrecting the candidacy of Arias once again in 1989 could likely generate an outcome similar to that of 1984, and further strengthen the hand of the PRD.

On the other hand, it is more than likely that if changes in the format of the civilian political landscape were to occur, the PRD would still yield an enormous amount of control wihtin the political arena. In this context, it may be presumed that any substantial changes within the Panamanian environment would need to come from within the PRD itself—or more likely, from the controlling arm of the PRD, the Defense Forces. And such a common thread runs through all of Latin America's transitions to democratic rule: namely, the critical issue of how to depoliticize the military. While past experience has shown us that there are no simple solutions, over the long term, there is perhaps one scenario which may come to pass within Panama.

In the current environment, many observers suggest that the recent barrage of attacks on General Noriega have only served to strengthen his hand in the conduct of domestic affairs. But other observers believe it to be entirely possible that over the long term, Noreiga's power base may be severely weakened.[9] Since the early 1980s, the Defense Forces have grown in numbers by approximately 35 percent, in anticipation of Panama's assumption of control over the Canal Zone.[10] In tandem, the Defense Forces' level of professionalism and education has also been expanded.

As a result, it is suggested that a "reformist junior officers-style" scenario may come to pass within Panama. In several Latin American (and by extension, Third World) nations, in a precipitious internal environment, as an institution the military has often shown an instinct for reform. In such cases, the armed forces have broken down into two principal factions: senior officers supporting the status quo, and junior officers supporting moves toward internal reform. And it has been precisely such actions which paved the road, in part, for the reinstatement of civilian supremacy in affairs of governance. In light of the current situation within Panama, there does remain the possibility that the Defense Forces could split into at least two principal factions, and in an ensuing power struggle bring to the fore sentiments within the Defense Forces which favor the institutionalization of civilian democratic rule. But at present, such a scenario does not appear imminent; rather, the two principal factions in the Defense Forces (represented by General Noriega and Colonel Díaz-Herrera) would appear to be supportive of the status quo.

Attempts to foresee the direction of future events within a crystal ball is less than promising. But since the early 1980s, Panama has made gains in its attempts to construct a viable civilian political arena. Quite naturally, domestic socioeconomic ills, as well as current political alignments, have made the task all the more arduous. But the basic elements exist for each a political transition to exist—what would appear to be needed at the present time is a convergence of such forces dedicated to the construction of a democratic polity.

PANAMA, THE UNITED STATES, AND THE CARIBBEAN BASIN

While an examination of domestic conditions in Panama is important in assessing the continued viability of the trend toward civilian democratic rule, Panama's political evolution must also be considered in the context of the dynamic situation inthe broader Caribbean basin. As indicated earlier, under the Torrijos regime, Panama sought to galvanize international attention to the issue of Canal negotiations. But due to Panama's important strategic location in the Basin, the attendant economic impact of the Canal, and commercial activities associated with the Colon Free Zone, the nation's political opening takes on new meaning.

As a by-product of the 1978 Canal treaties, Panama's attention to issues of internal security has been broadened. Through the nation's assumption of the role in defending the Canal, external defense of the nation has become a high priority. In this context, a new posture in national security strategy has been evolving. Thus, the Defense Forces have been thrust into a posture which has demanded increased attention to the possibility of low intensity threats relating to terrorist activity.

From the adoption of this posture, there has been a marked increase in Panama's visibility in the current regional turmoil. Beginning in the early 1970s, the Torrijos regime attempted to improve bilateral relations with Havana, in attempts to rally international support for the Canal Treaty negotiations. But from that starting point, Panama also increased its contact with radical elements in the region—predominantly through its support of the 1970 Nicaraguan revolution and subsequent consolidation of the Sandinista regime. While contact with such left-wing elements has been curbed through the 1980s, Panama City has maintained cordial relations with both the Nicaraguan and Cuban regimes.

On the other side of the equation, Panama has made concerted efforts to retain a role in regional negotiations. In this context, while the Contadora group and attendant regional support mechanisms have yet to yield any concrete results, Panama has gained much political capital in hosting the Group's sessions. Furthermore, in light of Panama's new external role relating to defense and operation of the Canal Zone, the nation has made concerted efforts to revive the Central American defense Council (CONDECA) in developing regional alliances, and forcing the region to pursue a security strategy.

Thus, it it can be stated that Panama City has pursued a balancing act to ensure the continuance of an internal political equilibrium, the same can be stated of the government's foreign policy. Relations with both moderate civilian and radical regimes in the region have been cautiously pursued in the hopes of reaching a security equilibrium. And at present, while a solution to the region's instability looms on the horizon, an equilibrium of sorts has been forged.

But in so doing, Panama City's relations with Washington have remained tense. The expanding influence exercised by the Defense Forces—and therefore felt through the policies of the current administration—on both domestic and regional levels has caused concern within Washington's policymaking community. Relating to domestic political developments, Washington's recent attempts to force changes within the Panamanian environment have hopelessly backfired, pushing the nation into a defensive stance, and strengthening the hand of antidemocratic forces. Thus, it remains clear that if Panama is to construct a viable civilian political arena, while the United States may be able to provide some assistance in this regard, the impetus for such reform will have to emerge from within Panama itself. In other words, only Panama can create a Panamanian democracy; Washington's role can only be in the provision of constructive and timely assistance. And yet, a continued drive toward the institutionalization of democratic rule does not appear imminent—generating increased concern over the direction of internal trends.

On a reginal level, Panamanian influence has been strengthened since the adoption of the Canal treaties, and the nation's newly institutionalized concern with external defense of the nation. In tandem, the current instability in the Caribbean basin has afforded Panama the capacity to play a larger role in regional developments. But once again, Washington's perceived unreliability of key segments of Panama's ruling elite, relating to the role of the Defense Forces has also hindered movement toward a solution to the region's instability. Thus, the search for a regional equilibrium has become inextricably linked to domestic Panamanian developments, and for the foreseeable future, the basic equation will remain unchanged.

In a final note, it should be underscored that the construction and instituionalization of democratic rule is not a pehnomenon which can be instantly received; a competitive political arena is by far the most difficult form of government to construct. Thus it is imperative that not only Panama, but the interntional community as well, remain supportive of fledgling advances made in this regard.

Over the long term it may well prove to be counterproductive to attempt to force nascent democracies into the pursuit of policies which may not only result in the eclipse of civilian rule, but, in the Panamanian case, trigger further instability within the Caribbean basin. Finally, in light of Panama's new regional role, it remains likely that the strengthening of the fragile democratic trend within that nation could well serve to strengthen the hand of democratic forces within the entire region.

NOTES

1. For an excellent analysis of not only underlying assumptions associated with transitions to democratic rule, but the political environment surrounding this entire process, see Guillermo O'Donnell and Philippe Schmitter, *Transitions from Authoritarian Rule: Tentative Conclusions about Uncertain Democracies* (Baltimore, MD: The Johns Hopkins University Press, 1986).

2. For a superb analysis of Panama's political development in an historical perspective, see Steve Ropp, *Panamanian Politics: From Guarded Nation to National Guard* (New York: Simon and Schuster, 1982). In addition, it is important to note that Ropp is regarded as one of the foremost observers of the Panamanian scene.

3. The seminal work on the construction of the Panama Canal remains David McCullough's *The Path Between the Seas: The Creation of the Panama Canal, 1870–1914* (New York: Simon and Schuster, 1977).

4. For an in-depth discussion of not only the U.S. congressional debate, but

the American political debate surrounding this issue, see J. Michael Hoga, *The Panama Canal in American Politics: Domestic Advocacy and the Evolution of Policy* (Carbonadal and Edwardsville, IL: Southern Illinois University Press, 1986).

5. For further discussion of the 1984 electoral exercise in Panama, see Terrence Modglin, *The Panamanian Presidential and Legislative Elections* (Washington, DC: Center for Strategic and International Studies, 1984).

6. Widespread reports appeared in the U.S. press just after the elections indicating such trends. For a Panamanian perspective on this issue, see Raul Arias de Para, *Asi Fue El Fraude: Las Elecciones Presidenciales de Panama, 1984* (Panama: Edicciones Tercer, 1984).

7. As reported in *Foreign Economic Trends and Their Implications for the United States and Panama* (Washington, DC: U,.S. Department of Commerce, 1986).

8. A series of articles appeared in mid-June 1986 in The New York *Times* under the authorship of Seymour Hersh.

9. One such noted observer who indicates the posibility of such a trend in Panamanian events is Steve Ropp, "General Noriega's Panama," *Current History*, December 1986.

10. Ropp, "General Noriega's Panama."

13
Grenada, the Caribbean Basin, and the European Economic Community
Scott B. MacDonald
and Albert L. Gastmann

INTRODUCTION

The continuing imbroglio in Central America, the debt crisis, the U.S.–led intervention in Grenada and dangerous flashpoints in the Caribbean have been substantial challenges to individual European states in the 1980s. Throughout most of the post–World War II period, European influence was largely limited to economic matters in the Caribbean and its periphery. However, in the 1980s several European nations have sought to develop a response and play a larger role in the region's affairs.

The Lomé convention of 1975, signed between the European Economic Community (EEC) and the Africa, Caribbean, and Pacific (ACP) group of nations, reflected the concern of Western European governments about a shifting international environment over which they no longer had control. Individual European states could not longer protect their vital concerns in a global system dominated by superpowers and powerful coalitions such as OPEC. Lomé offered much to the EEC and its Third World counterparts. The Community developed with 46 countries of Africa, the Caribbean, and the Pacific, a model for balanced cooperation between industrial and developing countries. Moreover, the progress of this "new and comprehensive type of agreement" hinged on European support for the New International Economic Order. Reciprocity became the linchpin in the new organization. In the Caribbean, the Lomé I and II (1979) conventions ultimately included the entire English-speaking community, including Guyana and Belize, Suriname, the Netherlands Antilles, the French Antilles, and French Guiana.

By the early 1980s, European influence in Central America and the Caribbean was on the upswing, even though Lomé had not become an entirely viable model for economic growth in the Third World, and new financial concerns, such as the lingering effects of the second oil crisis (1979) and international recession, struck the EEC. An indication of this new European presence was the September 1984 meeting in San José, Costa Rica where foreign ministers of five Central American states met with their counterparts from the EEC and associate members, Spain and Portugal.[1] The meeting raises several questions: Why have European nations, since the late 1970s, begun to reassert their influence in the Caribbean and Central America? What impact did the United States' invasion of Grenada in 1983 have upon European goals in the two regions? And what differences exist between Europe's and the United States' perceptions and approaches to the problems of Central America and the Caribbean?

HISTORICAL BACKGROUND

Four EEC members—Britain, France, the Netherlands, and Spain—exercised sovereignty over colonies in the region for more than four centuries. Denmark, with its colony in the Virgin Islands until 1917, played a brief historical role in the Caribbean. Though European influence waned in the Caribbean and Central America and U.S. influence grew in the late nineteenth and early twentieth centuries, Britain and, to a lesser extent, France and the Netherlands, maintained a presence.

In the late 1950s Britain began to grant independence to her Caribbean possessions whose economic orientation promptly shifted towards the United States. Moreover, after the Suez Crisis of 1956, Western Europe as a whole exhibited little interest in the Caribbean and less in Central America with the exception of British Honduras (now known as the nation of Belize). Guatemala's claim to more than half the nation forced Britain to maintain a sizable garrison there and slowed the path to independence. By the late 1970s, European influences remained in the Caribbean and Central America, but had paled in significance when compared with the power of the United States. This does not mean that the relevant European nations were slavishly subservient to every whim of U.S. foreign policy. Most followed the embargo against Cuba concerning items of strategic value, but many European nations maintained or later renewed diplomatic relations with Cuba.

The United States could control neither its European allies nor events in the Caribbean. The late 1970s and early 1980s were a time of political and economic instability in the Caribbean and Central America, marking an inability of the United States to control events in what was sometimes referred to as its "backyard." In Central America, Nicaragua underwent a brutal and fiercely fought civil war, which ultimately resulted in the victory of a broadly based coalition led by the Sandinistas. As the Sandinistas embarked upon the creation of a new society in 1979, civil wars were fought with renewed fierceness in El Salvador and Guatemala. In the Caribbean, the English-speaking community was shaken by its first coup, which occurred in March 1979 in Grenada. It soon became apparent that the direction of the New Jewel Movement's revolution was anti-United States and pro-Cuban. The "Sergeants Coup" in Suriname in February 1980 and the victory of a center-left party in St. Lucia were further blows to Washington's hegemony over an area it regarded as strategic. The changed and charged environment in the Caribbean and Central America, the erosion of U.S. influence and the emergence of new regional forces, posed new opoportunities for Europe in the region.

EEC—THIRD WORLD DEVELOPMENT AND THE CARIBBEAN BASIN

The EEC's interest in Third World development has, as Europeans perceive, the potential to offer a viable alternative for the countries of the Caribbean basin. It is felt that if the Caribbean nations could develop strong European economic ties and political support, the current bipolar tension between the United States and Cuba (and the Soviet Union) would be eased and more balanced and stable relationships could emerge. In a sense, the EEC could become a "Third Force" alternative to troubled nations, such as El Salvador and Nicaragua, and allow them to escape the confines of the East-West struggle superimposed on the region by the United States. Moreover, the emphasis would be to build economic linkages. As the *Times* of London noted, "European governments have tended to support the more moderate elements within the opposition forces in the region . . . while the U.S. has tended to opt for a policy of encouraging the forces of moderate change within existing governments."[2]

The EEC demonstrated its new interest in Caribbean development in February 1981 at the Europe-Caribbean Contacts meeting held in Pointe-à-Pitre, Guadeloupe. Hosted by the Chambers of Commerce of Martinique, Guadeloupe, and French Guiana, those who attended represented over four hundred government agencies and businesses. Also present were Eugenia Charles, the prime minister of Dominica, and ministers from Barbados, Jamaica, Guyana, Grenada, Suriname, and the Netherlands Antilles. Existing accords between the EEC and its Caribbean partners were discussed and it was agreed that the Lomé approach had helped to improve trade relations, stabilize export earnings and that financial aid, though limited, had been productive. One of the few areas of discord was EEC agricultural policy as it related to the importation of sugar and rum, two important Caribbean commodities that competed with European beet sugar and cognac and rum produced in France's overseas possessions.

While the Lomé accords provided a useful framework for ties between the EEC and a number of Caribbean nations, they had no jurisdiction over European–Central American trade relations and development programs. Consequently, a European initiative was advanced at the suggestion of then French Foreign Minister Claude Cheysson in September 1981. A plan was outlined by the European Commission in March 1982 which envisioned the augumentation of aid to non-Lomé Caribbean and Central American states. The former Spanish colonies were not Lomé members as those treaties had been signed well in advance to Spain's membership.

Problems arose, however, as to which nations should be included in the non-Lomé aid program and the original seven nations were reduced to four—Costa Rica, the Dominican Republic, Honduras, and Nicaragua. Haiti, Guatemala, and El Salvador were excluded because of the high incidence of human rights abuses. It was felt by many in European diplomatic circles that Haiti, which suffered under the Duvalier dictatorship, and Guatemala, under the control of the military, were clearcut examples of regimes to whom democratic nations could not lend their support. El Salvador's standing was less clear, but French Socialists who came into office in 1981 were opposed to the government and regarded it as a repressive U.S. puppet. Through the relationship with Nicaragua would later deteriorate, most Europeans felt that the heavyhanded nature of the Reagan administration was forcing the Sandinistas into the arms of the Cubans and Soviets. The extended European hand, through the EEC and by non–EEC members such as Sweden, was expected perhaps unrealistically, to be taken by a Nicaragua yet to emerge—one that was pluralistic, nonaligned, but pro-European. Europe as a "third force" between the Americans and Soviets, would offer support for political and economic change without the negative impact of the East-West struggle.

The EEC–Caribbean initiative was directed to governments rather than to the private sector and reflected in part the statist European approach to economic development. Aid was to be in the form of balance of payments support as finance to pay for imports, preferably from Europe. As with the U.S. Caribbean Basin Initiative (CBI), the overall package, proposed in 1982, was severly limited by domestic European concerns. The remaining scope of aid remained highly inadequate for the region's problems of stimulating trade and fostering economic development. The nature of the failure of the European initiative was both political and economic.

On a more political note, foreign aid was for individual EEC members a means of pursuing national interests. Britain, France, and Germany, with greater interests in the Caribbean basin, favored bilateral over multilateral aid. As one Mexican observer noted of the preference of the larger European states, "The reason behind this is that bilateral aid can be more easily controlled and can better serve the purpose of the donor."[3] Consequently, when the time came for the European program to be formulated and implemented, it lacked the financial scope originally intended. It also became clear that Central America's role in the EEC's collective foreign policy remained marginal and subservient to Europe's (through the North Atlantic Treaty Organization or NATO) national security concersn. As Esperanza Duran commented, "The stability of Latin America is not Europe's direct concern; its aim is rather to keep the U.S. free from unwanted distractions in areas that do not directly bear upon European defense needs"[4] Ireland, Belgium, Greece, and Luxembourg, however, with marginal interests in the area looked to multilateral approaches.

Europe's greater assertiveness in the Caribbean basin in the early 1980s was related to European national security concerns as well as a belief that the EEC as a third political-economic force had something to offer. Even though little action of a concrete nature occurred, the rhetoric was enough to occasionally place European and U.S. policies and actions at odds. The U.S.–led invasion of Grenada was a case in point: Though many European leaders were privately relieved that the "Grenada affair" ended, public condemnation was widespread in Western Europe. Britain, Belgium, France, Germany, Italy, and the Netherlands attacked the intervention, which ultimately prompted Washington to send then Deputy Secretary of State Kenneth Dam to Europe to explain Washington's motives and to ease the strains in the alliance. The German business newspaper *Handelsblatt* summarized one often-repeated concern: "One question is the credibility of the claim that the landing is the result of a call for assistance. Eastern actions of a similar nature are invariably cloaked in that justification."[5]

Most European nations were also irritated by the Reagan administratin's lack of consultation. This was especially the case for Britain because of Grenada's status as a Commonwealth country and Britain's "special relationship" with the United States.[6] As *The Financial Times* editorialized, "The U.S.–led invasion of Grenada raises profound questions about the confidence that the European allies can have in the responsibility of the Reagan administration. The more the U.S. indulges in ill-considered unilateral actions, the more essential it is that the European allies should concert their own policies."[7] European governments were also concerned that the intervention's unpopularity in their countries would hamper or delay the deployment of cruise and Pershing II nuclear missiles. Despite the wave of mistrust generated both by Grenada as well as the Reagan administration's Central American policies, the NATO defence plan proceeded on schedule.

Grenada also precipitated a division within the EEC over the kind of role of that organization in the Caribbean basin. France, West Germany and the Netherlands, as will be seen, maintained an active presence on a bilateral basis as well as playing a role in the multilateral process. On a more specific basis, Germany was active as a leader within the multilateral approach, while France developed a series of bilateral foci. The Netherlands' primary consideration was centered on Suriname and the Netherlands Antilles. Other EEC members—Belgium, Luxembourg, Ireland, Greece, Denmark and Italy—were distracted by developments closer to home. Simply stated, those EEC nations pursuing a multilateral approach had minimal interests in the Caribbean basin and there were no individual interests to stand in the way of collective action.

BRITAIN AND THE CARIBBEAN BASIN

Britain reassessed its role in the Caribbean basin after the U.S,. intervention in Grenada. Despite discussions over a renewed British presence in the region, the established low profile keyed to ties with its former colonies in the English-speaking Caribbean was reaffirmed. There were also a number of dependencies which demanded limited amounts of attention—Anguilla, Bermuda, the British Virgin Islands, the Cayman Islands, Montserrat, and the Turks and Caicos Islands. Only in Belize, which gained its independence in 1981, has Britain maintained a sizable military presence. A garrison of one thousand British soldiers and four Harrier jet aircraft defend that nation's borders against possible Guatemalan incursions. Guatemala claims most of Belize and has consistently refused to recognize it as a sovereign nation although that hard-line position softened in late 1986 and 1987. Consequently, the British role in Belize has been maintained as London has consistently supported its former colony in the border dispute. Though relations have not been as close with the government of Guyana, Britain has also continued to support that former colony's position in its border dispute with Venezuela.

In the post-Grenada period, Britain's Caribbean basin policy was largely opportunistic and cost-effective. Along these lines, the British Embassy was closed in Santo Domingo in 1985, with relations to be maintained through other United Kingdom embassies in the Caribbean. More importantly, trade relations with Cuba were expanded. British-Cuban trade was worth $92 million in 1985, less than Britain's trade with Jamaica and Trinidad and Tobago, but equal to that with Guyana and greater than that with Barbados, Belize, and the smaller countries in the Eastern Caribbean.[8] Though there remains an official caution vis-à-vis Cuba, British business missions went to Cuba in 1985, 1986, and 1987. By one estimate, some one hundred British companies visited Cuba since 1985, despite that nation's deepening economic crisis.[9] British companies were attracted to a market in which they did not have to compete with U.S. firms. Moreover, in terms of visible trade, Britain enjoyed a large surplus in 1986, with British exports to Cuba worth 59.3 million pounds against imports of 7.27 million pounds.

In a political sense, however, the British perception of Cuba was formed by its relationship with the Commonwealth Caribbean. Britain has clearly been disillusioned with Castro and has opposed, with a minimum of effort and cost, Cuban expansion in the area. London regards the United States, Venezuela and Mexico as more effective counterweights to contain any Cuban destabilizing efforts. The Thatcher government was concerned about Cuban involvement in Grenada and was critical of the New Jewel Movement's nondemocratic path of development. At the same time, Britain's major concerns in terms of foreign affairs were in Europe, not the Caribbean or Central America. Though opposed to the American intervention, Cuban activity in a Commonwealth nation had been brought to a halt and so satisfied one dimension of London's policy in the region. By late 1984, the Caribbean basin was again a marginal concern of Britain.

FRANCE AND THE CARIBBEAN BASIN

The significant French presence in the Americas began in the early 1600s. By the twentieth century only Martinique, Guadeloupe, French Guiana, and St. Pierre and Miquelon off the coast of Canada remained of France's possessions in the Western Hemisphere. The promulgation of the Law of March 19, 1946, made these remaining enclaves into overseas departments (*départements d'Outre-Mer* or DOMs). Decolonization in the Caribbean for the French meant no more than a new status for Martinicans, Guadeloupeans, and Guianese. French citizenship, with all the rights and liberties guaranteed under the French constitution, represented "liberation" from the colonial condition. Departmentalization, begun with widespread support and high hopes, did not transform the tropical islands and Guiana into carbon copies of temperate zone European departments. Although departmentalization improved the standard of living to a level above those of most Caribbean basin nations, there was a cost. Highly dependent on France, the Antilles and Guiana have been plagued by high unemployment (25–35 percent) and chronic trade deficits.[10] Furthermore, Antillean and Guianese enterprises have been subordinated to metropolitan industries, as in the sugar sector.

Dissatisfaction with France grew and in the late 1970s the French

Caribbean was torn by labor unrest, political terrorism, and a worsening economic position. The Grenadan and Nicaraguan revolutions, which were nationalistic as well as ideological, symbolically challenged a continued French presence in the region and raised important questions concerning equality and sovereignty. The conservative government of President Giscard d'Estaing pursued a polite but cool policy to both the New Jewel Movement in Grenada and the Sandinistas and other leftists in Central America. Moreover, to insulate the DOMs and their problems from a regional radicalism, Paris pressed aid on Dominica, St. Lucia, and Haiti to form a "cordon sanitaire."[11]

In June 1980, French policy changed radically as François Mitterand and the Socialists came to power. A new tone in relations was soon apparent as economic aid was given to Grenada and Nicaragua, diplomatic support was given to leftist groups in El Salvador and the minister of culture, Jack Lang, went lobster fishing with Fidel Castro.[12] At the same time, Régis Debray, one of Ché Guevara's close associates and an admirer of the Cuban Revolution, was made special adviser to Mitterand on Latin American affairs. In the French Caribbean, suspected proindependence terrorists were released, policy controls were relaxed, and independence for the DOMs was hinted. French policy placed a strong emphasis on the bilateral approach.

The Socialist envisioned a Caribbean Basin where France could play a progressive role in improving the quality of life. At the same time, those nations with reactionary regimes could be brought toward social democracy. U.S. hegemony could be balanced by a stable neutral region which leaned in the direction of the Non-Aligned Movement and progressive European governments like that of France. The Socialist regarded the EEC as a fruitful sphere of action, but placed a stronger emphasis on bilateral relations (at least in 1981 and 1982). The French approach also reflected a traditional need to exhibit independence from the superpowers and France's European partners. Along these lines, Paris maintained an open door to Grenada, Nicaragua, and Cuba, preferring its own policy of dialogue to the policy of confrontation of others.

The Mitterand government's approach to the Caribbean basin was undermined by three factors which increasingly hampered the scale of involvement: (1) Discontent, with some violent incidents, from both the right and the left in the Caribbean departments forced a reassessment of policy; (2) economic problems in Europe, including a growing national external debt ($70–79 billion) and a slump in production, raised serious questions about the amount of aid France could afford to give to the region; and (3) increased commitments in other parts of the world, in particular Chad and Lebanon, were more pressing.[13]

In the Caribbean, reforms to create greater local autonomy sparked heated debates in the French Parliament, helped rally right-wing parties in Martinique, Guadeloupe, and French Guiana, and ultimately helped set the stage for the 1982 exit of Henri Emmanuelli, President Mitterand's first secretary of state for overseas department and territories. Worse yet, proindependence groups claimed that the Socialists had not done enough to put the islands and Guiana on the road to independence. At the end of 1983 bombs rocked Paris and the French Caribbean, killing one person, injuring several and causing substantial damage to property.[14] Caught in a dilemma, Mitterand increased police activities in the DOMS and there were rumors of Cuban and Grenadian involvement in the training of the terrorists.[15]

The French Caribbean became a headache for the Mitterand administration. By 1983, when proindependence terrorists conducted a highly destructive bombing campaign in the Caribbean DOMs, there was considerable doubt about the future course of French policy. Such doubts were enhanced as the influence of the radical left within the Socialist party waned. This was especially true after the disclosure of plans within the Mitterand government to topple the government of Jean-Claude Duvalier in Haiti. In short, a more pragmatic line emerged. Georges Lemoine, who replaced Emmanuelli as secretary of state for overseas departments and territories, was representative of the change.

When the U.S. invasion of Grenada occurred, the pragmatists in the Mitterand government were in control. France was asked to participate, but declined and officially condemned the act.[16] Grenada clearly had an impact on French policy in the Caribbean. The demise of the Grenadan revolution, despite rhetoric to the contrary, was a relief to the government and a disappointment to the proindependence radicals in the Caribbean DOMs. To the government, the U.S. invasion removed a possible thorn in the French side, close to their overseas departments. After the invasion of Grenada, French ties to Dominica and St. Lucia were also strengthened.

The pragmatic policy also resulted in cooler relations with the Sandinistas and Fidel Castro. When Nicaragua's Interior Minister Tomas Borge visited Paris, French Foreign Minister Claude Cheysson received him for only five minutes, an obvious signal of a change in French policy.[17] Debray was also described as "extremely disappointed" by the turn of events in Nicaragua. The shift in French policy was related to the Sandinista government's earlier criticism of the international peace force in Lebanon, which included French troops, and expressed disapproval of the French role in Chad. Related to this was Nicaragua's close ties to Libya.

While Franco-Nicaraguan relations soured, the French Caribbean was rocked in October by another round of ARC bombings in Guadeloupe. An ARC statement followed a car bomb explosion in November: "Our actions, in their present phase, involve harassment of French occupation troops...we've chosen to devote ourselves to battle for the cause of independence for a free Caribbean and the Grenadian brothers in particular, and against American expansionism."[18] Though the government did not implicate Cuba in the violence, members of the Socialist party told reporters off the record that significant Cuban involvement in Guadeloupe was suspected.[19] Relations with Cuba remained cool.

The ARC's struggle against the French government in Guadeloupe finally resulted in the outlawing of the organization. The banning order, passed in May 1984, was an admission that the group had become a major problem. By placing the ARC in an illegal status, similar to the National Liberation Front of Corsica, the French government appeared to some as a colonial oppressor whose Central American policy now seemed contradictory and hypocritical.

Central America, however, was further away and allowed the Socialists a pragmatic (perhaps cynical) opportunity to vocalize their ideology. When Nicaragua sided with Libya, a challenger to French interests in Africa and the Middle East, the situation changed. To a certain extent Claude Cheysson reflected the French attitude vis-à-vis the Caribbean basin when he stated that the only chance to bring Nicaragua closer to the West and to accept Western concepts of democracy was by "closing our eyes" to the increasingly authoritarian nature of the Sandinista regime.[20] The alternative was another Cuba.

The French parliamentary elections in 1986 brought little change in the French policy in the Caribbean basin. The new "cohabitation" government of Prime Minister Jacques Chirac and President Mitterand brought an uneasy alliance of the Socialists and the Right to power as the former lost control of parliament. Despite this, France's disillusionment with the Sandinistas and rebel groups in El Salvador over their inability to form a united and democratic front, the lull in terrorist activities in the Caribbean DOMs in 1986 and early 1987, and the absence of a significant regional revolutionary movement like the New Jewel Movement, meant a lower profile for Paris in the Basin's affairs. In many respects, terrorist activities by Middle East groups in France, the ongoing war in Chad (with Libya on the opposing side), the state of the global economy (and the French economy's place in it), and New Caledonia and the South Pacific have weighed heavier on the minds of the government's foreign policy leadership. The major exception was the development in mid–1986 of a rebellion in Suriname, which borders French Guiana, the launching center for the European space Program. Though French officials denied involvement in supporting the rebel force, the Surinamese National Liberation Army, the government of Suriname (headed by the dictatorial Lt. Col. Desi Bouterse) accused Paris of involvement.[21] Considering that Libya developed a presence in Suriname in 1985 and was reported to have between 100 and 200 military advisers or commandos in the country, France was certainly concerned and increased the number of its troops along the border. Furthermore, refugees from eastern Suriname have fled into French Guiana, causing a strain on social and health services. Another possible exception was Haiti. In 1986, Jean-Claude Duvalier fled his nation after considerable pressure came from France which worked closely with the United States. In the end, the dictator went to an arranged exile in France. Suriname's civil war and Haitian affairs aside, France's focus on the Caribbean basin in 1986 and 1987 was blurred as more pressing matters demanded attention.

The high point of French Caribbean Basin policy occurred between 1981 and 1983 when the new Socialist administration sought to project a "third force" option and attempted to resolve the bitter conflicts in Central America and create a pro-French "progressive" sphere in the Caribbean which would function to buffer its DOMs from the radicalism of Grenada's revolution and, to a lesser extent, Cuban influence. In 1984 and 1985, French involvement declined both along multilateral and bilateral fronts. The Caribbean DOMs, especially Guadeloupe, became problems for the government in Paris as the earlier ideological perception of liberation gave way to traditional concerns of French national interests. National interests in the Caribbean basin meant a retreat from a proliberation stance on Central America and a return to military force in Martinique, Guadeloupe, and French Guiana to control terrorism. The retreat was further marked in 1986 and 1987, with the exception of possible involvement in the civil war in Suriname. It could be argued, moreover, that involvement in Suriname's war was a defensive response to instability in a neighboring nation and a growing Libyan presence.

THE NETHERLANDS AND SURINAME

The Netherlands was a founding member of the EEC and has consistently placed an emphasis on the Community as an important actor in global affairs. In the post–World War II era, the Dutch dismantled their colonial empire. Indonesia became independent and the remaining possessions in the Caribbean—the Netherlands Antilles and Suriname (also known as Dutch Guiana)—became part of the Tripartite Kingdom of the Netherlands as set forth in the Constitution of 1954. In 1975, Suriname left the Kingdom and became an independent nation. The six islands of the Netherlands Antilles, the largest of which was Curaçao, pursued a more gradualistic approach and became self-governing, within the Kingdom. In 1986, Aruba left the Federation of the Netherlands Antilles and assumed Suriname's old position as the third leg of the Tripartite Kingdom. Dutch concerns in the Caribbean basin have, therefore, been largely linked to their dependencies and Suriname.

The seizure of power by Bouterse in Suriname in 1980 caused a more active Dutch concern in the region as The Hague was clearly displeased by the destruction of its former colony's democratic system. Suriname's growing ties to Grenada, Nicaragua, and Cuba in 1981 and 1982, though not entirely regarded as a positive matter, were not a major source of concern by the center-right government of Prime Minister Rudd Lubbers. The Dutch were, in fact, supportive of EEC efforts in Central America and were not sympathetic to the activities of military governments in Guatemala or El Salvador. What did provoke a Dutch reaction, however, was the massacre of fifteen opposition members in December 1982 by the Bouterse regime. A substantial aid package was cut and trade to Suriname declined considerably.

The Netherlands has maintained a stormy relationship with Suriname since 1982 as ambassadors were recalled several times by both sides, Surinames liberation groups were formed in the Netherlands, and several private missions against the Bouterse regime were organized and launched from Amsterdam via French Guiana. The slaughter of opposition leaders and other questions about human rights violations in Suriname were raised by the Dutch at the European Parliament.[22] The Dutch government also indicated that if Bouterse were removed from power it would increase the level of aid to the nation from the initial agreed amount at the time of independence.

The Netherlands' role in the Caribbean basin is likely to place an increased emphasis on the multilateral approach offered by the EEC. The Dutch are gradually pushing their remaining island dependencies forward to independence despite local resistance to the idea. Suriname, however, presents the Dutch with special problems best handled bilaterally. Surinamese exiles in Netherlands are one such problem. Moreover, if and when Bouterse falls from power, there are many questions as to what type of government will emerge. In this possible scenario, the Dutch stand to play an important role as the nation's major foreign aid donor. They might also assist certain parties to create a democratic environment. The United States is likely to follow the Dutch lead not only because it recognizes the important linkages between the mother nation and former colony but also because it would not want to disrupt U.S.–Dutch relations vis-à-vis defense policy in Europe. Beyond Suriname and the gradual push to independence of the Dutch islands, The Hague's regional role is likely to remain as it was before Grenada, narrowly focused on its former colonies. The multilateral EEC approach is of secondary importance.

THE GERMAN INITIATIVE

The conservative government of Helmut Kohl, which came to office in 1982 and was reelected in 1987, not surprisingly demonstrated little sympathy for leftist forces in the Caribbean basin. Aid, in fact, was terminated to Nicaragua and resumed to El Salvador in 1983. In April 1984 a top West German foreign ministry official admitted: "Central America for us Europeans is not a priority region."[23] The same could be said for the Caribbean. Although the German public was skeptical about U.S. motives for intervening in Grenada, the Kohl government had little to say on the matter beyond a cursory condemnation of the use of violence. Bonn was wholly absorbed by the future of Ostpolitic, the installation of U.S. missiles, and the relations with other European nations. The German government's main concern in the Caribbean basin was the effect of the region's political instability had on NATO's unity. As one leading German official commented, "If you got American intervention in El Salvador, that would weaken and split the alliance. It could divert U.S. attention from vital areas such as the Middle East and Europe, and you'd get anti-European feeling in the U.S."[24]

In July 1984 West Germany's role in the Caribbean basin appeared to change abruptly as the Kohl government became the first European nation to accept an invitation to the Euro-Central American conference held on 21–22 September in San José, Costa Rica. The idea was proposed by West German foreign minister Hans-Dietrich Genscher, who hoped to create a "pact" between the two regional bodies along the lines of the Association of South East Asian Nations and the EEC. Its goal was closer political and economic cooperation.

Why the shift in German policy? The underlying reason was that the Germans had reassessed both their perceptions of events in Central America and saw a possible German role. This, in turn was influenced by the release by the ruling Christian Democratic party (CDU) of a resolution for economic cooperation that called for a more active German presence in international finance. It was believed that political and ecomonic stability in Central America would lead to a more stable international financial environment. German trade with Central America (and Panama) was worth a little over $600 million annually.[25] Between April and July, therefore, the Kohl government reassessed its role in Central America and decided that as the region's political and economic problems continued, there was an opening for a stronger West German (and EEC) role. The Germans, multilaterally, through the EEC and bilaterally, could fill the gap caused by the shortcomings in U.S. diplomacy. As Genscher stated, "These countries don't want to be under the thumb of just one power, be it Washington or Moscow. For this reason they are particularly attracted to Europe."[26] This was, in part, a German response to the CIA–aided mining of Nicaraguan waters that began in the Spring of 1984 and was regarded with considerable apprehension by European governments.

There are other reasons for the shift. One of the most significant was

the Christian Democrat party'svictory in Guatemala's July 1, 1984, con-
stituent assembly elections. The Guatemalan Christian Democrats, led
by Vinicio Cerezo (later to become president), won, but this was only a
small step toward democracy. Yet it was the first time the military had
allowed the party to win an election over the past decade. The West
German CDU, therefore, found that a sister party was in need of support.
As a sister party, the CDU and other Christian Democrat parties provided a small amount of assistance and applied diplomatic pressure
through European and Latin governments for open elections.

Another important factor in the shift of West German policy was the
visit to Bonn of Salvadorean President José Napoleon Duarte in July
1984. Kohl praised Duarte's efforts to "achieve peace and rebuild his
country's economy and El Salvador's contribution to the Contadora peace
initiative."[27] In turn, Duarte criticized Nicaraguan leader Daniel Ortega's
statements of solidarity with El Salvador's guerrillas made on West German television. Duarte termed the remarks "interference in El Salvador's
internal affairs."[28] Although Germany's Social Democrat party (SDP) was
silent about Duarte's visit, the Salvadorean president left Bonn with some
$15 million in aid.

There were two other reasons less important but notable for the German government's fresh approach. There were communities of Germans
living in each nation, especially Costa Rica and Guatemala, and the opposition Socialist Democrat party had organized international ties to
philosophically similar Central American parties.

Shortly before the San José meeting, the Kohl government announced
that there were new priorities for West German aid to the Dominican
Republic, Jamaica, Haiti, Costa Rica, and Honduras.[29] While increases
to Haiti and Honduras were determined by humanitarian concerns (as
they are the first and second poorest nations in the Western Hemisphere), assistance to the Dominican Republic was also important as that
nation was Germany's largest trade partner in the Caribbean after Cuba.
Jamaica was also of relative importance in the region for German trade.
It was also a strategically located nation which was led by the pro-Western
Seaga government.

German aid was earmarked for programs which emphasized education
and vocational training, technology transfer and the development of
medium-sized enterprises. Like the Americans, the Germans also advocated a reduced state role in the economy. The Germans, unlike the
Americans, did not provide military aid: Bonn's aid package to Honduras, for example, gave $17 million for power lines, roads, agrarian
development, and worker training.[30]

The San José meeting emphasized that the EEC, pushed by the Germans, was also a player in Central America's peace efforts. The core
issue, however, was the region's future economic development which

was linked to meeting basic human needs and ultimately peace. For El Salvador, Nicaragua, Guatemala, Honduras, and Costa Rica, the meeting was an opportunity to reactivate the regional economy by helping to revive the long dormant Central American Common Market (CACM). Interregional trade had declined from over $1.2 billion in 1977 to under $700 million in 1982.[31] Central Americans indicated that if the region's shortage of hard currency could be overcome with EEC aid, CACM could be resuscitated, which would help generate the growth their export-dominated economies needed. Furthermore, the EEC would have to increase its volume of trade with Central America, especially in stimulating regional exports. At the time, the EEC with West Germany leading the way was Central America's largest market (24 percent) after the United States.

Central Americans also pressed for European political support to obtain the "softest" possible terms of debt repayment in the renegotiation of the region's external debt of $11 billion.[32] Some of the aid figures presented to the Europeans ranged between $1 billion for short-term capital to $20 billion for the medium term. The European response to Central American proposals did not match expectations. No specific commitments were concluded and most issues were left "open." Though financial issues dominated the discussions, a letter from U.S. Secretary of State George Shultz to the Europeans transformed the meeting into a contest over European influence and the region's future. On one hand, the United States had announced the CBI and established a financial blockade of Nicaragua; on the other hand a German-led EEC initiative included Nicaragua. Shultz' proposal asked the Europeans not to commit aid to the Sandinista government but his request was firmly rejected. Even the United Kingdom, a firm U.S. ally, rejected the U.S. position.

The San José meeting was a positive movement for those forces favoring a new multipolar orientation for Central America. On the positive side, the Europeans, led by West Germany, emphasized that for them cooperation was with the region as a whole, not only with U.S.–approved states. In addition, Central American nations were brought together in a neutral forum that asked them to act collectively for mutual benefit. This was an important step in creating some degree of regional cooperation. Finally, the Europeans demonstrated that they, too, could play a progressive role in a politically troubled region.

On the negative side, the Europeans offered much less aid to Central America and the Caribbean than did the United States. European priorities for aid, including West Germany, have traditionally been in Africa and Asia, a situation not expected to change. Even the geographical focus of West Germany's aid programs did not change radically despite Kohl's rediscovery of America. For the Kohl government, Ostpolitic with Eastern Europe remains a more important concern. The West Germans did manage to expand the EEC's role in the Caribbean basin, and the EEC, in all likelihood, will continue to be an important force. If, however, the Germans want to maintain their position or project greater influence, they will have to be willing to maintain their position or project greater influence, they will have to be willing to provide greater economic aid and possibly some form of military assistance. Significantly, Bonn did not resume foreign aid to Nicaragua on a bilateral basis, but only through the EEC.

SPAIN AS A "BRIDGE"

On January 1, 1986, Spain and Portugal became members of the European Economic Community, expanding that organization's membership to twelve nations. For Spain, entry into the EEC was a major step forward in its consolidation of democracy and in its recognition as part of the developed community of nations. Moreover, the entrance of the two Iberian nations into the Community created a "bridge" for Western Europe to Latin America. Many Latin American nations did look to Spain (and to a lesser extent Portugal) as a model for political change. Spain had moved from the Franco dictatorship in November 1975 to democracy in the late 1970s. Though Spain's role in Latin America, and more narrowly in the Caribbean basin, was reviewed in light of this change, an activist role was not developed until the victory of the Socialist party (PSOE) in the fall of 1982. PSOE leader Felípe Gonzalez, the nation's first Socialist prime minister since the Second Republic, perceived that Spain had a role to play in the Western Hemisphere.

Spain's ties to Latin America were founded upon a shared linguistic, cultural, political, historical, and religious past rooted in the Iberian nation's role as the colonial motherland. For the Caribbean basin nations, in particular, the ties had lasted longer as that region marked the entrance of Spanish imperial power in the New World and witnessed its final exit in the Dominican Republic, Puerto Rico, and Cuba. Spain's decline as a global power was marked by the gradual distancing of the motherland and its excolonies which gave way to the then greater commercial and political vitality of France, Britain and, in the late nineteenth and early twentieth centuries, the United States. The various political experiments which ultimately culminated in the birth and death of the Second Republic, the Civil War, and the long period of authoritarian rule of General Franco, left Spain politically isolated from the Latin American Republics.

One exception to Spain's isolation from the Caribbean basin was Cuba. Franco had insisted on retaining diplomatic relations with Castro's Cuba despite obvious ideological differences. For the fascist general and the revolutionary Cuban leader, the relationship benefited national interests.

Both nations gained by trade and diplomatic contact as both were regarded as pariahs in the 1960s: Spain was regarded as a brutish authoritarian regime alien to the new, postwar democratic Western Europe, and Cuba was perceived as a revolutionary leper, capable and willing to export radical revolution to the rest of the Americas. Another reason for this relationship was advanced by Alistair Hennessy:

It is puzzling in view of Franco's anti-Communist stand that Spain should have opted for the European rather than the American line toward Cuba, but in doing so he chose the lesser of two evils. The godlessness of a lapsed Catholic state was preferable to the godlessness of Protestant materialism. In right-wing Spanish thought—especially that stemming from Donoso Cortes—Protestantism has always been regarded as the prime threat, not only for historical reasons but also because Communism is deemed to follow from Protestantism as surely as night follows day.[33]

The revitalization of Spanish democracy in the 1970s and entry into the EEC renewed an interest in the Caribbean basin. The Gonzalez government did not share the viewpoint of the Reagan administration of the roots of the problem in Central America and how to approach Cuba. Appalled by the U.S. intervention in Grenada, the Spanish government perceived Central America's problems in the context of economic development, and an outmoded class system. The Spanish role was to help the promotion of positive change and not cast questions of development into the North American perceptual context of the East-West struggle.

The Spanish approach to the Caribbean basin was based on the understanding that Madrid had influence in the region as opposed to power and, consequently, was prepared to play a supportive role for the advancement of democratic regimes. At the same time, the door was to be left open to Nicaragua and Cuba. Madrid did not seek a confrontational stance with the United States over the region which had previously scuttled French and Socialist International peace initiatives.[34] The Contadora peace initiative, launched by Panama, Colombia, Venezuela, and Mexico provided an opening for Spain. On one hand, it allowed the Spanish to support a group of progressive Latin American nations in a quest for peace in Central America. On the other hand, the door was kept open to Fidel Castro on a bilateral basis. In 1983, Cuba's and Spain's cultural ministers exchanged visits, while Spain hosted a meeting entitled "Ibero-America: Democratic Encounters 83," which was attended by political moderates of both the left and the right. This was followed by Gonzalez' visit to the nations of the Contadora group and the Dominican Republic.

Though Spain's support for the Contadora group did not dwindle, the group's inability to make substantial progress in combination with a recession in the Iberian nation's economy in 1983–1984, left the major impact of Madrid's trade and foreign policy to be found in bilateral relations, especially in 1985 and 1986. Madrid's relations continued to develop with Cuba. Despite a degree of irritation caused by a Castro speech in which he condemned Spain's imperialist past and by the defection of a high-ranking Cuban official and his attempted kidnapping in Madrid, Castro visited Spain and Gonzalez in turn went to Cuba.

Spain's ties with other Caribbean basin nations in 1985 and 1986 concentrated on the reestablishment of relations with Guatemala. Madrid had broken relations with Guatemala as a result of an attack on the Spanish embassy by the Guatemalan security forces in which 39 people died, among them the Spanish diplomat Ruiz del Arbol.[35] The Gonzalez government watched the redemocratization process with approval in 1985 and accepted an invitation to attend the inauguration of Christian Democrat Vinicio Cerezo as the first civilian president in 25 years. In mid-January 1986, the Spanish minister of foreign affairs was present at the inauguration. Later in 1986, Cerezo visited Spain, marking the resumption of formal diplomatic relations between Spain and Guatemala. To further bolster Cerezo's position, the Spanish government supported the Guatemalan president's neturality in the Central American conflict. On Cerezo's visit the Spanish king, Juan Carlos assured the Guatemalan leader that Spain would continue to act in international circles as the patron of legitimate Latin American aspirations as exemplified by the return of democracy in that Central American nations for the first time in a quarter century.[36]

To argue that Spain has abandoned the multilateral approach would be a misnomer. Spain, like the rest of Europe, pursued multilateral policies so long as their own vital interests were not effected. In this sense, bilateralism reveals a policy of opportunity. As one Spanish government publication noted in 1986: "The setting up of a summit between Spain and the countries of Latin America to pave the way for dialogue with the European community, has been followed by official visits to Spain by the Guatemalan and Venezuelan presidents and a private visit by the Argentinian Head of State."[37]

Moreover, the Spanish foreign minister who had attended Cerezo's inauguration as president of Guatemala also visited Costa Rica and Nicaragua. In the former, Fernandez Ordonez met with the Spanish ambassadors assigned to the region as well as those assigned to Mexico, Cuba, Haiti, Jamaica, and the Chargé d'Affaires in Panama. At this meeting the foreign minister stated: "Spain will continue to support every promising lead to achieve peace in Central America, but without interfering in the work of Contadora."[38] In Nicaragua, the Spanish official expressed to Daniel Ortega the hope of his government that the Sandinistas would advance toward internal democratization. Nicaraguan resistance to any substantial liberalization of the political system, because of the war waged by the contras and by their own desire to not to share power, was a source of friction with Madrid. Hence relations were to evolve along a cordial, yet not close basis.

Spain's foreign policy vis-à-vis the Caribbean basin since the Grenadan intervention has largely been characterized by both a multilateral and bilateral emphasis. The bilateral ties to Cuba were maintained as an important part of Madrid's relations with the Western Hemisphere dating back to the colonial past. Relations with other Caribbean nations were of less importance given the limited resources of Spain and the emphasis placed on relations with the rest of Latin America and, in particular, with the Central American republics. With Central America, Spain pursued its objectives through both the EEC as a bridge and through bilateral means. In a sense, Spain has rediscovered Latin America and in the future is likely to continue to play a role in the affairs of Central America and the Hispanic Caribbean.

EUROPE AND THE CARIBBEAN BASIN: WHAT WILL THE FUTURE BRING?

The EEC's Central American policy has not been forgotten. In November 1985 and February 1987, "San José II" and "San José III" were held respectively in Luxembourg and Guatemala City. Major topics of discussion at both meetings were foreign aid and protectionism. At the second meeting protectionism was the main agenda item. In January 1987, EEC foreign ministers extended the "Comprex" scheme to nine "least developed countries." Most of these nations, with the exception of Haiti, were in Asia. This development occurred despite Spanish resistence. Since November 1986, Spain had lobbied hard to include Latin American nations in the Comprex program. The majority, however, felt that Latin America, and especially Central America, should be assisted within existing aid budgets and perhaps some asistance could be extended on certain commodities. Spain, with its greater interest in the region, has sought to change the system of non-Lomé aid to developing nations: In 1986 75 percent of non-Lomé aid went to Asia and 25 percent to Latin America. Spain has sought a 50–50 parity, which would help Central American nations. The thrust of the San José meetings and Spanish diplomacy within the EEC has been undermined in Central America as progress has been slow and the ACP countries have fought hard to maintain their share of the aid pie, not wishing to share it with any newcomers. Moreover, protectionism has hurt: In 1987 Italy and the United Kingdom suspended imports of bananas from Latin America in a bid to protect imports from the African, Caribbean, and Pacific nations. While nations like Jamaica, Dominica, St. Lucia, Grenada, and

Suriname (all Lomé signatories) have benefitted, two Central American nations, Costa Rica and Panama, were hurt and probably stood to lose several million dollars in export earnings. These developments in 1986 and 1987 have raised some serious questions about the European role in the Caribbean basin.

The Caribbean basin offers a challenge to the European community. Collectively, the European nations would like to have a peaceful region that is democratic and economically linked to North and South America and Europe in an equitable interdependent trade system. Peaceful change is decidedly preferred over revolution and coups, which many regard as being the instruments of the radical left and reactionary right.

Europe's role in the Caribbean basin is important as it offers a democratic, tolerant, and flexible political force as a counterweight to the bipolar approach of the United States. As Tom Adams, the late prime minister of Barbados stated, "But certainly we do look at Europe and I expect that at the forthcoming Heads of Government Conference... that we must witout delay improve the political structure of the CARICOM Treaty and make it more like the Treaty of Rome and the ancillary treaties."[39] The influence of creating regional trade blocs, with possible long-term political implications, was not lost on the Central American nations that attended the San José meeting.

Of the European nations, Germany and France are the most competitive in the Caribbean basin and have the greatest resources to project an influence. Consequently, it is likely that the other nations within the Community will follow the lead of one or the other or both, with the possible exception of Spain which has a special relationship with the Hispanic nations as a former metropole. Two important distinctions exist between France and Germany and their respective roles: France has possessions in the region and will protect them from external influences and regional meddling by Cuba. West Germany leans closer to the United States in its perception of economic development. The conservative Kohl government is also politically akin. The Germans feel that private enterprise and a smaller public sector are needed.

In reviewing Europe's "rediscovery" of the Caribbean basin it is important to note that there has been an emphasis on interdependence. Most Europeans perceive that the Lomé accords and trade agreements with Central American states are, in the words of Ellen Frey-Woutersm, "the latest step in a slow historical process from colonial domination toward mutual cooperation and equality."[40] François-Xavier Ortoli, former president of the European Communities Commission, observed, "The Community must commit itself wherever possible to cooperation based on the search for long-term economic interdependence, which is a better guarantee of progress and unity than any treaty."[41]

For Europe to achieve its interdependence and to avoid the conditions for another Grenada or Nicaragua, its role will have to be on a much grander scale that at present. It will also have to be more carefully weighed in context to policies within the Lomé system. Though U.S. hegemony remains a factor, the Caribbean is no longer an American lake, especially as the EEC countries have extended a greater influence in the region since the Grenadan and Nicaraguan revolutions in 1979. That role, however, remains secondary to the United States. Furthermore, it is doubtful that EEC agreements will result in a new string of pro-Western European nations in the Western Hemisphere. The future, however, may provide the nations of the EEC an opportunity to exert a progressive influence in the development of the region.

NOTES

1. Spain and Portugal were associate members of the European Economic Community in 1984 and had applied to become full members. On January 1, 1986, both Iberian nations became full members and the Community expanded from a membership of ten to twelve.

2. The *Times* (London) July 21, 1982, p. 4.

3. Esperanza Duran, *European Interests in Latin America* (London: Routledge & Kegan Paul Ltd., 1985), p. 46.

4. Duran, *European Interests*, p. 76.

5. Quoted from *World Press Review*, December 1983, p. 18.

6. Duran, *European Interests*, p. 76.

7. *The Financial Times*, October 27, 1983, p. 22.

8. International Monetary Fund, *Direction of Trade Statistics Yearbook 1986* (Washington, D.C.: International Monetary Fund, 1986), p. 148.

9. Frank Gray, "British Business Finds Cuba a Tempting Prospect," *The Financial Times*, January 6, 1987, p. 4.

10. "Nous aussi, nous avons nos Falklands," *The Economist*, January 22, 1983, pp. 40–41.

11. *Latin American Regional Report Caribbean*, January 16, 1981 and *Caribbean Monthly Bulletin* 14, 9–10 (September/October 1980): 56.

12. John Vinocur, "Will French Culture Be More French?" New York *Times*, January 9, 1984, pp. H1, H20.

13. New York *Times*, January 6, 1984; and *The Amex Bank Review*, 7 (September 17, 1984): 19–21.

14. *Latin American Weekly Report*, April 13, 1984, p. 4.

15. *Kessing's Contemporary Archives*, September 1983, p. 32379.

16. *Latin America Weekly Report*, April 13, 1984, p. 4.

17. Stephan Kinzer, "Disillusion with Nicaragua Grows in Europe," The New York *Times*, November 16, 1983, p. A7.

18. John Vinocur, "Unrest Poses Questions for French Possessions," The New York *Times*, 4 December 1983, p. A5.

19. Vinocur, "Unrest Poses Questions," p. 5.

20. *Latin America Weekly Report*, April 6, 1984, p. 4.

21. "Charges, Confusion, Bullets Fill Suriname Air," *The Times of the Americas*, December 24, 1986, p. 3.

22. "Euro-parlement zal politieke situatie in Surinem onderzoeken," *NRC Handelsblad*, February 18, 1986, p. 6.

23. *Latin America Weekly Report*, April 6, 1984, p. 4.

24. *Latin America Weekly Report*, April 6, 1984, p. 4.

25. International Monetary Fund, *Direction of Trade Statistics Yearbook 1986*, pp. 188–89.

26. *Latin America Weekly Report*, July 20, 1984, p. 4.

27. *Latin America Weekly Report*, July 27, 1984, p. 2.

28. *Latin America Weekly Report*, July 27, 1984, p. 2.

29. *Latin America Regional Reports Mexico and Central America*, August 17, 1984, p. 7.

30. *Latin America Weekly Reports*, September 21, 1984, pp. 6–7.

31. *Latin America Weekly Reports*, September 21, 1984, pp. 6–7.

32. *Latin America Weekly Reports*, September 21, 1984, pp. 6–7.

33. Alistair Hennessy, "Spain and Cuba: An Enduring Relationship," in Wiarda, *The Iberian-Latin American Connection: Implications for U.S. Foreign Policy* (Boulder, CO: Westview Press, 1986), p. 370.

34. David Eugene Blank, "Spain and the Andean Republics," in Wiarda, *The Iberian-Latin American Connection*, pp. 325–26.

35. "Strengthening of Links with Latin America," *Spain' 86* (Madrid), No. 160, November 1986, p. 3.

36. "Strengthening of Links," p. 3.

37. "Strengthening of Links," p. 3.

38. "Spain Supports Peace in Central America," *Spain' 86*, February 1986, p. 2.

39. "Interview with Tom Adams," *The Courier*, No. 57 (September–October 1984), p. 25.

40. Ellen Frey-Wouters, *The European Economic Community and the Third World: The Lome Convention* (New York: Praeger, 1980), p. 3.

41. As quoted by E. Wirsing, "Towards New Economic Relations," *The Courier*, 31 (March 1975), p. 3.

14
Soviet-Cuban Foreign Policy in the Caribbean: Was Grenada a Setback?
John W. Merline

The U.S. invasion of Grenada on October 23, 1983 sent shock waves across the globe. Right-wing supporters of the Reagan administration were overjoyed that the most conservative president in decades had taken action against a Marxist government in the hemisphere. Many liberals were appalled at the transgression against a legitimate government and the breach of international law. Most importantly, however, the Soviet Union and its ally in the Caribbean, Cuba, suffered a major setback in the region. Its importance as a defeat can be measured by its importance while as an ally of Cuba and the Soviet Union. Grenada offered both Cuba and the Soviet Union tremendous strategic and political advantages, and its loss, given the size of Soviet/Cuban investment in the New Jewel Movement's government, was substantial.

Before advancing further, however, the parameters of the discussion must be clearly marked. Space austerities require that various complexities surrounding the issue of Cuban/Soviet policy in the region not be studied in minutia, and that certain assumptions be understood as underlying the discussion.

The first of these assumptions is that the Soviet Union and Cuba have a particular view of the world that is predominantly geopolitical. The Soviet Union in particular has little reason to be interested in the Caribbean other than as a means to further long-standing strategic goals. Intertwined with strategy, however, is the play for a superior political and psychological position with the West. How these all fit together is the subject of several volumes, but it should be noted that above all else, the Soviet Union views the world with military spectacles.

The second assumption lies within the belief that, historically, what is said and done by the principal actors carries greater weight than imputed intentions. The "real" reason President Reagan decided to send Marines into Grenada might be debated ad nauseum, but historians must reisgn themselves to study what was said and agreed upon prior to the action. A study of the Grenada invasion's effect on the Caribbean, then, should assume that the documents recovered after the invasion bear witness to the intentions of the New Jewel Movement (NJM), and the role played by its Soviet/Cuba mentors. Speculation about nationalistic impulses and noninternationalistic foreign policy fall by the wayside when confronted with statements by Maurice Bishop in support of the struggle for a socialist transformation of Grenada's Caribbean neighbors and his belief in Marxism-Leninism. We cannot overlook the fact that Grenada was becoming the focal point of leftist revolutionaries in many of the newly independent Caribbean States. Nor can the importance of agreements reached between the NJM and the Soviet Union for future arms shipments, or the armaments already in place when the government was destroyed be downplayed.

Grenada presents the historian with a unique opportunity to understand how a government was formed, how it viewed itself, and how it perceived its place in history. The 35,000 pounds of documents recovered present a picture rich in detail. They reveal not only how Grenada under the NJM viewed itself, but how important Grenada was in Soviet and Cuban planning.

A discussion of Grenada's place in Cuban/Soviet policy in the Caribbean can overlook, if only for the need to be succinct, claims that Bishop was a moderate, and that, had the United States acted differently, we could have avoided (1) an invasion and possible breach of international law, (2) the termination of a socialist and nationalist experiment in the Caribbean, and most importantly, (3) the use of Grenada as a forward base for Soviet expansion in the United States' "backyard." Bishop himself expressed full solidarity with the goals of the Soviet Union and Cuba: including "the same convictions against imperialism, colonialism . . . and Zionism, [and agreed] that the many-sided relations of cooperation be governed by the widest and justest spirit of cooperation, solidarity, and internationalism."[1] The Soviet Union and other Eastern bloc countries were highly motivated to oblige once Grenada's position in the Caribbean became secure.

It can be argued that Bishop had set in motion a machine over which he lost control. One does not reasonably spend time psychoanalyzing the inventor of a bulldozer designed without brakes, after it begins wrecking new buildings. Bishop paved the way for the radicalization of Grenada and its further stabilization in Soviet orbit. The exact nature of the government, and its subtle differences from the Cuban model are also unimportant for our purposes. In the United Nations, Grenada voted with the Soviets and their allies over 92 percent of the time in the General Assembly, including the vote on Afghanistan—a pro-Soviet record exceeding even that of Nicaragua's Sandinista government.

STRATEGIC IMPORTANCE

The Caribbean and Gulf of Mexico maritime routes carry about 55 percent of the imported petroleum to the United States, as well as approximately 45 pecent of all U.S. seaborne trade. More than half of all NATO resupply would be shipped from Gulf ports and would have to pass by Cuba in the event of the breakout of war between NATO and Warsaw Pact countries.[2]

Because of its location, it can be argued that Grenada posed a threat to the very lifeblood of the Western Hemisphere's economies: its oil supplies. During the 1970s a dramatic shift occurred in where the United States obtained its oil. As recently as 1979, nations in the Persian basin accounted for close to half the West's oil production, but their role was diminished, while that of Western Hemisphere nations has increased. Mexican oil exports to the United States represented as much as 20 percent of all oil purchased abroad. Venezuela, too, is one of America's most important sources of crude, and refineries in several Caribbean nations are major sources of U.S. gasoline and other petroleum products. During the period of January to June, 1980, U.S. imports of crude oil from Latin America and the Caribbean was 6,011,000 barrels per day, with 1013 thousand coming from Venezuela alone. Therefore, anything that even potentially threatens the Caribbean oil traffic poses a clear threat to the U.S. economy.[3]

Grenada sits astride the favored trade route for tanker traffic from Venezuela. It is ideally positioned to serve as a base for submarines seeking to interdict tanker traffic. Grenada is a perfect location for a base to operate against shipping in the region, and there were growing indications that Moscow had just such a plan in mind for the island.[4]

Moreover, MiG 27s operating in Grenada could strike the totally unprotected refineries in southern Trinidad within 10 minutes; the major Venezuelan oil fields are only 17 to 25 minutes flying time away, and the essential refineries and storage facilities in the Netherlands Antilles could be reached in about 35 minutes. The island also is an invaluable staging post on the air route to Southern Africa.[5]

By the 1970s, the USSR and Cuba had formulated a coherent strategy in the Caribbean designed to achieve specific ideological, security and political goals.[6] In terms of ideology, the Soviets hoped that Grenada would gradually follow Cuba's path toward Leninism. Some Soviet analysts in early 1983 even suggested Grenada and Nicaragua possessed a "people's democratic state order" the label used by the Soviets in the late 1940s to refer to the now Leninist East European countries.[7]

THE SOVIET UNION AND THE CARIBBEAN

The leaders of the Soviet Union, who have comprehended the advantages of dominance in the Caribbean wish to succeed in this region on three distinct levels: strategic, political, and psychological. Cuba has been as close to a complete success as they could hope for on all three levels. According to a briefing by the Department of State and the Department of Defense:

The Soviet Union sees in [the Caribbean] an excellent and low-cost opportunity to preoccupy the United States—the "main adversary" of Soviet strategy—thus gaining greater global freedom of action for the USSR. They are attempting to foment as much unrest as possible in an area that is the strategic crossroads of the Western Hemisphere. Working through its key proxy in the region, Cuba, the Soviet Union hopes to force the United States to divert military resources to an area that has not been a serious security concern to the United States in the past.[8]

The Soviets have defined their strategic goals to include the Caribbean. In 1971, for instance, the Soviets were noted to have publicly announced that Latin America was the most active National Liberation Front. They then regarded, and presumably still do, the Caribbean as a serious commitment, one that could balance the presence of the United States in areas of close proximity to the USSR's borders. In any case, the Caribbean was devirginized as soon as Castro took power and became the Soviets principal ally in the region. Previous to Castro's victory over Batista in 1959, the Soviet Union had no meaningful presence in the Caribbean. It was a region in which the United States was thought to have had maximum control and an area believed to be essentially impenetrable. After the Cuban revolution, Moscow repeatedly made the point that U.S. defenses had been penetrated. In a sense, the Soviets were able to knock on the United States' back door.[9]

In Cuba alone, the Soviet Union has 7000 civilian advisers, a 2800-man combat brigade, another 2800 military advisers, plus about 2100 technicians at the Lordes electronic intelligence facility. Cuba, in turn, has supplied its own citizens to fight overseas in the advancement of Soviet influence. These places include: South Yemen, Ethiopia, Mozambique, the Congo, and Angola.

Cuba also affords the Soviet Union a priceless base for intelligence gathering and military maneuvering within a hundred miles of U.S. soil. According to the U.S. Departments of State and Defense, the Lordes facility is the most sophisticated Soviet collection facility outside of the Soviet Union itself.[10]

In addition to strategic interests, the Soviet Union has profound political reasons for supporting allies in the Caribbean. The Soviets can now claim to have spheres of influence in nearly every region of the world. The projection of Soviet power in the Caribbean accelerates the process of disintegration of the U.S. position, imposes constraints on U.S. freedom of action, and encourages similar developments in other countries within the Caribbean and Latin America. Bishop, for instance, had said, in a speech celebrating the first anniversary of the NJM insurrection in Grenada: "The greatest debt of gratitude [is] owed to the Cubans... if there had been no Cuban revolution in 1959 there could have been no Grenadian revolution in 1979."[11]

Cuba, with Nicaragua and Grenada following, demonstrated to radical elements throughout the region, especially in the Caribbean nations struggling with economic problems, that success promised worldwide recognition and support. Revolutionaries met in Grenada a number of times, and Grenadans were trained in Cuba and the Soviet Union. Support for liberation movements would begin at the early stages of a revolution, and once victorious, a Marxist government could reasonably expect permanence. The United States appeared to be unwilling or unable to act in response to the takeover of governments by groups hostile to its interest—until 1983, at least.

The Soviet Union viewed Grenada as a place of geostrategic importance and was steadily expanding its involvement with the island. Senior Soviet officials perceived Grenada as a bridgehead in the war to penetrate the traditional U.S. sphere of influence in Latin America and the Caribbean. A document reporting on a meeting between top Soviet and Grenadan military commanders states:

The Marshal said that over two decades age, there was only Cuba in Latin America, today there are Nicaragua, Grenada, and a serious battle is going on in El Salvador. The Marshal of the Soviet Union stressed that United States imperialism would try to prevent progress but that there were no prospects for imperialism to turn back history.[12]

Grenada was important militarily to the Soviets as a potential exporter of communist revolution and as a base for the overt projection of tactical power:

Of all the regional possibilities, the most likely candidate for special attention is Suriname. If we can be an overwhelming influence on Suriname's international behavior, then our importance in the Soviet scheme of things will be greatly enhanced. *To the extent that we can take credit for bringing any other country into the progressive fold, our prestige and influence would be greatly enhanced.*[13] [Emphasis mine]

CUBA AND THE CARIBBEAN

Cuban goals for the Caribbean have been obvious for years. Only purposeful obfuscation or ideological blinders could lead serious scholars to doubt that Cuba under Fidel Castro hopes to nurture and support mini-Cubas throughout the Caribbean. A reasonable argument could be advanced that Cuba's goals do not differ significantly from those of the Soviet Union. One must be careful, in this instance, not to confuse goals with methods. While there might be some room for argument over who decides what the Cuban methods in the Caribbean and Latin America will be, it can still be argued that Castro is not deciding, for himself, what he hopes to see accomplished in this region, or that these goals are not different from the Soviet Union's in any important way. The Soviet's huge investment in Cuba was not taken because they wanted a place for Russian tourists to visit.

In any case, Castro rarely says or does things that would seriously jeopardize the flow of goods from Russia. With Soviet backing, Cuba becomes a power known around the world. And, with Cuban client states in the region, Castro gains credibility in the eyes of his Socialist brethren in Moscow and the Eastern bloc. Cuba saw in Grenada an opportunity to enhance their prestige as a leader of the Third World revolution and increase their influence in the Caribbean.

The documents recovered after the Grenada invasion by the United States indicate that Cuban influence on Grenada was substantial. It was the only country in the region capable of giving the NJM real moral and material support in the early days of the revolution. By the end of their first month in power, the NJM had received 3800 infantry weapons and 36 artillery pieces, as well as military advisers. According to a report from Grenada's embassy in Havana, by 1980 there were "22 different areas of collaboration with Cuba plus seven areas requiring constant consultation."[14]

Castro's assistance to guerrilla movements in Latin America has also been well documented. Since the early 1960s, Cuba has attracted guerrillas from virtually every country in the region. Castro has given logistical and financial support to thousands of these guerrillas as well as providing them military training, usually in courses lasting three to six months.[15] In one document recovered from Grenada, the relationship between the two countries is clearly spelled out:

The Government of the Republic of Cuba in agreement with the request formulated by the People's Revolutionary Government of Grenada, will maintain

Cuban military specialists in that country...Grenada will give facilities to the chief of the Cuban military specialists in the work places and for using the communication means existing in the country...[and] will take all measures depending on them in order to assure secrecy of the permanency of the military personnel in both states and the character of the activities.[16]

For Cuba, Grenada presented a chance for prestige and victory difficult to find in the rest of the Caribbean, or Latin America. Cuba has been isolated from its neighbors—much easier to accomplish when only one Cuba exists. Castro had failed to make inroads in some countries, and others were predisposed to show a strong aversion to the Cuban model of development. Jamaica under Michael Manley had developed close ties with Castro, later severed after Edward Seaga came to power in 1980. Other islands had been turning Westward. Conservatives Tom Adams and Milton Cato were both reelected in Barbados and St. Vincent respectively, as were Eugenia Charles in Dominica, Vere Bird in Antigua, Sir Eric Williams and his successor, George Chambers, in Trinidad and Tobago.

GRENADA AND THE CARIBBEAN

Under Cuban sponsorship, and with plenty of Soviet hardware and assistance, Grenada underwent a rapid transformation from a small, little known, former British colony into a heavily armed, militant island with designs on spreading its revolution to neighboring states. When the NJM took power in 1979, Grenada had a British-style constabulary and a small and lightly armed defense force. By October 25, 1983, Grenada had a regular army approaching six hundred supplemented by a militia estimated at between 2,500 and 2,800 members. The size and sophistication of the armed force of Grenada can be measured by a comparison with those of Jamaica. Grenada, having only one-twentieth of the population of Jamaica, had mobilized an army that was one and a half times as large as the Jamaica Defense Force.

When the NJM was removed in 1983, Grenada had plans to field three more active battalions and hold nine more battalions in reserve. A July 2, 1982, request by the People's Revolutionary Armed Forces of Grenada (formed in January, 1981) to the Armed Forces of the Soviet Union reads:

The plan for the development of the Armed Force during the three year period 1983 to 1985 for which the assistance is required as follows:

1983—(i) Further consolidation of:
      (a) One Permanent Infantry Battalion.
      (b) Five Reservist Infantry Battalions plus assurance and support units.

(ii)   The creation of:
    (a)   Two more regular Infantry Battalions.
    (b)   Four more reservist Battalions plus assurance and support units.
1984—Formation of one additional regular Infantry Battalion together with two reservist battalions plus assurance and support units.
1985—Formation of three additional reservist battalions plus assurance and support units.

The proposed eighteen-battalion force, even if organized into relatively small battalions along Cuban lines, would put 7200 men and women under arms. Battalions of more conventional size would raise this to some ten thousand or more, excluding personnel on the general staff and in other support functions. In proportion to population—over 10 percent of the population under arms—this would have given Grenada the largest military force of any country in the world.[17]

There was a maritime facility going up along the shores of Egmont Harbour, one of the finest protected anchorages in the Southern Caribbean. The encampment housed some four hundred personnel, including two platoons of Soviet Army "advisers" who were rotated bimonthly from their parent brigade in Cuba.[18]

Documents found subsequent to the invasion also revealed that Grenada had signed at least five military assistance agreements: three with the Soviet Union, one with Cuba, and one with North Korea. Taken together, the Soviet, Cuban, North Korean, and a possible agreement with Czechoslovakia provide for delivery by 1986 of the following:

• About 10,000 assault and other rifles, including Soviet AK–47s;
• More than 4500 submachine and machine guns;
• More than 11.5 million rounds of ammunition;
• 294 portable rocket launchers with more than 16,000 rockets;
• 84 82mm mortars with more than 4800 mortar shells;
• 12 75mm cannon with about 600 cannon shells;
• 7000 land mines;
• 50 GRAD-P howitzers with 1800 122mm projectiles;
• 4 costal patrol boats;
• 156 radio stations;
• 15,000 hand grenades, plus other assorted armaments and weapons.

The weight of these agreements and the hardware already on the island by 1983, led a former senior Defense Department official who served during the Carter administration to say: "The amount of aid specified in the agreements was far more than Grenada could absorb for its own use, suggesting that the weapons were going to be reexported or used for training paramilitary forces from other nations.[19] Prime

Minister Maurice Bishop also secured agreements for assistance from Libya, Algeria, Syria, and Iraq, and Algeria pledged to supply all the oil and gas used by machines on Grenada's international airport project.

The Point Salines airport project was another example of Grenada's movement to increasing strategic importance for the Soviet Union and Cuba. Soviet financing and equipment was channeled through Cuba for the construction of the Point Salines airport, being built by Grenada by more than six hundred Cuban workers. Once completed, the airport's runway could handle any aircraft in the Soviet fleet. There is some dispute as to the nature of the project, but this should be dispelled once one reads that Bishop had acknowledged the potential strategic uses for the airport. In an interview with *Newsweek* magazine, Bishop did not rule out the possible military use of the airport: "Suppose there's a war next door in Trinidad, where the forces of fascism are about to take control, and the Trinidadians need external assistance. Whey should we oppose anybody passing through Grenada to assist them?" At an April 15, 1983, meeting with Soviet Foreign Minister Andrei Gromyko, Bishop emphasized the benefits of the airline project, commenting that "There is also the strategic factor which is well known!" At a conference of the Worker's party of Jamaica in December 1981, the NJM's Selwyn Strachan stated that the Point Salines airport would be available for use by Cuba and the Soviet Union. Also, a diary belonging to Central Committee member Liam James contained the notation from a March 1980 meeting: "Airport will be used for Cuban's and Soviet's military."[20]

The airport facilities at the time of the invasion showed few signs of commercial feasibility—the airport turned out to be nothing less than a sophisticated military camp. All the signs and directions were in Spanish, none in English. Facilities were present throughout for the storage of arms, and there was no evidence of provision being made for any normal commercial or civilian aircraft. Furthermore, the installation was filled with places to hang rifles, even in the bathrooms.[21]

There are other elements of the airport's construction that belie claims that the airport was to be used strictly to boost the tourist trade. Only one airline had responded to PRG feelers on the site of the airport. Eastern Airlines had reportedly told the PRG that a minimum of 2100 rooms would be required to justify regular service. Grenada had under a thousand rooms, and there was no evidence of a major effort to build more.[22]

In addition, a CBS poll taken one week after the October 1983 invasion revealed that 65 percent of the Grenadan people agreed the airport "was going to be used mostly for Cuban and Soviet military purposes."

It is also interesting to note that, prior to victory in 1979, the NJM had opposed the construction of the airport. Ironically, Bishop argued "The importance for the military circles in the Pentagon is also obvious, given Grenada's strategic position in the Caribbean and on the routes to Africa and Europe." Had the Point Salines airport been operational in April 1983, for instance, the Libyan aircraft detained in Brazil, which plane's cargo contained military supplies destined to Nicaragua, could have refueled in Grenada instead of in Brazil.[23]

The NJM was also helpful in Havana's efforts to cultivate contacts between small island states. Representatives from Cuba were invited to "party-building seminars" and youth group meetings hosted by Grenada for the various leftist organizations of the region, and Grenada provided briefings and documents to the Cubans on political conditions in the Eastern Caribbean.

Grenada acted consciously as an agent of world revolution in the Caribbean. The NJM's International Relations Committee supported the activities of leftist movements throughout the Caribbean and offered Grenada as a training ground and safe haven for those movements.

In Jamaica, for example, the PRG had close ties to the Workers' Party of Jamaica (WPJ) led by Trevor Munroe. As early as October 1979, Munroe sent a team of WPJ members to Grenada to work with the NJM and receive security training. Munroe was later to advise Bishop on how to handle the unions in the wake of the 1981 public workers' strike; he was drafting his Jamaican colleagues to serve responsible posts for the PRG; and he was recruiting elsewhere.[24]

Among its nonsocialist neighbors, the NJM cultivated close ties with leftists in Trinidad, particularly Michael Als of the People's Progressive Movement and Allan Alexander, an important source of legal advice to the PRG. On January 9, 1980, the *Trinidad Guardian* alleged that Trinidadians were being trained as guerrillas in Grenada. Geddes Granger, leader of the black power–oriented National Joint Action Committee of Trinidad, was a frequent guest of the government of Grenada. Ralph Gonsalves of the St. Vincent United People's Movement was, Richard Jacobs told the Soviets, "a clear, consistent and reliable Marxist-Leninist" who "can be helped at all levels without fear of compromise." The NJM also worked closely with Tim Hector of the Antigua Caribbean Liberation Movement (ALCM). A top secret report of Grenada's security service recounted Hector's assistance in procuring sensitive Antigua government documents, and recommended that two ALCM comrades be brought to Grenada for security training.[25]

The NJM also recognized close ties with the government of Nicaragua, and organized rallies for El Salvador, briefed the FMLN guerrillas there on the Caribbean political situation, and advised them on ways to participate in the 1983 CARICOM summit meeting.[26]

The People's Revolutionary Government of Grenada was constructed along doctrinaire Leninist lines using the NJM as "the vanguard party" and adhering as closely as possible to the Soviet Union's political system.

"It is clear," a recovered document reads, "that our objective as Marxist-Leninists must in the first instance be to construct socialism as rapidly, but scientifically as possible." Bishop and his comrades were dedicated believers in the Soviet model of Communism formulated by Lenin—which included a frighteningly dogmatic belief that no other worldview was correct. "Being a communist," the same documents reads, "means becoming a different kind of person.... We believe firmly that the path we have chosen is the *only* correct one."[27] [emphasis in original]

Grenada under the NJM showed no signs of reservation about the assumption of their policy goals into those proposed by the Soviet Union and the Communist camp. In fact Bishop planned to:

Build rapidly our links with the Socialist World, especially with the Soviet Union. And here I should hardly have to say more; when I had just come back from an important visit to the land of Lenin. The Soviets in the last two days have arrived, nine of them including the Ambassador, and their embassy is about to be opened and so on. So these links and relations are building reasonably satisfactorily.[28]

Bishop clearly pledged solidarity with his Marxist neighbors. He said "We give our solemn pledge that we will unhesitatingly fulfill our internationalist responsibilities. Imperialism [referring, of course, to the United States, primarily] must know that if they touch Cuba, they touch Grenada, and if they touch Nicaragua, they touch Grenada."[29]

THE CARIBBEAN REACTION

There is little evidence, however, to show that Grenada's neighbors felt unconcerned about the developments on the island. It is clear that, if Grenada had no plans to export its revolution, it did very little to reassure countries in its vicinity, or even inhabitants of Grenada itself. Opinion polls have confirmed that the people of the English-speaking Caribbean strongly supported the invasion. In Jamaica, a national poll revealed 58 percent in favor and 34 against the U.S. action, while in Trinidad and in Grenada itself the support levels for the invasion were 61 percent and 90 percent respectively.[30] In testimony before the U.S. Senate on March 27, 1984, Dominica's Prime Minister Eugenia Charles stated that, "In 1981 and 1982, we began to be very upset by the information we were getting that there was an arms buildup in Grenada. It was obvious to us that there was an arms buildup in Grenada far in excess of anything that would be required for the Grenadian Government to keep Grenadians within the tight and narrow path that they had set forth. We could only realize that this buildup of arms was meant to be used against all of our islands."[31]

The invasion initiative was promoted initially by Barbados, Dominica, Jamaica, and the United States. The prime ministers of Jamaica and of Dominica (as head of the Organization of Eastern Caribbean States [OECS]) played key roles in convincing the members of the OECS (St. Vincent, St. Lucia, Montserrat, Antigua, and St. Kitts–Nevis) to join and support the U.S.–led invasion. The OECS voiced the fear that "military forces and supplies are likely to be shortly introduced to consolidate the position of the regime and that the country can be used as a staging post for acts of aggression against its neighbors."[32]

The response from U.S. congressmen was surprisingly favorable, at least after most of the information recovered from the invasion was made public. Michael Barnes, for example, a Democratic representative from Maryland, and chairman of the House subcommittee on Western Hemisphere Affairs, said in an op-ed in the Washington *Post* (November 9, 1983): "I believe that the OECS request was genuine. Certainly the OECS nations felt they were threatened by the circumstances in Grenada."

CONCLUSION

The evidence above suggests the following: (1) Grenada was becoming a militarized island with plans to obtain more weaponry than it could absorb, and with more arms than it could possibly need for security, given the lack of arms possessed by its neighbors. This move towards militarization included the building of an airstrip—capable of handling any plane in the Soviet arsenal—with clear and self-admitted strategic uses. (2) The Grenada revolution, as its nature came into focus, was not popular with the people of Grenada or its neighbors. (3) To NJM enjoyed close ties with the Soviet Union and Cuba, and expressed a desire to see more Soviet-style states develop in the region. (4) The Soviet Union, for its part, saw Grenada as an opportunity to gain a further strategic and political advantages over the United States in the latter's "sphere of influence."

Given these four points, it become clear that the loss of Grenada was a serious setback for both countries. Cuban and Soviet arms supplies and military training had turned Grenada into a garrison state with military capability to defeat all of the English-speaking Caribbean states combined. This drastic alteration of the balance of military capability in the region combined with the perceived Marxist threat (to weak mini-states without effective armies or other security forces) left the door open for U.S. leadership to assume the role of protector of small and militarily weak democratic states against international Marxist insurgency and military threats.

The U.S. action, while fulfilling this role, also negated a recent Communist gain. Cuba, meanwhile, continues to support revolutionary movements in Latin America, and as Nicaragua consolidates its power, it too will be in a position to take a more active role in events in the Western Hemisphere.

Some losses, temporary and fleeting at best, were evidenced soon after the invasion. Psychologically, the success of a revolution in Grenada would bolster similar movements elsewhere in the region. The removal by force proved, in a small way, that the United States was not a "sleeping giant" and was therefore clearly a setback for both Cuba and the Soviet Union. Revolutionaries could no longer expect permanence once they obtained victory. A recipe for caution—on the part of the revolutionaries themselves, and their Cuban/Soviet supporters—who are dependent on the success of leftist movements within the countries. A Reagan administration official said of Grenada's neighbors, for instance, that "they have been inoculated against Communism, at least for a while."[33]

Cuba, it should be noted, suffered more directly as a result of the invasion. As reported by the Los Angeles *Times* (October 27, 1983): "In the wake of the invasion, a second Cuban ally in the area, Suriname, abruptly suspended its cultural and economic agreements with Havana. After a decade of assiduous attempts to Castro to win friends around the Caribbean, one senior diplomat in Havana said, the two reversals were 'probably the biggest defeat for Cuba since the elections in Jamaica,' when Seaga defeated Cuban ally Michael Manley."

Castro's credibility in the region was not enhanced by the discovery of Cuba's heavy involvement in Grenada, either. His attempt last fall to convince Latin countries strapped with debt burdens to boycott payments was a resounding failure. A Havana conference on the subject attracted only a handful of precommitted leftists—but no government representatives.[34]

Nevertheless, for those concerned with U.S. interests in Latin America and the Caribbean, there is little to be cheery about. Although Cuba has not altered its agenda vis-à-vis Latin America or the Caribbean, it has succeeded in bringing itself back into the mainstream of Latin America's political life. According to Nelson Valdes, who spoke to the World Affairs Council of Maine on August 12, 1986, "The second most important element in Cuban foreign policy is a persistent, sophisticated, multidimensional effort to forge connections with the rest of the world. In the early 1960s Cuba was almost alone. In the Western Hemisphere it had relations only with Canada and Mexico. Today, Cuba has relations of some sort with all but four nations in the Americas: Chile, Paraguay, El Salvador and Guatemala."

Peru and Cuba, for example, are now said to have "similar viewpoints on the current situation in Latin America, [including the belief that] the United States is the main obstacle to peace in Central America because it seeks to thwart negotiations and impose a military solution in Nica-

ragua with the help of the contras and the threat of invasion," according
to Cuban Vice President Carlos Rafael Rodriguez at a meeting in Lima.
Peru and Cuba restored their diplomatic relations at the ambassadorial
level in March, and will, according to Rodriguez, "soon begin cooperating
in the fields of cattle raising, citrus production, and sugar cane farming,
among other areas." Alan Garcia, meanwhile, was quoted in the press
as saying his country will aid Nicaragua, granting them a $10 million
credit line and rescheduling Managua's debt to Peru over a period of
twenty years with three percent interest.[35]

On June 25, 1986 full diplomatic and economic relations were reestablished between Cuba and Brazil. Brazil had difficulty explaining the
refusal to deal with Cuba, particularly when other Latin American nations were improving their links to Havana. An editorial in *O Globo*, Rio
De Janeiro, however, lamented that "Nothing has changed concerning
Cuban behavior in Central America. And . . . nothing has changed concerning the overwhelming Cuban presence in Angola. . . . Angola's geographic location has a bearing on maritime routes that are vital to the
security of the hemisphere because it guarantees the movement of fuels
and other supplies."

Cuba and Uruguay also recently signed a trade agreement. The document signed by the foreign ministers of the two countries noted that
they are both "interested in economic cooperation and trade based on
the principle of national sovereignty and the spirit of Latin American
integration." It also stated that Cuba and Uruguay will grant each other
most-favored nation status regarding customs and regulations pertaining
to import and export operations.

A Cuban delegation attended the July 24–25, 1986, meeting of the
Latin American Integration Association (ALADI) held in Acapulco,
Mexico. The Cuban director of international organizations in the Ministry of Foreign Commerce, Eduardo Delgado Bermudez, announced
that Cuba is interested in reentering the Latin American economic community after being isolated for 23 years.[36]

Nicaragua has become a major player in Latin America. Their efforts
to support elements friendly to the interest of Cuba and the Soviet Union
continues, though at a lower level since the invasion of Grenada.[37] Nevertheless, according to a former ranking member of the largest guerrilla
faction in El Salvador, rebels fighting in El Salvador continue to receive
about three-quarters of their ammunition supplies from Managua and
virtually all their supply of explosives. The Sandinistas continue to control the distribution of the supplies, approving and disapproving the
requests from individual guerrilla groups.

In April 1985, the Sandinistas were caught trying to provide support
for the Honduran guerrilla groups. Seven Nicaraguans were arrested
in Paraiso department trying to infiltrate arms to Chinchoneros based

in Olancho department. The leadership of Honduran guerrilla groups continues to reside in Nicaragua and U.S. intelligence reports current training of Honduran guerrillas in Managua.[38]

According to Alvaro José Baldizon Aviles, who was formerly chief investigator of the Special Investigations Commission of the Nicaraguan Ministry of Interior, a group of approximately 45 members of the Costa Rican Popular Vanguard party were training for guerrilla warfare on the property of the African Oil Palm Cultivation Project near El Castillo in southern Nicaragua.[39]

Nicaragua is also building a new airbase, one of the largest in the Western Hemisphere. Called Punta Huete, it is three meters thick and 3040 meters long. The Punta Huete airfield can handle any plane in the Soviet inventory, Bearcat and Backfire bombers, and of course any MIG. Punta Huete will also give the Soviet Union the capability to conduct aerial intelligence reconnaissance flights of the West Coast of the United States with the inviting intelligence targets of Silicon Valley and the U.S. nuclear submarine base in Washington State. The Soviets, thanks to Cuba, have been able to conduct similar missions along the East coast of the United States.[40]

The Soviet Union, for its part, continues to supply Cuba with more than $4 billion annually in economic aid—or one-quarter of Cuba's GNP—along with 2800 military and some seven thousand civilian advisers.[41] Tonnage of Soviet arms deliveries to Cuba has tripled over the past three years; Soviet Tu–95 Bear D and Tu–142 Bear F naval reconnaissance and antisubmarine warfare aircraft fly regular missions from Cuban air bases; Cuba's Cienfuegos naval base regularly services Soviet submarines.[42] The Soviet Union is the primary supplier of modern military hardware to Peru, and provides more official scholarships to Latin America than does the government of the United States. The Nicaraguan gunships and more than twenty major new military facilities have been constructed with financing and technical asistance from the USSR, Cuba, and other Soviet bloc nations.[43]

In short, while the Grenada invasion had some psychological as well as military benefits to the United States, it did not change the basic goals of Cuba of the Soviet Union. Both continue, with the help of Nicaragua, to pursue gradually the goal of dominating the Western Hemisphere. As Bayardo Arce noted on May 6, 1984, "We cannot cease being internationalists unless we cease being revolutionaries."[44] This is being carried out in Central and Latin America as well as the Caribbean.

N●TES

1. "Cooperation and Exchange Plan Between the Communist Pact of Cuba and the New Jewel Movement of Grenada, for the 1983 Period" October 1, 1983 (GD 100016).

2. Timothy Ashby,"Grenada—Threat to America's Caribbean Oil Routes," *National Defense*, May–June 1981, pp. 53–54.

3. Milton Copulos, "Grenada and Oil Security," The Washington *Times*, November 10, 1983.

4. Copulos, "Grenada and Oil Security," p. 54.

5. Copulos, "Grenada and Oil Security," p. 54.

6. James Theberge, ed., "Russia in the Caribbean: A Conference Report," October 7, 1971.

7. Jiri Valenta, "Grenada: A Friend the Russians Couldn't Protect," The Boston *Globe*, November 14, 1983.

8. "The Soviet-Cuban Connection in Central America and the Caribbean," The Department of Defense and the Department of State, March 1985, p. 3.

9. Theberge, p. 12–13.

10. "The Soviet-Cuban Connection," p. 3.

11. Maurice Bishop, "Forward Ever! Three Years of Revolution," (Sydney [Australia]: Pathfinder Press, 1982), p. 114.

12. "Meeting Between Chiefs of Staff of Soviet Armed Forces and the People's Revolutionary Armed Forces of Grenada," March 10, 1983 (GD 000008).

13. Richard Jacobs, "Grenada's Relations with the USSR," July 11, 1983, (GD W2).

14. Embassy of Grenada in Havana, "General Report," dated (by hand) September 17, 1980 (GD 000425).

15. "Cuba's Renewed Support of Violence in Latin America," U.S. Department of State, Special Report #90, December 14, 1980.

16. Page from Liam James notebook, dated March 22, 1980.

17. "Grenada: A Preliminary Report," The Department of State and the Department of Defense, December 16, 1983, p. 18.

18. Ashby, "Grenada—Threat to America's Caribbean Oil Routes," p. 53.

19. "Experts Say 5 Arms Pacts Suggest Moscow Had Designs on Grenada," New York *Times*, November 6, 1983, p. A5.

20. "Grenada: Tiny Exporter of Revolution?" *Newsweek* 95, 13, p. 44 (GD 004708); Liam James' notebook.

21. Jeane Kirkpatrick, "The U.N. and Grenada," Congressional Record–Senate S 3271, March 27, 1984.

22. Gregory Sandford and Richard Vigilante, *Grenada: The Untold Story* (Lanham: Madison Books, 1984), pp. 103–4.

23. "The Soviet-Cuban Connection," p. 13.

24. Grenada, NJM National Youth Organization, "Document of the 2nd Meeting of the Anti-Imperialist Youth and Students of Caribbean," September 1982, (GD 102521); "Report of Mission to Moscow" (GD 103068), December 10, 1981, p. 16; Letters to "Comrade Maurice Bishop" signed Trevor Munroe, October 16, 1979, March 11, 1981, (GD 104729, 104260).

25. "Report of Mission to Moscow," pp. 7–9; "Grenada's Relations with the USSR," p. 5. Also GD 100285, 104061, 104366.

26. "Line of March for the Party," presented by Comrade Maurice Bishop, chairman, Central Commitee, September 13, 1982.

27. "Line of March."

28. "Line of March."

29. "The Foreign Policy of the Grenadian Revolution," *Bulletin of Eastern Caribbean Affairs* 7, 1, p. 4.

30. Carl Stone, "A Political Profile of the Caribbean," *Political Profile of the Caribbean* (Washington, D.C.: The Woodrow Wilson International Center for Scholars, 1985), p. 8.

31. Congressional Record–Senate, March 27, 1984, S 3261.

32. William Giandoni, "Grenada Neighbors Closer Witnesses," *The San Diego Union*, November 13, 1983.

33. Otto Reich, at reporter luncheon, Washington, D.C. (June 1985).

34. *The Times of the Americas* 29, 17, August 14, 1985.

35. *The Times of the Americas* 29 17, June 11, 1986, p. 3.

36. *The Times of the Americas* 29, 17, July 23, 1986, pp. 3, 6; June 25, 1986, p. 6; August 6, 1986, pp. 2, 9.

37. "Revolution Beyond Our Borders: Sandinista Intervention in Central America," U.S. Department of State, September 1985, p. 23. It reads: "According to Napoleon Romero, formerly the third ranking member of the largest guerrilla faction in the FMLN who defected in April 1985, his group was receiving up to 50 tons of material every three months from Nicaragua before the reduction in deliveries after U.S.–Caribbean action in Grenada."

38. "Revolution Beyond Our Borders", pp. 25, 38.

39. "Inside the Sandinista Regime: A Special Investigator's Perspective," U.S. Department of State, p. 25.

40. Robert R. Reilly, "Components of Soviet Global Strategy: The Case of Central America," March 1986, p. 12.

41. "Moscow's Latin Connection," The American News Service, Washington, DC, March 1985.

42. The Heritage Foundation, "Briefing Book for President Reagan's Summit Meeting in Geneva, November 19–20, 1985," p. 16.

43. American News Service.

44. "Commandante Bayardo Arce's Secret Speech Before the Nicaraguan Socialist Party," U.S. Department of State, March 1985, p. 4.

15
The Reagan Years
Timothy Ashby

While the October 1983 U.S./Organization of Eastern Caribbean States (OECS) intervention in Grenada can be justly considered the emotional and ideological highpoint of Reagan administration policy toward the Eastern Caribbean, the operation appears as an anomaly in a generally benign policy based overwhelmingly on development assistance and diplomacy. While in most respects the Reagan administration's policy toward the region differed little from its predecessors in the White House, there was renewed emphasis on a restoration of the Monroe Doctrine.

U.S.–GRENADA RELATIONS

The best illustration of a basic continuum in U.S.policy toward the Caribbean is provided by an analysis of U.S. relations with Grenada during the island's rule by the People's Revolutionary Government (PRG), an era overlapping the last two years of the Carter administration and the first two years of the Reagan administration. Ambassador to the Eastern Caribbean Frank Ortiz, a career diplomat, exhibited cautious moderation in his recommendations to Washington regarding relations with Grenada in the immediate aftermath of the New Jewel Movement's (NJM) March 13, 1979, coup d'état. Ortiz felt that the U.S. reaction to Grenada "should be guided in both degree and in rapidity of design and execution by the responses from Britain (the former colonial power) and Commonwealth Caribbean governments."[1]

Although Ortiz felt that events in Grenada should be viewed with concern, he nonetheless told his superiors in Washington that he believed the assumption of power might moderate some of the extremist ideas which the NJM had advocated in its publications and speeches. The U.S. ambassador also thought that the NJM leaders, although ideologically predisposed against much of U.S. policy, might prove to be open to contact with the United States. Ortiz therefore recommended that the U.S. government "Reciprocate the NJM leadership's expressed desire for a 'non-confrontational relationship' to create a space of time in which undesirable aspects of Grenadian events, notably the unconstitutional nature of the transition and the Marxist ideology of the new leaders, might be influenced in a direction more in accord with U.S. interests in the Eastern Caribbean region."[2]

In light of what transpired in 1983, it is interesting to note that the United States, in the person of Ortiz, was being pressured by "leaders of several Caribbean democracies [apparently Barbados, St. Lucia, and Dominica] into taking extreme measures to bring down the PRG." Ortiz feared that the Carter administration "would somehow be pressured into taking precipitate action which would not serve its own or Commonwealth Caribbean interests."[3] At this stage, Ortiz was ready to accept in good faith the PRG's promises of early elections, nonalignment, and due process for political detainees. As a result, the United States "recognized" the People's Revolutionary Government on March 22, 1979, only nine days after the coup. Following his meeting with Maurice Bishop and Unison Whiteman on the same day, Ortiz reported to Washington that "if we expect to have a significant constructive influence on the course of events, we shall have to play for time showing forebearance and patience and avoiding unnecessary confrontation until the new government is more comfortable in its relationship with us, and we understand its ultimate design better."[4]

As the undemocratic nature of the PRG became evident in succeeding weeks, U.S. State Department officials consulted with other Caribbean leaders such as then Jamaican Prime Minister Michael Manley to express their "puzzlement and dismay" over the PRG's actions. Praising the moderate U.S. policy, Manley said that "the NJM was, like his own party, engaged in the dificult task of instituting new policies while keeping the Communists out."[5]

The tenuous U.S.–Grenadan relationship was deliberately ruptured by Maurice Bishop on April thirteenth, during the Grenadan leader's "Back Yard" speech denouncing Ambassador Ortiz and the United States for allegedly trying to dictate to Grenada what policies it should adopt and of total unresponsiveness to the PRG's requests for economic aid and arms. The speech had in fact, followed both the infiltration of Cuban intelligence and military operatives into Grenada as well as the unloading of weapons shipped both from Cuba via Guyana and directly from Cuba. The day after Bishop's speech, Grenada and Cuba established diplomatic relations.

Ortiz's successor, Sally Shelton, "turned herself inside out in her effort to deal with Grenada," yet her diplomatic efforts were to no avail because the "PRG had already set its course toward Cuba and . . . the Soviet Union and its allies."[6] Regardless of the PRG's blatant hostility toward the United States, and the resultant hardening of U.S. policy towards Grenada, the Reagan administration remained open to any overtures for improved relations with the revolutionary government.

The most dramatic example of this occurred in June 1983 when Maurice Bishop met in Washington, DC, with U.S. National Security Adviser William Clark, Undersecretary of State Kenneth Dam, and U.S. Ambassador to the Organization of American States William Middendorf. Although Bishop had hoped for a meeting with President Reagan or Secretary of State George Schultz, the meeting with Clark and the other officials was amicable, and PRG notes of the meeting record that the Americans were open to better relations with Grenada if the PRG moved away from its embrace of the Soviet bloc. The notes say that National Security Adviser Clark agreed to another "off the record meeting, a secret meeting," and that Maurice Bishop was [e]ncouraged by this response, that they are willing to accept talks on the normalization of relations."[7]

This meeting may have precipitated Bishop's downfall, for the Soviet officials responsible for Grenadan affairs were highly displeased that Bishop had not informed them of the meeting beforehand and that he had ordered the PRG's ambassador in Moscow to keep its details secret.[8] During remarks apparently based on still classified intelligence reports, Prime Minister Eugenia Charles of Dominica revealed that during the two weeks prior to the execution of Bishop and his supporters by members of the PRG's Coard faction, there had been an unusual amount of movement between Soviet Caribbean embassies and Grenada by members of the Coard wing.[9] Although the pertinent records remain classified, there have been reports that, following Bishop's house arrest by a rival PRG faction, the United States had planned to rescue the deposed prime minister with a special forces team of U.S. SEALS. Bishop was executed before the operation could take place, and the SEALS were allegedly dispatched instead to rescue Grenadan Governor-General Sir Paul Scoon.[10]

Reviving the Monroe Doctrine

The emergence of a Cuban-allied regime in Grenada, followed closely by the July 1979 Sandinista victory in Nicaragua and Senator Frank Church's "discovery" of a Soviet brigade in Cuba the next month, served to sharply focus U.S. attention on the Caribbean as the election year of 1980 opened. Ronald Reagan came to office determined to halt the tide of communism which appeared, from Washington, to be lapping at the United States southern shores. Mr. Reagan's opposition to the Carter administration's Panama Canal treaty stemmed from his perception of "the Soviet Union and Cuba egging on the dictator of Panama to insist that we give him the canal."[11] Contrary to that assertions of Reagan's critics, who viewed his more assertive Caribbean policy as arising from outdated jingoism and an unwillingness to accept the erosion of U.S. economic and political dominance in the region, the president's over-riding concern was the strategic threat to the United States posed by the Soviet Union's unprecedented advances in American's "back yard."

Such a policy also had strong precedents. Although the United States had always considered the Caribbean to be a strategically important region, the opening of the Panama Canal gave it added significance. In the late nineteenth century, the U.S. naval strategist Alfred Thayer Mahan noted Cuba's command of the major Caribbean chokepoints of the Yucatan Channel and the Straits of Florida, through which all sea traffic from the Gulf of Mexico had to pass.[12] President Theodore Roosevelt's military experiences in Cuba, followed by U.S. acquisition of the Panama Canal route in 1903, inspired his Corollory to the Monroe Doctrine, which gave notice that the United States would employ force to prevent extrahemispheric aggression against fledgling democracies in the Caribbean and Latin America. U.S. covert actions in Guatemala in 1954, the Cuban Missile Crisis of 1962, and the Johnson administration's military intervention in the Dominican Republic in 1965 are all manifestations of the Monroe Doctrine.

Although alluded to in policy pronouncements, the Monroe Doctrine was not given as a justification for the 1983 Grenada intervention, and was not officially invoked until the Reagan administration's second term. Even then, it fell to Defense Secretary Caspar Weinberger, rather than to the White House or the State Department, to enunciate the administration's formal resurrection of the Monroe Doctrine. In the context of reports that a Soviet ship might be carryng MiG fighter aircraft to Nicaragua in November 1984, Weinberger said: "We shouldn't forget that the United States' policy for many decades has been governed by the Monroe Doctrine."[13]

THE CARIBBEAN BASIN INITIATIVE

The Caribbean Basin Initiative (CBI) can be seen as the Reagan administration's corollary to the Monroe Doctrine. Unveiling the CBI in a speech to the Organization of American States in February 1982, President Reagan said: "Make no mistake, the well-being and security of our neighbors in this region are in our own vital interest . . . we will do whatever is prudent and necessary to insure the peace and security of the

Caribbean area. In the face of outside threats, security for the countries of the Caribbean and Central America is not an end in itself, but a means to an end."[14]

Recognizing that stable democracies and unrestricted economic growth represent the best obstacle to communist expansion, the Reagan administration introduced the Caribbean Basin Economic Recovery Act of 1983, which codified the CBI. Conceived as a means of coupling increased economic aid with one-way free trade for most Caribbean exports, the CBI had the potential of being one of the most important measures in U.S. economic policy of the twentieth century, comparable to the 1934 Reciprocal Trade Agreements Act and the 1947 General Agreement on Tariffs and Trade (GATT). Within the context of the CBI, the Reagan administration sought to stimulate private investment in the Caribbean via tax breaks and risk insurance provided by the Overseas Private Investment Corporation (OPIC).

Unfortunately, the Caribbean Basin Economic Recovery Act (which went into effect on January 1, 1984), was crippled from the start. The version of the bill actually passed by Congress had been stripped of its most important features through special interest lobbying and political compromises to the extent that *Business Week* called it "more a symbolic gesture than the ambitious program for economic stimulus" originally designed by President Reagan.[15] A wide range of items, some of which were considered primary export products by Caribbean nations, were excluded from preferential treatment. These included textiles and garments, petroleum products, canned tuna, frozen citrus juices, and leather goods such as footware and luggage. Heavy lobbying by the AFL–CIO also succeeded in clocking President Reagan's proposal for 10 percent tax credit for new investments in the region.

Regardless of trade restrictions, the CBI has stimulated some new investment in the region, while its promotional campaigns indirectly benefitted the Caribbean tourist trade. An increase in some agricultural exports to the United States, such winter vegetables from Jamaica and melons from Honduras, can be directly attributed to the CBI. While overall Caribbean exports have declined, certain categories of manufactured goods, such as high technology devices and chemicals, grew at an annual rate of 11.4 percent between 1983 and 1986. Although still rudimentary, the most positive impact of the CBI has been its stimulus for broadening and diversifying the production and export base for countries with economies still largely based on eighteenth century colonial systems.

A 1986 U.S. General Accounting Office (GAO) investigation of the CBI found serious errors in the Commerce Department's claims that some 285 new investments worth $300 million had been generated in the region as a result of the CBI legislation. A report issues by the GAO found that "about half of the 285 businesses were not related to the CBI trade provisions," and the Commerce Department did not even "have addresses for 274, or 96 percent, of the businesses or telephone numbers for 253, or 89 percent of the businesses."[16]

DEVELOPMENT ASSISTANCE

Aside from the CBI, other forms of Reagan administration development assistance to the Anglophone Caribbean had disappointing results, despite the fact that the billions of dollars given to the Caribbean in economic aid since 1981 was more than five times the amount of U.S. security assistance.

Jamaica. The coincidence of Ronald Reagan's 1980 election with that of Jamaican Prime Minister Edward Seaga made Jamaica a natural place to become the centerpiece of the Reagan administration's new activist policy toward the Caribbean. As Grenada slid further left, the Reagan administration sought a conservative counterweight for the English-speaking Caribbean. In the mistaken belief that Edward Seaga shared President Reagan's commitment to free market economics, the administration crafted a policy designed "to make Jamaica an example of what could be accomplished when assistance was provided to a government that shared the U.S. belief that private sector growth could lead to economic development."[17] Jamaica was also chosen to be the fulcrum of the CBI. The U.S. plan to cure Jamaica of its economic morbidity was based on a combination of foreign direct investment, CBI-generated trade preferences, and greatly increased bilateral and multilateral assistance.

In January 1981 Prime Minister Seaga was received at the White House as President Reagan's first foreign visitor. Under Ronald Reagan's guidance, a U.S. Business Committee on Jamaica was launched for the specific purpose of promoting private investment on the island. Headed by then–Chase Manhattan Bank chairman David Rockefeller, the Committee was composed of 25 top U.S. corporate chiefs, including the chief executives of Bank of America, Hilton International, United Brands, W. R. Grace, and Reynolds Metals.

Including the aid appropriation for Fiscal Year 1987, U.S. bilateral assistance given to Jamaica since Seaga took office totaled more than $1 billion, making Jamaica the second highest per capita recipient of U.S. assistance in the world after Isreal. The Reagan administration also used its influence to increase multilateral assistance for Jamaica. For example, in 1981 the World Bank provided $133.1 million to Jamaica (three times the previous year's amount); President Reagan also authorized the purchase of $67 million worth of Jamaica bauxite for the U.S. strategic stockpile to help the island's depressed mining sector.

Despite such unprecedented U.S. generosity, the Jamaican government did not follow through with its stated commitment to free market development which the assistance was supposed to fuel. U.S. businesses introduced by David Rockefeller's now-disbanded committee encountered so many bureaucratic restrictions and other problems that only a handful actually established operations in Jamaica. A portion of the Reagan administration's aid largesse, designed to provide Seaga with a "cushion" to allow him to make major structural and sectoral adjustments without undue political or social upheaval, actually proved to be counterproductive. The PL 480[18] and U.S.–subsidized Jamaican food stamp program (the latter of which fed almost half of the island's population) proved to be disincentives for domestic food production, while an Agency for International Development (AID) funded government housing program, coupled with the reimposition of rent controls, undercut private construction financing.

Jamaica's poor economic performance proved an embarrassment to the Reagan White House in light of Prime Minister Seaga's statement that his nation "was the best example of what the Caribbean Basin Initiative can accomplish."[19] Mr. Seaga also angered U.S. officials in other ways: Despite the prime minister's generally strong support for U.S. regional policies, Jamaica's United Nations voting record seemed at variance with this. In 1985, for example, Jamaica voted against the United States 77.3 percent of the time, more than even the socialist government of Greece.[20] As a result of Reagan administration disillusionment with the Seaga government, aid levels were cut and U.S. officials began building a cautious *entente cordiale* with Seaga's socialist predecessor and likely successor, former Prime Minister Michael Manley.

Grenada. In the aftermath of the October 1983 joint United States/Organization of Eastern Caribbean States (OECS) intervention in Grenada, the Reagan administration concentrated an impressive amount of economic and political resources to make the island a model of the benefits of parliamentary democracy and free market development. In November 1983, less than three weeks after the landing of U.S. forces, a U.S. government interagency team traveled to Grenada to examine general economic and private sector conditions. Other teams followed, and the White House Office of Private Sector Initiatives gave Grenada high priority status until the beginning of 1985. During the course of the year leading up to Grenada's December 1984 general elections, the centrist coalition New National Party (NNP) received financial and technical assistance from the National Endowment for Democracy (NED), the National Republican Institute for International Affairs, the American Institute for Free Labor Development (AIFLD), and other organizations supportive of Reagan administration policy toward the region.

Although Grenada returned to parliamentary democracy, the island's economic performance fell short of expectations. The bulk of nearly $100 million of U.S. aid between November 1983 and the second quarter of 1987 went to complete large-scale construction projects such as the Point Salines international airport and the highway system, and to maintain the Grenada government's solvency in the face of a persistent shortfall in budget revenues. Despite the determined promotional efforts of the quasi-governmental U.S. Overseas Private Investment Corporation (OPIC), U.S. businessmen seemed unwilling to risk capital in Grenada. Two of the early U.S. investments sponsored by OPIC, a wooden toy factory and a spice bottling enterprise, went out of business. The unemployment rate remained unacceptably high, even though the overall economy grew at an average rate of 3 percent per annum.

Completion of the Point Salines airport failed to spur the hoped for expansion of the island's tourism industry. By the end of the 1986–1987 tourist season, this vital sector of the economy had yet to recover to its levels of the early 1970s. With less than seven hundred hotel rooms, major air carriers refused to add Grenada to their scheduled stops, and air service remained erratic. As a result, the island's hotels registered an unhealthy 41 percent occupancy rate during the 1985–1986 tourist season.

Friction also developed between the Reagan administration and the government of Grenadan Prime Minister Herbert Blaize, largely over Grenada's inability to wean itself of dependence on U.S. aid (which provided 85 percent of the government's finances in 1986), and for slowness in making structural economic reforms advocated by U.S. AID.[21]

Elsewhere in the Eastern Caribbean. The Reagan administration moved decisively in making it clear that the United States would not support the continuance in power of Haitian dictator Jean-Claude "Baby Doc" Duvalier—a diplomatic stance that was a major factor in forcing a change of government in Haiti. Recognizing Haiti's vulnerabilities as the poorest nation in the Western Hemisphere, the United States increased its economic assistance and actively worked to ensure a smooth transition to parliamentary democracy.

As a result of U.S. Assistant Secretary of State Elliot Abram's attendance at the funeral of Guyanese president Linden Sampson Forbes Burnham in August 1985, strained U.S. relations with Guyana gradually improved. Limited U.S. economic assistance resumed, and Burnham's successor, President Desmond Hoyte, adopted a more centrist course in domestic and foreign policy. In Barbados, the landslide election of Errol Barrow in 1986 resulted in a loosening of ties with the United States—a process that showed signs of being repeated elsewhere in the English-speaking Caribbean in the final months of the Reagan administration.

REGIONAL SECURITY ASSISTANCE

The Reagan administration's regional security assistance to the Caribbean region also is a continuation of programs begun by the Carter administration. Following President Carter's October 1979 "revelation" of a Soviet combat brigade in Cuba, a U.S. forces Caribbean Command was created to be based at Key West, Florida. U.S. and NATO exercises in the Caribbean were also expanded during the final year of the Carter presidency, and continued at similar levels during the Reagan administration. The United States also supported the creation of the Regional Security System (RSS) in October 1982, which at that time included Antigua-Barbuda, Barbados, Dominica, St. Lucia, and St. Vincent.

Following the successful cooperation between the United States and OECS forces during the Grenada intervention, U.S. security assistance to the English-speaking Caribbean was increased. St. Kitts–Nevis and Grenada joined the RSS, and both the United States and Britain contributed technical and material assistance to the creation of a regional Coast Guard. The United States also assisted in raising, training, and equipping company-sized Special Security Units (SSUs) based on the smaller islands such as Grenada. The SSUs were organized as an elite, counterinsurgency force, and recruits were given special training to instill a respect for democracy and the rule of law.

CONCLUSION

The heightened U.S. involvement in the Caribbean during the Reagan administration is due more to greater awareness of the region's strategic importance than to a political philosophy distinct from the predecessor administration. A renewed U.S. government emphasis on security interests in the Caribbean was largely inherited by the Reagan White House, as demonstrated by President Carter's authorizing of both the U.S. forces Caribbean Command and covert military assistance to Nicaragua rebel forces. Although the Reagan administration's policy towards the Caribbean has produced mixed results, it has wholly succeeded in giving this strategically vital region the foreign policy prominence it deserves.

NOTES

1. Lawrence Rossin, *U.S.–Grenada Relations Since the Coup: A Background Paper*, American embassy Bridgetown (drafted January 17, 1983), U.S. Department of State case control number 8402598, p. 1.

2. Rossin, p. 2.

3. Rossin, p. 2.

4. Rossin, p. 10.

5. Rossin, p. 16.

6. Rossin, p. 33.

7. U.S. Departments of State and Defense, *Grenada Documents: An Overview and Selection*, "Notes on Bishop's Meeting in Washington with Judge Clark, et al.," No. 32, Washington, DC, September, 1984.

8. *Grenada Documents*, "Grenada's Relations With the USSR," No. 26., p. 4.

9. *Presidential Documents: Administration of Ronald Reagan.* "Situation in Grenada: Remarks and a Question and Answer Session with Reporters," October 25, 1983, p. 1488.

10. This plan was originally revealed by the late Tom Adams, prime minister of Barbados, in the aftermath of the October 1983 U.S./OECS intervention in Grenada. The man reportedly responsible for planning the Bishop rescue mission was former National Security Council staffer, Lt.-Col. Oliver North.

11. "Address to the Foreign Policy Association, New York, June 9, 1977." *A Time for Choosing: The Speeches of Ronald Reagan 1961–1982* (Chicago: Regnery Gateway, 1983), p. 213.

12. Admiral A. T. Mahan, *The Interests of America in Sea Power Present and Future* (Boston: Little, Brown and Company, 1898), p. 289.

13. David Ronfeldt, "Rethinking the Monroe Doctrine," *Orbis* (Winter 1985), pp. 685–86.

14. "Speech to the Organization of American States," *A Time for Choosing*, Washington, DC, February 24, 1982, pp. 294, 302.

15. "Whittling Away at the Caribbean Initiative," *Business Week*, July 11, 1983, p. 28.

16. U.S. General Accounting Office, *Caribbean Basin Initiative: Need for More Reliable Data on Business Activity Resulting from the Initiative*, August 1986, p. 2.

17. U.S. General Accounting Office, *AID's Assistance to Jamaica*, April 19, 1983, p. 1.

18. PL 480 was set up for the purpose of creating overseas markets for U.S. rice, wheat, corn, vegetable oils, and fortified blended foods.

19. Edward Cody, "Luster off Jamaican 'example'," The Washington *Post*, January 21, 1986, p. A11.

20. The Heritage Foundation, *National Security Record* 93, (July 1986), p. 4.

21. "Grenada Survey," *Financial Times*, December 11, 1986, p. 1.

Index

About the Editors and Contributors

TIMOTHY ASHBY was formerly the Deputy Director of the Spitzer Institute for Hemispheric Development at the Heritage Foundation in Washington, DC. He is currently the Director of the Office of Mexico and the Caribbean Basin, at the International Trade Administration, the United States Department of Commerce. Dr. Ashby is widely traveled and has lived and worked in Grenada and the United Kingdom. He received his Ph.D. in International Relations from the University of Southern California, and his M.A. from the same institution. He is widely published and his first book was *The Bear in the Back Yard: Moscow's Caribbean Strategy* (1987).

G. POPE ATKINS is a Professor of Political Science at the U.S. Naval Academy. He has lived and worked in the Caribbean and Latin America, was a Visiting Professor at the University of Guayaquil, Equador, and was a guest scholar at the Institute of Latin American Studies, University of London. He has written widely on Caribbean affairs and is the author of *Latin America in the International Political System* (1979).

WENDELL BELL is a Professor of Sociology at Yale University, New Haven, Connecticut. He has written extensively on Caribbean affairs, especially on nationalism.

VICTOR J. BONILLA is a Foreign Service Officer at the Management Operations of the United States Department of State with fourteen years experience. During his earlier tours of duty, Mr. Bonilla lived and traveled extensively in the Caribbean and Central America. He has an M.A.

in International Studies from the University of Miami, Florida, and a Diploma in Law from the University of Madrid, Spain. Mr. Bonilla has also done postgraduate studies at Harvard Business School. In addition, he has written a number of articles in such publications as *The World and I* and *The Times of the Americas*, and has done consulting work for the Center for Strategic and International Studies in Washington, DC.

EDWARD DEW is a Professor of Politics at Fairfield University in Connecticut. He received his Ph.D. from University of Los Angeles in Political Science, and an M.A. in Government from George Washington in Washington, DC and an M.A. from Yale in International Relations. He is widely published in the *Caribbean Review*, *Comparative Politics*, and the *Latin America and Caribbean Contemporary Record*. His first book was *Politics in the Altiplano: The Dynamics of Change in Rural Peru* (1969), and his second book, *The Difficult Flowering of Suriname Ethnicity and Politics in a Plural Society* (1978).

GEORGES FAURIOL is a Senior Fellow and Director of Latin American studies at the Center for Strategic and International Studies in Washington, DC. He received his M.A. and Ph.D. in International Relations from the University of Pennsylvania. Dr. Fauriol has lived overseas and written extensively on the Caribbean and Latin America. In addition, he was a U.S. government election observer in several Central American countries in recent years. He is the author of *Foreign Policy Behavior of Caribbean States: Guyana, Haiti and Jamaica* (1984) and coauthor of *The Cuban Revolution: Twenty-five Years Later* (1984) and the forthcoming *Guatemala: A Political Puzzle*.

ALBERT L. GASTMANN is a Professor of Political Science at Trinity College in Hartford, Connecticut. Dr. Gastmann received his B.A., M.A., and Ph.D. in International Relations from Columbia University in New York. He is the author of numerous articles in such publications as the *Caribbean Review* and *Journal of Caribbean Studies*. A native of the Netherlands, he has traveled extensively and taught in the Caribbean, Latin America, and Europe. Dr. Gastmann is the author of two books, *The Politics of Suriname and the Netherlands Antilles* (1968) and *Historical Dictionary of the French and Netherlands Antilles* (1978).

PAUL B. GOODWIN, JR. is Professor of History at the University of Connecticut, and served from 1979 to 1987 as Director of its Center for Latin American and Caribbean Studies, which sponsored the conference "Grenada: A Post Mortem" that served as the genesis of this book. He received his M.A. and Ph.D. from the University of Massachusetts. He has written extensively on Latin America, focusing on Argentina and

Anglo-Argentine relations. He is the author of *Los ferrocarriles britanicos y la Union Civica Radical, 1926–1930* (1974) and two editions of *Global Studies: Latin America* (1984, 1986), as well as numerous articles in *Hispanic American Historical Review* and *Journal of Latin American Studies*. He is currently at work on *The Sixth Dominion: A History of Anglo-Argentine Relations in the Twentieth Century*.

ERIK KOPP is a free-lance journalist who has written on the Caribbean and Central America, especially Costa Rica. He was an intern at *The Times of the Americas*. He is currently an M.A. candidate in journalism at American University in Washington, DC. His articles have appeared in *The Times of the Americas* and several Spanish language publications.

JONATHAN LEMCO is an Assistant Professor of Canadian Studies at the Johns Hopkins University School of Advanced International Studies, Washington DC. He received his M.A. and Ph.D. from the University of Rochester, NY, and has published a number of articles on Canada's relations with Central America which have appeared in the *Times of the Americas* and the *Journal of Interamerican Studies and World Affairs*. He is currently editing a special issue of the *Journal of Asian and African Studies* entitled *The State and Economic Change in Comparative Perspective*, forthcoming.

DAVID E. LEWIS is a Ph.D. candidate in International Relations at the University of Pennsylvania. He has lived and traveled through most of the Caribbean, and his first book, *Reform and Revolution in Grenada, 1950 to 1981*, was published by the Cuban publishing house, Ediciones (1984). He is currently conducting research in Nicaragua for his dissertation.

EVA LOSER is a Ph.D. candidate in International Relations at the Johns Hopkins University School of Advanced International Studies in Washington, DC. She received her M.A. in Comparative Government from Georgetown University. She also is a Research Associate at the Center for Strategic and International Studies in Washington. Ms. Loser has testified before the U.S. Congress on Panama and has contributed to a number of books and journals. Her most recent effort with Georges Fauriol is a coauthored volume *Guatemala's Political Puzzle* (forthcoming). In April 1987, she addressed a conference sponsored by the Association of Panamanian Business Executives (APEDE) on the Panama Canal and Internal Political Development.

SCOTT B. MACDONALD is the Chief International Economist at Maryland National Bank in Baltimore, Maryland and a consultant on Caribbean, Latin American, and Asian affairs. Before his current position at Maryland National Bank, he was the International Economist at American Security Bank in Washington, DC and prior to that, the International and Specialized Industries Unit Manager/Senior Country Risk Analyst at Connecticut National Bank. He received his Ph.D. from the University of Connecticut in Political Science and his M.A. in International Relations in the Far East from the University of London's School of Oriental and African Studies.

MacDonald has traveled extensively and lived overseas. He has published articles in the *Caribbean Review*, the *Latin America and Caribbean Contemporary Record*, *The Financial Times* (London), *The Times of the Americas*, *Export Today*, *The International Trader*, and is the author of *Trinidad and Tobago: Democracy and Development in the Caribbean* (1986). He is also the author of *Dancing on a Volcano: The Latin American Drug Trade* (1988).

JOHN W. MERLINE is the former Assistant Editor of *The Times of the Americas* in Washington, DC. He is currently the Executive Editor of *Consumer's Research* also based in Washington. Mr. Merline has published a number of articles on Suriname and the Caribbean and is a consultant on Soviet/Cuban policy in the Caribbean basin.

ROBERT A. PASTOR was formerly a National Security Advisor during the Carter administration. Currently, he is a Professor of Political Science at Emory University and Director of the Latin American and Caribbean Program of Emory's Carter Center. He is the author of *Condemned to Repetition: The United States and Nicaragua* (1987).

HARALD M. SANDSTROM is Associate Professor of Politics and Government and Director of African-American Studies at the University of Hartford, Connecticut. He received his M.Sc. (Econ.) in International Relations from the London School of Economics and Political Science, University of London, and his Ph.D., also in International Relations, from the University of Pennsylvania. He is author of "Race and Class in Grenada and Jamaica: The Self-Destruction of Two Black Power Movements," in *Proceedings* of the Eleventh Annual Third World Conference (1985) and "The New International Economic Order and the Caribbean: The External/Internal Nexus," in *The Restless Caribbean: Changing Patterns of International Relations*, ed. Richard Millett and W. Marvin Will (1979). He is working on his first book, *Third World Underdevelopment and Development: An Eclectic Introduction to Problems, Issues, and Theories* (forthcoming), and is editing another on *Race, Class and Gender in Comparative Perspective: The United States, the Caribbean, and South Africa* (also forthcoming).

AARON SEGAL is a professor of Political Science at the University of Texas at El Paso. He has written extensively on Africa, the Caribbean and Latin America. His books include *The Politics of Caribbean Economic Integration Population Policies in the Caribbean, The Traveler's Africa,* and *Haiti: Political Failures, Cultural Successes.*

SALLY SHELTON-COLBY was the Deputy Assistant Secretary of State for Latin America and the Caribbean 1977–1979, and Ambassador to the Eastern Caribbean 1971–1981. Following these positions, she was a Fellow at the Harvard University Center for International Studies and lectured at the Kennedy School of Government. Ambassador Shelton-Colby has an M.A. in International Relations from the Johns Hopkins University School of Advanced International Studies. She has published numerous articles on Latin America and the Caribbean, and is currently a consultant for several banks on the Latin American debt problem.